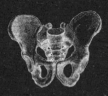

THE
TRUTH

AN UNCOMFORTABLE
BOOK ABOUT RELATIONSHIPS

NEIL STRAUSS

CANONGATE
Edinburgh · London

FULL DISCLOSURE

This book covers a period of approximately four years, during most of which my life was a roller coaster and many pledges of anonymity were required, particularly from men who wrecked their family's lives and women whose lives I wrecked. In order to compress it into a manageable length, reduce the complexity, get at the truth of relationships, and preserve anonymity, incidents, people, locations, and situations were moved, removed, compounded, or compressed, and certain identifying details, including names, have been changed. If you are reading this and believe you recognize yourself, think again. Your story is the same as that of most others in this book: You cheated and got caught.

Published in Great Britain in 2015 by
Canongate Books Ltd, 14 High Street, Edinburgh EH1 1TE

www.canongate.tv

1

THE TRUTH

www.neilstrauss.com

First published in the United States in 2015 by Dey St.,
an imprint of William Morrow Publishers.
HarperCollins Publishers, 195 Broadway, New York, NY 10022.

Interior book design by Laurie Griffin
Illustrations by Bernard Chang, except for the really shitty ones, which are by the author
Additional image credits on p. 432

British Library Cataloguing-in-Publication Data
A catalogue record for this book is available on
request from the British Library

ISBN 978 1 78211 094 1
Export ISBN 978 1 78211 095 8

Printed and bound in Great Britain by Clays Ltd, St Ives plc.

MIX
Paper from
responsible sources
FSC® C018072
www.fsc.org

*T*o my mother and father.

They say a parent's love is unconditional.

Let's hope that's still true after you read this book.

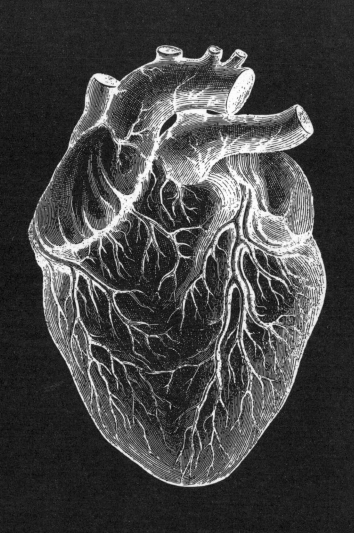

*P*EOPLE ARE MADE
TO NEED EACH OTHER.
BUT THEY HAVEN'T
LEARNED HOW TO LIVE
WITH EACH OTHER.

—RAINER WERNER FASSBINDER
The Bitter Tears of Petra von Kant

⚠ WARNING

The following pages contain one of the most terrifying and obscene words in the English language: *commitment*. Specifically the type of commitment that often precedes or follows love and sex.

A lack of commitment, too much commitment, a poorly chosen commitment, and misunderstandings about commitment have led to murders, suicides, wars, and a whole lot of grief.

They have also led to this book, which is an attempt to figure out where so many people go wrong, again and again, when it comes to relationships and marriage—and if there's a better way to live, love, and make love.

This, however, is not a journey that was undertaken for journalistic purposes. It is a painfully honest account of a life crisis that was forced on me as a consequence of my own behavior. Like most personal journeys, it starts in a place of darkness, confusion, and foolishness.

As such, it requires sharing a lot of things I'm not proud of—and a few things I feel like I should regret a whole lot more than I actually do. Because, unfortunately, I am not the hero in this tale. I am the villain.

WARNING FOR INGRID

If you are reading this, please stop now.

Do NOT turn the page.

Ingrid,

If this is you, really, don't read this.

Don't you have email to check or something?
Or have you seen the video with that
cat who's doing a human-like thing? It's
hilarious--maybe you should watch it. This
book isn't very good anyway. I've written
others that are much better. Go read one
of those.

Seriously, stop reading now. THIS IS YOUR
LAST CHANCE.

CONT

Prologue

THE HAND YOU ARE DEALT FACE DOWN

Every family has a skeleton in the closet.

You may know your family's skeleton. You may even be that skeleton. Or you may think that your family is different, that it's the exception, that you're one of the lucky ones with a perfect set of parents and no dark family secrets. If so, then you just haven't opened the right closet door yet.

For most of my life, I, too, believed I was one of the normal ones. But then I found the right closet door.

It was in my father's room. The door was white, with chipped paint along the outer edge and a brass doorknob burnished by my father's large hand. I twisted the knob, emboldened by the hope of finding pornography, my hand over the mark of my father's.

I was a late-teenage virgin, my parents were out, and I craved the female skin I so desperately lacked access to in real life. I'd found a *Playboy* and a *Penthouse* in my father's magazine stack before, so it stood to reason that in a deeper recess of his room, there existed a superior form of pornography: the kind that moves. Real porn.

In the back of his closet, beneath rows of blue cotton-polyester dress shirts with monogrammed pockets, dulled nearly white from years of washing, I found three brown grocery bags filled with VHS tapes. I sat on the floor and examined each one meticulously, careful to return them in the exact reverse order in which I'd removed them.

There were no videos labeled as porn, but I knew my father wouldn't be that stupid with my mother around. So I set aside all the unmarked tapes. Since I was never allowed to have a television set of my own, I brought the videos into the family room, where there was a small TV and VCR, old presents from an old uncle.

I felt like I was about to explode.

I loaded the first video, and was disappointed to find a Dizzy Gillespie jazz concert recorded off PBS. I pressed fast-forward, hoping it was just camouflage for a nubile blonde-on-blonde scene. But what came next was an episode of *Newhart*, followed by *Masterpiece Theatre*. It was spectacularly unmasturbatory.

The next tape was a recording of *The Philadelphia Story*, followed by a tennis match, and then nothing but static.

I placed the third videotape into the VCR and watched it sink slowly into the machine. I pressed play, and as soon as I saw what was on that tape, my excitement instantly drained, my skin went cold, and my image of my father as a meek, passive businessman changed forever.

I saw images I didn't even know existed in this world.

And suddenly, as if I'd accidentally opened a theater curtain to reveal the rigging, I realized that the reality of my family was very different from the façade.

"Promise you won't tell anyone, not even your brother or your father," my mother instructed when I asked her about what I'd found.

"I promise," I reassured her.

And I never told anyone what I learned that day about my father's secret life.

That is, until that secret became an acid, corroding my relationships. Until it burned straight through my sense of right and wrong, leaving me alone and despised. Until it landed me in a psychiatric institution, where I was told that for my own sanity, freedom, and happiness, I needed to break my promise and reveal the contents of that tape.

And so I faced a decision: How far would I go to protect my parents? Is it better to betray the people responsible for my existence or to betray that existence itself?

It is a decision that everyone, at some point in life, must make.

Most make the wrong one.

Maybe your dad is living a double life. Maybe your mom is. Maybe one of them is secretly gay or cross-dressing or having an affair or paying for hookers or going to strip clubs or watching Internet porn or just not in love. Maybe both are. Maybe it's not your parents, but you or the person you love. But somewhere, there is a skeleton. And that skeleton has a penis. And it will fuck your life.

Door

1

INFIDELITY

STAGE I

▪ Wounded Child ▪

*W*HAT WE DO NOT KNOW,
CONTROLS US.

—JAMES HOLLIS
Under Saturn's Shadow

1

Across the aisle from me on the plane is a thin girl with black hair. She could be anywhere from seventeen to twenty-three. And she has *it:* dark eyeliner, fake lashes, a small round tattoo on her lower back, pink headphones, and the permanent pout of someone who is angry at Dad but will fuck any insensitive asshole who reminds her of Dad.

Next to me is a middle-aged woman with large imitation designer sunglasses and a sundress showing milky white cleavage. In just twenty minutes of conversation, and with the artful positioning of a complimentary airline blanket, maybe I could have my hand inside there.

In front of me is a thin redhead with a beat-up face. Probably an alcoholic. Not my type, but I would.

Inside my head, there is a map. And on that map, there is a small LED bulb marking where every reasonably attractive or slightly sexually compelling female is sitting. Before the plane has hit cruising altitude, I have already thought of ways to approach each one, stripped her naked, imagined her blow-job technique, and fucked her in the bathroom or the rental car or her bedroom that night.

This is it: the last time I'm allowed to lust, the last time I'm allowed to even entertain the thought of sleeping with a new woman. And my mind is going crazy. I'm attracted to everyone. Not that I ever wasn't, but this time it hurts somewhere deep—in the core of who I am, of my identity, of my reason for living.

I have nothing with me: no computer, no cell phone, no technology. They are not allowed where I'm going. It feels liberating to be alone with my thoughts—most of which involve debating whether to start a conversation with the aforementioned, possibly jailbait girl in the row to my right or the pock-faced redhead in front of me.

When the plane eases to a stop at the gate, a bespectacled man stands up and makes his way to the aisle. He looks the black-haired girl up and down. He is not hitting on her; he has stared at her too long for that. He's capturing the image, imprinting it in his memory to save it for later, when he can use it.

Why am I putting myself through this? I wonder. This is normal male behavior. That guy's probably worse than I am.

As I walk through the terminal, I pull a folded piece of paper out of my pocket: *Your driver will meet you as soon as you pass security. He will be wearing a badge with a* D, *so as not to identify where you are going.*

Suddenly, a guy in his twenties—at least six feet tall, muscular, square jawed, basically the opposite of what I see when I look in the mirror—freezes in front of me. His mouth drops open, like he's seen a ghost. I know what's about to happen, and I want to get rid of him. He is not my driver.

"Oh my god, are you . . ."

For some reason, he can't seem to get the next words out of his mouth. I wait for him to spit it out, but nothing happens.

"Yeah," I tell him.

Silence.

"Well, nice to meet you. I have to go meet a friend." Fuck, that's a lie. I swore to stop lying. Lies just roll off the tongue so much easier than the truth sometimes.

"I read your book," he says.

"Just recently?" I ask, for some reason. Walking away from people who show interest is not one of my strong points. That's why I'm here. Along with the lying.

"No, three years ago."

"That's great." He doesn't look like the kind of guy who ever needed my advice.

"I met my wife because of you. I owe you everything."

"That's great," I say again. I think about the prospect of marrying someone, of spending the rest of my life with her, of not being allowed to fuck anyone else, of her aging and losing interest in sex and me still not being able to fuck anyone else. And the next words just slip out of my mouth: "Are you happy?"

"Oh yeah, totally," he says. "Seriously. I read *The Game* while I was in the Army in Iraq, and it really helped me."

"Do you plan on having kids?" I'm not sure what I'm doing. I think I'm trying to scare him. I want him to show a little fear or hesitancy or doubt, just to prove to myself that I'm not crazy.

"My wife's actually about to give birth to our son," he says. "I'm flying home to see her."

His answer hits me right where it hurts: in my self-esteem. Here I am, incapable of having a relationship and starting a family, and this guy read some book I wrote on picking up women and three years later he's got his entire life figured out.

I make my excuses and leave him standing there, no doubt thinking, He's much shorter than I imagined.

On the other side of security, I see a man with a gray ring of hair around his head and a badge with a *D* on it. He must see all kinds of people rolling off the plane, either half dead or wasted or trying hard to pretend they're a normal adult, which is, I think, what I'm doing.

I feel like an impostor. There are people who need to go to this Level 1 psychiatric hospital because without it they are going to die. They're going to drink or snort or inject themselves to death.

All I did was cheat on my girlfriend.

2

Los Angeles, Six Months Earlier

They say that when you meet someone and feel like it's love at first sight, run in the other direction. All that's happened is that your dysfunction has meshed with their dysfunction. Your wounded inner child has recognized their wounded inner child, both hoping to be healed by the same fire that burned them.

In fairy tales, love strikes like lightning. In real life, lightning burns. It can even kill you.

My girlfriend is sitting on the floor of the guesthouse where we live, packing to go with me to Chicago today. It's her birthday. She's going to meet my family.

I look at her and appreciate every inch of her, inside and out. "I'm excited, babe," Ingrid says. She is pure joy, pulling me out of my dark, solipsistic world every morning. She was born in Mexico, but to a German father, and somehow ended up living in America and looking like a petite Russian blonde.

And so she embodies all the elements: the intensity of fire, the strength of earth, the playfulness of water, the delicacy of air.

"I know. Me too."

I try to push the night before out of my head. There is no evidence of it anywhere; I made sure of that. I showered. I checked the interior of the car. I inspected every item of my clothing for stray hairs. The only thing I can't clean is my conscience.

"Should I bring these shoes?"

"It's only five days. How many pairs do you need?"

Sometimes I get annoyed by how long it takes her to get ready, the amount of clothing she needs to pack for even the shortest trips, the way her high heels prevent us from walking more than a few blocks when we go out. But deep down, I love her femininity. I am a slob and she gives me grace. When I told her last night that I had to go see Marilyn Manson, a musician I'd written a book with, about a new project, I looked into the hazel-green of her eyes and I saw love, happiness, innocence, peace.

Yet still I went through with it.

"So how was last night?" she asks as she struggles with the zipper of her suitcase.

"It was kind of frustrating. We didn't get much work done." That's for sure.

As she places a small, confident hand on top of the overstuffed bag and pushes the two rows of zipper teeth into contact, I can't help but think of two separate lives being forced together—and how, if just one element pops out of place, everything starts to fall off the tracks.

"Aw, babe, you can sleep on my lap on the plane, if you want."

She is reliving her mother's relationship with her cheating father. I am reliving my father's secret sex life. We are repeating a pattern handed down by generations of lying, cheating assholes and the poor fools who trust them.

"Thank you," I tell her. "I love you." At least I think I love her. But can you really love someone if you just fucked one of her friends in the parking lot of a church, and now six hours later you're lying to her about it? My mind is so clouded with guilt, I don't know anymore. Somehow, I doubt it.

There comes a time in a man's life when he looks around and realizes he's made a mess of everything. He's dug a hole for himself so deep that not only can't he get out, but he doesn't even know which way is up anymore.

And that hole for me is, and has always been, relationships. Not just because I cheated on Ingrid, but because yet another fairy tale is teetering on the brink of an unhappy ending.

The last fairy tale concluded with my ex locking herself in her apartment with a gun, and yelling that she was going to splatter her brains all over the wall and I shouldn't go to her funeral.

But this one is different. Ingrid isn't crazy, she isn't jealous, she isn't controlling, she's never cheated on me, and she's talented and independent, working in a real estate office by day and designing swimsuits by night. I'm ruining this one all by myself.

And that's because I am the king of ambivalence.

When I'm single, I want to be in a relationship. When I'm in a relationship, I miss being single. And worst of all, when the relationship ends and my captor-lover finally moves on, I regret everything and don't know what I want anymore.

I've gone through this cycle enough times to realize that, at this rate, I'm going to grow old alone: no wife, no kids, no family. I'll die and it will be weeks before the smell gets strong enough that someone finds me. And all the shit I spent my lifetime accumulating will be thrown in the trash so someone else can occupy the space I wasted. I'll have left nothing behind, not even debt.

But what's the alternative?

Most married people I know don't seem to be any happier. One day Orlando Bloom, an actor I'd written a *Rolling Stone* profile about, came over to visit. At the time, he was married to one of the world's most successful and beautiful women, Victoria's Secret supermodel Miranda Kerr, making him one of the most envied men on the planet. And the first thing out of his mouth? "I don't know if marriage is worth it. I don't know why anyone does it. I mean, I want romance and I want to be with someone, but I just don't think it works."

My other married friends haven't fared much better. Some even seem content, but after a little probing they admit to feeling frustrated. Several cope by being unfaithful, others white-knuckle it, many surrender passively to their fate, and a few simply live in denial. Even the rare friends who've remained happy in their marriages admit, when pressed, to being unfaithful at least once.

We expect love to last forever. Yet as many as 50 percent of marriages and even more remarriages end in divorce. Among those who are married, only 38 percent actually describe themselves as happy in that state. And 90 percent of couples report a decrease in marital satisfaction after having their first child. Speaking of which, more than 3 percent of babies are not actually fathered by the male parent who thinks he did.*

Unfortunately, it's only getting worse. Thanks to technology, we now have more dating and hook-up options than at any other time in human history, with countless desperate men and women just a click or swipe away, making fidelity—or even committing in the first place—yet more of a challenge. In a recent Pew Research survey, four out of ten people believed that marriage was an obsolete institution.

Maybe, then, the problem isn't just me. Perhaps I've been trying to conform to an outdated and unnatural social norm that doesn't truly meet—and has never met—the needs of both men and women equally.

So I stand here, packing for Chicago, riddled with guilt and confusion, with one foot in the best relationship I've ever had and one foot out of it, wondering: Is it even natural to be faithful to one person for life? And if it is, how do I keep the passion and romance from fading over time? Or are there alternatives to monogamy that will lead to better relationships and greater happiness?

Several years ago, I wrote a book called *The Game* about an underground community of pickup artists I joined in search of an answer to the biggest question plaguing my lonely life at the time: Why don't women I like ever like me back?

In the pages that follow, I attempt to solve a much tougher life dilemma: What should I do *after* she likes me back?

Like love itself, the path to answer this question will be anything but logical. The unintended consequences of my infidelity will lead me to free-love communes, to modern-day harems, and to scientists, swingers, sex anorexics, priestesses, leather families, former child actors, miracle healers, murderers, and, most terrifying of all, my mother. It will challenge and ultimately revolutionize everything I thought I knew about relationships—and myself.

If you're interested in getting more out of this odyssey for yourself, notice the words and concepts that most excite or repel you. Each gut reaction tells a story. It is a story about who you are and what you believe. Because, all too often, the things that we're the most resistant to are precisely what

---

*Sources for these and other facts in this book can be found at www.neilstrauss.com/thetruth.

we need. And the things we're most scared to let go of are exactly the ones we most need to relinquish.

At least, that will be the case with me.

This is the story of discovering that every truth I've desperately clung to, fought for, fucked for, and even loved for is wrong.

Appropriately, it begins in a modern-day insane asylum, sometime before I escaped against medical advice . . .

A hairy man in green hospital scrubs takes my luggage, stretches a pair of latex gloves over his hammy fists, and starts searching for contraband.

"We don't allow books here."

The only other place I've been where books are confiscated is North Korea. Taking away books is a tactic of dictators and others who don't want people to have an original thought. Even in prison, inmates are allowed to have books.

But this is my punishment, I tell myself. I'm here to be retrained, to learn how to be a decent human being. I've hurt people. I deserve to be in this hospital, this prison, this asylum, this convalescent home for weak men and women who can't say no.

They treat all addictions here: alcohol, drugs, sex, food, even exercise. Too much of anything can be a bad thing. Even love.

Their specialty is love addiction.

But I am not a love addict. I wish I were. That sounds much more socially acceptable. There's probably a special place in heaven for love addicts, along with all the other martyrs.

The attendant drops my nail clippers, tweezers, razor, and razor blades into a manila envelope. "I'm going to have to take these too."

"Can I shave first? I didn't have time to shave this morning."

"New arrivals can't use razors for three days while on suicide watch. After that, you need your psychiatrist's permission."

"But how can you commit suicide with nail clippers?" I'm not very good with rules. That's another reason I'm here. "Mine don't even have a file attached."

He is silent.

You can't fix most problems with rules, any more than you can with laws. They're too inflexible. They break. Common sense is flexible. And I'm clearly in a place devoid of it. "If I wanted to kill myself, I'd just use my belt. And you didn't take that."

I say it with a smile, to show I'm not angry. I just want to let him know that this system doesn't work. He looks me up and down, says nothing, then writes something in my folder. I'm never getting that razor back.

"Come with me," insists a green-smocked woman—rail thin and sinewy, with unkempt blond hair and sun-damaged skin. She introduces herself as a nurse technician and leads me to a private room.

She wraps a blood pressure cuff around my arm. "We need to take your vitals four times a day for the next three days," she says. Her eyes are dull, the words mechanical. This is what she does all day, every day.

"Why is that?" I ask. Too many questions. I can tell they don't like them here. But I'm just trying to understand. This isn't how I thought things were supposed to go. When I visited rehab to see a rock guitarist I was writing a book with, it seemed like a cross between a country club and overnight camp.

"We get a lot of people withdrawing and we want to make sure they're going to be okay," she explains. She listens to my pulse and lets me know my blood pressure is high.

Of course it's fucking high, I want to tell her. I've never been so uncomfortable in my life. You're taking away all my shit and treating me like I'm going to die. Withdrawing from sex isn't going to kill me.

But I stay quiet. And I submit. Like a good cheater.

She gives me a pager I'm supposed to wear at all times, in case they need me in the nursing station. Then she thrusts one form after another in front of me—patient rights, privacy, liability, and the rules. More fucking rules. One paragraph forbids me from having sex with any patient, nurse, or staff member. The next says that patients may not wear bikinis, tank tops, or shorts—and must wear bras at all times.

"So I have to put on a bra?" I joke, futilely trying once more to show how stupid their rules are.

"It's kind of silly," the nurse concedes, "but we have sex addicts in here."

The words escape from her mouth with scorn and fear, as if these sex addicts are not normal patients but creepy predators to beware of. And suddenly I realize that the alcoholics and junkies have nothing on me: They harm only their own bodies. I am after the bodies of others. I'm the worst of the worst. Other addicts can't find drugs in rehab, but my temptation is here. It is everywhere. And anyone in flirting distance must remain vigilant, lest I prey on them.

"Do you have any suicidal thoughts?" she asks.

"No."

She clicks a box on the computer and a form appears titled *Promise Not to Commit Suicide*.

She thrusts a small digital pad and a stylus toward me and asks me to sign the form.

"What are you going to do if I kill myself? Kick me out for lying?"

She says nothing, but I notice her dig the nail of her index finger into her thumb. I think I'm annoying her. It's the questions. The fucking questions. They don't like them here. It's because questions are powerful: The right question can expose the flaws in the system.

But I sign. And I submit. Like a good cheater.

She looks over my file on the computer, sees something that evidently surprises her, then turns the monitor away from me and quickly types a few words. I've only been here twenty minutes, and on relatively good behavior considering, and I'm already in the doghouse. And that's fine with me, because so far I hate the whole process. This is not about making me better. This is about covering their own asses from lawsuits, so they can tell the victim's family, "Well, he promised us he wouldn't hang himself. See, we have his signature right here, so it's not our fault if he lied to us."

"Do you have any homicidal thoughts?" she asks.

"No." And in that moment, I have a homicidal thought. It's like saying, "Don't think of a pink elephant."

She moves to the next question. "What are you here for?"

"Cheating."

She says nothing. I think about that word. It sounds lame. I'm in a fucking mental hospital because I couldn't say no to a new sex partner. So I add the other reason I'm there: "And I guess to learn how to have a healthy relationship."

I think of Ingrid, whose heart I broke, whose friends threatened to kill me, who never did anything wrong but love me.

The nurse looks up to face me. It is the first time she's made eye contact.

I see something soften. I'm no longer a pervert. I've said the magic R word: *relationship*.

Her lips part and moisten; her whole demeanor is different now. She actually wants to help me. "Of course," she says, "the first part of that is finding someone to date who's healthy."

"I found that person," I sigh. "She's totally healthy. That's what made me realize it's just me."

She smiles sympathetically and continues looking through my intake folder. I ask her if she thinks I'm really an addict. "I'm not an addiction specialist," she says. "But if you're cheating on your relationship, if you're visiting porn sites, or if you're masturbating, that's sex addiction."

She opens a drawer, removes a red square of paper, and writes my first name and last initial on it in black marker. Then she slips it into a small plastic sleeve and loops a long piece of white string through it. It's the ugliest necklace I've ever seen.

"You're in red two," she says. "You're required to wear your badge at all times."

"What does red two mean?"

"The tags are color coded. Red is for sex addicts. And the red two group is in therapy with"—she pauses and flashes a brief, uncomfortable smile—"Joan."

I can't tell whether it's fear or pity in her expression, but for some reason the name fills me with a crawling dread.

She then picks up a large poster board from the floor and holds it on top of the desk, facing me. There are eight huge words on it:

JOY
PAIN
LOVE
ANGER
PASSION
FEAR
GUILT
SHAME

"This is called a check-in," she says. "You'll be required to check in four times a day and report which emotions you're feeling. Which ones are you experiencing right now?"

I scan the display for crawling dread, for utter worthlessness, for total confusion, for intense regret, for rule-hating frustration, for the impulse to jump up and run away and change my name to Rex and move to New Zealand forever.

"I can't find my emotions on the list."

"These are the eight basic emotions," she explains with practiced patience. "Every emotion belongs in one of these categories. So select the ones you feel the most right now."

I don't get this. I feel like someone just made this shit up. It's completely arbitrary. It makes me feel . . .

"Anger."

She types it in my file. I am now officially institutionalized. I feel another emotion coming on.

"What's the difference between guilt and shame?" I ask.

"Guilt is just about your behavior. Shame is about who you are."

"And shame." Lots of shame.

She leads me back to the reception desk, where I see a woman with her arm in a blue fiberglass cast being led out of a nursing station: another new arrival. She has pasty skin, blue-black hair, lots of piercings, and the look of a vampire who seduces men to their doom. And I'm instantly attracted.

From the other direction, an even more alluring woman, with long blond hair pouring out of a pink baseball cap, saunters to the reception desk. She's wearing a tight black T-shirt that clings to every contour of her body. And I think what I always think, what every man always thinks. What was puberty for if not to think these thoughts? What is testosterone for if not to feel a sudden rush of chemicals priming the neuroreceptors in the medial preoptic area of the brain right now, impelling me forward to action?

"What are you here for?" I ask the blonde. Her tag is blue.

"Love addiction," she replies.

Perfect. I ask if she wants to get dinner.

Check-in: guilt.

And passion.

4

My roommate also has a red tag around his neck. As soon as I walk through the door, he looks me up and down, and instantly a wave of inferiority washes over me. He's tan and muscular; I'm not. His face is chiseled; mine is soft and weak. He was the most valuable player in a football championship, if his T-shirt is to be believed; I was always picked last for sports teams in school.

"I'm Adam," he says and crushes my hand in his. He speaks with confidence; my voice is nervous and fast.

"Neil." I extricate my hand. "So what are you in for?" I ask with forced ease. If I looked like Adam, I would have had girlfriends—or at least some sort of sexual contact—in high school and probably wouldn't be lusting after every woman on the street, on the plane, in rehab, in a fifty-yard radius of wherever I am. I'd have some fucking self-esteem.

"Neil, I'll tell you." He sits down on his bed and sighs. "I'm here for the same reason you are, the same reason every guy is: I got caught."

Or maybe I still wouldn't have self-esteem. Suddenly, I like him. He speaks my language.

The room is sparse: three small cots, three locking wardrobes, and three cheap plastic alarm clocks. I claim a bed and a closet as Adam tells his story. The bed is so low to the ground that his knees are almost at his chest.

Adam is a hardworking, God-fearing, patriotic American man clipped right out of a 1950s magazine ad for aftershave. Married his college sweetheart, bought a small house in Pasadena, sells insurance, has two kids and a dog, goes to church on Sundays.

"But my wife," he's saying, "she doesn't take care of herself. She lies around the house all day and does nothing. I come home from work and she just sits there reading a magazine. I'll ask if she wants to hear the five-minute version of my day and she'll say, 'No thanks.' She doesn't even have dinner ready for the kids." He drops his chin into his hands and takes a deep breath into his probably perfect athlete's lungs. "It's not that I want her to be a housewife or anything, but I'm exhausted. So I'll make dinner for everyone and she doesn't even clean up. You know, Neil, I call her every afternoon and tell her I love her. I send her flowers. I do everything to show her I care."

"But do you care or are you just doing a duty?"

"That's just it." He anxiously twists his wedding band. "I play football and help run the local leagues, and there's this woman who started coaching one of the teams, and there was something there between us. It was maybe seven months before anything happened, but when it did, let me tell you, Neil, I'm not kidding, it was the best sex I've ever had. It was real passion and it developed into real love. But then my wife hired a private eye and that was the end of that."

Perhaps marriage is like buying a house: You plan to spend the rest of your life there, but sometimes you want to move—or at least spend a night in a hotel. "So if you were so happy with this other woman and so unhappy with your wife, why didn't you just get divorced?"

"It's not that easy. I have a mature, established relationship with my wife. And we have children, and you have to think about them." He pushes himself off the bed and rises to his feet. "Wanna keep talking while we jog?"

I look at his legs, built by some super genetic stock and, probably, by a strict dad who loved him only when he scored goals. It would take me four steps to keep up with just one of his.

"That's all right. I have dinner plans."

"See you around, then." He starts to leave the room, then turns back. "Anyone warn you about Joan yet?"

"Joan?" And then I remember.

"She runs our group. A real ballbuster. You'll see."

And off Adam goes—healthy, wholesome, and fucked.

In the cafeteria, there's no sugar or caffeine, just food that won't make anyone high. At a table in the corner, seven women with eating disorders sit with a staff counselor, who makes sure they swallow their allotted calories and don't purge in the bathroom.

So far I haven't seen any women with red tags. Evidently, women have eating disorders, men have sex addiction. I suppose both share the same obsession: women's bodies.

I sit down next to the love addict, who's with the broken-armed vampire from reception. Turns out they're roommates. The love addict introduces herself as Carrie; the vampire as Dawn, an alcoholic and indiscriminate drug fiend. Whenever Dawn needs more sugar-free dessert or caffeine-free coffee, Carrie gets it for her, until the counselor from the eating table walks over.

"Stop getting food for other people," he reprimands her. "That's codependency, and it's against the rules here. No more caretaking! Got it?"

After he leaves, Carrie gives me a helpless look. "But her arm's broken! What am I supposed to do?"

"You're enabling my cast addiction," Dawn jokes. And we laugh as if everything's normal. But as we do, I look down and see the red tag dangling over my solar plexus like a scarlet letter. And I start to falter, to get nervous, to wonder if they've noticed that, of all the people to talk to here, I've chosen them—the youngest ones, the most attractive ones, the only two I shouldn't be sitting with.

If they don't know yet what this red badge means, they will know soon: Keep away. This man is a pervert.

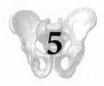

5

On a bulletin board outside the reception area, there's a list of twelve-step meetings taking place that night: Alcoholics Anonymous, Narcotics Anonymous, Sex and Love Addicts Anonymous, Overeaters Anonymous, Gamblers Anonymous, Crystal Meth Anonymous, Co-Dependents Anonymous. A menu of dysfunctions to choose from.

I've never been to any of these meetings, so I choose the most relevant: Sex and Love Addicts Anonymous. It's in the patient lounge, which serves primarily as a library of tabletop puzzles to keep obsessive-compulsive patients busy wasting their lives. In a circle of couches and chairs at the far end of the room, there's a group of three men and three women, including Carrie, led by a sad but dignified gray-haired man with a binder open in front of him. He looks like a newscaster who's fallen on hard times.

"My name is Charles, and I'm a codependent depressive sex addict with PTSD and OCD," he tells the group.

"Hi, Charles."

"I was treated for sex addiction ten years ago and then relapsed two months ago. Because I didn't want to raise kids around my addiction, I've passed up the chance to have children with my wife. We're both too old now, and I really regret that. And I'm scared for her to come for family week, because I don't want to lose her."

When he's finished, he looks to Carrie. She's changed into another tight T-shirt. This one says DAMAGED GOODS on it.

"My name is Carrie, and I'm a love addict and trauma survivor." Hi, Carrie. "I just got here today. I spent the last two years chasing after an abusive guy who wasn't even interested in me. If a guy gives me just a little bit of attention, I get obsessed. I don't feel pretty, and I see him as a challenge. And because I want approval and love so much, I have sex before I should—and a lot of times when I shouldn't at all."

The thought occurs before I can stop it: These groups are a great place to meet women. Carrie is sitting here divulging the exact strategy by which she can be seduced. There's nothing a man with low self-esteem loves more than a beautiful woman who doesn't know she's beautiful.

I need to control my mind. I suppose that's why I'm here.

Next up is a man in his early fifties: gray hair, gray beard, slight belly, red cheeks, like a skinnier, sex-addicted Santa Claus. He stares at his stomach and slowly, reluctantly tells his story. "I started out just going to strip clubs, but then I went to Tijuana and found this whorehouse and started going there all the time."

He sucks in a lungful of air like it's cigarette smoke, and lets out the saddest sigh I've ever heard. "And I got an STD." He pauses, as if considering whether to share the rest of the story, then squeezes his eyes shut for a moment and shakes his head side to side. "And I haven't told my wife about it yet." He waits for a reaction, but it's so quiet you could hear a syringe drop. "I'm going to have her come for family week and tell her then, I guess. Twenty-five years of marriage, and the whole house of cards is about to come tumbling down."

He looks like his neck is in a guillotine and he's waiting for the blade to fall. No one seems to have much of a problem with cheating here, just with getting caught. Many a man has shot himself in the head rather than face up to the consequences of what he's done in his secret life.

Yet the consequences are rarely death, violence, or prison. The consequences are that other people will know about it, and they'll have feelings and emotions about it that he can't control. Santa Claus's wife isn't going to kill him. She's just going to be really, really, really pissed off. Lying is about controlling someone else's reality, hoping that what they don't know won't hurt you.

Suddenly I notice that everyone's eyes are on me.

"My name is Neil."

"Hi, Neil," they all echo flatly.

And then I hesitate. If I check in as a sex addict, that could ruin my chances with Carrie.

But I'm here to ruin my chances with Carrie. I'm here to ruin my chances with everyone. If I have sex in rehab, then I'm really doomed.

But Carrie aside, am I even a sex addict? I'm a fucking man. Men like to have sex. That's what we do. Put a beautiful woman in a tight dress in a bar on a Saturday night, and it's like throwing raw meat into a den of wolves.

But I ate the meat while I was in a relationship. And I lied to and hurt someone who loves me, or loved me—I'm not sure which anymore. I suppose that's what addicts do: They want something so badly, they're willing to hurt others to get it.

"And I'm a sex and love addict."

Okay, so I softened it a little.

Everyone is listening, no one is judging. They've all got their own problems. "I never thought I'd be in a place like this. But I made some bad decisions and I cheated on the woman I love. So I guess I'm here to find out why I'd do something like that and hurt her so much. And because I want to become healthy enough to have a committed relationship, hopefully with her. I don't want to end up destroying a marriage and traumatizing my children because I cheated."

Santa Claus shakes his head and his eyes well up with tears.

I stop there. I decide not to mention the other option I'm debating: to just say, "Fuck it, this is my nature," and not get in another monogamous relationship, to be free to go out with who I want, when I want.

Since adolescence, we've been trained as men—by our friends, by our culture, by our biology—to desire women. It seems unreasonable to expect us to just shut it off forever once we get married. Legs are long, breasts are soft, and forever is a long time.

After everyone else shares, Charles asks if anyone is attending their first meeting. I raise my hand and he passes around a coin for me. I've seen friends who were junkies get these coins for sobriety and treat them like Olympic gold medals. Now I've got one. I look at it. It means nothing to me, except that today I've become one of them. One day sober.

Never in my lifetime did I think I'd be a patient in a place like this. In fact, I always thought that I was normal, that I was lucky to have parents who stayed together and never beat me, that my father's secret had nothing to do with me, that I had no use or time for therapists, that I was a journalist who wrote about other people's problems. I'm not sure what made me finally realize I was the one who was crazy.

Maybe it was Rick Rubin.

6

Pacific Ocean, Five Months Earlier

So let me get this straight: You love your girlfriend, but you went and had sex with someone else?

Yes.

And you knew that would hurt her, so you lied to her about it?

Yes.

Well, look on the bright side: If she finds out and breaks up with you, you're not really in a relationship anyway. With all the lying, you've been in your own world the whole time.

Rick and I are paddleboarding in the Pacific Ocean. He's one of the best music producers in the world, and for some reason he's taken me under his wing. At first I thought he befriended me so I would write about him in Rolling Stone, *but I soon realized that nothing could be further from the truth. He doesn't like to be written about, to go to parties, or to be in any situation outside his comfort zone. Yet at the same time, he has no problem telling bands like U2 that some new song they've recorded sucks.*

So do you think I should just tell her what happened?

Of course. If you'd committed to always telling her the truth in the first place, you would have thought twice before cheating on her. So start now, and maybe it's not too late to include her in your relationship.

I don't think I can do it. It would hurt her too much.

Well, was it worth it?

Definitely not.

Every other day for the last year, Rick and I have paddled from Paradise Cove to Point Dume together and talked about our lives. He's older than me but faster, always a few strokes ahead. Shirtless, with a long gray beard, he looks like some kind of water mystic leading a young acolyte.

Our paddles together are a far cry from my conversations with Rick a few years ago. Back then, he was 135 pounds heavier and rarely got off his couch. Every movement seemed like hard labor to him. Now, every day he's either working out, paddleboarding, or trying some new exercise regimen. I've never seen anyone go through such a rapid transformation. And today, I suppose he's trying to help me do the same.

Do you know what kind of people can't control their behavior, even when they don't enjoy that behavior anymore?

Weak people?

Addicts.

I don't think I'm an addict. I'm just a guy. It's not like I do this all the time.

Spoken like a true crackhead. Didn't you just get finished telling me that you lie to the people you love to get your fix, that you don't even get high from it anymore but still do it?

Yes. But what if Ingrid just isn't the right person for me? If she was, maybe I wouldn't cheat. She gets on my nerves sometimes, and she can be really stubborn.

You had the same kind of complaints about your last girlfriend. When things get hard for you, you start blaming the person you're with. None of this has anything to do with her. Just you. Can you see that?

I don't know.

He rolls his eyes.

Sometimes I feel like I'm an experiment of Rick's, that he gets off on persuading people to do the exact opposite of what they enjoy, that this is a sadistic attempt to see if he can make the guy who wrote The Game *let go of the game.*

I will go as far as to say you probably have never experienced a true connection, sexually or otherwise, before in your life. Rehab may be exactly what you need to cure your fear.

What fear?

That in a healthy monogamous relationship, you're not enough for the person you're with.

Either that or he's actually trying to help me.

I'll have to think about that.

You don't have time to think. If you ever want to be truly happy in this lifetime, you have to recognize that you're using sex like a drug to fill a hole. And that hole is your self-esteem. Deep down, you feel unlovable. So you try to escape from that feeling by conquering new women. And when you finally go too far and hurt Ingrid, all it's going to do is reinforce your original belief that you're not worthy of love.

As he speaks, Rick appears almost messianic. His eyes burn brightly and he seems to be receiving the truth from some higher place, a place I've never been. I've seen him get like this before—and when I ask him later to repeat what he said, he usually can't remember.

I see what you're saying. But I also just like trying new things. I love traveling, eating at different restaurants, and meeting new people. Sex is the same: I like getting to know different women, experiencing what they're like in bed, meeting their friends and family, and having the adventures and memories.

Fill the hole and have sex when you're whole, then see how that feels.

Maybe you're right. It wouldn't hurt to try that.

There's a place I know where you can go for sex addiction. It's a month-long program. If you go now—and write Ingrid from rehab, tell her the truth, and explain that you're dealing with your problem—I think she'd forgive you.

I can't go now. I have a couple of really big deadlines coming up.

If you got hit by a car today and you were in the hospital for a month, you wouldn't miss out on anything by not being able to write during that time. That excuse is just the illness having free rein with you. Nothing's going to change until you take deliberate and committed action to change it.

I promise myself that I'll be faithful to Ingrid from now on, that I'll make sure she never finds out what I did, and that I'll prove to Rick I'm not an addict. Yet at the same time, there's a voice inside me, telling me that somewhere out there, like Bigfoot or the Loch Ness Monster, there are smart, attractive, and stable women who want commitment without requiring sexual exclusivity.

Listen, there's a lot of truth in what you're saying. And I'm going to think about it and try to do the right thing. But I really don't think I'm a sex addict. It's not like I'm blowing all my money on hookers or fondling altar boys or anything.

Maybe you're not ready yet. Like a junkie, you need to hit rock bottom first.

There are ten chairs pushed against the side and back walls of the room, each filled with a broken man, including my roommate Adam. Charles, who led the twelve-step meeting the previous night, is here. So is Santa Claus, slumped in his chair, his forehead creased with stress, his eyes cinched tight. He's in the room in body only. His mind is elsewhere, suffering. Against the front wall is a rolling chair, a desk, and a file cabinet filled with the sins of countless sex addicts.

On the wall is a large chart titled "The Addiction Cycle," with four terms—*preoccupation, ritualization, acting out,* and *shame & despair*—arranged in a circle. Arrows point from one word to the next in an endless loop.

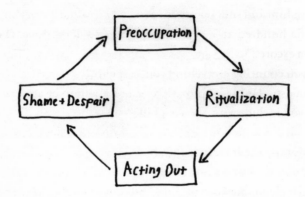

As I'm studying it, the door swings open and a tall woman with a pear-shaped body walks in. She has brown hair, unwashed and pulled back in a tight bun. She's wearing a loose-fitting flowered top over brown slacks and flat shoes. The corners of her lips are pulled slightly downward in a permanent frown. She looks the group over, careful not to make eye contact with anyone or acknowledge his individuality. Whatever the opposite of sex is, she embodies it.

She lands with a thud in the rolling chair. Sifting through a stack of manila folders, she shows no tenderness, no humanity, no humor. She is our doctor and judge, the stern mother we've been fucking women to try to escape from and the bitter wife who's caught us.

Her name is Joan. And her mere presence ripples through the flesh of each man in the room like a violent chill.

"Have you completed your assignment?" she asks a man in his mid-thirties. He's thin and blond, with a sweet, boyish face, ruddy cheeks, and the beginnings of an oddly incongruous potbelly.

"Yes," he says nervously. "Should I read it?" His red name tag identifies him as Calvin.

"Please." There's no warmth or caring in her voice, only authority and a drip of condescension. In fact, everything she does and says is so measured that her personality seems artificial, like a mask she puts on before walking into a room to face ten male sex addicts. And she fears that if she drops it, if she gives up any ground, she'll lose control of these predatory animals she must tame and civilize.

"These are the ways in which my sexual addiction has hurt my life," Calvin begins. "I lost my house and my brother. I booked a trip around the world with him and snuck away to see escorts in almost every city. I've spent a total of a hundred and twenty-five thousand dollars over the course of my life on escorts."

"Are you counting everything you've spent?"

"I think so." He braces himself as if he's about to be attacked.

"Did you include your Internet bill?"

"No."

"Do you use the Internet to find escorts?"

"Yes."

"Then include your Internet bill. And your phone bill, if you called any of these women you dehumanized." She spits out the last word like a preacher damning him to hell. "Include the money you spent on taxis to see these women and the money you spent on condoms and the entire cost of any trip where you saw them."

"Okay, then maybe it's two hundred and fifty thousand?"

A quarter of a million dollars is still not enough for Joan. As she pushes him to add up every penny even peripherally involved in the pursuit of sex, I think about how I've made my living off my so-called sex addiction. My sex addiction pays for my phone, rent, and health insurance. It pays for breakfast, lunch, and dinner; for movies, books, and the computer I'm writing on; for socks, underwear, and shoes. Fuck, I couldn't afford to be here getting treatment without it.

When I look back on my childhood, I see a malnourished nerd wearing cheap black-rimmed plastic glasses, too big for my little face yet too small for my gigantic ears. And I see greasy brown hair chopped awkwardly short—at my request. I hated my curls. Everyone else had straight hair and I wanted to fit in. Even my own mother called me a follower.

My losing streak continued not just through high school—where my junior prom date left the dance with another guy and my longest interactions with attractive women were during haircuts—but through college and my twenties. I sat on the sidelines, watching other people have fun. Eventually I made that a full-time job and started writing profiles of musicians for a living. When things got particularly lonely in the long droughts between girlfriends and I craved female touch, I'd go to an Asian massage parlor. And even there, I got the feeling they were making fun of my awkwardness behind my back.

But one day, everything changed. I embedded myself with the world's greatest self-proclaimed ladies' men, hoping to turn my losing streak around. After living with them and traveling the world with them for two years, I finally developed the confidence to talk to women I was attracted to and, for the first time in my life, the ability to attract them to me. The book I wrote about my education at the hands of these unlikely Lotharios became so infamous that it eclipsed everything I'd done before. And so my pursuit of sex didn't destroy my life, it made my career.

How frustrating, then, to find myself in rehab some five years later, trying to unlearn everything I've spent so much time and energy learning.

"Do you realize that you're harming these women when you use their bodies to masturbate with?" Joan admonishes Calvin. She senses he's on the verge of tears, then tries to bring him over the edge. "They don't care about you. These are hurt and abused women. And you're reenacting their childhood trauma. You are their father, their first boyfriend, the predator who raped away their innocence."

And that's it. Calvin is done. His head rolls down and he covers his eyes with his palms as the tears spill out. Victorious, Joan takes a verbal lap around the room, asking different patients to report on what their sexual addiction has cost them, breaking down each of their defenses, stripping them of the last vestige of ego and pride they've retained from any affair or adventure or transaction.

When a thin, laid-back patient with thick black hair and a cratered face mentions a girl he had an affair with, Joan recoils and spends ten minutes lecturing him on the use of the g-word. "As a therapist, when I hear the word *girl,* I have to automatically assume that you're talking about a minor. And I'm obliged to report that."

The air in the room thickens with confusion and discomfort. Finally, the accused replies, "I'm a sex addiction therapist also. I've been practicing for fifteen years. And I have never heard that interpretation of the word *girl* before in my life."

Joan raises her head like a cobra about to strike: "If I hear you use that word again, I will report you. And you will not make it to your sixteenth year as a CSAT."

That shuts him up. Another man down.

A CSAT is a Certified Sex Addiction Therapist, a designation invented by Patrick Carnes, the Johnny Appleseed of sex addiction. While working with sex offenders in the seventies, he began to view sex as an addiction like alcohol and he believed it could be treated with the same twelve-step program. So in the decades that followed, he started lecturing, writing books, setting up treatment centers, studying thousands of sex fiends and their families, and crusading to get psychiatrists to recognize sex addiction as a mental disorder.

On the wall over Joan's desk, there's a small framed photograph of Saint Carnes himself in a majestic dark suit and striped tie, forehead shining below his receding hairline like the halo of an angel, wedding-band-consecrated left hand resting in the foreground. He's smiling crookedly and looking down beatifically on the room of sex addicts prostrate before him.

Except for Calvin, who's never had a serious girlfriend and is here because he got a Brazilian hooker pregnant, every other sinner seems to be in the room for cheating—some regularly for decades, others once or twice. And so they come here, trying to work off the sins of the flesh and hoping Saint Carnes can perform a miracle and save the family that is both their greatest achievement and their greatest burden.

Looking at abject Adam and scared Santa Claus and penitent Charles, I think: I need to fix this problem now. Because otherwise I'll be right back here like them after I'm married, fighting to keep my family together.

When Joan releases us, I stand up to head to the cafeteria, but she stops me. "You need to stay and sign some paperwork." She makes no eye contact.

Instead, she turns to her computer and pulls up my file, then studies it carefully.

"So how long have you been taking Zoloft?" she asks.

"I've never taken Zoloft."

"It says here in your file that you do."

"Well, that's probably a mistake. I've never taken any psychiatric medication in my life."

"So you don't take Zoloft?" Her eyebrows rise incredulously and she types into my file: "Denies taking Zoloft."

It's interesting how someone will believe a document more than they'll believe a human being—even though the words didn't get on the document by themselves. For the rest of my life and even after it, whenever people dig through my records, they'll think I have a chemical mood imbalance because of this hack.

She closes my file, then calls up another document. I look over her shoulder. The bold print at the top of the screen freezes my heart: CELIBACY/ABSTINENCE CONTRACT.

Evidently I'm about to become a priest.

She reads it sternly.

I WILL REFRAIN FROM THE FOLLOWING:

- Masturbation

- Implicit or explicit pornographic material

- Flirtatious, seductive, romantic, or suggestive comments
  or behavior

- Seductive attire

- Sexually overt or covert contact with another person or myself

- Secretive sexual fantasizing: I will report objectifying,
  fantasizing, or obsessing to appropriate staff members

- And cross-dressing.

"This contract is effective for twelve weeks," she informs me.

"But I'm only supposed to be here for four weeks."

She fixes her eyes on mine. Her pupils are brown and glassy, with as much empathy as a snail shell. "This is for your own benefit. It takes three months for your brain to return to normal after all the imbalances caused by the constant high of sex."

"So I can't even have sex when I go home?"

"Not if you want to recover."

I sign the contract. Like a good cheater.

"Thank you," she says dryly, waving me out of the room.

Check-in: the feeling your balls get when you jump in a really cold lake.

San Francisco, One Month Earlier

I'm standing at the baggage claim in San Francisco when the call comes. I've just pulled my roller bag off the carousel.

"I got an email from Juliet," Ingrid says.

The blood drains out of my face and my bones feel hollow. Something in me has just been cut loose. It is fear. It is panic. It is sadness. It is guilt. It is pain. It is every bad emotion at once. I'm as light as cotton, yet I don't have the strength to move.

"Is there anything you need to tell me?" she asks. I can hear the hurt in her voice, the shock, the disbelief. Her world has just come apart at the seams. What she thought was golden thread has turned out to be polyester. She needs me to say it's not true. And, more than anything, I want to give her one more soothing lie to keep the fabric of our reality stitched together.

I open my mouth to speak and nothing comes out. I can't compound the injury with one more deception. But I can't bring myself to admit the truth either. I have only one other option.

"Can I call you back?" If truth is not on my side, at least time can be. "My plane was delayed and I'm late to my talk."

I'm speaking at a big tech company about my books. And right now, it seems so fucking unimportant, all this writing, all this time spent hunched over a glowing screen, all this convincing myself that any of it matters. People are what matter, not things.

And I have destroyed the person who matters most to me.

Just the night before, Ingrid texted me a photograph. She was on stage in a bar, holding an immense trophy aloft, a huge silly grin on her face as a crowd applauded her. Somehow, she'd won an annual rock-paper-scissors championship against a hundred other people, even though she'd barely played the game before. Looking at that image, I felt as excited as if she'd won an Oscar. That's my girlfriend. She's a champion. She can figure anything out and crush it.

Well, now she's figured me out.

As I'm driving to the lecture, my heart pounding and mind racing, Ingrid forwards the message she received from Juliet. I glance at it, see "we had sex in his car, in my bed, and in my shower," and can't read anymore. All I can imagine is how Ingrid must have felt when she read those words.

This pause, this procrastination of the inevitable, is like the fuse on a bomb. I see it burning and I'm scrambling to find a way to extinguish it before it reaches the detonator. But there's too much evidence Juliet can provide: dates, times, texts, techniques. I don't know what made me believe I could get away with it or why I even put myself and Ingrid in this position. The first time I did it out of desire. The second time I did it out of guilt. The third time I did it out of fear: She'd threatened to tell Ingrid. Then I didn't do it the fourth time.

And that's when the gates of hell opened.

At a generic office building, a generic man in a generic shirt leads me to a generic room filled with more than a hundred generic employees. I take a deep breath and spend the next hour telling them to enjoy their lives and be their best selves, while in my chest I feel my life caving in.

When I get to my hotel room, I plug my dying cell phone into the wall. The cord is short, so I have to lie on the floor beneath the desk.

"I just got off the phone with Juliet," Ingrid says when she answers. "She told me about your birthmark." My birthmark is a splotch of raised red bumps, kind of like the six on a die, on the left side of my ass. When I was ten, I read the book *The Omen* and became convinced that my birthmark was the mark of the Antichrist. Ingrid had a more positive interpretation: She once took a thin black marker and connected the bumps like islands on a pirate treasure map, with an X at the end.

"I also talked to Luke," she says. Luke is a friend of ours. Juliet is his ex-girlfriend. "He's really upset."

"I know, I know, I can explain," I weakly protest.

"Neil, I am so hurt and in shock. I'm leaving. And I don't want to see you again. I don't want to talk to you again. That's it."

Then she hangs up and I collapse crying on the floor. Just sobbing out loud. Tears drip out of my eyes and my stomach heaves. I fucking blew it. I blew it. I blew it.

And then the texts come: Luke says he's going to punch me in the face when I get home. Ingrid's girlfriends want me dead. And I'm worried that her stepbrothers are going to beat the shit out of me.

Not that I don't deserve to be disfigured. At least my outside can match how I feel inside. It's not just the pain of losing Ingrid, it's the pain of knowing I've hurt her. In this life, we don't meet many people who truly love us, who accept us for who we are, who put us before themselves. Maybe a parent or two if we're lucky, perhaps a couple of previous partners. So what kind of person rewards someone's love with lies, betrayal, and pain?

A selfish person. A coldhearted person. A thoughtless person. An asshole. A liar. A cheater. A guy who thinks with his dick. Me.

As soon as I regain a semblance of control over my motor functions, the next call I make is to Rick to ask for the name of the program he recommended.

9

As I walk through a drab yellow hallway to the cafeteria, I feel a pain in my groin, a psychologically induced ache. I've signed my soul to Joan and turned my dick into an appendage, doomed to dangle desolately between my legs and just piss occasionally.

"Let me ask you," I nudge Charles, joining him in the food line. "Do you think it's male nature that makes us want to sleep with other people or is it really an addiction?"

"It's definitely an addiction," Charles says authoritatively. "And the day I finally admitted I was powerless over it was the happiest day of my life. Suddenly I was no longer responsible. If I saw a beautiful woman on the street and was attracted, I knew it wasn't my fault. I just looked away and said, 'This is a disease and I'm powerless over it.'"

At a table near the caffeine-free-coffee maker, I spot a fashionably dressed brunette with a red tag. She's the first female sex addict I've seen. So of course I sit next to her. She's tall and graceful, like a Siamese cat but with a forehead as big and shiny as a car mirror. Her name, according to her tag, is Naomi.

She's sitting next to a heavyset woman with short black hair, a lumpy sweatsuit, and several chins and growths on her face. Charles refuses to sit with us.

"We signed a contract," Charles admonishes me.

"We're not hitting on them. We're just eating with them."

"We're not supposed to talk to female patients."

"Says who? It's not even in the contract."

"You're threatening my sobriety," he warns.

Naomi laughs as Charles walks off, indignant. It's the first music I've heard since checking in. The laughter of a woman is a high unto itself.

As we eat, I ask Naomi about her story. She says she cheated on her husband seventeen times. "I remember the first time I slept with someone else. I got my first client on my own at work and my boss took me out to congratulate me. We started drinking, and he leaned over and made out with me. That acceptance was like a high for me. My head was just spinning. I've cheated since then looking for that high again, and it's always the same situation: wanting acceptance from powerful men."

As she speaks, I think about how easy it would be to fuck her. She's got a nice body, and she seems to have a wild side.

Shit, now I definitely broke the contract. Maybe Charles was right. A shiver of remorse runs through me: Why am I trying to patch things up with Ingrid when I'm still clearly not capable of the commitment she expects? But I suppose that's why I'm here: to become capable.

Check-in: shame.

Guilt is about breaking the rules. Shame is about being broken.

"My therapist gave me a really big insight today," the person I just accidentally fantasized about is saying. "I always put a lot of thought and care into the clothes I wear. But she told me that dressing to get attention is a form of acting out and part of my disease."

These therapists must be stopped. If they succeed in bullying women out of dressing beautifully, we might as well all move to Iran.

"She explained that sex addiction is different for women," Naomi continues. "Female sex addiction is usually about seeking love."

She tells me that roughly 90 percent of sex addicts entering treatment are men because guys tend to act out, while roughly 90 percent of people with eating disorders are women because they tend to act in.

The woman next to her, Liz, has a purple tag, which she says is for post-traumatic stress disorder. Because Naomi is the only female sex addict here, they're in the same group. "They diagnosed me as a sexual anorexic," Liz says.

I've never heard the term before, so Liz explains that it means she avoids sex. She tells us she was raised in a cult and repeatedly gang-raped. Eventually she ran away. And since then, she's compulsively eaten a lot, neglected to care for herself, and dressed sloppily to keep men away. All those chins may look soft on the outside, but in actuality they serve as a strong shield, keeping her body safe.

After lunch, as I walk along the path to the dorms, the sex-addicted sex addiction therapist from Joan's group spots me and motions me over with his finger.

"Your last name is Strauss, right?" he asks when I join him on the lawn. His name tag reads TROY.

"Um, yes."

"I read your book."

"Do me a favor and don't tell anyone who I am," I plead. "It's too ironic."

"So why *are* you here, man? I thought you'd be out living the life."

"I was. I learned all that stuff and it was fun. But at some point I want to get married and have a family, so I have to shut it off if I want to do that."

"I'll tell you something," Troy whispers conspiratorially. "As a sex therapist, I've heard every story there is out there." He gestures away with his right arm. It doesn't matter which direction he's pointing: All roads lead out of here and to the real world. "And after fifteen years in this job, I don't know if I believe in monogamy."

I clap him on the back and breathe a sigh of relief. "Let's talk some more about that," I tell him.

I've found either an ally in truth here or a partner in crime.

10

I've been sitting in this room with Joan for three straight days now and I've barely spoken a word or learned a thing. Today, Calvin is in trouble again. In the meantime, a new patient has joined us: a gay crystal meth addict from Las Vegas named Paul. He sits in his chair, unshaven, scratching his short brown hair, probably wondering why he's here as Calvin tells Joan, "I was doing equine therapy and there was this girl"—Joan glares at him and he corrects himself—"I mean, woman, there. Carrie."

"Oh man, that's my arousal template right there," Troy mutters, patting his chest.

Joan's neck suddenly reddens. "Are you aware that undressing someone with your eyes is covert sexualized violence?" She doesn't yell—that would signify a loss of control. Her weapon is severity. She knows just how to reduce a man to a boy: become his mother on her worst day.

"Sorry, I am aware of that," Troy says obediently.

I, however, am not aware of that. I want to ask her: Since when did thinking become an act of violence? If you see a bank teller counting a huge stack of bills and imagine taking it when she's not looking, is that covert bank robbery? And what are the charges?

"Go ahead, Calvin," she says icily, "tell everyone how you pornified Carrie."

"I don't know. I just noticed that she had riding boots on and was talking about how she liked horses, and I do too. So I was fantasizing about riding away on a horse with her and getting married."

I always thought that sex addicts would be lecherous criminals, not overgrown boys who fantasize about getting married to women who share their interests. The first time I heard of sex addiction was when I saw a news exposé as a teenager. It followed a sex addict who drove around the city in a van with a mattress in back and somehow talked women into hooking up with him in there. He was very ordinary looking and plainly dressed, and I was envious that his sheer determination to have sex could actually produce results when my desire was getting me nowhere with the ladies.

I guess the moral is: Be careful what you wish for.

When I tune back into the room, Charles and Troy are bickering about pronouns. Joan asks them to sit in chairs opposite each other and talk using what she calls the communication boundary. She holds up a poster board reading:

When I saw/heard _____.

The story I told myself about that was _____.

And I feel _____.

So I would like to request that _____.

Charles tries it: "When I heard you say that 'we're not monogamous by design,' the story I told myself about that was that it's not true for me. I'm here to get better. And I feel angry. So I would like to request that in the future, you use *I* to refer to yourself instead of *we*."

"Well done," Joan says. Then she turns to Troy, her voice saccharine sweet: "Now you need to respond using the communication boundary."

I look around and see Calvin drifting off again, no doubt fantasizing about Carrie. I see Adam sitting next to him, probably wondering how to convince his wife he's been cured. And I see Santa Claus retreating further into his mental hell, desperate for attention and advice. No one's problems are being dealt with. They're going to leave rehab the same as they walked in, just with more guilt and an awkward way of communicating. I can't take it anymore.

My voice cracks as I open my mouth to speak for the first time, and the question spills out clumsily: "How is this helpful to us?"

"The way that we're communicating in here is how people should be communicating with their spouses," Joan responds coolly.

"And that's going to stop them from sleeping with other women?"

It's a serious question, but everyone laughs. Joan's face trembles for a moment, as if nervous she's about to lose control of the room. But then she regains her composure and answers, "You learn to love yourselves by learning to be relational with each other." She emphasizes the word *relational* as if it's a magical healing salve.

I don't completely understand her answer, but it sounds like an important concept. "I'm not sure I understand what you mean by 'relational.'"

"Being relational is being in the moment—in the here and now—with someone else. Here's a tool you can use: Your mind can only do two things at once. So if you can sit and feel your breath go in and out as you listen to someone else, you are in the moment, in action. And when you're not in action, you're not relational: You're in reaction."

Finally, she appears to be teaching us something relevant. "So you're saying that if we're relational with people, then we won't want to cheat?"

She sizes me up for a second, trying to ascertain whether I'm a threat or not. It's the first time she's actually looked me in the eye. "What I'm saying is that if you have true intimacy with your partner, you won't need to seek sex outside the relationship."

She holds me in her gaze for a moment longer, then slowly scans the room. "This is the reason all of you ended up here. If you're addicted to sex, you're probably co-addicted to something else, like drugs or work or exercise, and this is because you're afraid of intimacy and you're afraid of your feelings."

I'm trying to get something out of this. I really am. But the accusations and diagnoses fly around so quickly that it's hard to accept them just on faith. You come in as an alcoholic or a sex addict, and you leave as an alcoholic codependent sex addict love avoidant with PTSD, OCD, and ADD. We're all suffering from low self-esteem, so I don't see how making us into walking DSMs helps.

Joan writes the words s.a.f.e. sex on the blackboard. The acronym was devised by Patrick Carnes, she explains, and it means that sex must never be "*secretive, abusive,* a way to alter *feelings,* or *empty* of a committed intimate relationship."

Before I can ask what's wrong with casual, consensual sex, Joan announces that a counselor named Lorraine is going to speak to us after lunch about something called *eroticized rage*. Then she curtly dismisses us to eat.

"I kept this to myself, but there was more to my fantasy," Calvin whispers as we rise to leave.

"What's that?" I ask.

"I'm glad I didn't tell her about the picnic."

In the hallway, Adam and Troy are waiting for me. "Hey, man, I like the way you stood up to Joan," Troy says under his breath. "We all have those questions, and it's cool that you're asking them."

"Thanks." From the corner of my eye, I notice Charles speaking with

Joan in the therapy room. I'm pretty sure he's telling on me. Some folks live to say, "I told you so."

"Don't give in to her," Troy encourages me as we head to the cafeteria. "She's going to try to break you so you can be like Charles. But you have to stand up for us."

"Why don't you guys just speak up for yourselves?"

"You know, we just want to make it through to the end of the program." He and Adam exchange glances. Troy is here because his wife caught him having an affair with an import model he met on a website for women seeking sugar daddies. "Joan, she doesn't forget. And when our wives come for family week, we don't need her making things any more difficult for us, if you know what I mean."

I've heard other guys here mention family week like it's the equivalent of an IRS audit, so I ask them about it. They explain that the program is divided by weeks here. In week one, you do your timeline; in week two, you go through a psychological head trip known as chair work; in week three, parents and wives visit so your therapist can help heal your family system; and in the final week, you design a recovery plan for when you leave.

For sex addicts, the family-week process includes something called *disclosure*, which requires coming clean with a partner about past affairs and transgressions. Ideally, once these final wounds heal, the couple can build a new relationship from a place of truth and intimacy. With a therapist who's not tactful, though, or one who has a hidden agenda, disclosure can quickly turn into disaster—and the next time the addict sees his wife will be in court.

11

Los Angeles, Two Weeks Earlier

I haven't been able to cry since this happened. I keep trying. My friends have cried for me, but I can't. I gave him my heart and my soul and . . . everything.

This is the first time I've seen Ingrid since she said she never wanted to see me again. It took countless emails, flowers, and coaxing from mutual friends to bring her to couples therapy. And now that she's here, I can see what I've done. She's pale and emaciated. Her eyes stare ahead vacantly and her skin seems devoid of nerve endings, like a combat veteran with post-traumatic stress disorder.

Do you think you can trust him again?

I don't trust him. I just don't. I feel hopeless.

And it rips me apart to know that I was the traumatic stress.

Did you trust him before all this happened?

Yes, of course. I had 150 percent trust in him before. I thought our relationship was the best thing that ever happened to me. It was like I was on ecstasy every day. I was walking on a cloud.

And how did you feel, Neil?

I felt the same way.

Ingrid shakes her head slowly and a distant voice inside her replies.

That's not possible. There must have been something wrong for you to do that.

There wasn't, I swear. It had nothing to do with you. I just got . . . weak.

Ingrid, what would you need to even consider being in this relationship again?

I just need three things.

What are those?

Honesty, trust, and loyalty.

The therapist turns to me. I know what she's going to ask. The only question I don't want to answer.

Do you think you're able to give her those things?

This is it: I must make a choice. The truth or the lie. Just one word either way. If I choose the truth, I risk losing her forever. If I choose the lie, I get to stay with her, but I continue living in deceit and risk hurting her again.

I start to speak. It's hard to get the words out. It's hard because I've opted for the truth.

I can't say for sure that I'm strong enough yet to resist every temptation out there. This is why I'm going to rehab. So I can work on myself and make sure this never happens again. I need to understand how I could have done this to someone I love so much.

Suddenly, Ingrid throws her arms around me and we embrace tightly, with as much pain as passion. Tears spring from both our eyes and make trails on the other's cheeks.

The first tears are sadness. The second are relief. And the third are the most dangerous of all: They are hope.

12

Lorraine is a bird-like woman in her fifties with long shaggy gray hair, taut lips, a big beak, and incongruous thigh-high black boots. The wounds of whatever struggle she went through still show in the lines on her face.

"I'm here to tell you that sex addiction goes away," she announces to us. "The compulsion stops. It's not like alcohol. You can get past this. Recovery, if you work at it, will take you three to five years."

At first, the words sound reassuring. But then I realize that if you work hard enough on almost any behavior, it can be changed in three to five years. I suppose another term for recovery is just behavior modification. There could be twelve-step programs for biting your nails, picking your nose, saying "I'm sorry" when you're not really sorry, and, perhaps more dangerous than cheating on a spouse, texting while driving.

Lorraine tells us, as she's probably told every addict who's passed through here for the last decade, that her alcoholic father would lock her in a closet for hours at a time when she was three; that she was molested by a priest at age twelve; and that she spent most of her adult life as a codependent, stuck in a marriage to an abusive, alcoholic husband. She was one of those women who couldn't leave the man who beat her—until he drank himself to death.

When Lorraine was here twenty years ago, her tag was blue.

"What I just presented to you was my timeline," she explains. "And all of you are going to do your own timelines this week. Who here has child-hood trauma?"

Everyone raises his hand except for me, Adam, and Santa Claus, who probably didn't hear the question.

Lorraine stares at us incredulously. "Trauma comes from *any* abuse, neglect, or abandonment. Think of it this way: Every time a child has a need and it's not adequately met, that causes what we define as trauma."

"But by that definition, is there anyone in the world who doesn't have trauma?" I ask her.

"Probably not," she replies quickly. "We link and store any experience that brings us fear or pain because we need to retain that information to survive. All you have to do is touch a hot stove once and your behavior around hot stoves changes for the rest of your life—whether you remember getting burned or not. So think of anything in your childhood that was less than nurturing as a hot stove, and when you encounter something similar as an adult, it can trigger your learned survival response. We have a saying here: *If it's hysterical, it's historical.*"

I look around the room. Everyone seems to be drinking this in. I suppose we're all broken in some way, whether or not we choose to admit it to others—or to ourselves.

"Most people think of trauma as the result of a serious assault, disaster, or tragedy," Lorraine continues. "But a small trauma, like a parent criticizing you day in and day out, can be just as damaging because it's happening on a regular basis. Think of it this way: If one big-T Trauma is a ten on the scale and a little-t trauma is a one, then ten little traumas can be just as powerful as one big Trauma."

Lorraine is blunt and severe, perhaps even more so than Joan, but there's something about the way she speaks that I trust. She doesn't seem to have a chip on her shoulder, nor does she sound like a member of the Moral Majority. And at least I'm finally learning something, though I'm not yet sure how it will help me be faithful to Ingrid.

"When children experience trauma, they tend to absorb the feelings of their abusers and store them in a compartment in their psyche that we call the shame core. It contains the beliefs *I am worthless, I am unlovable, I don't deserve.* Any time you feel *one down*—or inferior—to someone or you feel *one up*—or superior—those are false beliefs generated by your shame core. Because, in reality, every person in the world has equal worth and value."

Charles interrupts, "But I'm thinking of you as better than me because you're an expert on this topic and you know so much more than me. So what should I do?"

"And how do you feel about that?" Lorraine asks. "I'm standing here, a middle-aged widow, telling you how to live your life. I'm telling you I know more than you do and I'm one up to you."

"I feel anger," Charles says.

"Exactly. To survive painful beliefs and feelings, we often mask them with anger. That way, we don't have to feel the shame behind it."

I look at Joan. She's watching Lorraine with a frown, rapping her pencil against her knuckles. "The payoff of anger is mastery, control, or power," Lorraine continues. "So the anger makes you feel better and one up. And when you use sex to restore power or feel better about yourself in a similar way, this is what's known as eroticized rage."

Eighty-eight percent of sex addicts, she tells us, came from emotionally disengaged families. Seventy-seven percent came from rigid or strict families. And sixty-eight percent say their families were both distant and strict.

"Being overcontrolled as a child sets you up to lie as an adult," she concludes. "So the theory of sex addiction is that when you feel out of control or disempowered, you sneak around and act out sexually to reestablish control and regain your sense of self."

This is where she loses me. "Can you give a specific example?" I ask.

"Well," she replies with what appears to be a touch of condescension, "what's your story?" Or perhaps it's not condescension, it's caring, and my shame core is just flaring up.

"I cheated on my girlfriend."

"Strict mother?"

"Yes."

"Mom wasn't emotionally available, so you're taking out your dick and using it to look for love. And sex is healing the anger at Mom for not being available." She speaks quickly and confidently, as if my story is exactly what she knew it would be.

"So I fuck other women to get back at my mom?"

"And to have an emotionally safe way of getting the affection, acceptance, and comfort you never got from Mom."

"I don't know. It felt like my mom was always there for me."

She strokes her hair, which is as prodigious and thick as Rick Rubin's beard, and asks a question that will alter my entire understanding of my childhood: "Was she there for you . . . or were you there for her?"

STAGE II
▪ Adapted Adolescent ▪

"I SEE ANOTHER LAW IN MY MEMBERS, WARRING AGAINST THE LAW OF MY MIND, AND BRINGING ME INTO CAPTIVITY TO THE LAW OF SIN, WHICH IS IN MY MEMBERS. O WRETCHED MAN THAT I AM!"

—St. Paul
Romans 7:23-24

13

Chicago, Thirty Years Earlier

You know the drill, right?

Yes, Mom.

Then let's go over it again.

My younger brother and I are at the kitchen table, eating cereal. My mom sits in a chair backed against the wall, her mismatched legs dangling from her housedress at different heights off the ground. She observes us carefully as we speak, trying to ascertain whether we can be trusted.

If you die, we're not allowed to tell anyone.

What do you do if Uncle Jerry calls?

Don't say anything until afterward.

Right.

Then we go get you cremated.

What if Daddy tells you I should be buried? He wants that, you know. He doesn't care.

We don't listen to him. We make sure you get cremated. Then we put the ashes in a Marshall Field's box.

And then what?

We take the box to Lincoln Park and scatter the ashes.

Right. And no funeral. No obituary. No grave. Nothing. Don't tell anyone I've died until after it's done, in case they try to stop you.

Can we keep the box?

Yes, you may keep the box.

And then we're going to meet you at the bookstore, right?

We'll meet at Kroch's & Brentano's in Water Tower. In the magazine aisle.

Should we meet at the guys' magazines or the girls' magazines?

Either one is fine.

I'll be looking at the music magazines, okay? I'll wait for you all day. In case you're late.

You may not know I'm there, but I'll be there. I'll try to find some way to let you know.

I imagine her as a ghost, in another plane where she can see me but I can't see her. And I hope that if I stay alert, I'll be able to sense her presence in a cool gust of air or a sudden rustling of magazine pages or . . .

Maybe you can whisper something in my ear.

I'll try to do that. Now hurry up and wash the dishes. The school bus will be here in ten minutes and you're always late.

Yes, Mom.

Don't ever forget what I told you today.

14

When Lorraine finishes her lecture, Joan's lips curve into something resembling a smile. She walks to the front of the room, then lets us bask for a moment in the knowledge that we are now not just sex addicts but rageaholics. We fuck women because we hate our mothers.

Although pleased with the net effect of the talk, Joan also seems resentful of Lorraine's easy command and sway over our minds. She motions brusquely for Lorraine to leave, then turns to us and speaks. "One of the other therapists tells me that the male sex addicts have been talking to her female sex addict. I told her that it can't have been my guys, it must have been her patient. But then"—she raises her eyebrows in feigned shock—"I was told by a member of this group exactly what happened and who was responsible."

I flash Charles a dirty look and turn back to feel Joan's glare heating my face. "Do you see women as human beings or do you see them as a collection of body parts?" she asks.

It's such a loaded, judgmental question that I don't feel like answering it. I stay silent to see if I can get away with pretending like it's rhetorical, but she just repeats the question. So I tell her, "I see them as human beings. I'm not a serial killer."

"I would beg to differ," she responds, as if she really believes that eye-fucking someone should be punishable by lethal injection.

I want to be a better person. I want to have a healthy relationship. I don't want to cheat and lie and cause pain. But outside of Lorraine's talk, the lifesaving healing and lessons in intimacy that Rick said I'd experience here are nowhere to be found. I'm trying to have an open mind, but Joan keeps filling it with garbage.

"As a consequence of your behavior," Joan continues, "I'm going to have to take more extreme measures with all of you."

She holds up several slips of paper, each with the words MALES ONLY on it. "I'm requiring all of you to wear this in your badge, displayed prominently at all times. From this moment forward, you are not allowed to even say *hi* to a woman."

What if she says *hi* first? I wonder. But Joan's already closed the loopholes, with the exception of one: Paul, the lone gay member of the group, also has a badge that reads MALES ONLY. "Just point to your badge if they say anything." She slams her pencil onto her desk. "If any of you are seen talking to a woman, I *will* hear about it."

Now we don't just have the scarlet letter, we've been muzzled. It's hard to tell if they're healing our shame core here or adding to it.

"What about you?" Charles asks. "You're a woman. Are we allowed to talk to you?"

And that's the last straw for me. I'm not like Charles. I can't just blindly obey. It needs to make fucking sense to me. It's like going to a church to be a better person, but then being told that the only way to do it is by worshipping a god you don't believe in. Maybe I've come to the wrong place to learn how to be intimate and decide if a sexually exclusive relationship is right for me. So far, this program is as effective at teaching monogamy as prisons are at teaching morality.

"Is the underlying principle of all this the idea that if we have true intimacy in our relationship, we won't seek outside sex?" I ask Joan.

"Yes," she says, with some satisfaction that I appear to be getting it.

I ask again, just to make sure. I want everyone in the room to hear exactly what she's saying. Troy's advice from earlier echoes through my head: I'm not going to let her break me. I'm going to be the voice of sanity. Of reality.

"If you had true intimacy in your relationships," she repeats, "you wouldn't be seeking sex outside your relationships."

"I have this thing that's been going through my head all day. Is it all right if I ask it?"

"Please." The word drips with disdain.

"Is it okay to use the blackboard?" I don't know any other way to explain it.

Her back stiffens. She senses something unpredictable may be about to happen. She shoots me a stern look, trying to melt my resolve as I approach the blackboard.

My hand starts shaking as I pick up a piece of chalk. I write her words on the board:

If true intimacy, then no outside sex.

"That's your theory," I begin. "If you boil it down to the basic idea behind it, what you get is this . . ."

If true X, then no outside Y.

"And the problem is, this equation just isn't true." In school, I never thought I'd actually have to use algebra in real life. I was wrong. "Even if you make both X and Y the exact same variable, it still doesn't work."

I continue writing:

If true X in the relationship, then no X outside the relationship.

"Let's say, for example, that your wife is the best cook in the world. Then according to what you're saying, you'll never want to eat anywhere else."

Joan remains quiet, watching me, letting me write on her blackboard, rattling me with her lack of reaction.

If true cooking in the relationship, then no cooking outside the relationship.

"But that's just not true. Sometimes you want to go to a restaurant for a change."

The guys are watching intently. Calvin is on the edge of his seat. Troy has a big smile on his face. Charles's brows are deeply furrowed.

This is it. This is the moment where I disprove all the bullshit Joan's been feeding us. She can have her revenge afterward, whatever it may be.

"Now let's go back to your original premise. And let's make it even stronger."

If true intimacy, then no outside intimacy.

"Even that statement isn't true. You seek intimacy with your parents, your siblings, and your friends. No matter how you look at it, what you're telling us doesn't add up."

She says nothing. I press on.

"The other issue is that you're telling us intimacy and sex are related like this . . .

"But for men—and not just the guys here but every man I know—they're like this . . .

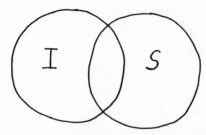

"So what are we supposed to do with all the rest of our sexual needs?"

The guys are staring openmouthed now, big dopey grins on their faces—except for Charles, who's looking at Joan imploringly. I must be interfering with his recovery again.

"Here's what I'm starting to think," I press on. "People are under the logical fallacy that when their partner wants sex outside the relationship, it's harmful to their intimacy together. We are all here because we don't believe that's true, but we do believe that lying and deceit harm intimacy. So instead of being retrained to accept a relationship on our partners' terms, we could just as easily retrain them to accept the relationship on our terms."

Troy dares to applaud. Calvin pumps his fist into the air in solidarity.

Joan doesn't change her expression. She's stone cold. "Cross out *if intimacy, then no outside intimacy,*" she instructs me. I do as she says. "Now cross out, *if cooking, then no outside cooking.*" I do that. "Now go back to your seat." I do that too.

She stares at the board. "I'm processing," she says.

The room is completely silent. It's like a chess match. And everyone's wondering if it's checkmate.

Finally, Joan turns to me. "You need to define *intimacy.*"

"Would you like me to do that now?"

"You can do that on your own time."

I'm disappointed, because I know the answer. I heard it recently in the patient lounge, where someone was quoting Pia Mellody, who's the Patrick Carnes of codependency: *Intimacy is sharing your reality with someone else and knowing you're safe, and them being able to share their reality with you and also be safe.*

"The definition doesn't have any bearing on what I've said, anyway," I tell her.

"I think you're intellectualizing to be able to control the overall addiction," she responds.

That's all she's got: to tell me to stop using my brain? "That's what dictators like Pol Pot and Hitler and Stalin say. They burn books and kill intellectuals so no one can question them."

The response comes out more confrontational than it's meant to be. I'm not trying to rebel. All my relationships have been disasters and something clearly needs to change. "So help me," I add, beseechingly. "I *want* to be wrong. I *want* to recover. But I need to reconcile this contradiction. What you're teaching us needs to actually make sense to me."

"This is your addict fighting against recovery and not letting go," she says sharply. She looks at the clock and rises to her feet. "You're all late for dinner."

She walks to the desk and starts gathering papers, holding her head high as if she's prevailed. Yet everyone, possibly even Charles, is aware that not only did she fail to defend her thesis, but quite possibly she couldn't.

"Neil," her voice rings out as I'm leaving, loud enough for everyone to hear, "why don't you present your timeline to the group tomorrow?"

15

At dinner we all sit together, the red demons of the round table. We are bonded now in brotherhood, in celibacy, in shame, in sickness, in punishment, in victory, and by the fact that we're all wearing signs that read MALES ONLY around our necks.

Nearby I see the anorexics in their workout clothes; Carrie, the love addict; Dawn, the alcoholic; and Naomi, the female sex addict. And they are ghost-like to me, creatures in an alternate dimension I can't communicate with.

The mood at our all-male table is jubilant and conspiratorial. If the guys could carry me on their shoulders, they would. I am their white knight, their sacrificial lamb, their dick in shining latex. In the meantime, from my perspective, something has shifted. This whole notion of sex addiction is unraveling for me. And quite possibly for everyone else. I came here with such high expectations from Rick, but all rehab has done so far is make me even more ambivalent about relationships and monogamy.

"You know, I've been thinking about how Joan made me add up all the money I spent," Calvin says. In the outside world, he's a day trader who writes about conspiracy theories online. "And most of it was worth it. I was with a porn star from Serbia once. She was a ten. Cost a thousand dollars—and she worked me over. It was the best experience of my life. I wouldn't trade it for anything." He pauses and reflects. "I've probably wasted more money on bad food."

"And bad dates," adds Troy, the sex therapist. He tears open three bags of sugar substitute and pours them into his coffee substitute.

"Okay, here's my main question about this place," I begin. "I think helping us understand our childhoods and heal our wounds—that will help our relationships. But I don't know if I buy the idea that wanting to sleep with other people is an unhealthy response to that trauma. I mean, they told me when I checked in that if I masturbated, I was a sex addict."

"Let me tell you, Neil, just be glad you're not in one of the sex addiction programs run by the church," Adam says. "My wife made me go to one of those before I came here. They consider you a sex addict if you have premarital sex."

Troy flashes a big grin. "We're guys. We like sex. Everywhere you turn, you're shown pictures of gorgeous women who look like they want to cater to your every desire. And then what? If you think about sleeping with them, suddenly you're sick and unhealthy?"

Adam nods. "You know, I don't think there are many guys who, if they were staying alone in a hotel and a beautiful woman wanted to have sex with them, would turn it down."

Suddenly Charles slaps the table, as if trying to snap us out of a trance. "This is your disease talking right now, guys. You can't trust your thoughts. Your addiction will say anything so it can keep controlling you."

"How old's your wife, Charles?" Troy asks.

"She's forty-eight."

"And do you find her attractive?"

"I don't know. She's a beautiful person."

"So when's the last time you had sex with her?"

"Eight years ago. But I brought that on myself."

"Adam, what about you?" Troy asks.

"Things were okay at first," Adam says. "But when we had kids, every-thing changed. She just let herself go. We tried having date nights once a month, but all she'd do is worry about the kids. So we stopped doing that too. And"—he hesitates—"I'll tell you honestly: I like sex that's exciting, you know, and sometimes a little rough. And she just lies there like once every three months, and basically lets me have sex with her."

And I wonder: Is this the reality I'm here training for? To cut off my dick in a sexless marriage, and then pathologize myself as a sex addict if I break down one night and sleep with a woman at the office or an ex-girlfriend while I'm traveling or even a hooker, just so I can remember what it feels like to have my dick sucked?

"So what do they expect?" Exasperation pushes the words out of me with unexpected force. "It's just common sense. If your partner hasn't had sex with you for a year, you should be allowed to get it elsewhere without having to throw away your entire relationship."

"Sex isn't something you're entitled to just because you want it," Charles admonishes me. "Pretending like this is common sense and natural is a form of denial. If you want any hope of overcoming this, you have to recognize and intervene on your distorted thinking. When I see another woman, for example, I just tell myself, Bright red apple, wrong orchard."

As the guys laugh over Charles's orchard, I'm overwhelmed by a crushing anxiety. A vision forms in my head before I can stop it. I grab my notebook and sketch it for the guys. They gather around to look:

THE MALE DILEMMA

1. Sex is great.

2. Relationships are great.

3. Relationships grow over time.

4. The sex gets old over time.

5. So does she.

6. Thus the problem.

It's a horrible thing to write or even think. No one could ever say this in regular society. They'd be destroyed for it. But it seems to be the reason most of these middle-aged guys are here. "That just about sums it up," Adam says sadly.

Troy shakes his head resolutely. "You wanna hear something tragic? I was still having sex with my wife four times a week when I started my affair."

"And that's the problem with what Joan's been telling us." Calvin flashes a big, guilty grin. "Sex isn't always about intimacy. Sometimes you just want some dirty sex."

Charles jumps out of his seat and announces, "This is not good for my recovery." He grabs his tray and walks away, looking for another table without women.

The counselor supervising the anorexics turns around and scowls at us, so we take it down to a whisper. We're rehab insurgents plotting a revolution. "Wanting variety is natural," Troy says quietly as the guys lean in. "Look at porn: Guys don't watch the same girl every time."

I think about one of the books the attendant confiscated when I checked in: James Joyce's *Ulysses*. The main character is an advertising salesman with a gorgeous wife at home. And he wanders around Dublin, worried that she's cheating while he gawks at and fantasizes about women of all ages, shapes, and sizes. At one point he starts wondering what his problem is, until he concludes very simply, "The new I want."

Santa Claus looks up from his food and speaks for the first time today, acknowledging morosely, "That's why I kept going to Tijuana. You could walk around a club with sixty women and have any one of them. And the things they could do . . ." Then he drops his head again.

"You know who the best girlfriend would be?" Calvin interjects, his eyes lit up as if he's just had the perfect picnic. "That mutant from *X-Men* who can turn into anyone she wants. I'd never get bored of her! You could have sex with Megan Fox one night and Hillary Clinton the next."

"Hillary Clinton?!" Troy asks for all of us.

"Why not? Just for the experience," Calvin says. "Don't tell me you've never thought about it."

None of us has.

I'm intoxicated by the discussion. But in the back of my mind, I wonder: Are we a bunch of junkies in denial—addicts bonding over our favorite drug—or is this just a natural by-product of high testosterone? In a book on evolution I once read, the writer cited research claiming that gay women have fewer than ten partners on average in their lifetimes whereas gay men have more than a hundred. So I ask Paul about it.

"I've been with over a thousand guys," he confirms. His voice is raspy and gruff, and he has the permanent look of someone who's had a rough night partying. "But it's different in our world, because everyone wants to have casual sex. So, literally, guys would come over to my place and instead of hooking up, they'd go online and invite more people. I'd have a dozen guys fucking each other in my living room sometimes."

"I once interviewed a woman who was going through a sex change to become a man," I tell him. "And she told me that as soon as the testosterone therapy kicked in, she suddenly understood men, because she wanted to fuck everything that moved."

"Imagine if women were wired like men," Calvin says dreamily.

"It would be sexual pandemonium," Troy replies with a big smile.

I ask them the ultimate question: "So if your wife allowed you to sleep with other women, would you allow her to sleep with other men?"

And much to my surprise, every guy except Adam says yes. "I wouldn't like it, but I guess I'd have to suck it up," Troy says.

Adam appears uncomfortable. We may have gone too far for him. Unlike the rest of us, he doesn't yearn for casual sex or variety; he just wants the love and passion his marriage is lacking. "Here's the thing you're all missing," he says, laying his huge hands on the table. "We're not here because we had sex. We're here because we lied, because we wanted sex so badly that we violated our own moral values."

He has a great point. No one is actually here for promiscuity. They're here solely for cheating. Except for Calvin, of course, and for Paul, who came to get off crystal meth but was placed in our group when he mentioned sex parties in his intake interview. "You're right," I tell Adam. "If we were single and behaved exactly the same, we wouldn't be here. It wouldn't be considered an addiction. If the rule was that you're not allowed to eat sushi once you're married, we'd all be here as sushi addicts."

"So maybe the answer to your male dilemma is that you sacrifice," Adam replies. "You tough it out and stand beside your wife, for better or worse, as a choice that you're led to by faith in your family and God."

"But why should you have to make that sacrifice?" I ask. "A relationship should be about what you both want, not about what you both don't want each other to have. There must be some way in which we can have freedom and our partners can have security—or we can all have both freedom *and* security."

Troy points a long finger at me. "See, that's the kind of thinking they want to stop here." He stretches an arm along the back of Charles's vacant chair. "The problem with therapy is that they try to normalize everyone and keep them in the middle of the road. But if you do that to a society, there's no innovation. Nothing new is created. You need that one caveman who said, 'We can't just keep waiting for lightning to strike every time we need fire. We have to make fire ourselves.' They probably thought he was crazy, rubbing rocks and sticks together. Today they'd diagnose him as obsessive-compulsive. But then he gave them fire, and all of a sudden everyone was doing it. You can't get anywhere as a civilization without that kind of original thinking and focus. It's people with compulsive behaviors who change the world."

As Calvin fist-bumps Troy, I wonder if maybe life has led me here not to cure my supposed sex addiction, but to take on a mission for the betterment of my peers and the world: to redesign relationships so that the needs of both sexes can be met. Because they don't seem to be working as it is.

16

Chicago, Twenty-Eight Years Earlier

Sigh. You're the only one I can talk to around here.

What about your friends?

I can't trust them.

Not even Denise?

She's the worst of all. Never tell her anything. She can't keep her mouth shut.

Okay.

I'm lying in bed wearing Star Wars *pajamas, a comic book and flashlight tucked under the covers. My mom's sitting in a small desk chair pulled up to the side of the bed. Sometimes, when she's really upset at my dad and has no one else to talk to, she comes to me. This is one of those times.*

I've just had it up to here with your father.

Is that why you guys were fighting?

Do you hear the way he swears at me—in front of you and your brother? He's a monster. I don't think he has any feelings.

He must have feelings.

He doesn't. He's like a rock. I remember I returned from my honeymoon and asked my mother if I could divorce him. And she said she wouldn't let me come back home if I did that. So I stayed with him, that selfish bastard.

You don't have to stay with him now, though. You're an adult.

Where am I going to go? Who's going to take care of me?

I'll take care of you.

You're not old enough. Where are you going to get the money?

I don't know. Maybe you can find someone else with more money than Dad. Then you can be happy.

Maybe when I was younger. I had a lot of confidence then. I even entered a beauty contest. A lot of men wanted to date me, if you can imagine that. But your dad has ruined me. You know he could only get it up twice: once for you and once for your brother.

Really?

Really. Listen to me, Neil: Whatever you do, never grow up to make anyone as miserable as your father makes me.

17

After dinner, I walk across the grounds to the art room to work on my timeline. I'm supposed to present the story of my life from birth to age eighteen, which Joan doubtless plans to use to pathologize me as a sex addict and troublemaker. And if that's the truth, so be it. I'll give her everything she needs.

I grab a long sheet of butcher paper and a black marker. Then I read a handout with instructions. I'm supposed to write my family message along the top of the butcher paper; words describing the different members of my family down the sides; and, along the bottom, a list of my family rules, my most prevalent feeling growing up, and the role I played in my family system.

Then I'm supposed to draw a long horizontal line from one side of the paper to the other, and to write positive memories above it and negative memories below it in chronological order.

Carrie sits two chairs away from me working on her own timeline, her nipples practically jutting through her shirt. "How's it going, Neilio?" she asks with a friendly smile.

I show her the slip of paper in my badge and trace a fake tear out of my eye. She pretends to catch it and put it in her pocket. This feels a lot like flirting.

I turn away instantly, exercising too little self-control too late. Next to me, a large-jawed, broad-faced man in a white T-shirt and jeans is working feverishly with a charcoal pencil. He looks like he could play the romantic lead in a Hollywood film, except for his forehead and his posture. The former is deeply furrowed, as if his brain is in pain; the latter is rigid, almost bristling, as if the slightest touch will send him into a fit of tears or violence or both.

I look at his drawing. It's a very detailed rendering of a demonic, childlike face behind bars. And it's beautifully done—good enough to sell to Goth kids. He notices me admiring it and I avert my eyes. Too late.

"Have you heard the story about the kid who wanders into the forest and gets captured by a witch?" he asks, his voice monotone.

"Hansel and Gretel?"

"No, this kid was bound with a golden cord. And when he got free and told people, no one believed him."

"I don't think I know it, but . . ."

"That's me," he says laconically, pointing to the creepy child face. "The bars are what separate me from everyone else. And no one can see through them to the monster I'm hiding inside."

His tag is purple for post-traumatic stress disorder. His name is Henry. It's clear someone did something horrible to Henry—probably repeatedly— and no one believed him when he sought help.

Henry says he runs a furniture-manufacturing company. As we discuss our lives, I'm aware that Carrie is nearby, listening to every word. And although I'm speaking to Henry, I'm also talking for her benefit. I'm following the rules but missing the point.

"Guys don't shoot themselves in the heart," Henry is telling me. "They shoot themselves in the head because they're trying to shut their brain up."

I try to focus on my timeline. I write a few words describing how I saw my mother when I was a child, then a few words about my father.

MOTHER

Punishing

Strict

Secretive

Complaining

Suffering

FATHER

Distant

Unemotional

Selfish

Temperamental

Alone

As I review the list, I realize that my family fits neatly into the sex addict mold that Lorraine taught us: Mother is strict and punishing (i.e., rigid) and father is distant and unemotional (i.e., disengaged).

I press on, writing down my most prevalent feeling growing up ("misunderstood") and my family role ("the black sheep"). Next I'm supposed to list my family rules.

And that's when I get stuck. Not because I can't think of any rules, but because there were so many of them. Too many rules to think about right now.

I feel a rush of anxiety and decide to postpone this part of the assignment. In the meantime, I start filling in the timeline with childhood memories that had a strong impact or imprint. Until I explored my father's closet, I never thought of my childhood as particularly bad or unusual. Although my parents were strict and at times eccentric, they loved me and provided for me. But as I start unpacking my memories, a small black cloud drifts into the idyllic picture.

I remember that some days my mother told me never to be like my father; but other times, when she was mad at me, she'd say I was just like my dad. And this was a man she apparently hated. She complained about the way he smelled, the way he slouched, the way he chewed his food, even the way he put his hands in his pockets. She'd call him temperamental, selfish, awkward, embarrassing, and a loser with no friends.

Suddenly, I notice that her constant admonishments that I'm just like my father are not only the root of my self-esteem problems, but that every word

I used on the timeline to describe him was a word I've also used to describe my negative qualities: distant, unemotional, selfish, temperamental, alone.

For a moment everything in the room goes silent, and I feel an old wound begin to tear open. I shake it off and try to focus my attention elsewhere, like on Carrie.

"I'm running a meeting tonight for incest and rape survivors, if you want to come," a monotone voice tells my ear. It's Henry. And suddenly my tiny black cloud seems like a small white wisp compared to big-T Trauma.

"Okay." Anything to avoid having to think about this stuff.

As I put away my supplies and prepare to walk out with Henry, Carrie writes something on a piece of paper and hands it to me.

I read it instantly: "When I'm in L.A., we have to hang out."

I nod yes. And then I realize: If I can't control myself around her, then maybe I do have an addiction. This is my chance to demonstrate that I'm not powerless. I resolve not to give Carrie my number, and to resist doing anything else that will violate my celibacy contract for the rest of the time I'm here.

I hurry out of the art room with Henry like Lot escaping Sodom. If I look back, I'll turn into a pillar of addict.

When we get to the meeting, two women are already there: Dawn, my other temptation, and a sickly looking freckle-dusted brunette in her thirties. Henry arranges us into a square of four chairs. He picks up a binder with instructions and readings for twelve-step meetings, then sets it aside. "Let's not do this," he says, speaking slowly, as if each word requires effort to utter. "Let's just talk. I can begin."

He pauses for five long seconds, the corners of his mouth trembling, then continues. "I snuck out to the street last night. I stood there and looked at the cars passing by in the dark. And I thought about throwing myself in front of one. I stayed there for an hour. I wanted so badly to end it all. It wouldn't take much effort. Just a little bit of courage to take that leap."

Not only did he almost get himself killed, I think, he almost got himself sued for violating the Promise Not to Commit Suicide form he signed.

"You don't worry about losing your life when you don't have one, when it was taken from you," he continues. He's silent again for several seconds, his brow furrowing and unfurrowing. "I remember the first time my brother raped me. I was in my room, and he came in and held me down. He choked me while he did it and said he was going to kill me if I made a sound or ever told anyone."

Henry goes on to talk about an evening, years later, when his father caught him molesting a horse in the barn and beat him. "For a long time, I'd seek out prostitutes, usually men, to whip me and beat me," he continues. "I got into some dangerous situations. My wife doesn't know any of this. Not even about my brother. When I told her I was going to rehab for post-traumatic stress disorder, she just looked at me and said, 'That explains it.' That really hurt me."

Dawn volunteers to speak next. Her story is also horrifying. She tells us about two memories of her father fondling her. A decade later, he was arrested for sexually abusing other underage girls. She testified against him and now he's serving time in prison. Then the freckly woman tells us how her adoptive father would come home drunk, stagger into her room, and molest her.

"I called him last night and asked him to come for family week to help me heal," she says, her eyes and nose filling with tears and mucus. "And he actually agreed to come."

As a culture, we voraciously consume horror movies about vampires, ghosts, zombies, and other supernatural beings. But people are much scarier than any monster we can make up. It's not just the acts of horror they perpetrate on each other, but even when they spare the person's life, they still take their soul, their spirit, their happiness. These offenders are the kinds of people I used to think of when someone mentioned sex addicts, not guys like Adam and Calvin.

"I just want me back," Henry is saying, his eyes ringed red. "I want to know who I am."

Then he looks at me and waits. I'm the only one who hasn't spoken. And I haven't been an incest or rape victim. But then I remember: One day, when I was in seventh grade, the school bully fondled me, then tried to have anal sex with me. The next day, he and his friends began a relentless bullying campaign against me. I lived in terror for the rest of the school year.

"I'm not supposed to talk to women," I tell the group. "But I guess this is okay." I then share the story, which I've never told a single person before. It was my first sexual experience, I conclude, and perhaps my obsession later in life with seduction was a way of overcompensating and proving to myself that I was straight.

As the three of them respond supportively, I still feel like an impostor: My trauma is woefully inadequate compared to theirs.

Even here, in a hospital of misfits, I don't fit in.

18

Chicago, Twenty-Six Years Earlier

Take off your shoes.

I know, Mom.

And put them on the mat, not the carpet like last time.

Yes, Mom.

Now go wash your hands before touching anything. It's too hard for me to keep cleaning your dirty fingerprints off the walls.

Okay, jeez.

And don't forget: Dinner is at six o'clock sharp. Don't be late or you won't get dessert.

I walk to my room to wash my hands. There is no television there, no phone, and no technology except a small stereo. It used to be the Beatles whose music soothed me, but now that I'm a little older and my voice is starting to change, hardcore seems to fit my temperament better.

I'm in the mood to play the Damned's "Smash It Up," but I smashed the record in a fit of anger after I was grounded for a weekend for putting my feet up on the kitchen counter. So instead I crank Suicidal Tendencies as loud as I can without getting into trouble: "They just keep bugging me and they just keep bugging me and it builds up inside."

And I wash my hands. Like a good son.

A few minutes before six, I hear my mom's voice:

Dinnertime.

I enter the kitchen and see her sitting at the far end of the table, my father on her left, and my brother at the end closest to me. I'm the last to arrive, as usual. The black sheep. I sit down in my appointed seat.

Neil, elbows off the table. Ivan, you too!

Her voice is gentle for me, but harsh for my father. He is the blacker sheep. I feel bad for him. But my mom constantly tells me, "You're your father's favorite," as if that's a bad thing, so I try not to show him any sympathy.

You'll never believe what your father did to me this time. He told Robin in his office that we were going to Sarasota for vacation. I have half a mind to just cancel the trip. You two haven't told anyone, have you?

No, Mom. Of course not. But it isn't . . .

When everyone in school brags about where they're traveling for Christmas break, it's hard not to tell them where I'm going. But my mother forbids it. She's worried that while we're gone, someone will break into the house. Before every trip, she hooks up lights to timers to fool all the criminals she imagines lurking outside. My father and I then leave the house and pretend to wave goodbye to my mother and brother. Afterward, they wait until the coast is clear, then sneak into a taxi to follow us. Even at my age, I know we have very little to steal: just two small television sets, two stereos, and one VCR.

I'm also not permitted to know my mother's age, where she went to school, what her past jobs were, or why her leg is deformed. And I'm not allowed to have keys to the house—and never will be—because she's worried I'll lose them. However, my brother is sometimes trusted with the keys to the house. It doesn't seem very . . .

. . . fair. Sam's going to Jamaica and he's allowed to tell everyone.

I've always been jealous of Sam. His parents are divorced and he's a latchkey kid, which means he gets the keys to his house. He can also stay up as late as he wants. Until recently, my bedtime was seven thirty.

Well, Sam's parents don't care what happens to him. And he's just like his parents. I don't want you hanging out with Sam, Neil. He has a big mouth. Anything you tell him, everyone in the neighborhood is going to know. Do you understand me?

Yes, Mom.

He's not your real friend anyway. Now what did I tell you about switching your fork to your other hand after cutting your meat?

. . .

That's better. Who's your mother who loves you very much?

You are.

As I write the family rules on my timeline, I suddenly realize: No wonder I hate monogamy. It's just another irrational rule I have to put up with.

19

In the art room the next morning, I quickly finish my last rule—"Don't trust other people: They are out to hurt you"—and race to join the guys in group therapy. Joan storms into the room a few minutes later carrying a stapled printout. My picture is on it. She looks at me and blurts, "Are you here for research?"

"Research?"

"I looked you up online. I know who you are." She seemed merely to dislike me before, but now she may actually hate me. She knows what I've written: articles and books about sex-crazed rockers, porn stars, and players. A sex addict's oeuvre. And evidently she thinks my sole purpose here is to undermine her.

"I'm one hundred percent here for me," I tell her truthfully. What I don't tell her is that if I were undercover writing about sex addiction, I wouldn't be in this genital detention camp. I'd be with the sex addicts in the real world—having fun in Thai go-go bars and Brazilian termas and German FKK clubs.

"The truth is, this is the last chance for me to have a normal relationship," I continue. "If I can't be convinced that monogamy is natural and healthy, and wanting to be with multiple women is a symptom of dysfunction and trauma, I don't think I'll ever want a regular marriage."

Joan's arms are folded. She studies my every micro-expression closely, waiting to see if I'll smile or break eye contact or show any sign that I'm lying. When I don't, she clucks sharply, "Are you aware that any man who courts a woman with the goal of having sex is an addict?"

I tell her I wasn't aware of that, and she goes on to explain that couples should have seventeen dates and fully get to know each other before initiating any physical contact.

But sex, I think, is part of getting to know someone. What if you commit to a relationship and she's horrible in bed, smells like balsamic vinegar, and refuses to give blow jobs?

She waits for me to challenge her, but this time I keep my thoughts to myself. She then uncrosses her arms and nods her head. "Go ahead and present your timeline."

I unroll the butcher paper—it's the size I was when I was ten—and sit on the floor next to it. I tell her about the rules, the paranoia, the punishments—and the tough but compassionate babysitter who came to live with us when I was two and became like a second mother to me. When I get to the story about my mom's wish that my brother and I cremate her and leave no memorial, my face swells and I feel tears approaching.

Joan responds to the possibility of tears in the room like a shark to the scent of blood in the water. "What are you feeling?" she asks, as if inviting me to cry. She has me right where she wants me: submissive, vulnerable, open.

"Pain," I tell her. "Because just saying that makes me realize how sad she must be inside, how lonely and empty she must feel that she just wants to disappear from the world without any trace of her existence left behind."

I inhale, clamp down on my emotions, and try to suck back the tears through the sides of my eyes. I will give Joan the story, but I won't give her my soul. I don't trust her with it.

When we move into my teenage years, I tell her about my parents never trusting me with the keys to the house, not letting me go on my first-ever date, and grounding me for most of my high school years.

And then, suddenly, I stop presenting my timeline. I've reached the part I've been dreading.

"I have a family skeleton in the closet here," I explain. "But I promised my mother I'd never tell anyone about it. So I don't know what to do. I don't want to lie or break that promise."

"This is *your* recovery," Joan replies. "And you're as sick as your secrets. You can't keep old promises if they're not healthy for you."

"Yes, but I have my own value system. Just like we've taken a pledge of anonymity here, I pledged secrecy to my mother."

"Then we will all make a pledge of secrecy to you," she says. And they all promise.

"One more thing," I add.

"Just say it," she snaps, annoyed.

I ask more questions, buying time so I can determine what's right. I crave the release, but I dread the betrayal. And then, as I look at the faces of the other guys who've shared their secrets in this room, I decide that, after two decades, I just need to let it go. Maybe it's been holding me back, keeping me stuck in the past and riddled with confusion. And so I share what I've never told anyone—not Ingrid, not even my brother.

"Okay. So one day, I was in my father's closet looking for porn." The words start slowly, as if waking from a deep slumber. "And I found this videotape. The first thing on it was a tennis game with people in wheelchairs. Then there was a clip from a movie with a woman in a wheelchair begging in the streets for change. Then a swimming race with these people with no limbs just wriggling in the water. And at the end were all these old film clips of"—it's hard to go on; everyone is silent—"amputees. All these models in bathing suits with missing legs and shit. That's when I first realized"—again, my throat tries to choke the words back down—"my father's got a thing for cripples."

The words fly out between tears and spittle. "And my mom's a fucking cripple. She had no idea he had this obsession when she married him. That's why she hates him so much. She thinks she's like the prize of his collection."

I tell the group that after I found the video, I asked my mom about it. She seemed relieved she had someone to talk about it with and told me what she already knew about his obsession, like the pictures she'd found of my father when he was younger, bending limbs behind his back to look like an amputee. Eventually, we began investigating him together, and we found detailed inventories that he'd made of his photo collection of men and women with different amputations and birth defects.

Everyone in the room is silent, even Joan. I press on, telling them that my mom's never told my dad that she knows about this, that she made me promise never to say a word about it to anyone, that she constantly calls me to discuss new evidence she's found, that she's paranoid that he has cameras hidden in the house to record her, that she believes he meets regularly with a secret club of men who share his fixation, that she thinks he brings them photos of her and random disabled people he photographs in the streets, that she has such an overwhelming feeling of shame that she won't allow herself to be photographed and thinks anyone who stares at her must have a thing for her bad leg.

"She even found a film of their honeymoon he'd edited so that it only contained scenes of her limping." I talk and talk and don't stop talking. "I try to tell my mom that if she were a blonde with big breasts, people would stare and take photos and she wouldn't have a complex about it, so she should just think of it as an attractive feature."

And finally, when the story is as exhausted as I am, I skid to a halt and return to my body.

"Was that so bad?" Joan asks.

I want to answer: Yes, it was that bad. I don't feel unburdened at all. I'm still carrying the secret; the only difference is that now nine proven liars also know it. I feel vulnerable and sick to my stomach.

"Are you aware that sex addiction has a genetic component?" she goes on.

"I don't know." I wish I hadn't told her: She's already using it against me. Just like my mom warned me people would do.

"I know," she says firmly, as if a point has been proven. "However, there's an issue here that's even bigger than your father's addiction and him leaking that energy all over the house."

"What do you mean?" My face is crimson from fear, guilt, stress, fatigue.

"It's your bond with your mother—the way you keep secrets for her, the way you both investigated him together." I can perceive the faint outline of something important on the horizon of her words, but I can't seem to identify it. "If you put what you just shared together with all the other pieces of your childhood, a clear pattern emerges."

"Which is what?"

She starts to speak, then stops herself. "I don't know how you're going to take this."

"Just say it," I snap, imitating her, just to be an asshole.

This gives her the resolve she needs. She sucks in a breath of air, then exhales. "Okay, I'll just say it." The pause is long, the room is quiet, my heart is hammering, and then she says it. "Your mom wants to be in a relation-ship with you."

It hits me like a ton of bricks. I sit there dazed, and a cold wind blows from somewhere inside me. Images from my life flutter in the current, each one a disturbing fragment of evidence: Why else would my mom come into my room at night and tell me all her problems? Why else would she not let me go on my first date? Why else was I grounded all the time and told that my classmates weren't really my friends? Why else wasn't I allowed the keys to the house when my brother was? Why else did she cut off all support and communication when I moved in with my first girlfriend, even though I was in my twenties? And what was I in this whole investigation of my father if not her intimate partner?

The tears come fast now. The statement seems so preposterous, yet some-thing in my body recognizes the truth in it.

Joan's got me. She's won. The pride, the ego, the defenses, the algebraic equations are all gone. I am at her mercy. And that's when she hammers once more on the stake she's just driven into me: "That's why you're unable to be in a healthy relationship."

"Now it makes sense why there was a double standard between my brother and me," I choke out between sobs, regressing with each one. "Like, after college, he could have his girlfriends spend the night at my parents' place, but I never could. Even to this day."

"And why was that?"

"She said they were never good enough for me. That I chose badly."

"It's not that you chose badly." She's found the blood in the water now. "It's that you didn't choose Mom."

My head is spinning. My mom didn't do this intentionally, I'm sure, but it was unconscious. She hated Dad, she didn't trust her friends, and I was the oldest, most reliable male around. So she probably wanted me all to herself, or at least safely under her control.

"When your mom is emotionally dependent on you and has intimate discussions with you that she should be having with her spouse, there's a name for that." Joan looks at me like a prizefighter sizing up a dazed opponent, then lands her final blow. "It's called emotional incest."

And I'm done.

STAGE III

▪ Functional Adult ▪

HE TRUTH MAY BE OUT THERE,
BUT LIES ARE INSIDE YOUR HEAD.

—TERRY PRATCHETT
Hogfather

20

Mexico City, Many Years Earlier

"Ready for school, princess?" her father asked.

She glanced up at him. He was wearing a dark suit and looked like a movie star. An actor. She hated it when he talked to her like that. He had no right. He was rarely around and had never taken her to school before.

He bent down and found her hand. She let it lie limply in his, like dough in an oven. She couldn't remember ever feeling the warmth of his hand before.

Instead of taking her to the front door of the school, he led her to an alley alongside the building, where he met a short-haired brunette woman in a pencil skirt with high heels. He kissed her, but not the way the girl's grandmother kissed people. They kissed like lovers in the movies.

In the days that followed, she conducted an investigation of her father, like in the detective shows she'd seen on TV. In an evidence box underneath her bed, she collected her father's beeper, full of messages from random women; his scheduling book, documenting appointments with them; and, finally, tape recordings her father was secretly making of her mother talking on the phone.

When she was ready to make her case, she sat her mother down and handed her the box. The little girl was nervous, not because of the effect it would have on her mom, but because the phone recordings contained evidence that she and her brother had been prank-calling the butcher. ("Hello . . . do you have pig's feet?" "Yes." "Why don't you wash them!" *Click*.)

Her mother didn't say a word as she went through the box. First she looked confused, then uncomfortable, and finally she started crying.

The next day, her mother started her own investigation. In addition to discovering that her husband had several girlfriends on the side, she found out that not only had he never divorced his previous wife, but he was actually still living with her—and having more children with her. So she confronted her husband about his double life and told him it was over between them.

That night, the little girl was woken by screaming and a loud crash from her parents' bedroom. She ran to their door and pushed against it, but it was blocked by a broomstick. The doorknob had fallen off a few weeks back, so she looked through the hole to see what was going on.

Her father was sitting on top of her mother, his face red and twisted as if possessed. His hands were over her mother's mouth and nose, squeezing tightly. She struggled to breathe, her hands clawing at his. Her eyes, grotesquely enlarged, appeared to turn toward the little girl, pleading, "Help me!"

"Please don't kill her!" the little girl yelled between sobs as she tried to open the door. She rushed to her older brother's room and woke him up, and he ran into the hallway and slammed his body against the door. Over and over again.

As the door burst open, her father released his grip from her mother's face and backed away, telling his children that they were just playing. Her mother stumbled toward her—gasping violently, her face pale blue, her eyes blood red—and the little girl grabbed her hand and ran into the bathroom with her. She locked the door, and the two of them cried together.

The boy ran to the phone to call their mom's brothers. They were all big men and very protective of their sister. But as the boy was yelling "Help!" into the receiver, his father tore the cord out of the wall, pulled open the window of their fourth-floor apartment, and threw the phone outside.

Ten minutes later, the girl emerged from the bathroom. The house was completely still. She heard classical music coming from the kitchen. There, she saw her dad sitting at the table, his legs crossed gracefully. He was holding a glass of cognac, swirling it slowly, gazing at it with a look of complete peace as he breathed in the notes of the drink, the music, the night air.

She yanked the needle off the record. "What are you doing?!" she yelled, furious, confused, terrified.

"I'm waiting for my death to arrive," he said calmly.

That was the last time Ingrid saw her father.

21

I wake up alone in the rehab dorm, the sun diffusing through a small dirt-filmed window, the muffled mating calls of birds and cicadas announcing another morning, and a raging hard-on pressing against my boxer shorts.

My mind drifts to an image of Carrie and the suggestive way she handed me her note. I remember she's roommates with Dawn and I start picturing a threesome with them. I think about how her caretaking qualities must extend to the bedroom and I imagine her using her breasts in considerate ways. Some guys are ass men; others are into breasts, legs, or faces. My theory is that it has to do with the sexual position you prefer. If you like it doggy style and you're looking at a woman's ass when you come, you're going to associate your sexual pleasure with that part of her body. If you like missionary, maybe you're a face man. And if you like her on top, you've usually got an eyeful and a handful of breasts when you orgasm. And if . . . fuck, I just made a mess in my boxer shorts.

I waddle to the bathroom and wipe up. I feel like an alcoholic who's smuggled a fifth of vodka into rehab and just guzzled it.

As I get ready for the day, I think about a book Rick Rubin once showed me. It was about a seventies commune called the Source Family, which was run by a bank robber, vegetarian-restaurant owner, and aspiring rock star known as Father Yod. In the book, there was a photo of him—looking eerily like Rick—sitting outdoors in his commune in the Hollywood Hills with thirteen of his hippie wives and lovers gathered around him, at least two of them pregnant with his children.

And I wonder what it would be like to live in an environment of open and unrestricted sexuality, with friends and lovers coming in and out freely, no one claiming ownership of another's body as if it were a personal possession.

That's when I realize why today, of all days, my mind is spinning out of control: It's Sunday and Ingrid is coming. The force of light, monogamy, stability, marriage, children, and a normal life is on her way. And now my "disease" is blossoming like mold.

Check-in: guilt. And shame.

Guilt is about making a mistake. Shame is about being a mistake.

And fear.

Two days earlier, when I was lying in a puddle in group therapy, seething over the violence of the phrase *emotional incest*, Joan suggested a couple of things. The first was that I call Ingrid and tell her what I'd learned about myself and why I'd cheated on her. The second was that I ask my parents to come for family week to work on healing our trauma and dysfunctional relationships with one another.

As I masturbated, Ingrid was driving hundreds of miles to see me for the first time in weeks and talk about my recently diagnosed intimacy issues. I think of her driving so far all alone, and I'm touched she would do that for me after what I did to her. And how do I show my gratitude? By plotting orgies.

I'm not a bad person, I tell myself. I'm just scared of intimacy.

Unlike reaching out to Ingrid, calling my parents and telling them I was in rehab for sex addiction wasn't liable to be greeted with the same degree of support. So, like anyone faced with doing something emotionally difficult, I put it off until later.

Every Sunday, all patients are required to attend family-week graduation. So I walk across the property to a large classroom, where a dozen addicts and trauma survivors sit with their families in the front of the room. One after another, sons, daughters, parents, siblings, and spouses stand up and talk about how the week has begun a much-needed healing process for them.

"A lot of times, people in a family think it's just one person who causes all the trouble," Lorraine, the therapist who lectured us on trauma, is telling the assembly. "But a family is a system, and a sick person is the product of a sick system."

As the ceremony continues, I feel a dry, sticky crunching in my navel hair. Evidently I didn't wash away my sins well enough. I look around to see if it's possible to slip away, but then the freckly woman from Henry's rape-and-incest meeting rises from her seat and turns to face us. She's wearing black slacks and a blue cardigan, and looks much less sallow than before—almost upbeat, bordering on charismatic. She's standing next to a man in his late sixties with a large red face, a porcine body, and huge, crevassed hands. It is the adoptive father who molested her.

I don't sense any hatred from her, nor any warmth. Someone looking at a photo of the two of them might think it was of a schoolteacher giving an old janitor an award for forty years of dedicated service.

"If some of you remember, when I first arrived, I was very depressed and cried a lot and thought about killing myself," she is saying. "I don't think I talked to anyone for my first two days here. But thanks to family week, I feel like a human being again."

She turns to her father and everyone sits stock-still, waiting to hear what he has to say. "It was very hard for me to make the decision to come here," he says. No shit: You're staring at a room full of trauma survivors who hate you. "I feel very bad about what I've done. And I think Laura is an incredibly brave woman for being here and for allowing me to be here. I know nothing I can do or say will take away the past, but I'm happy that Laura can have a future now. I think I've grown more as a person with the therapists here than I have in my entire life."

Listening to him, I resolve to call my parents. Since the day I left home for college, I've called my mom nearly every Sunday; the few times that I haven't, she's given me a guilt trip to remember. And it is a Sunday.

Besides, if this woman could invite the monster who molested her to come, then surely I can ask a woman who merely grounded me a lot. Not only would it be good for my parents to face the truth—my mother and I have never told my dad that we know his secret—but maybe the family healing will relieve me of whatever is hanging over my head and standing in the way of having a happy, honest relationship.

Rehab, One Hour Later

You're not a sex addict, you're a man. If someone wants to play with you, you're not going to walk away. What are you, a dork? You're going to play back.

The voice belongs to my mother.

Yes, but not when I'm in a relationship.

In my book, that's how men do it. I believe in honesty in relationships, but if you're going to cheat, you gotta keep it to yourself. As a woman, I've been asked out for coffee a couple of times and I say no thanks. But that's because I'm a woman and that's not my nature. Though if he were a multi-millionaire and he wasn't married, maybe I'd get coffee with him.

As I listen to her talk, I'm floored. I've never heard her views on fidelity before, except when she's disclosing the latest piece of evidence supporting her conviction that my father is having an affair. Yet here she is on the phone, making the exact same argument I've been making all week—except she's doing it her way.

She continues . . .

I don't think you need treatment. Everything about you is going to be in those hospital files for the rest of your life and the world is going to know about it. All you're addicted to is life and living it.

It's too late now. But I'm learning some things that will help my life. And the week after next, they have something called family week, when the parents of the people here visit. It really completes the healing process and I wanted to see if both of you could come for it.

To go there would be useless.

I really need you and Dad here. It would mean so much to me. And it would help me a lot.

Listen, you're an unusual but normal person. If it were a life or death situation, we'd do it.

My father is also on the phone, but he doesn't say a word—except to apologize when my mother tells him he's breathing too loudly into the handset. No wonder I'm scared of marriage. Whenever someone I'm dating starts treating me worse than they treat a stranger, that's always the beginning of the end for me.

What if I have a therapist from here call you and explain why it's important?

Don't you dare give anyone my phone number.

Okay. Please, Mom. I don't know what to say.

There's nothing you can say. Physically, it's just very difficult to travel.

If they have therapists in Chicago they recommend, can we all go see one together?

I don't think so. There's nothing we could do or add. We don't feel you have a problem. Whatever problem you have, you know and we know.

It would help us connect. Remember my ex-girlfriend Lisa? When she saw us together, she said it didn't seem like there was any warmth or love between us.

Lisa was just with us for one meal. I wasn't comfortable with her. She wasn't friendly or smiling. She didn't relate to us at all.

Joan's words ring in my head as she speaks: another example of the women I date not being good enough for my mother. The implicit message is that sex and affairs are okay, but don't get a real girlfriend because that would be competition.

I try using her own weapon against her: guilt.

As a mother, it would be one of the best things you could ever do for me.

How would it help you exactly?

It would help me be happier, healthier, and capable of having a functional relationship and starting a family of my own.

Charlie Aaron didn't get married until he was in his seventies, and he was never happier. And he didn't need any kids.

My breath catches in my throat. I've never heard of a mother who didn't want to be a grandmother. Every word coming out of her mouth seems to support Joan's horrific diagnosis.

But remember Irvin from high school? He said he didn't even know the meaning of the word love until he became a father.

Irvin was your brother's friend?

No, he was my friend.

That's not possible. You were a dork. You didn't have any friends.

Why would a mother ever say that to her son? I wonder. Then I realize that I just recently learned the answer: She's keeping me in my place. I beg and plead for them to come, countering objection after objection, until she says flatly . . .

I have some really valid reasons why we can't come. We love you, and we'd do anything else for you.

Hard to believe that right now.

Can just Dad come then?

No way, José.

He says nothing. He has no voice in the relationship. I try one last angle, my ace in the hole: promising to keep the secret.

Whatever you're worried about, and I think I know what it is, we don't have to discuss that.

I know who I am. I know who my parents are. I had an idyllic childhood. I think I turned out to be a great mother with two wonderful kids. I wouldn't change you an ounce. But if you're not satisfied with you, then you can help you by yourself. I'm not coming for personal reasons—very personal—and that's it! Tell them not to call.

The words fall like a sledgehammer, breaking the ground around me, isolating me, sending me spinning off into space alone. I reach for a lifeline.

Can I ask you to just send me a copy of the keys to the house instead? They said it would give me a sense of closure if I could wear them around my neck as a symbol that I can be trusted.

I realize that since leaving home for college, I've always had an odd key fixation. I've never thrown one away, even to old dorm rooms, cars, and apartments.

Sorry, Charlie. It's not you, it's me. I don't feel safe. And, besides, you're absentminded. You lost that tape recorder when you were twelve and a million other things. And I can't endanger my feeling of safety.

Okay, thanks for listening. Bye, Mom.

We can hire two people and send them to family week instead if you want.

That's okay.

Enjoy your incarceration.

The world I once knew, the one I thought I grew up in—strict, yes, but full of love and sacrifice from the parents who conceived, nurtured, and supported me—is gone. What she's saying, ultimately, is that her issues are more important than my wellbeing. And they always have been.

It could be worse, though. At least she has a sense of humor.

23

I shower for a second time, making sure to use a washcloth, soap, and pressure, then trudge to a men's circle in progress on the lawn. The thirty or so guys there are using what they call a talking stick, and only the person holding the erect-cock-sized piece of wood can speak. When he's done, he says "aho," which is some sort of macho Native American sound, and hands the wooden dick to the next lunatic.

"Hi, I'm Calvin and I'm a sex addict. And I'm feeling a lot of fear right now, but also joy, because Mariana"—the Brazilian prostitute he impregnated—"just told me she wants to keep the baby. Aho!"

He hands me the stick. It's my turn to check in and I want to get it over with quickly: "I'm Neil and I'm tired of labels and I'm fine. Aho!"

Everyone sucks in air or exclaims "ooooh" like I've just stepped in shit.

"What?" I ask.

Charles gestures for me to hand him the stick. I shake my head in annoyance and hand it to him. Idiotic rule.

"Fine stands for fucked up, insecure, neurotic, and emotional," he says. "That's about right."

The men glare at me in silent accusation: I spoke without holding the talking stick. You'd think I just shot someone.

Charles hands me the talking dick and I place it on the ground next to me. "I love how someone can just make up a random fucking rule and you all follow it like sheep," I tell them as I walk off. "I've been in a fucking men's circle all week anyway. Aho!"

No one responds because no one is holding the talking stick.

I'm aware, as I walk away, that I'm not really mad at them. And I'm not mad at the talking stick. It's actually a decent rule. If I'd had the chance to speak uninterrupted as a child and express myself and truly be heard, I'd probably be much healthier.

What I'm mad about is that some people's parents *can't* come to family week because they're dead or broke or in prison, but my parents just *won't*. A guy who molested his daughter has the balls to show up here. As for my father, he doesn't even have the balls to speak up for himself on the phone.

Check-in: fucked up, insecure, neurotic, and emotional. And rethinking everything I thought I knew about my childhood, my life, and who I am.

The perfect frame of mind to see Ingrid after all this time apart.

24

She is too pure for this place.

She stands in the nurses' area, where I'm now allowed the occasional use of my razor under supervision only. She's wearing a fitted blue plaid button-down shirt that's open to reveal a triangle of flawless skin, and black jeans that stop just above her high heels. No one wears high heels in this place. It's not healthy for the fragile libidos here.

She stiffens as she sees me and everything comes up at once in her face—the love, the hate, the desire, the fear, the hope, the hurt—and pushes through the scab covering it all.

The words "Oh my god" escape from her mouth. Then the tears roll. When we hug, it seems like she's dissolving into me. But when I feel her shirt rubbing against my chafed navel, a sense of unworthiness sweeps over me. Here I am, lusting after every slightly attractive inpatient I see, while she's come all this way hoping I've changed. I guess I'm here because I want to be as good a person as Ingrid is.

What I'm feeling right now is another symptom of my trauma. It's shame again. I am putting myself one down.

Where I belong.

Suddenly, a fragment of my past comes rushing back. I'm a teenager lying in bed, imagining what my life will be like in the future. It's always the same scene:

My brother is living in a large suburban house with a big green lawn and a beautiful blond wife. I visit and ask if I can stay for a while because I have nowhere else to go. My clothes are dirty and wrinkled, and my face is unshaven. I crash on his couch, emitting a funny smell and watching TV, until one day his perfectly put-together wife asks him, as politely as can be, "Is your brother ever going to get a job? He can't stay on this couch forever."

And now, two decades later, I actually manage to achieve the happy life I never thought possible—a home, a job, a girlfriend oddly similar to the wife I imagined my brother with—and I wreck it. It's as if the prediction didn't come true, so I willed it to be. I fucked it to life.

"What are you thinking about?" Ingrid asks.

"I'm just happy you're here."

There's an energy between us. It's a stronger feeling than I get with any-one else, like the pull of two magnets held just slightly apart. "What's in your hand?" she asks.

"It's my timeline. I want to explain it to you, so you can know who I am."

We walk to the lawn and sit in the grass near where the men's circle was. It's just below the patient lounge and I notice the sex addicts clustered along the outdoor benches above. They also seem taken in by Ingrid's magnetism. I wonder if they're thinking of being with their wives or of cheating on their wives.

Ingrid listens closely as I walk her through each event on my timeline. But when I reveal the punch line—emotional incest—she strains to under-stand. "How is that incest?"

"I know. I hate the term. Everything is diagnosed as some sort of crip-pling psychological disorder here." It feels so good to be talking with her, sharing with her, smelling her again that, despite the subject matter, I'm giddy with happiness. "But this is what pertains to us: They say here that if you tell them what kind of relationship you had with your opposite-sex parent as a child, they can tell you what kind of romantic relationship you're going to have as an adult. Unless you're gay, in which case it would be the same-sex parent."

"I don't know. That sounds oversimplified."

"Maybe it is. I have no idea what's true anymore." Ever since presenting my timeline, my head's been a mess. So I explain to Ingrid what I've learned since that afternoon . . .

They say here that there are three ways of raising children. The first is functional bonding, in which the parents or primary caregivers love, nur-ture, affirm, set healthy limits with, and take care of the needs of the child. I turn over my timeline and sketch it for her:

This creates a child who has healthy, secure self-esteem and relationships.

But then there's neglect, when a caregiver abandons, is detached from, or doesn't appropriately nurture the child. This can range from a parent who isn't physically present, to a parent who is physically present but emotionally distant, to a parent who doesn't provide adequate care or safety, to a parent lost in a work, sex, gambling, alcohol, or other addiction. If you grew up feeling unwanted by or unimportant to a parent, this is a sign that neglect likely occurred:

This creates wounded children, who are often depressed and indecisive, see themselves as flawed and less valuable than others, and feel they can't face the world alone. In relationships, they tend to have what's called anxious attachment. They may feel like they're not enough for their partners; become so wrapped up in their relationships that they lose sight of their own needs and self-worth; and be emotionally intense, passive-aggressive, or in need of constant reassurance that they're not being abandoned. Here, they call this type of person a love addict.

As Ingrid listens intently, I look for any recognition in her eyes. After all, she was abandoned by her father throughout her childhood, even before he tried to kill her mother and narrowly escaped her uncles. When I see none, I move on to explain the third type of parenting: enmeshment. This is my upbringing.

Instead of taking care of a child's needs, the enmeshing parent tries to get his or her own needs met through the child. This can take various forms: a parent who lives through a child's accomplishments; who makes the child a surrogate spouse, therapist, or caretaker; who is depressed and emotionally uses the child; who is overbearing or overcontrolling; or who is excessively emotional or anxious about a child. If you grew up feeling sorry for or smothered by a parent, this is a sign that enmeshment likely occurred:

In the process, enmeshed children lose their sense of self. As adults, they usually avoid letting anyone get too close and suck the life out of them again. Where the abandoned are often unable to contain their feelings, the enmeshed tend to be cut off from them, and be perfectionistic and controlling of themselves and others. Though they may pursue a relationship thinking they want connection, once they're in the reality of one, they often put up walls, feel superior, and use other distancing techniques to avoid intimacy. This is known as avoidant attachment—or, as they put it here, love avoidance. And most sex addicts, according to this theory, are love avoidants.

I tell Ingrid that I asked if there was a fourth category for physically or sexually abusive parenting, but was told that this could register on a child as either neglectful or enmeshing. They explained that a rule of thumb to use is that when a parent's abuse disempowers a child, that's neglect; when it's falsely empowering, that's enmeshment.

Ingrid blinks back tears, places her rock-paper-scissors-playing hand warmly over mine, and says, "I would give up anything to see you healed and free of the enmeshment that's keeping you from living."

In the past, I would have thought this was the most beautiful thing in the world to say. Now, instead, I worry that wanting to give up "anything" for someone else's happiness is a dysfunctional symptom of love addiction and codependence. Then I worry that being scared by her selfless caring is a symptom of my own love avoidance. They're really screwing up my mind in here.

"I'm working hard on it," I tell her. Wait, that's not completely true. "Some of the stuff here is a little too over-the-top for me, though." That's better.

"I think this is going to be the best thing that ever happened to you," she responds. And for the first time since I cheated on her, I see the light return to her eyes.

"Do you really think so?"

"I know it. I've never told you this, but I was in rehab for two years."

25

"So all you really want in a relationship is freedom?" Ingrid asks as we walk to the cafeteria for dinner later that day.

"Yeah, I think so."

"I'd like to give you more freedom, then."

"Really?"

"Yes, starting now." She grabs my jeans playfully and starts pulling them down. "This is what freedom feels like!" An impish smile, which I've sorely missed, spreads across her face. "Why don't you show everyone here your freedom?" she mocks, pulling next at my boxer shorts.

I yank the waistband up to keep from exposing myself: If Joan saw this, she'd probably add *compulsive exhibitionist* to my permanent record. But Ingrid keeps fighting to remove my clothing, yelling "Freedom!" at the top of her lungs.

We walk into the cafeteria, grinning ear to ear. She's making a joke out of the issue all us red demons have been tying ourselves in knots over. Perhaps the best cure is just to lighten up. I don't need Zoloft. I have her.

"Miss, you're going to have to button your shirt higher," the dining-hall counselor and anorexic-feeder barks when he sees her, as if the sex addicts are going to break into spontaneous public masturbation when they see that extra inch of cleavage.

We each grab a plate of flavorless chicken parts over soapy rice and walk to the sex addict table. Troy claps me on the back and says idiotically, "You didn't tell us how hot she was." Maybe the counselor was right after all.

Charles doesn't leave the table as we sit down, which means visitors are presumably exempt from the "males only" rule. Ingrid asks each guy in the group about his story and each speaks freely of his sins, except for Charles.

Then she tells them her family's story: "My grandfather cheated on my grandmother all the time, but she always loved him. After he died, she started having recurring nightmares about him cheating. So every morning, she goes to his room and yells at his ashes, '*Dios mío*! Even in death you are still cheating on me. Can't you let me be, you dirty old man?'" The guys laugh all too knowingly. "Then, a few hours later, she returns, apologizes, dusts the room, and refreshes the flowers on his nightstand."

And so, even in death, in relationship with a memory, the ballad of the love addict and love avoider continues.

Ingrid's mother was just as obsessive a love addict. "She used to be beautiful and independent and have her own TV show in Mexico, but when we moved to America, she became a domestic slave to my stepfather," Ingrid tells the guys. "I'd try to get her to leave him because he was so emotionally abusive, but she'd always say, 'I can't. What am I going to do when you both turn eighteen? I'm going to be left alone.'"

"Maybe that's the female dilemma," Troy cuts in. "She marries someone who's giving her love and romance, but over time she gets taken for granted or turned into a maid or becomes a baby factory or gets cheated on. There's not a single emotional need of hers that's filled by her husband. Then he has the nerve to complain that she's not sexual or attractive when he's drained the life out of her."

As the guys nod in sad recognition, Ingrid quickly summarizes her teenage years, some of which she'd never shared even with me before: Her stepfather treated her worse than a servant—making her do backbreaking work, refusing to let her dine at the table with the rest of the family, and giving her an unheated garage without any furniture as a room. Ingrid soon slid from a straight-A student to a straight-F student.

Eventually, she ran away, started doing meth, and spent two years living in rehab because her stepfather wouldn't let her back in the house. She ended up becoming the youth spokesperson for the treatment center, appearing on the news and speaking at events with the mayor.

Yet despite separating from her family and accomplishing so much on her own afterward, she still followed in her mother and grandmother's footsteps and fell in love with a cheater.

After dinner, the anorexic-feeder curtly tells Ingrid that visiting hours are over. As we head back to reception, Henry, my new friend from the art room, falls in step with us and starts speaking in his slow monotone, ignoring Ingrid. "They talk about how there are eight emotions here, but I think there are nine."

"What's the other one?"

"The ninth emotion is the death emotion. It's just feeling nothing."

We're fragile beings, I think as I see the pain in his face. Even when the body heals, the soul remains scarred. As we talk, he slowly becomes aware of Ingrid's presence and asks if she's my girlfriend.

I turn to Ingrid and our eyes search each other's for an answer. I've done my penance and shown a willingness to change by checking in here; she's shown her forgiveness by driving here to see me and sharing her own secrets.

"Yes," she tells him. "I am."

Relief and gratitude flow through me. I'm done fantasizing about the women here. I've been given a second chance not to be Ingrid's father and grandfather—or to be them and perpetuate the multigenerational pattern of cheating men and the women who love them. The sins of the parents are the destinies of their children. Unless the children wake up and do something about it.

"I trust your boyfriend," Henry says. "I feel like I can talk to him."

Of course he can, I think. I must give out some sort of enmeshment signal, letting everyone know they can confide their crazy shit in me. That's probably why I ended up profiling rock stars for *Rolling Stone,* why all those mistrustful celebrities felt comfortable divulging private thoughts to me that they'd never shared with anyone else, why my editors clapped me on the back afterward and put the story on the cover.

Childhood trauma may sneak up from behind and fuck you in the ass when you grow up, but at least it leaves a tip on the nightstand.

"Who was that poor guy?" Ingrid asks as Henry drifts away, talking about his latest suicide plan: He's identified the most dangerous patient here and is planning to pick a fight with him.

"He had sex with a horse."

"And the horse got jealous and told his wife?" she jokes, though there's a barb in there that I ignore.

As we hug goodbye in reception, I try to imprint the softness of her breasts against my chest, the ridges of her spine beneath my fingertips, the warmth of her cheek against mine, so I can remember them when I get weak.

"My biggest wish is that you find your inner peace and happiness," she says as she pulls away.

"Thank you for believing in me," I tell her—my girlfriend, my lover, my jailer.

After she leaves, I sit on a bench outside the patient lounge and tears come to my eyes. She seems to love me unconditionally, but I fear that I love her conditionally. I look at her sometimes and worry that she's going to get wide hips like her mother, or I wonder if I'll still be able to make love to her when she's fat and wrinkly. Other times, I pick apart her existing features, looking for flaws and imperfections. The sad thing is, I certainly have a lot more imperfections she could pick apart: I'm short, bald, bony, and big-nosed, with huge greasy pores. I'm lucky to have her. And I wonder: Am I even capable of love? Have I ever truly loved anyone?

I can't tell whether my tears are for the beauty of her love or the sadness of my incapacity to feel worthy of it.

26

As a journalist, I've met a lot of so-called experts. Most are just people with a little experience and a lot of confidence who've given themselves a title with which they can fool the suggestible and dim-witted. But every now and then, I come across someone who has the experience, knowledge, and calling to be not just a teacher dispensing information but a guide leading others to themselves. And Lorraine seems to be one of them.

"Self-deprecation is still self-worship," she is telling Calvin. "It's the flip side of the same coin. It's still about *self*."

It's our second week here and the staff has divided us into smaller groups to experience a Gestalt-like therapy they call chair work. Adam, Calvin, Troy and I—the troublemakers—have, to our relief, been placed under Lorraine's care in a nearby building. And she's in the midst of prepping us to undergo this intense form of trauma healing.

"I suck at self-deprecation," I whisper to Calvin.

Lorraine overhears and says sternly, "Remember that humor is a wall. It's a form of denial, just the same as repression, rationalization, globalization, and minimization."

Yes, I think she is one of those experts. It's clear she's dealt with enough stupid smart people that she can read me like a book.

That afternoon, Lorraine rips open everyone's minds. As she lectures on the human psyche, sex addicts' faces illuminate intermittently, like fireworks, as they realize the origins of their behaviors, their feelings, and the beliefs that have kept them estranged from others and ultimately themselves.

Unlike traditional talk therapy, in which a therapist sits with a client in an office for an hour every week for years or even decades, addiction treatment *has* to change people quickly. Lives are at stake. That next drink could lead to a burst vein; that next injection could be a hot one. What matters is what works today, not what's been studied and accepted by the mainstream psychiatric community. And so some say the techniques here, many of them adapted from the decades-old work of a former nurse, Pia Mellody, who as of this moment doesn't even have her own Wikipedia entry, are problematic; others say they are the pinnacle of personal transformation—if you're lucky enough to get the right counselor.

And we were lucky enough to get Lorraine, the only person I've encountered here so far who doesn't seem burned out or embittered by the Sisyphean task of healing damaged minds she can't touch or see.

As Lorraine explains the model they use here, she asks us to take a deep breath, listen carefully, and drift back to the way we saw our parents—and the world—at age eight or twelve and not as we understand them now. And this is what we hear. Maybe, if you choose to do the same, you'll recognize someone you know . . .

EVERYTHING THAT'S WRONG WITH YOUR BEHAVIOR AND WHY IN 1,800 WORDS OR LESS

In the beginning . . .

You were born.

And like all infants, you were completely vulnerable and dependent, with a new developing brain and no understanding of the world.

In a perfect world . . .

Your parents would be perfect. They would be dedicated full-time to taking care of your physical and psychological needs, always making the right decisions, setting the healthiest boundaries, and protecting you from all harm, while preparing you to eventually take care of your needs without them.

But in the real world . . .

No one is perfect. Neither your parents, nor the other people who play a role in your upbringing. Therefore, along the way, some of your developmental needs don't get met.

And the problem is . . .

When one of your needs doesn't get met, however big or small, it can leave a wound.

These wounds are known as childhood trauma. Each instance or pattern of trauma can create specific core personal issues and relation-ship challenges—and if these are left untreated, you're likely to pass your wounds on to the next generation. Since this trauma occurs early in life, it can affect social, emotional, behavioral, cognitive, and moral development.

It's not always overt or intentional . . .

Most commonly, people think of trauma as coming from hateful perpe-trators who are knowingly and willfully abusive. But even parents who think of themselves as loving or well-meaning make mistakes, cross boundaries, or simply do their best with the limited internal resources they have. And this covert, often unrecognized abuse can, through its constant repetition, leave wounds just as deep as those created by a single malicious act.

It can be an emotional scar . . .

In your earliest years, you're the center of the universe. Everything revolves around you. So wounds can come from caregivers who are either out of control or completely detached from their emotions around you. When Mom is always full of anxiety as she's breast-feeding, Dad comes home in a rage every time he has a rough day at work, or Stepdad is depressed by his money problems during the rare moments he spends with you, you soak up these emotions like a sponge, often erroneously taking the blame or responsibility for them. Even if a parent falls ill and passes away, it can seem like abandonment or something you made happen if you're too young to understand death.

It can be physical . . .

Most people understand that it's not okay to physically harm or even spank a child. But here's an example that's not as obvious: Any invasive medical procedure—even something as commonplace as a circumcision or getting stiches—may register the exact same as physical abuse if you experience it in your first few years of life. You may even start to distrust your caregivers for bringing you to an unfamiliar place and not keeping you safe.

Often it's intellectual . . .

After the first few years of life, you start to separate from your parents. In this period, it's their job to help you become your own person and confidently stand on your own two feet in the world. Here, a whole new set of problems can arise—especially when parents try to over-control you, habitually criticize you, or unreasonably expect you to be perfect. Other families adhere to such rigid rules that any manifestation of a child's individuality is immediately attacked as a threat. All these can lead to esteem problems later in life.

Or it can take over your entire identity . . .

Within a dysfunctional family system, each child tends to play a different role that helps the family survive and detracts from its real issues. These can include the revered *hero*, the troublemaking *scapegoat*, the neglected *lost child*, the people-pleasing *placater*, and the mood-lifting *mascot*. Later in life, these roles (as well as birth order) can lead to corresponding personality issues, whether it's the hero's judgmental perfectionism, the scapegoat's explosive anger, the lost child's low self-esteem, the placater's denial of personal needs, or the mascot's impulsive irresponsibility.

But it's not easy to see your own core issues . . .

Your oldest beliefs, behaviors, and adaptations have not just been reinforced by decades of habit, but are built deep into the architecture of your brain, which is busy building new neural connections at an astounding rate in early life. As the saying goes, "Cells that fire together, wire together." So trying to see yourself with any objectivity can be like trying to touch your right elbow with your right hand.

But if you can detach from yourself a little bit, you'll notice that the things you do and think don't just come out of nowhere. Here are a few techniques and tools you can use to better understand the way your past can interfere with your happiness, your relationships, and your life today.

You can work backward . . .

Are you relentlessly driving yourself to succeed and beating yourself up when you fail? Maybe that's because when you were a teenager, your parents made you feel as if your worth as a human being was dependent on your grades, touchdowns, or accomplishments.

Are you out of touch with your emotions because Stepdad always told you to toughen up when you cried? Do you feel deep down like you don't matter because you were often ignored growing up? Are you always trying to save or care for others because you were never able to save Mom from her depression or addiction? Are you in complete denial that anything was wrong with your family because Dad acted as if he were infallible and must be unquestioningly obeyed, so criticizing him would be like blaspheming God?

Are you getting the hang of this yet?

You can excuse my language . . .

Some of you have a big bag of shit you're carrying around. And every time you encounter a situation in which you can possibly get more shit to put in the bag, you grab it and stuff it inside. You'll even ignore all the diamonds glittering nearby, because all you can see is the shit.

This shit is known as "the stories you tell yourself."

Examples include generalizations like "I make bad decisions," "If people saw the real me, they wouldn't like me," or, conversely, "No one is good enough for me." Each of these beliefs can be formed in childhood by, respectively, fault-finding parents, abandoning parents, and parents who put you on a pedestal.

As a result, you can spend much of your life misinterpreting situations and thinking you've found more evidence to support these false conclusions formed in childhood. One way to recognize when you're stuck in your own story is whenever you feel less than or better than others.

You can examine this chart . . .

Wounded Child (emotionally 0–5)	Adapted Adolescent (emotionally 6–18)	Functional Adult (emotionally mature)
Worthless	Arrogant	Esteemed from Within
Extremely Vulnerable	Invulnerable	Healthy Boundaries
Extremely Needy	Needless	Communicates Needs
Feels Bad / Naughty	Feels Blameless / Perfect	Honest and Self-Aware
Out of Control	Hypercontrolling	Flexible and Moderate
Fears Abandonment	Fears Suffocation	Interdependent
Seeks Attention	Seeks Intensity	Lives in Integrity and Harmony
Idealizes Caretakers / Partners	Disillusioned by Caretakers / Partners	In Reality About Caretakers / Partners

Then ask yourself: In a given week, do you exhibit any of the wounded child or adolescent behaviors here? If so, you may have either gotten stuck somewhere along the way in your emotional or behavioral development, or certain situations are causing you to revert to those ages.

Any time you overreact to something—by shutting down, losing your temper, sulking, feeling hopeless, freaking out, disassociating, or any of numerous other dysfunctional behaviors—it's typically because an old wound has been triggered. And you're regressing to the childhood or adolescent state that corresponds to that feeling.

Note that the wounded child tends to directly internalize the messages that caretakers give; the adapted adolescent tends to react against them.

However, not everyone reacts to the same trauma in the same way . . .

And children are born with different predispositions and resiliencies.

So if you remain loyal to people who abuse and mistreat you, that's called *trauma bonding*.

If you only feel normal if you're doing something extreme or high-risk, that's *trauma arousal*.

If you've developed intense self-loathing, you've got *trauma shame*.

If you find chemical, mental, or technological ways to numb yourself and your feelings, that's *trauma blocking*.

And it goes on and on. One pattern of trauma; many different possible responses to it. We've only scratched the surface. But at least you know the model we're working with here.

It's not about blaming but understanding . . .

In summary, we each spend our adult lives running on a unique operating system that took some eighteen years to program and is full of distinct bugs and viruses. And when we put together all these different theories of attachment, developmental immaturity, post-traumatic stress, and internal family systems, they make up a body of knowledge that allows us to run a virus scan on ourselves and, at any point, to look at our behaviors, our thoughts, and our feelings, and figure out where they come from.

That's the easy part. The tough part is to quarantine the virus, and to recognize the false self and restore the true self. Because it isn't until we start developing an honest, compassionate, and functional relationship with ourselves that we can begin to experience a healthy, loving relationship with others.

"And that," Lorraine concludes, "is what chair work is all about."

27

At the Sex and Love Addicts Anonymous meeting that night, Carrie plops down on the sofa next to me, her bare arm resting gently against mine. I move my arm away. This is the new me.

"I can't believe that bitch still won't let you talk to me," she says.

"It's for your own safety. I'm too dangerous for women."

Charles, who's sitting across from me, makes a slashing motion over his neck. He's right. Even that little is too much. I leave the room, return a few moments later, and sit somewhere else. Although it seems like a sensible thing to do and respectful of Ingrid, this kind of distant, uninterested behavior is probably only going to make Carrie like me more. This is, until she hears my check-in.

"I broke my contract Sunday morning," I confess when my turn comes. "I feel weird saying this in front of everyone, but I masturbated. I just woke up in a certain condition and couldn't help myself."

The words ring in my head: "I couldn't help myself." That sounds exactly like something an addict would say. To reassure myself, I ask if anyone else has masturbated.

There's total silence and then one hand sheepishly rises. "I have," Calvin whispers.

Suddenly, I'm the most out-of-control sex addict in the room. Calvin was probably masturbating about his picnic. "I realized afterward," I continue, "that I was masturbating because I was terrified of my girlfriend coming to visit. However, it turned out to be incredible having her here, and it made me want to take my recovery more seriously and become a better person."

As we walk out of the lounge after the meeting, Charles falls into step with me. "Let me give you some advice so you don't break your contract again," he says. "Believe, behave, become: Believe in you and Ingrid. Behave for Ingrid. Become a nuclear family."

It's good advice. The three steps.

"If you ever decide to admit you're powerless over your addiction, you can look me up in L.A. when you leave," he continues magnanimously. "I can get you into a private therapy group with one of the best CSATs in L.A."

Evidently I said the right thing in today's meeting. I decide to ask him

how he relapsed, since he shared the details of his story with the group before I arrived. "I was in New Zealand, where prostitution is legal," he answers. His voice is melancholy, yet despite himself, a guilty smile creeps across his face. Joan calls this *euphoric recall.* "And I ended up going to this place where they had a menu of services and had a threesome with two very attractive women for four hundred and fifty dollars."

We stand silently at the edge of the dormitory for a moment, both dialing up the visual, a crack of desire appearing in Charles's austerity. "And that was bad," I say. "Very bad."

"Yeah, very bad."

That night, I dream that Ingrid and I are in a hotel room in Las Vegas with a priest we're paying by the hour.

"I now pronounce you man and wife," the priest says.

As soon as the words leave his lips, a cold shroud of fear envelops me. Something irreversible has taken place in just seconds and I'm overcome with regret because I know I can't reciprocate what Ingrid feels. I wake up with a sense of doom hanging over my head.

Charles's words ring in my head: "Become a nuclear family."

What's so great about a nuclear family? I wonder, before I can stop myself. All the word *nuclear* makes me feel is a fear of annihilation.

28

Chicago, Twenty-Three Years Earlier

Ring. Ring.

Hello.

Is Todd there?

It's a girl calling for my younger brother. They always call for him. Never for me.

No, he's out.

This is Rachel.

Hey.

I'm with Julia and we were calling to invite him over. We're having a special party. Julia, why don't you tell him about it?

They both giggle. It's a sound only teenage girls can make. It is their mating call.

Yeah, Jonas and Craig were over, but they can't get it up anymore.

What do you mean? What are you guys doing?

We're really horny. Want to come over?

This is it: finally, a chance to lose my virginity. And I need to become a man before college.

There's only one problem.

I can't. I'm grounded.

We'll make it worth your while.

How?

We'll give you—*and here she whispers*—a blow job.

Together?

If you want. We'll do you so right if you do us right.

God, I want to come over so much.

I can't believe they're offering to have a threesome with me. This would be the Super Bowl of teenage sexual experiences. But I stayed out too late one night without calling my mom, so I got grounded for two months. I've spent most of my teenage life punished. The year before, my mom somehow found out that I'd gone to a rock concert I wasn't allowed to attend, so she grounded me for six months.

Hurry. Julia wants to have sex with you.

Really?

She wants you, Neil.

Fuck, I want her too. But I don't think I can today.

Or any day for the next seven weeks.

Why not?

I told you. I'm grounded.

Just sneak out.

I can't. I don't have the keys to the house.

You're no fun.

Wait.

Let's call Alex. Hey, do you have Alex's number?

Looking back on that phone call—the only time I ever got propositioned in high school or college—I don't know why I never rebelled, why I never just went out anyway, why even at that age I put up with being constantly imprisoned. Senior year of high school, second semester, when you've already been accepted to college—that's supposed to be the best time of your life. At least for teenagers who aren't enmeshed.

Lorraine tapes several sheets of butcher paper across the wall and asks me about my relatives as far back as my great-grandfather. As I speak, she maps my family tree, diagramming everything I know about each relative, from their birth order to tragedies in their lives to the power balance in their marriages. This is called a genogram. She's looking for patterns. And she finds several.

"I've been doing this a long time, and this is one of the most narcissistic mothers I've ever come across," she tells me when we get to my parents and my relationship history. "She suffocated you, so you set up a wall with her that you kept in place through anger and sneaking around behind her back. And you're still using that wall to keep from being suffocated by Ingrid."

Everything she says lands in my head like the sweep of a broom, knocking away cobwebs and uncovering lost brain cells, like the years of anger and regret I harbored over being grounded and missing out on my only high school sexual opportunity.

"There's one thing that's been bothering me," I tell Lorraine. "I can't understand why I never stood up for myself against her strictness and just rebelled or ran away?"

She looks at my genogram for a moment, then responds: "Because your example was your dad, and he never stood up for himself. And his father didn't stand up to his mother either."

The rest of the guys nod in agreement as I wonder whether my grandfather had a secret sex life too. Probably. "And you'll notice," she continues, "that they didn't model a healthy relationship for you. It's no wonder you have fear when it comes to Ingrid. You don't want to end up in a relationship like the one your parents have."

Growing up, I often wished my parents would have affairs. When my mother and I found photos of my father out with a woman we didn't recognize, I was happy he'd apparently found some romance and excitement outside his desolate marriage. It's no wonder cheating came so naturally to me. I'd given myself permission long before I'd ever had a girlfriend.

Lorraine spends the rest of the morning and most of the afternoon doing everyone's genograms. When she finishes, she tells us that before we start our chair work tomorrow, she wants to teach us about the relationship between the love addict and the love avoidant—or, as she prefers to put it, the codependent and the counterdependent.

"If you think of intimacy as *into me I see and I share that with you*—that's intimacy," Lorraine begins.

I've heard the word *intimacy* constantly here, spoken as if it's the holy grail. And all these fun things—from sex to drugs to ambition to even dressing attractively, reading novels, or having intellectual thoughts—are supposed to be eliminated because they're barriers to it.

"Intimacy problems come from a lack of self-love," she continues. "Someone who fears intimacy thinks, unconsciously, If you knew who I actually was, you'd leave me."

"I always think that!" Calvin says, raising his hand for a high five. It goes unslapped.

"I'd classify all of you as intimacy avoidants," she presses on. "The avoidant is very good at seducing, in the sense that he has an uncanny ability to find out what his partner needs and give it to her. Because he was usually enmeshed, he gets his worth and value from taking care of needy people."

"So are guys love avoidants and women love addicts?" Calvin asks.

"No, I've seen both. What happens in either case is that we choose partners who are at our age of emotional development and maturity, and whose issues are complementary to ours. Your wives may think they sent you here because you're sick and they're normal, but I've never worked with a couple where one of them had it all together and the other was a screw-up. They've got just as many issues as you do. Proof of this is the fact that they're still with you."

"Can I please get you on the phone with my wife to tell her that?" Adam asks.

"This is exactly what I'm talking about," Lorraine responds. "That's the enmeshed child in you speaking. You should be in recovery for you, not for her. And that's typical of your marriage as a whole. Because when a love avoidant and a love addict begin a relationship, a predictable pattern occurs: The avoidant gives and gives, sacrificing his own needs, but it's never enough for the love addict. So the avoidant grows resentful and seeks an outlet outside of the relationship, but at the same time feels too guilty to stop taking care of the needy person."

"By outlet, you mean an affair?" Adam interrupts.

"It can be," Lorraine says. "But it can also be obsessive exercising or work or drugs or living on the edge or anything high-risk. He will also compartmentalize it because the secrecy helps kick that intensity up a notch. In the meantime, as the avoidant's walls keep getting higher, the love addict uses denial to hold on to the fantasy and starts accepting unacceptable behavior."

As she speaks, I think of one of the most classic myths of our civilization: *The Odyssey*. Odysseus cheats rampantly on his voyage home from the Trojan War, even shacking up with a nymph for seven years, knowing full well that his wife, Penelope, is waiting for him. Meanwhile, Penelope stays pure for twenty years, even though she thinks he's dead. Yet Odysseus is the hero of the tale and even slaughters all 108 of Penelope's suitors for daring to court her. In here, they'd diagnose Odysseus as a love avoidant—off adventuring, warring, and intensity-seeking—and Penelope as a love addict, living in fantasy. This relationship is as old as time.

"But the avoidant's behavior has consequences," Lorraine continues, "and chief among them is something most of you are familiar with: getting caught. And that shatters the fantasy for the love addict, who experiences her biggest nightmare: abandonment, which replicates her original wound."

One thing Odysseus did right is that he didn't get caught. That's because they didn't have paparazzi, social media, mobile phones, and the Internet back then. It was easier to compartmentalize.

"The pain and the fear are so intense for the love addict that she often develops her own secret life as well. Where the avoidant wants the highs, the addict typically goes for the lows. She wants benzodiazepines, alcohol, romance novels, shopping till she drops, or anything that depresses the central nervous system. If she acts out sexually or has an emotional affair, it's not for intensity, but to numb the pain and get away from the agonizing hurt. Soon, the relationship is no longer about love for either partner, but about escaping from reality."

Lorraine draws a diagram of the unhealthy relationship she's been describing:

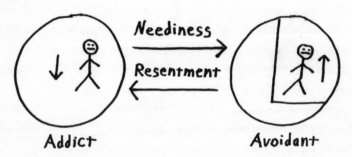

"Is everybody one or the other?" Calvin asks. "I feel like I'm both."

It's a good question: I've always seen myself as more ambivalent in my relationships than avoidant, but perhaps doubt is just a form of avoidance because it prevents me from ever fully committing to anyone.

"Some people have elements of both or play different roles at different times," Lorraine responds. She then draws a picture of a healthy relationship:

"A healthy relationship is when two individuated adults decide to have a relationship and that becomes a third entity. They nurture the relationship and the relationship nurtures them. But they're not overly dependent or independent: They are interdependent, which means that they take care of the majority of their needs and wants on their own, but when they can't, they're not afraid to ask their partner for help." She pauses to let it all sink in, then concludes, "Only when our love for someone exceeds our need for them do we have a shot at a genuine relationship together."

"Can I ask a question?" I blurt. For some reason, whenever someone starts telling me what's right and wrong, or making life sound so black-and-white, I get uneasy. My fellow red demons give one another a look. They know where this usually leads. I walk up to the blackboard as Calvin rubs his hands together gleefully.

In her model of an unhealthy relationship, I erase the arrows and the words *neediness* and *resentment*. Then I erase the other person, until all that remains is one person in a box with an excitement arrow:

"If we eliminate one half of the dysfunctional relationship, the dysfunction is gone," I explain. "What's left is a single guy enjoying life and its pleasures. Why is the option with two people in a reciprocal nurturing relationship any better than this option?"

"If it's not outside your value system and there aren't any negative consequences, then live it up," Lorraine replies. "But I would question why you'd choose intensity over intimacy."

"Because intensity's more fun."

This time, I return Calvin's high five as I take my seat. I'm not doing a very good job of taking my recovery more seriously, but in her depiction of a relationship, all the highs and peak experiences of life have to be sacrificed in the name of intimacy. And that doesn't seem like a goal worth aspiring to.

"I'd be willing to bet that after the high of the intensity, there's a comedown, and you feel not so great and you need that next hit of intensity," Lorraine responds coolly. "So ultimately, you can live your life like a hamster on a wheel, chasing after the next hit to keep yourself spinning. Or you can realize that ultimately it's all a distraction to avoid the harsh reality that you are not connected to yourself."

The jubilation in the room dies down. Her blows are well aimed and hard. Unlike Joan, Lorraine doesn't seem to be trying to win, but rather to help—and her position is not only less dogmatic, it actually makes sense.

"There's an unconscious part of ourselves we want to defend," she continues, "and it's been useful and helped us survive the difficult stuff we went through with Mom or Dad or the priest or the coach. But we don't want it driving the car anymore." She looks at me and Troy and Adam and Calvin, then concludes: "Life's not worth living if you're living someone else's life."

Calvin starts crying.

30

Today I saw myself. For perhaps the first time in my life.

The day after Lorraine's lecture, we walk into the treatment room to find six chairs carefully arranged. There are two chairs near one wall. The first is for Lorraine, the second for her first victim—which I soon find out is me. There's a third empty chair facing mine on the other side of the room. The seats for the rest of my libidinous brethren are lined up against the wall on my left side, as if out of the range of fire.

Each chair has a box of Kleenex next to it.

"You're going to want to imagine that you have wetsuits on," Lorraine tells the rest of the guys. "And zip them up tight, because it's going to get very emotional in here and I don't want any of you affected."

I brace myself for what's to come as she tells me, "Before we start this process, I'd like you to know that there are married men who are not only faithful, but don't even think of cheating."

Before the adapted adolescent in me can respond with something cynical like, "And there are also men born with eleven toes," she tells me to close my eyes and shut off my thoughts. "Pay attention to the feeling of your feet on the ground and the gentle in and out of your breathing," she says, her voice slowing and softening. "Notice how every time you exhale, you become more relaxed."

I know what she's doing: She is putting me into a trance. And I trust her, so I try to relax and let go. She asks me to imagine my eight-year-old self sitting next to me, watching the events that are about to unfold. As I try to visualize that skinny, awkward kid with the cheap glasses, I recall Joan saying that fantasizing is a defense against intimacy. So I wonder what she'd have to say about this.

Shit, I need to stop thinking critically for this to work.

Focus on breathing, come back to the moment.

There.

"I want you to imagine that your dad is outside the door. Picture him as he looked when you were growing up."

I summon an image of my father: He is bald, wearing a faded blue mono-grammed dress shirt tucked into black pants. There's a gentleness to his face, but also a distant look, as if he's not completely present. In short, I see him exactly as he was when I was eight.

"Call him into the room and ask him to sit down in the chair across from you."

I do as she says and try to imagine my father walking into the room. It's eerie how easy it is to feel like I can see him. The imagination is a powerful thing. Of course, I've had plenty of practice with it, but it usually involves that threesome I missed out on.

"What's he doing?" she asks.

"He's just sitting there, kind of disconnected."

"I'd like you to talk to him. Repeat what I say: *Today I am calling you into this room and holding you accountable for the way you raised me.*" She speaks the words loudly and forcefully—as if she is the parent and my father the child, as if she is the judge and he the accused. I try to match her tone, repeat her words, and not sound too ridiculous in front of my fellow addicts in their imaginary wetsuits.

"*This is not about you, Dad,*" she says. "*This is about me.*"

I repeat.

"*This is about your behaviors, not about who you are as a person.*"

I repeat, and she urges me: "Louder! Really speak up and tell him off." She shifts into her accusatory voice. "*You were never there for me, Dad. When Mom punished me, you chose to stay silent, even though you knew her punishments were arbitrary and unfair.*"

I try to own each phrase, to feel it as deeply as I can, to release it as explosively as possible. And it goes on:

"*You never protected me.*"

"*You neglected me.*"

"*I'm not going to act out for you anymore, Dad.*"

"*I'm not going to medicate anymore by seducing women.*"

I throw the words with force at my dad, but as I do, a voice in my head goes, "Wait a minute. I worked hard to learn how to seduce women!"

She's still feeding me: "*I'm not going to medicate anymore with cheap sex in some club bathroom.*"

I repeat, but the voice in my head grows louder. "Hey, those are among my most treasured life experiences. What is she implanting in me while I'm in a trance?" Then another voice reminds me, "Go with it. That's why you're here." So many voices. Joan can add dissociative identity disorder to my file now.

And the tirade continues:

"I'm angry."

"Shout it: *'I'm angry!'*" I try, but it's not enough for her. She has me scream it over and over until I'm really summoning wrath and hurling it at him.

"Tell your father what it was like being punished by him!"

I do as she instructs: "The only time you ever punished me was when you spanked me because I made you late to watch a TV show. I was only a kid and I was having fun on the walk home. You didn't punish me to make me a better person. It proved everything Mom said about you being selfish."

"That was wrong, Dad!" she has me repeat. My eyes well with tears, with the sadness that I never allowed myself to show at the time. She's getting to me. *"You were shameless! And I give you back your shame!"*

As I tell him off for not being a father, for being checked out, for never standing up for me, I hear Calvin sobbing in the background. Evidently he didn't zip his wetsuit up high enough. As for me, I have no wetsuit. I'm in the moment, yelling at my father, flushing out the loneliness and sadness of childhood. It's as if a heavy load is lifting off me.

"You had a secret life, Dad," I'm telling him now. "You lied to all of us and it wasn't fair. You disappeared on Thursdays, and no one knew where you were or what you were doing. You traded photos with a group of guys who shared your obsession. You kept it in the closet and it was more important to you than any of us."

"Let go," she encourages me. "Tell him how shameless it was for him to teach you to lie and sneak and hide things."

The next word doesn't make it out of my throat. All that emerges is a sudden, uncontrollable sobbing. I can't remember the last time I cried this much.

"What just happened?" she asks.

"I realized why he has that obsession," I say, each word escaping after a heave of my chest. "Because that's how he feels inside, like a cripple. He's emotionally crippled."

And then I really break down.

When I recover, she tells me to return his problems, behaviors, emotions, and neglect to him so that I can shrink my shame core. She asks how he's receiving all this, and when I respond that he's taken it in as best he can, she has me tell him to leave the room.

"Now I'd like you to imagine your mother standing outside the door," she says.

Anxiety bursts from my chest and buzzes through every nerve in my body like a swarm of insects. This is the moment I've been dreading.

31

It's much more difficult to imagine my mother outside, because just a few days ago she refused to come here. So I know she'd never walk into a room full of strangers to air personal problems.

"Order her in, then," Lorraine instructs. "Tell her she has no choice."

I do as she says and eventually I see my mom limp into the room.

"What's she doing?"

"She's sitting down and she has a sort of joyful, happy face on. But it's just a mask."

"Can we see through it?"

"It's pretty convincing."

"Let's see how it holds up. Tell her she told you things she shouldn't tell a kid."

I do as she instructs, but for some reason, it doesn't sound very assertive.

"You made me your surrogate spouse," she cues me.

I repeat her words and try to match her tone, but it rings hollow.

"You enmeshed me, Mom."

I can't seem to find the inner strength and conviction to yell at her about all this. Besides, she doesn't know what enmeshment means. I didn't even know myself until a week ago.

"You committed emotional incest."

This is where I draw the line. "I can't say incest. Can I call it emotional abuse?"

"That's fine. But is anything else wrong?"

"Yeah, as I'm saying these things, I'm hearing her voice in my head telling me, 'I did my best to raise you. And I talked to you because I had no one else to turn to.'"

"Are those things true?" Lorraine asks.

"They are to her."

"Are they to you?"

"No."

"Then tell her what it was like growing up with her. If it's easier for you, simply list the things she did."

I suck in air and prepare myself. Ever since I presented my timeline, the thread holding together the first eighteen years of my life has been completely ripped apart, with strands swirling through my memory, trying to coalesce around the new narrative that Joan and Lorraine see so clearly. So I just let it all out.

The room, and the world, seem to freeze as I vomit out every single memory of being overcontrolled, overwhelmed, and overshared with: The constant groundings. The warnings that everyone was out to hurt me. The criticisms of all my friends and girlfriends. The belittling of my dad as a husband and lover. The prohibiting of my first dates. The withholding of keys to the house. The insistence that I report to her room after returning home at night to tell her everything I did. The abandonment when I chose to live with a girlfriend. The request to not bring girlfriends when I visited home. The refusal to let them stay at the house when I did. The comments that she'd rather live to see my next book than to see a grandchild. The constant admonishments that I don't take care of things and I lose everything and I can't be trusted and on and on and fucking on.

I pause. "There's more, but that seems like enough for now."

"Tell her what you think of all that," Lorraine says.

The narrative is disturbingly clear. "I didn't want to believe the counselors here at first, Mom, because it's so weird, but you've been trying to keep me all to yourself. And since you can't do it physically anymore, you continue to do it emotionally. Why?"

"Do you want to know why?" Lorraine asks.

"Please."

"She wants a monogamous relationship with you. So when you're in a relationship with someone else, you're being unfaithful to her. And if you don't take your emotional life back, you'll be in a relationship with your mother until the day you die."

She has me yell at her, *"Shame on you, Mom, for scaring away women so you could have me to yourself!"*

Despite all I've learned, I still feel guilty for hurting my mom this way and for bursting her bubble. But Lorraine keeps encouraging me to defeat my resistance with volume, until I'm roaring her words: "This is your pain I've been carrying, Mom! I'm giving your pain back to you." My voice fills the room until it feels like there's no space for air. "I'm very angry. And I have a right to be angry!"

"Tell her how it felt when she told you never to make anyone as miserable as your father makes her."

"It fucked me up, Mom. It made me avoid relationships and made me fear the future. It made me scared that I would make someone I loved miserable, that I was bad for them, that we'd end up hating each other like you and Dad."

And all of a sudden I collapse into tears. Fuck.

"What are you feeling?" Lorraine asks.

"I haven't been connecting with Ingrid." The tears come harder. I can't believe I'm bawling like this. Again. "Every time I have sex with her, I'm thinking about some random woman I didn't have sex with. I'm not letting her in." I'm crumpled in my seat now. I can hear Calvin and the other guys crying. I feel the support and encouragement of all the sex maniacs in the room. "It's not fair to her."

"Do you know why that is?"

"No."

"Because your mother has taught you to fear women. So you avoid intimacy by not being present and connected when you're with Ingrid."

Before I can process that concept, she has me yelling, *"I'm not letting you scare me away from women anymore, Mom. I'm going to love who I want, and you can find someone else to be your confidant."*

It's preposterous, but I really feel like my mom's sitting there and I'm telling her all these things. Tears pour down my face. Until this moment, I'd maintained a small reserve of skepticism about the concept of emotional incest. But now there's no doubt. I feel the truth of it in every cell of my body. *"I'm not going to be afraid of intimacy for you anymore, Mom!"*

And when it seems like everything's come out, that there are no more tears and snot left inside, Lorraine asks if I have anything else to tell my mother.

"Yes." I take a deep breath and let the last thing out: "I'm not keeping your secrets for you anymore, Mom." And fuck if I don't break down again.

Lorraine asks what I'm experiencing. I tell her, "I realize that she feels on the outside how Dad feels on the inside: like she's deformed." And then I have a fucking breakdown within the breakdown. I don't share this next epiphany, but I recognize that they do belong together: two trauma-bonded cripples who are comfortable in their walls of secrecy and silent suffering,

who are even more afraid of intimacy than I am, and who are mortally terrified of anyone knowing who they are.

It turns out it wasn't me who was the black sheep. That blackness came
from them. That's how they feel on the inside, underneath the mask.

I thought that the tears were done and dried, but they're back again. This
time, though, they're accompanied by a feeling of lightness and freedom
in my chest. I can't remember the last time I saw the truth. This is more
cathartic than any drug experience I've ever had. All my anxiety and fear
and guilt have peeled away, as if they were layers of clothing I didn't know
I was wearing. I thought they were part of my skin the whole time, but it
turns out they were someone else's hand-me-downs.

So that's what they mean by my false self.

I used to think that intelligence came from books and knowledge and
rational thought. But that's not intelligence: It's just information and interpretation. Real intelligence is when your mind and your heart connect.
That's when you see the truth so clearly and unmistakably that you don't
have to think about it. In fact, all thinking will do is lead you away from
the truth and soon you'll be back in your head, groping with a penlight in
the dark again.

"How's your mother feeling right now?" Lorraine asks.

"It got through to her. Her walls are crumbling and she's realizing she
wasn't actually a good mother after all." Somehow I feel set free by the thought
that I was heard and understood. To the brain, the difference between reality and imagination can be minor. After all, the information travels down
similar neural pathways. So I suppose it doesn't matter that she actually
didn't hear a thing and may never understand. My brain thinks she did,
and that's good enough.

Lorraine directs me to send my mother out of the room, then has me tell
my eight-year-old self, who's been sitting next to me and watching the whole
time, that I'm firing his parents—and that from now on I'm taking care of
him. She guides me through a visualization in which I imagine shrinking
him until he can fit in the palm of my hand and placing him in my heart.

"Now that you've re-parented your inner child, you're going to protect
him and look after him—and let him play with Ingrid's inner child," Lorraine instructs. She gives me a few moments to imagine this, then gently
says, "You can open your eyes when you're ready."

There's one thing I've been striving for all my life: with sex, with writing, with surfing, with partying, with anything and everything. And that is to be free. It's the one feeling I never had growing up.

When I open my eyes, I feel free like I never have before. I see the guys sitting against the wall, their cheeks shining with tears, and I can tell they've been on this ride with me. Then I see Lorraine, beaming at me like an angel. And I tell her, "You're doing God's work."

The words come out of my mouth before I have a chance to think about them. I've never used the word *God* in my life in a spiritual context. In fact, the week before, I even had an hour-long debate with the spiritual counselor here, trying to dissuade him from the belief that there's a higher power who cares about the fate of every individual.

I once wanted to write a novel called *The Big Book of Negativity*. It would be about what life is really like, the cold hard truth. But in this moment, I'm so full of light, hope, and positivity that I wouldn't be able to put a single word on paper. I can't even connect to the idea anymore.

I need to hold on to the golden cord that, right now, is connecting my brain to my heart and illuminating the path to my authentic self—or, as the singer and poet Patti Smith once put it, "the clean human being that I was as a child."

"You look like you're floating on a foot of air," Calvin tells me.

Technically, this process is called post-induction therapy. Others call it ego-state integration. Joan calls it feeling reduction work. And Lorraine calls it an experiential. But those are euphemisms for what it really is: an exorcism. An exorcism of childhood demons.

"You've been letting the grounded teenager control your life," Lorraine says as I rise unsteadily to my feet. "And he wants to compensate for missing out on his adolescence by doing all the things and having all the women he was never allowed. But it's time to be an adult." She hands me a box of Kleenex. "It will wear you out if you don't live your authentic life."

I excuse myself from the room to get some fresh air. As I stand outside, experiencing the warmth of the sun and the cool of the wind and the smell of the trees through reopened senses, I think, I can't wait to connect with Ingrid. To look into her eyes and let her see into me—all the way—and not be afraid of what she might find there.

Door
2

EXCLUSIVITY

STAGE I

Love Avoidant:
Enters or Returns to Relationship out of
Obligation, Connecting Behind a Wall of Seduction

Love Addict:
Enters or Returns to Relationship to End Pain of
Abandonment, Connecting in a Fog of Fantasy

1

The problem with time is that it doesn't go backward.

Every word, every step, every action is irreversible. If we step in front of a moving car, if we sign a contract we haven't read, if we betray the person we love, the best we can do is try to clean up the mess. But no matter how hard we scrub, the stain on reality will never come out. The word you just read can never be unread.

And so I am back in the airport where I stood fifteen days earlier, on the way to the plane that will take me back to Ingrid, blinking in the light of a reality that is no longer the same.

Instead of glimpsing anonymous individuals hurrying by, I see different archetypal products of bad parenting. That meek old man with the blank stare was probably beaten senseless by his father; the sad-looking obese guy in an undersized T-shirt may have grown up with a mom who expressed love only through her cooking; the uptight businessman was likely raised by strict parents who never allowed him to be imperfect. Suddenly there seem to be very few adults in the world, just suffering children and overcompensating adolescents.

When I see a tempting mane of blond or black hair, I try not to turn my head and "pornify" this human being or see her as "a collection of body parts."

If the discharge papers in my luggage are to be believed, I am a very sick man.

According to my psychiatric evaluation, I have "Axis I sexual disorder, generalized anxiety syndrome, and depressive disorder," in addition to "problems with primary support group" and "problems related to social environment." As the coup de grâce, I have an Axis V rating of fifty out of a hundred—a score reserved for head cases who are either suicidal or so functionally impaired they're unable to form basic friendships. This diagnosis is followed by a three-page list of medications and treatments I'd supposedly been given in rehab, including an enema, none of which I'd taken or even requested.

I wonder for a moment if my mother was right. These medical opinions, most of them made up by someone who clearly has her own psychological issues, are now on my permanent record, where they could come back to haunt me at any time. I start to imagine going through a divorce trial in the future and a lawyer showing this evaluation to the judge as evidence that I shouldn't have custody of my children.

I have left rehab AMA—against medical advice. There was no reason to stay. After the chair work with Lorraine, we were back with Joan for family week. Since my parents weren't coming, and Joan said it wasn't necessary for Ingrid to return, and even Charles admitted that the final week mostly involved administrators trying to up-sell the hospital's aftercare program, there didn't seem to be much point in spending the money to stick around. The other guys who didn't have families to save—Calvin and Paul—said they were planning to break out early as well.

Before leaving, I stopped by Lorraine's office to get her contact information in case I needed to get in touch with her in an emergency. She gave me an hour of good advice on reentry into my relationship, explaining, most importantly, that in order to be emotionally free to commit to Ingrid, I need to limit contact with my mother. "Stick to news, sports, and weather," she advised with a smile.

Then I said goodbye to Joan, whose only words as she closed my file were a dismissive "good luck."

As I board the plane, I'm excited to use what I've learned about myself to heal my relationship with Ingrid and earn back her trust. However, as I'm buckling my seat belt, I see body parts: a pair of tan legs, long and toned, topped by tight cutoff denim shorts. I look up to see a frayed, loose-fitting gray sweater that, despite its bagginess, reveals the outline of what are clearly large breasts. The body part above them has flowing brown hair and a golden-hued face with very little makeup. The sum effect of all these parts is so naturally sexual that even a clown suit couldn't hide it.

I try to put myself back in the chair with Lorraine and imagine my inner child playing with Ingrid's. But it's too late. Out here, there's just too much reality: lights, colors, screens, signs, faces, fast food wrappers, yoga pants. My brain is working so hard just to keep up, it doesn't have time to pause and think about consequences. And now this woman has gotten in. I'm already imagining making out with her and putting my hand up her sweater. This is covert sexualized violence. I need to stop myself.

And so I think, Bright red apple, wrong orchard—and I look away. Damn you, Charles, that was actually decent advice.

I notice another side effect of rehab: I am no longer *attracted* to or *turned on* by random women; instead, I am *triggered* by them. It's the same thing, but being attracted is a natural human impulse; being triggered is an unhealthy plunge into the addiction cycle, into compulsive behavior, into the charts and diagrams hanging in Joan's office.

This may be the first step in my downward spiral. And I haven't even been free for three hours.

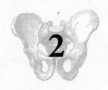

2

In the baggage claim of LAX, I see her. She's wearing an outfit that would have gotten her banned from rehab: tank top with no bra and tight jeans, with a wave of blond hair falling over the left side of her face. At first, she backs away a step—maybe out of shyness, maybe fear. Then joy washes over her face, as if a spotlight's been turned on overhead, and she rushes toward me.

"I'm ready to start something new with you," she whispers. The warmth of her breath fills my ear, carrying with it the implicit expectation that I've been cured.

"Me too," I reply. And I hope, for both our sakes, that I have changed.

We drive along the Pacific Coast Highway listening to electronic dance music and making up lyrics to each instrumental. The sun kaleidoscopes off the ocean, which stretches endlessly to the left, the silhouette of Catalina Island visible faintly in the distance like the promise of something new and transitory.

Our destination: the two-bedroom guesthouse in Malibu that we used to share. The day she found out I was cheating, Ingrid called two friends to help her move out, and she's been living with them since. Before leaving, her friends grabbed a permanent black marker and defaced not just the books I'd published, but cover samples for ones that weren't even out yet.

EVERYONE LOVES YOU WHEN YOU'RE DEAD

"I got you something special," Ingrid says with a wide, toothy smile as we walk inside. She pulls a small brass key out of her purse. "Everyone deserves a second chance."

"What's that?"

"Your mom wouldn't give you the keys to her house when you were in rehab, so I'm giving you my key."

"To what?"

"To my filing cabinet at work."

"Why not your house?"

"I have to be out soon because my friend's lease is ending."

She takes a small metal chain, threads it through the key, and gently fastens it around my neck like a charm for healing childhood wounds. No one I've dated has ever done anything this meaningful for me.

"This key," I tell her, "will serve as a reminder that I can be trusted and that I can tell the truth."

In bed that night, as I hold Ingrid against me and run my hands along her skin, I try to let go completely, to breathe and stay in the moment, to be open and vulnerable.

"Should we?" she asks.

"I don't know. It's up to you."

"I don't want you to break your contract."

"Well, are we really not going to do it for ten more weeks?"

"I can try to wait."

At this point, we're naked and our bodies aren't listening to us. As I enter her, a rush of chemicals floods my brain and bathes my body. It feels so relieving and uplifting, like I'm high, an alcoholic having his first shot after rehab. But unlike before, I find it easier to stay with Ingrid, remain connected, and look into her eyes and her being—to make love and not just have sex.

It's been a long time since I've seen and felt Ingrid this powerfully, and so my love is fleeting. As soon as I release, my body dissolves into weightless euphoria. I'm not sure if sex is an addiction or if it's just awesome.

When we shower together afterward, Ingrid starts making out with me. She rubs me against her clit—which I believe would qualify, in Joan's words, as masturbating using my body. However, I'm not hard enough to have sex with her again.

"I still haven't come," she pouts, trying to put it in. It's only fair that she also get off. So I look at her body and try to "pornify" her. When this doesn't work and I see Ingrid's growing distress, I decide to resort to more extreme measures: I think about the woman from the airplane.

I'm doing this for Ingrid, I tell myself. And I imagine Short Shorts sitting next to me on the plane, putting an airline blanket over us so she can guide my hands to her smooth tan legs, whispering to meet in the bathroom. It's starting to work. I think about walking into the lavatory and seeing her waiting for me, sitting on the toilet with her sweater off and the button of her cutoff shorts undone, the fly unzipped just enough to reveal her panties. She slides a hand under the waistband and starts touching herself while looking me in the eye . . . and, god, now I'm hard enough, now I can fuck Ingrid. I'm doing this for her. For her.

3

In the morning, I retrieve my phone from its resting place in my sock drawer. I insert the battery, wait for it to come to life, and punch in the password. A long parade of texts and emails rolls across the screen.

An Asian American tech entrepreneur, whom my friend Melanie once tried to set me up with, writes that she wants to get on Skype to "distract me." An Australian girl I hooked up with on a book tour says she wants to end six months of celibacy with me. A porn star I once had horrible sex with in a bathroom says she misses me. A social-networking friend from France whom I've never met asks when I'm going to be in Paris next, and attaches a photo of herself standing naked in a garden. And on and on: women sending sonar signals, waiting for a ping back so they know what their position is.

The women you've slept with, the ones you never did but primed for a future encounter, the ones who seemed interested but then suddenly stopped texting: Unless you do something horribly wrong, they never completely disappear. A lonely night, a cheating boyfriend, a sudden breakup, an attack of low self-esteem, an attack of high self-esteem—anything can, out of the blue, send them scrolling through their address book looking for validation, for security, for conversation, for adoration, for the fantasy of you filling some empty space in their life.

Exacerbating this problem, I included my email address on a whim in one of my early books, mostly because I didn't think anyone would read it. And so new temptation arrives to the inbox almost daily. The one that stops me in my tracks today is from a woman named Raidne who says she'd love to meet me. Unfortunately for my sobriety, she's attached a photo. She is of an ethnicity best described as Las Vegas: artificially constructed to make every cell in the male visual brain throb with desire—a blend of who-knows-what nationalities, beauty regimens, and surgeries, resulting in a perpetual tan and fake breasts that catch the light like brass Christmas ornaments.

I look at Ingrid's key. And it looks back at me.

They say that a man is as faithful as his options, and in this moment I know it to be true. So I switch the phone off. It's too much. Even Jesus had only three temptations.

STAGE II

Love Avoidant:

Feels Oppressed by Partner's Neediness
and Moves from Wall of Seduction
to Wall of Resentment

Love Addict:

Ignores Partner's Walls and Partner's Need
to Have a Life Beyond the Relationship

4

Pets are the gateway drug to children. As a general rule, when a woman over twenty-five gets a dog, it means she's ready to start a family.

Nearly three weeks after my return, Ingrid and I are at the West Valley Animal Shelter, where a diseased ball of black-and-white fur is balancing on its hind legs and ever so gently resting its front paws on Ingrid's kneecap.

This one is good: He knows just how to win her heart. It doesn't matter that he's got only one working eye, infected brown goo dripping out of both ears, and a stench worse than a homeless person on a New York subway. The deal is soon closed. This ten-pound runt, bred to be faithful to whoever feeds him, has been saved.

Usually the pound keeps adopted dogs so they can get neutered before being transferred to their new owner, but the receptionist just gives us this one. She's that eager to get rid of him. He has so many health problems, she suggests getting everything else fixed before neutering him.

On the way home, I check my post office box. Inside, amid the bills and junk, there's a square envelope addressed to me. I recognize the girly handwriting on it as my mom's.

I'm shocked when I open it to find this card:

GET
YOUR
SH*T
TOGETHER

Then I read the message inside:

Until recently, I used to think it was just her sense of humor when she called herself long-suffering. Now I see that every joke comes with a first-class ticket to a guilt trip. Clearly she's not happy that I abandoned my Sunday phone-call obligations after rehab.

It's been a while since I've spoken to her, so when we return home, I dutifully pick up the phone and dial her number. The conversation starts casually enough, but soon the part that Lorraine warned me about begins.

"I'm worried about the things they told you in rehab," she says. Her voice is upbeat, as if about to break into song. "People come out of psychotherapy thinking they have problems they don't." She seems to be mounting a defense against whatever I've been learning, like a publicist trying to spin-control a scandal.

"It's actually been very helpful, and I'm smart enough to separate the good from the bad." I wish she were receptive enough to discuss what I learned, but you can't expect the same person who wounded you to heal you. So I take a tip from my last conversation with Lorraine and suggest: "Let's talk about something else."

"One thing first," she says. "I want you to know that your father wasn't involved in your childhood. Marg"—the babysitter—"and I raised you. I was home all the time for you unless I had to go out for something." Her voice is warm and suffocating, coming at me in a torrent of words I can't stop. My hands and wrists tighten, as if telling me that I need to fight to save myself.

News. Sports. Weather.

"People always say how nice and sweet your father is. I think, if only you knew that he's just a piece of dirt. He does not have the ability to love or care. It's an act. I was on his computer the other day, and I saw that he was searching for *congenital leg deformity*. He's terrible."

"How's the weather been in Chicago?" It feels like I'm struggling to get a plastic bag off my head before I asphyxiate.

"You and your brother are the best things that have ever happened to me," she continues, talking right over the question as if she never heard it. "I wasted my life, is what I really did. So if everything is for nothing, then at least I have you two."

I need to end this conversation. She may think she's telling me how much she loves me, but what I'm hearing is that by not calling her on Sundays, I'm slowly killing her. One of the biggest indicators of enmeshment, according to Lorraine, is when a mother tells her children that she lives only for them.

"Hey, I gotta jump off the phone now."

"Why?"

"I have a bunch of work to finish before the day ends."

"And that's more important than your mother?"

"Mom, I have to go, okay?!"

"Okay." Her tone has changed. Now it's sad, bruised, on the verge of tears instead of laughter.

"Is everything all right, Mom?"

"Now I'm not going to be able to get to sleep tonight. You know how I—" The guilt is like a carcinogenic gas, seeping through the holes of the phone receiver, down my ear canal, and toward the folds and crevices of my brain.

"Havetogonicetalkingbye!" I hang up the phone.

That was a close one. I can't let her get back into my mind. I've got enough problems in there as it is.

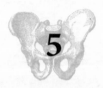

5

I join Ingrid on the couch, where she's sitting next to our used and abused new shih tzu. I pet him and he barely reacts outside of blowing snot from his nose, spraying my arm. Eventually he rises to his feet, stretches out his front legs, takes a few steps, pisses on the couch, walks in a tight pointless circle so that the urine gets all over his paws, then drops back onto his chin, exhausted from this evidently Herculean effort.

As I grab a roll of paper towels to clean the mess, I suggest calling him Hercules. Ingrid stares rapturously at his black-and-white face. "I love him," she says. "I love Hercules."

And I think: I can't believe how easy it is for her to fall in love.

And then I think: Why is that not cheating?

And then I think: Now she's going to neuter him.

For some reason, I'm disturbed hearing the word *love* roll out of her mouth so quickly and easily. Especially when I've been working so hard to be worthy of it. Maybe love isn't so sacred if we can attach it to any furry thing with a heartbeat, bad breath, and no bladder control.

She scoops the dog up in her arms and trots to the bedroom to take a nap. Now she's sleeping with him. Is this still monogamy?

I grab my computer, find an image of the Mexican flag, and print it. I have a small publishing imprint at HarperCollins, and decided recently to contact two anonymous news bloggers in Mexico about writing a book on the drug war there. Because the Mexican cartels have been trying to find out who they are and execute them, however, the journalists want me to verify my identity. So they asked me to email a photo of myself holding a Mexican flag in one hand and a newspaper with today's date in the other. Lorraine would say this is a way to find intensity outside the relationship without cheating. And perhaps she's right.

As the flag image prints, I start thinking about our new shih tzu, which makes me think of Asia, which makes me think of Asian women, which makes me think of the tech entrepreneur who wanted to Skype me. I decide to search the Internet to see how her start-up is doing, and I come across a photo of her in a bikini. Five minutes later, I'm on PornHub watching videos of Asian women who look like her while stroking myself.

I know I shouldn't be doing this. It's clearly compulsive. But it's too late to stop: That's how compulsions work. Besides, I went to rehab for cheating, not for porn. And I'm not breaking any promises to Ingrid. There's nothing wrong with jerking off occasionally. The whole notion that I can only have an orgasm with Ingrid's participation for the rest of my life is ridiculous. I've been home and well behaved for almost a month. I deserve this. I'm being interdependent.

I should send this image to the Mexican journalists.

A link underneath one of the clips leads me to an excessively pierced girl with bleached-blond hair who looks like an emo version of Ingrid. Suddenly I hear Ingrid's sleepy voice summoning me: "Babe?"

I quickly zip up, close my browser, grab my computer, and walk into the bedroom. But some combination of my flushed cheeks, overly innocent expression, and the laptop in my hand gives me away.

"Were you watching porn?"

She's not asking judgmentally, but I feel accused. I went to rehab to stop cheating, and so far I've succeeded. I've been working on my wandering eye, and that's been going well. I'm successfully tapering off my lust, one sin at a time. And today, these women are my sexual methadone.

"Were you or weren't you?"

This is my chance to be honest and intimate. If there's nothing wrong with watching porn, then I shouldn't have any shame in telling Ingrid about it. "Yes, I was. I thought you were sleeping and I didn't want to wake you."

She rolls over, picks up Hercules from the floor, and hugs him against her chest. I think she already loves that thing more than me.

And it looks like she's enmeshing him.

"Did you finish?" she asks.

"No, I didn't."

And here it comes. The knife in the gut, spewing hot guilt all over my insides: "You make love to those girls more than you make love to me!"

"That's not true." My heart clenches, my breathing gets shallow, and what feels like hot steel rods coalesce lengthwise from my forearm to my wrist. "This is the first time I've watched that stuff since I've been back."

She scoops up Hercules and walks out of the room. And I'm frustrated because I shouldn't have to defend myself if I want to have an orgasm without her. Sometimes my inner child is going to want to play with himself.

A text suddenly arrives on my phone from Belle, the Australian who wants to end her celibacy experiment with me: "It's my birthday today. I wish you were unwrapping me right now."

And I text back, "I wish I were too."

Instantly, I'm filled with remorse. I don't know why I just did that. Is it because I'm feeling smothered by Ingrid? Is it because I would have felt guilty letting Belle down on her birthday? Or is it because I need more intensity in

my life? Whatever the case, it was a stupid thing to do. And if it isn't technically cheating, it's definitely a violation of Ingrid's trust in me.

Which would make it cheating.

Fuck.

I can't believe how easy it was to slip up. That moment of blinding clarity during my chair work with Lorraine already feels so far away, like a
memory of childhood innocence, and I wonder if it wasn't actually a cure
but another high.

As I'm standing in the bedroom with my shame in my hand, Ingrid
stomps back in, stares at me for a moment with a hurt expression, and asks,
"What's wrong with me? Am I ugly?"

"No, you're not. You're beautiful." And she really is beautiful: The emo
girl I masturbated to had a body just like hers.

"Then why don't you want to sleep with me?"

"I do. I was just procrastinating on my work, and I felt like I smelled bad,
and—I don't know, I didn't want to bother you."

"You keep saying different things."

"No, I don't. They're all true."

I know she needs reassurance. She needs me to pick her up and sweep
her off her feet and make mad passionate reconnecting love to her. But
right now I can't. I feel too guilty. I'm spiraling into my shame core like an
oil prospector who's struck shit.

However, she does have a good point: Why would I rather masturbate to
a girl who looks like Ingrid than actually have sex with her in the flesh? Is
this intimacy avoidance or just normal male fantasizing?

And that's when I realize why I was oversensitive to Ingrid's affection
for Hercules, why I'm lusting after these women who aren't one-tenth the
person Ingrid is, why I'm jeopardizing my relationship for a single stupid
text. It's an unconscious reaction to my conversation with my mother. I'm
punching holes in the vacuum-sealed plastic bag of my relationship so I
don't suffocate. The physiological reactions to Ingrid's complaints about me
were almost the same ones I had to my mom's complaints about my father.

I drop onto the bed and explain this to Ingrid apologetically, along with
my fear of being trapped in a marriage like my parents'. Slowly she begins
to thaw, eventually sitting on the bed next to me and stroking my head like
I'm Hercules, a helpless creature to be pitied.

"Your problem is that you worry too much about the future," she says, her voice confident, her eyes wise, her hand tender. "You could die in a car crash, or there could be an earthquake right now and the house could collapse on top of us. There's no guarantee we'll be here tomorrow. So let's just love each other in this moment and appreciate each other in this moment. We can deal with the future when we get there."

She proposes taking a trip together when she can get time off work, some place where we can enjoy peace, nature, and each other. "I've always wanted to hike the Inca Trail to Machu Picchu," she suggests.

"Then let's do it!"

She smiles, clasps the key hanging around my neck, and utters the most beautiful words she's spoken since before my infidelity ripped our world apart: "I really trust you now. I don't think you'd ever do anything to hurt me."

A wave of joy fills my heart, but it crashes instantly on the shore of guilt. I just texted that Australian woman. If Ingrid saw my phone, she'd be devastated.

6

Malibu, One Day Later

You left rehab early?

There wasn't any point in staying longer.

And you broke your celibacy contract to sleep with Ingrid?

She's my girlfriend and she wanted to have sex.

And you fantasized about someone else?

Only so I could please Ingrid.

All I'm hearing are excuses for going only halfway. No wonder you're still cheating.

Rick and I are in his Range Rover, discussing my idiotic text. We park in the gravel driveway of a house available for rent. It looks like the kind of giant hippie tree house that Father Yod and his wives would have lived in.

I can explain.

I'm all ears.

Spoken with a wry smile, as if he's preparing to be deeply amused by whatever I say next.

There were two schools of thought in rehab. One was taught by a very compassionate woman named Lorraine: From her, we learned that we weren't there for our partners but ourselves. And the goal is to separate from our parents and our wounds so we can live our authentic lives.

And the other?

The other school of thought was more puritanical. It was taught by a very strict woman named Joan. And she believes that masturbation, pornography, seduction, fantasy, and casual sex are all unhealthy. And that basically anything other than lifelong monogamy is a symptom of sexual addiction and intimacy avoidance.

Why can't they both be right?

You gotta be kidding me. Then nearly every male in the country should be in rehab.

Who goes to rehab and just picks and chooses what they like? I think you have a false belief about how men are that you're using as a way of not feeling emasculated in the world. You were unhappy before in your old ways when you were single and you're unhappy now in a relationship. You can go on this way for five or ten years, and all you'll do is waste a lot of time sitting on the fence.

So what should I do? I'm so confused.

I see the look of pity in Rick's eyes, like I'm some sort of lesser life form, a two-dimensional creature trying to understand the concept of three dimensions.

Here's what I suggest: Go into sex addiction recovery all the way. Starting today, everything an expert tells you, just do it without challenging it. Even if all you find are therapists like Joan who you don't agree with, hand over control anyway. If they tell you no sex for ninety days, then don't have sex for ninety days. If they tell you no masturbation or porn, then cut those things out.

I know I need to do something drastic, but . . .

You want me to just go along with even the most extreme things these people say, without thinking about whether they make any logical sense or are true to myself?

Yes, exactly. How do you think I lost 135 pounds? I tried to lose weight for years, but I wasn't able to do it until I finally gave up control to a nutritionist and a trainer. I didn't think about whether anything they said was true. I didn't even believe it would work. But I just submitted to the process and did it without judgment.

I think back to the moment of clarity I had in the chair with Lorraine. What would that opened-up version of myself advise me to do?

He would say to just let go and love Ingrid.

Okay, I'll try it.

Don't try. Do it. Really get into recovery and feel it for at least ninety days. And if at the end of that time, you're still not happy, then do what you feel is right. Find an open relationship, go crazy, have all the sex with all the people you want and see how that feels. The goal is not monogamy or nonmonogamy. It's for you to be living a life that brings you happiness.

That sounds like a great way to get off the fence before I fuck up my relationship again.

It may be your last chance. If you can't stick with it, maybe God will find a way for you to stick with it.

What's that supposed to mean?

It means that if you can't control your lust, the universe will take care of it for you.

He says this ominously, as if lightning is going to strike my prick or it's going to get stuck in a blender if I don't keep it zipped up.

And so I'm back: facing the firing squad.

This time, the bullets are being loaded by Sheila Cartwright, Charles's therapist, supposedly the best in L.A. for sex addiction. She's an older woman with dreadlocks and beads in her hair like a teenage hippie, but she's sitting in a large armchair with a blanket over her legs like an old lady. In the spirit of Joan and Lorraine before her, she's another single woman surrounded by male sex addicts.

Adam is also here. So is Calvin. Evidently they were smart enough to stay in touch with Charles and join his private therapy group immediately on reentry. There are also five cheaters I don't know, three of whom have been in the group for over ten years.

"It's too bad there's no such thing as a woman who'll let you do what you want and still love you," Calvin says, nudging me in the ribs, as we sit in adjacent mismatched chairs in the therapy room.

It feels good to be with my dysfunctional buddies again, except this time, I need to be more like Charles and go along with the entire program.

The meeting begins with each addict checking in and letting Sheila know how his week went. Instead of lecturing us like Joan, she *feels* for us, in what seems like a tactic to get us more in touch with our own feelings. As Calvin tells us that he's thinking of returning to Brazil to be with his hooker when she gives birth to their son, she exhales slowly and melodramatically, and looks at him with big, soft eyes, as if trying to absorb the pain and the hurt that he's not even aware he has.

"I was alone with my wife last night, so I asked her if she wanted to fool around," Adam says during his check-in. "She got really mad, and she told me it was inappropriate and not intimate and not the way she likes to be propositioned. So it turned into a whole blowup."

After Sheila emotes for Adam and advises him to start with hand-holding, it's my turn to check in. I tell the group about the woman on the plane, the temptations of my inbox, the text to Belle, and renewing my commitment to recovery.

Sheila's response is a hiss of escaping air and a sad puppy dog expression. She looks like she's trying to send me love. And, for some reason, it makes me uncomfortable. I'm not sure if that's because she seems insincere or if, although I'm used to sex with no strings attached, I'm unaccustomed to emotion with no strings attached.

When I smile awkwardly at her, Sheila finally speaks, ever so slowly: "What you're doing is sexual hoarding. When there's a problem in your relationship, you feel shame—like something is wrong with you—and there's an immediate reaction to that called *defensive grandiosity*. And that's when you start checking your hoard of messages." She shifts in her chair and the blanket slides off her lap. "And that's fueled by anger, because it drives Ingrid away and makes you feel like you have power."

Sheila looks through a copy of the file from rehab listing all my ailments, real and imagined. She stands up slowly, placing her leg blanket back on the chair, then removes a book from a shelf and hands it to me. The title is *Silently Seduced*.

"Read this," she recommends. "It's you."

Charles leans forward in his chair and tells me, "Next time you see a woman like that one on the plane, use the three-second rule."

I'm stunned. The three-second rule was something I learned during my time with the pickup artists: It means that when you see a woman you're attracted to, you have three seconds to approach her—otherwise, either she'll notice you staring or you'll get too nervous to talk to her. "You mean I should start a conversation with her?"

"No!" he says, horrified. "The three-second rule means that as soon as you see someone and start objectifying them or fantasizing about them, you have a maximum of three seconds to focus on something else before the thought starts to get too strong and lead you into the addiction cycle. Remember"—he wags a finger—"bright red apple, wrong orchard."

As I walk back to my car after the meeting, I flip through the book Sheila gave me and read a passage. The author, Dr. Kenneth Adams, writes: "Covert incest occurs when a child becomes the object of a parent's affection, love, passion, and preoccupation. The parent, motivated by loneliness and emptiness created by a chronically troubled marriage or relationship, makes the child a surrogate partner. . . . To the child, the parent's love feels more confining than freeing, more demanding than giving, and more intrusive than nurturing."

Suddenly, a lost memory comes back to me. It arrives first as a scent of sweet petroleum, then a vision of white cream. When most of my classmates were going to bed at ten or eleven at night, my bedtime was seven thirty. However, my mother would let me stay up and watch TV until eight if I massaged her hands or feet. I'd pump moisturizer into my palms, then caress it into her olive, veined skin. When I finished, she'd tell me, "You're so much better than your father at this." At the time, I took it as a compliment, but now a shudder of disgust runs through me.

As a result of this confusing dynamic, Adams continues, when the child grows up, relationships often begin with "immediate and total commitment," but this is soon "followed by uncertainty and ambivalence." And, often, "having an affair is a way to be relieved of the struggle with commitment."

When I shut the book, I see Charles standing next to me. I have no idea how long he's been there. I thank him for getting me into the group. In response, he opens a satchel he's carrying and pulls out a copy of *The Game*.

"Alfred Nobel," he says.

I wait for the rest of the sentence. But evidently that's it. "What about him?"

"Know him?"

"Not personally."

"Alfred Nobel, the same guy who invented dynamite, went on to create the Nobel Peace Prize."

He looks at me, trying to make sure his point landed. And slowly what he's trying to say dawns on me: that a book about learning how to meet women is destructive, and a book about learning how to stop meeting them would be good for the world. And ironic.

"I understand," I tell him.

He tucks the book away and hands me a brochure for Sex and Love Addicts Anonymous. The first sentence reads: "We in SLAA believe that sex and love addiction is a progressive illness which cannot be cured but which, like many illnesses, can be arrested."

"Let me ask you something," Charles says sharply, watching me. "Have you finally recognized that you have a disease?"

I tell him, honestly, "I can recognize it as a disease in a metaphorical sense."

"No, it's a real disease. Because it's not a choice. It may start off as a choice, but if you do anything to cope with stress or pain, the structure of the brain changes and the behavior can go from an impulse to an addiction."

"If that qualifies as a disease," I respond, recalling my pledge to Rick, "then I guess I have it."

Charles seems unconvinced. "Let me do you a favor and prove to you that this is a disease. I'm going to set you up with a friend of mine, Dr. Daniel Amen. He's a brain expert specializing in addiction. He'll scan your brain for free, and show you exactly where the disease is in your head and how to treat it."

And I think, This is crazy. But I say, "Thank you."

8

Dr. Daniel Amen is a small, balding man—the son of a Lebanese grocery mogul—who has become, according to the *Washington Post*, "the most popular psychiatrist in America."

In the waiting room outside his office, a PBS TV program featuring the good doctor plays on infinite loop. I try to tune out his well-scripted patter about using brain scans for behavior assessment and modification while I work up the courage to go through the messages I've been ignoring on my phone.

I scroll down the list and start politely responding to each tempting text, making sure to mention my girlfriend.

Belle, the Australian who I didn't unwrap for her birthday, says she's going to be stuck in Los Angeles on an overnight layover and wants to know if I'll be in town. I tell her, "Don't know yet. But I have a gf, so can see you only as a friend."

Anne, my online temptation from France, has sent another nude photo, this one of her pole-dancing, her body curving in the air like tinder feeding the fire of my fantasy life. I write back, "Have enjoyed corresponding with you. Wish I'd met you in person, but in a relationship now."

Each reply is painful, like hammering a nail into my scrotum. But I do it: Because I believe. Because I'm behaving. Because I want to become.

I'm interrupted by a thin, sultry receptionist who calls me in to meet with Amen. His office staff seems to consist solely of attractive women in their twenties and thirties. I start to wonder if he has some undiagnosed sexual compulsiveness himself.

When I enter Amen's office, he's sitting in a high-backed swivel chair, swallowed in oversized clothing as if his body doesn't matter, only his brain. The walls are decorated with pictures of penguins, which have something to do with a children's book he wrote on positive reinforcement. In his hands, he's holding a sheaf of papers with green splotches on them that look like Hercules's snot stains. They are, collectively, my brain, and it looks like this:

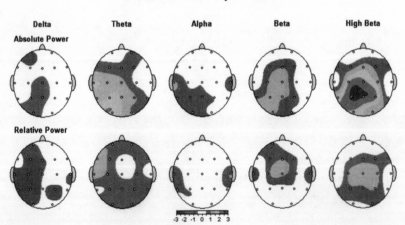

Though Amen specializes in a type of brain scan that involves injecting patients with a radioactive isotope, I opted instead for a safer-sounding EEG test, which was performed earlier by a tall blond neuroscientist in high-waisted leggings.

"Is that a pervert's brain?" I ask Amen.

"Have you ever been knocked out?" he inquires, ignoring the question—or maybe answering it.

"Only once." I tell him about an afternoon more than a decade before when a group of guys attacked me for no apparent reason as I was walking to my apartment in Manhattan.

"Where exactly did they hit you?"

"I think the blow that knocked me out was here." I touch the upper left side of my skull.

"That could be important."

"In what way?"

"Your brain is really soft and your skull is really hard, and inside your skull there are a whole bunch of ridges. The incidence of head trauma in sex addicts is huge, and nobody knows that because most addicts see therapists. And the problem with therapists is, they tell you all about your brain, but they never actually look at it."

"So do I have brain damage?" Fuck, another item to add to the grocery list of what's wrong with me.

"Your scan showed some mild evidence of injury." He studies the images again, decoding a language few understand. "You also have, and this is sort of funny, high slow-wave activities. Do you know about ADD?"

"I know about it."

"Did anybody ever suggest you had it?"

"No, never."

"I think a lot of your behavior is classic ADD stuff, especially the excitement seeking and the conflict. Wanting to be with new women is a biological drive to keep the species going, but it's totally destructive when you can't pair-bond appropriately and then be involved in raising a family."

As he speaks, I realize that's the exact problem: These two contradictory evolutionary desires—for variety and for family—have been tearing me apart. And on the journey to reconcile them, not only am I getting neither, but I'm discovering I'm insane.

Two months ago, I was just a jerk who cheated on his girlfriend and felt really shitty about it. I'd never seen or even wanted to see a therapist in my life. Now all of a sudden I have generalized anxiety syndrome, depressive disorder, socialization problems, brain damage, ADD, sex addiction, eroticized rage, developmental trauma disorder, emotional incest syndrome, Axis V impairment, and who knows what else. It's a miracle I can function in society at all.

"I'm also noticing here that when your eyes were open, the back part of your brain fired up a lot more. Which is a bad thing."

"Why is that?" I don't think I can take another disorder. I might as well just get a lobotomy at this point.

"Because that means you notice everybody who passes by."

"Yeah, that's been somewhat of a problem."

"When your visual center is turned on all the time like that, it can be painful to your partner if you're not careful." He laughs. I laugh. We relate. We are men. I look down and notice his wedding ring. "How does your girlfriend react when you're out and do that?"

"She's been good about it, but I really haven't done it lately. Except . . ." I tell him about my recent lapses.

"Well, part of it is patterning," he replies. "You worked so hard to figure out women that you're still like a hunter. It's so deeply ingrained, you're not going to be able to just walk out of here and stop it. The other problem is that your prefrontal cortex, the part of your brain that's supposed to act as the brake, is a little weak. So when you see a really pretty girl and you go, I'd love to have sex with her, your frontal lobe then plays it out."

It's confirmed: I've got a mind like a streaming-porn site. I have a future as a dirty old man to look forward to when my prefrontal cortex deteriorates even more with age. "So does my brain suggest sex addiction, then?"

He flips through my EEG results and concludes: My prefrontal cortex is weak, making it difficult to repress my instincts; my anterior cingulate gyrus (which he describes as a gear shifter that helps the brain switch between different thoughts and activities) gets stuck, making me obsessive about women I encounter; and my emotional lobes are overactive, so I can easily be provoked into acting out by something Ingrid says or does—even if I'm not conscious of the exact trigger.

Finally, he says grimly: "The brain has safety circuits that form when we experience repetitive physical and emotional caretaking from nurturing, predictable, secure figures. If your mom is handicapped and had to hire a babysitter after failing to take care of you on her own, that means there's probably little or no safety-circuit formation in your brain. So you can fall in love for the short term, but long-term emotional attachment may be harder to achieve and sustain."

In other words, on top of everything else, half the lobes and circuits of my brain are fucked up. "Do you think there's any truth to the saying that a man is as faithful as his options?" I ask, hoping for a small reprieve.

"I don't think that's true," he replies adamantly. "You're as faithful as you decide to be if your brain is healthy. If your brain is not healthy, then you're as faithful as your options. And we're going to make your brain healthy."

He then prescribes a lengthy regimen to heal my screwed-up head: neurofeedback to retrain my brain, herbal supplements to improve my frontal lobe functioning, a healthy diet to keep my blood sugar balanced, omega-3 and vitamin D to reduce my cravings, and, yes, more sex addiction therapy.

He sends me away with a cardboard box loaded with his books, audio programs, and branded supplements. When I return home, I look up local sex addiction meetings to attend, order a Patrick Carnes recovery kit, research neurofeedback clinicians, and call Charles about finding a sponsor.

This is my new life.

STAGE III

Love Avoidant:

Further Engulfment by Partner Leads to Withdrawal
from Relationship and Intensity Seeking

Love Addict:

Experiences an Undeniable Incident or Awareness
that Ends the Fantasy

9

Fast-forward through ten months of meetings and step study groups, working to curb my lust with my fellow former philanderers. Ten months of group therapy, learning to be emotional and powerless with Sheila Cartwright. Ten months of one-on-one therapy, reporting my every carnal thought to an additional sex addiction therapist. Ten months of neurofeedback and supplements and everything else Daniel Amen prescribed. Ten months of filling out Patrick Carnes's workbooks and reading his daily meditations and talking to sponsors and letting go to higher powers and making inventories of my sex life.

And where am I?

The sun is setting and I'm taking a short break from reading *Facing Love Addiction* by Pia Mellody, which my sex addiction therapist recommended finishing before our next session, to answer a call from Adam. Suddenly, I hear Ingrid's steps outside. Purposely loud. Each obnoxious stomp of her heels on the wood forms a word in a sentence: "I'm . . . coming . . . home . . . stop . . . whatever . . . you . . . are . . . doing . . . and . . . pay . . . attention . . . to . . . me!"

Adam and I have been talking every night, and I've come to admire him. I don't think he's even looked twice at another woman since leaving rehab. He's just been trying to get his wife to look at him.

He's in the middle of telling me that his football team was practicing with one of the women's teams, and even though there was nothing inappropriate about it, his wife saw this, got jealous, and flipped out. She said she doesn't trust him anymore to play football.

"So what are you going to do?"

"You know, Neil, I looked at my wife and I understood. I thought, How could someone want to be with me after what I've done? I always think, How can I give her back what I've taken away from her by my affair? So I'm gonna stop playing football for a while. I want to show her that our relationship is what's most important to me."

Now Ingrid's knocking—even though I gave her the house keys when she moved in. The rapping is nonstop. It's not polite, like a neighbor, or even impolite, like someone delivering a package. It's just annoying, like someone hitting a pipe with a hammer when you're trying to sleep.

"I gotta go, Adam. But I don't think you should quit doing the things you love just because she feels threatened by them. Let's talk later."

I slip the phone in my pocket and walk to the door to let Ingrid in.

"Wanna watch *The Twilight Zone*?" she asks, bursting inside, grinning ear to ear. She places Hercules on the floor and stomps in circles around him, trying to make me laugh.

"Not right now. I have to read for a little."

Her face drops. Following the advice in *Silently Seduced*, I've been making an effort to put my needs first in the relationship to avoid feeling enmeshed. But so far all it seems to be doing is intensifying Ingrid's own abandonment fears, because now she thinks I'm falling out of love with her and is constantly seeking reassurance.

"Skittykitts?" she chirps. It's a card game a friend of ours invented.

"When I'm done with this chapter, okay?" I find it easy to say no once, but after two or three requests, I start to feel guilty and lose my resolve. Sheila tells me that continuously complying with someone else's priorities at the expense of my own is called *pathological accommodation*.

"Okay!" She hugs me. I hug her back. At each point where her body makes contact with mine, a nerve ending freezes and stiffens. The chain reaction builds all the way to my heart until, finally, she releases me.

When Ingrid and I were at a rooftop bar last week, she was tipsy and clingy—and I was seized by an inexplicable impulse to hurl myself over the divider and into the void below. That's when I understood why some people spontaneously jump off rooftops and bridges and window ledges: They do it because it's easier than almost everything else in life. It's easier to jump than divorce your wife, easier to jump than try to win a girlfriend back, easier to jump than ask your boss for a raise, easier to jump than deal with your growing pile of unpaid bills, easier to jump than face your wife and kids after letting them down, easier to jump than spend every day in meetings and therapy trying to be someone you're not. It's easier—and quicker. It solves every problem with certainty, swiftness, and finality.

I sit on the sofa and continue reading the book, hoping Ingrid will get the hint. Instead, she sits next to me, cranes her head over my shoulder, and reads the page out loud, her voice histrionic and staccato, trying to be funny: "Resentment is the anger the Avoidant feels because of thinking he or she has been victimized by the partner's neediness or by the partner's 'demands' for connection in the relationship."

She tries to make eye contact, which I don't return. "Do you feel like that?"

My sponsor advised me to always be honest and vulnerable, no matter how difficult it may be. So I tell Ingrid, "I'm feeling it right now." I force a smile so the words don't seem too harsh.

She touches her temple and closes her eyes for a moment, taking it in. "Can I ask you a question?"

"I don't know. Can it wait?" Her face starts to fall. I can't take an argument right now, so I pathologically accommodate. "Okay, what is it?"

"Why is this relationship different from your other ones?"

It seems not just like a need for reassurance, but an accusation. "Because I enjoy being with you. I appreciate you inside and out. And you make me laugh."

She folds her arms across her chest. "So I just make you laugh. Is that *it*?"

"No, I love you." And I really do. Just not right now.

"What do you love about me?"

"It's a feeling. I get it in my heart when I'm with you." Just not right now. She's silent.

"What's the problem? I feel like I'm being cross-examined, but I don't know what I'm being charged with."

She bites her lower lip and gazes down at Hercules. Then she hits me with it: "So why are you working so hard to stay in this relationship?"

It's a good question. One I've been asking myself lately. I think back on my past girlfriends: I broke up with Kathy because she was constantly jealous. I broke up with Katie because she kept cheating on me. And I broke up with Lisa, my most serious relationship before this, because she started to remind me of my mother.

But with Ingrid, I can't find anything hopelessly wrong with her, any way to use her behavior or shortcomings as an excuse to flee. Sure, she's being a pain in the ass right now. And she shuts down when she's angry, smothers me with affection, demands my attention when I want to work, can be needy due to her abandonment issues, and has some understandable insecurities because I cheated. But these are all things a guy can live with.

So if I can't find anything significantly wrong with her, then I must accept the only other conclusion available: the problem is still me. And after months of working on me, I'm a bigger mess than I was when this whole thing started. When I was dating Ingrid and cheating behind her back, everything was in stasis. She was happy. I was happy enough. We were living in ignorant bliss.

Those were the good old lies.

But now, everything I once thought I liked about myself has been turned into a symptom of something wrong with me. I'm told over and over by addiction experts not to trust anything I say, think, or feel. They tell me I need to build self-esteem from within. Yet in order to do that, I have to accept that I'm broken, shattered, stigmatized, diseased, and traumatized— and all that does is make me want to throw myself off a rooftop so I can start all over again.

And so instead of being healed, I've become raw, edgy, irritable, and moody. The blood flowing through my veins feels like it's filled with sand and broken glass. And my sexuality is boiling over. Despite using the three-second rule, I'm attracted to any woman under three hundred pounds and some cartoon characters. I feel like the drunk who can't get any booze, then starts chugging mouthwash and rubbing alcohol. I'm ready to scrape the bottom of the barrel. And Ingrid's become so sensitive to my moods that I'm sure she's aware of this.

"Well, why?" she asks again. Didn't I tell her thirty times already that I wanted some alone time to read? How am I supposed to take care of my needs when she won't listen to me?

As I'm trying to figure out how to respond without creating a worse scene, my phone beeps. I check it quickly: It's a text from Calvin, who's just returned from Brazil and sent a picture of his baby boy. I return the phone to my pocket without answering him.

"Who was that?"

"That was Calvin. From my therapy group."

She frowns and squints at me. "It seems like you're hiding something."

"No, I just thought it would be rude to respond to him while we were talking."

"Well, it seemed sneaky."

I want to tell her to lay off me, to remind her that she said she trusted me, to ask to see her fucking phone. But I manage to stay—just barely—in the functional adult. "It really was Calvin. You can check my phone. I've been totally good." Actually, I think I'm in the punished-adolescent ego state.

"I don't need to do that."

She strokes my face lightly, so soft it feels more irritating than soothing, like a fly buzzing around my cheek. "I'm sorry," she says, looking into my eyes, hoping for something in return.

But all I feel is a rising tide of revulsion. In the last ten minutes, we've gone through a whole mini–soap opera of love, suspicion, and reconciliation. I'm emotionally exhausted.

I look into her eyes and try to stop the enmeshed monster inside me from taking over, but it's too late. The love I see shining there is like a bear trap, snapped shut on my soul to keep me from straying. I am a prisoner of fear. And in that moment, I realize that the self-destructive impulse I've had lately is not actually about wanting to hurt myself. It's about freedom. It's about not wanting to live under constant scrutiny, to be responsible for her feelings, to feel guilty if I happen to have a sexual thought that's not about her, to feel like my every word or expression is a red-hot brand that may scar her.

Once again, my girlfriend has turned into my mother: Ingrid doesn't trust me, she doesn't give me space, and her happiness seems to depend almost entirely on my behavior.

Things could be worse, I futilely try to console myself. At least Ingrid trusts me with the keys to the house.

I head to the bathroom to be alone for a few moments, first setting the phone on the table so Ingrid doesn't think I'm sneaking any texts in there. I close the door and stand in front of the mirror, staring blankly at the face staring blankly back at me. There are crow's-feet forming around my eyes; the creases of worry in my forehead are starting to turn into actual wrinkles; and I'm getting gray hairs in my beard. Maybe I've passed my peak. The decaying process has begun.

When is this sex addiction recovery going to start working? I can't go on like this forever. Pretty soon, I'm going to be too old to be a good dad who can still relate to his children and play ball with them. It's been almost a year and I'm definitely not happy. It seems more like I'm repressing my authentic self than becoming it.

When I return from the bathroom, Ingrid's sitting at the kitchen table with my phone in her hand. Her eyes are blazing and her jaw is thrust out, but I have no idea why she looks so angry. I've done nothing wrong.

"Who's Belle?"

Except for that. I get a hollow feeling in the pit of my stomach. Passwords are useless when you have a suspicious girlfriend who likes reading over your shoulder.

"What are you doing looking at my phone?" I snap. If only she'd have let me read in peace.

"Who is she?" Ingrid asks again. Angrier, louder, more abrasive. I try to answer, but my breath catches in my throat and burns there with shame.

Guilt is about the way you breathe. Shame is about the fact that you breathe.

"She's just some girl I slept with a long time ago, before I ever met you," I finally manage to utter. "I don't know why I stayed in touch with her. I'm so sorry. It was really dumb. I have a weak prefrontal cortex."

"Give me my key back."

"No, not that!" The key around my neck, the symbol of trust. Anything but that.

"I can't believe you would do that, Neil. Give me my key."

She grabs the necklace and pulls hard on the chain, trying to break the clasp.

"Okay, okay, just let go."

She's right. I don't deserve it. I don't deserve her.

I'm not angry anymore. At least not at her. I'm pissed at myself. I remove the necklace and give her the key to her file cabinet back. I told Belle I was in a relationship, but she kept sending flirtatious messages. And though I didn't encourage her again, I didn't do enough to discourage her either—and I definitely fantasized about her a lot. I should have ignored her or blocked her number, and had the courage to immediately apologize to Ingrid after I fucked up the first time.

Perhaps relationships are like heart surgery: Even the smallest mistake can be fatal. And now I've undone almost a year of earning Ingrid's trust back. It must have been my enmeshment or pathological accommodation or sex addiction or ADD or damaged brain or all of them working together in a symphony of self-sabotage.

Ingrid takes the key, storms out of the house, gets in her car, and drives away.

And now I've gotten my wish: I'm alone. I can breathe. I can read. I can do whatever I want.

And it sucks.

10

"I can't go on like this," I tell Calvin as we sit at a Japanese curry restaurant a week later, discussing the situation.

"I've gone through a lot of emotions about this stuff too," Calvin replies. "There's no end to it. It's not like, 'Go do this work for a few months or years, then you'll be better.' They want us to be in meetings and therapy for the rest of our lives."

He reaches into the back pocket of his jeans and pulls out a folded piece of paper. "Look at this."

It's a printout of an article about a guy named Robert Weiss who runs a treatment center in Los Angeles called the Sexual Recovery Institute.

"Not another place."

"Read it," Calvin urges. "Troy emailed it to me. Rob Weiss used to work with Patrick Carnes, but their egos clashed or something so he broke off and started his own center."

I read that the Sexual Recovery Institute was sold to Elements Behavioral Health, a big rehab chain, and they're planning to take Weiss's institute nationwide, with luxury sex addiction centers around the country for, as the article puts it, "wealthy sex addicts," and two-week outpatient programs "for those of lesser means."

"Can't you see what's going on?" Calvin presses. "Think about it: If you add up all the people who've cheated in their relationships, that's tens of millions of customers in the U.S. alone. Now add to that the even huger number of people who watch porn, and this is the smartest business plan in the world. If they turn being male and horny into some kind of brain cancer that's covered by health insurance, they'll be billionaires."

"It would be one thing if the treatment worked," I gripe. "But it's taken over my entire life. Like half the time, I'm too busy going to meetings and reading books on intimacy to actually be intimate with Ingrid."

After finding the texts with Belle, Ingrid spent the night sleeping on the sofa in her office. Though we talked it through for hours when she finally came home, she's shown no signs of forgiving or forgetting.

"It's no joke," Calvin replies. "There are a bunch of websites about this.

Remember when Joan made me add up all the money I spent on sex? Well, if I keep doing this, I'll end up spending even more money on recovery."

I hate that everything he's saying makes sense . . . and I'm relieved that everything he's saying makes sense.

"Most people who go to rehab relapse," he continues. "So what's the point? And Sheila doesn't want me to bring Mariana and Flavio"—his Brazilian and their baby—"over here, because it's not good for my recovery. But that's my son, and I have to do what's in my heart. That can't be wrong, right?"

"I don't know what's right anymore, man. I don't know. But despite my frustration, I have to say, the enmeshment stuff really fits me like a glove."

"That part may be true, but remember: This is the same profession that said homosexuality was a disease and gave gay people electroshock treatment and lobotomies. And, you know what, back then, therapists probably blamed it on smothering mothers also. Maybe we're just different sexually but the world hasn't accepted it yet."

He's making a good argument, too dangerous to consider. When I grew up, there were two women in my life: my mother and a live-in babysitter. So maybe it's natural for me to want multiple female caregivers. And who's to say that this broad definition of sex addiction we've been learning isn't just modern-day quackery, with Carnes as the Kevorkian of the male libido?

Doctors used to claim there was a disease called drapetomania—a disorder in which slaves were seized by the irrational and pathological desire to be freed from their masters. They're all just words, made up by people with degrees, to enforce social norms.

"You may be right," I respond noncommittally. "It could just be the way we're wired."

Perhaps sex addiction is the new ADD or Asperger's syndrome. It's very real for some people, but it's also massively overdiagnosed and anyone who doesn't fit a certain unrealistic standard of behavior is labeled with it. Pretty soon, just like there are six-year-old kids taking Ritalin and Adderall, some poor child who strips a Barbie doll naked will be getting sex addiction treatment.

"We got sucked into a weird fringe pseudoscience." Calvin stabs a fork into his chicken cutlet. "Most of this stuff has never been proven. Talk to scientists. Talk to doctors. Talk to other therapists. Talk to any single person except for Patrick Carnes and his minions. Even that brain doctor you went to isn't taken seriously by most of the medical community."

Rick told me to trust the experts, but maybe I just chose the wrong ones.

"Sex addiction isn't even in the DSM," Calvin goes on, his ovoid face heated red. "It was considered and completely rejected! We've been chasing a ghost."

11

One of the benefits of writing for *Rolling Stone* is that I can get just about anyone on the phone. So after talking to Calvin, I go on a rampage for knowledge, contacting as many of the world's most credible relationship experts as I can to get their point of view on the issues we discussed.

I start with the anthropologist Dr. Helen Fisher. For more than two decades, she's been studying love, sex, and marriage across cultures, species, and time—becoming, in the process, arguably the most cited living researcher on the science of relationships.

Her conclusion: "We're an adulterous animal."

In her book *Anatomy of Love,* she explains the origins of this behavior: "During our long evolutionary history most males pursued trysts to spread their genes, while females evolved two *alternative* strategies to acquire resources: some women elected to be relatively faithful to a single man in order to reap a lot of benefits from him; others engaged in clandestine sex with many men to acquire resources from each. This scenario roughly coincides with the common beliefs: man, the natural playboy; woman, the madonna or the whore."

Based on her current research, however, Fisher feels a little differently about that passage in the book. "I think I would amend that if I could write it now," she tells me. "Among men and women under the age of forty today, women are just as adulterous as men."

Fisher explains that our ancestors unfaithfully pair-bonded just long enough to conceive and raise a child until it developed some degree of autonomy, then they moved on to raise a child with (and cheat on) someone else. She describes this as a dual reproductive strategy: serial monogamy plus clandestine adultery.

So, I think as she explains all this, if my goal is to be in a relationship that's true to my authentic self, then cheating on Ingrid was the way to do it. Now all I need to do is marry her, father a couple of children, start cheating again, be cheated on, and divorce. This is evidently love among *Homo sapiens*. Call it *fauxnogamy*.

However, even if Fisher's theory is true, there's a problem with this lifestyle in the modern world. As the red demons and I unfortunately discovered, it causes a lot of pain, destroys any hope of intimacy, and traumatizes everyone in the family. In addition to the ethical issues, with keystroke-capturing software, phone bills, credit card statements, and social-networking profiles with tagged photos all easily accessible, it's almost impossible for a cheater not to leave a technological slime trail for a determined partner to discover.

So I ask Fisher how to best overcome our evolutionary past and have a successful, lasting relationship today. She responds by explaining that we've developed three different primary brain systems for mating: one for sex, another for romantic love, and a third for deep attachment. And after the initial intensity of a new relationship, our romance and sex drives often swing toward other people, while our attachment drive remains connected to our primary partner.

However, before I can draw any conclusions, Fisher says that this natural ebbing of romance and sexuality can be prevented. The solution, she elaborates, is for couples to do novel and exciting things together (to release dopamine and get the romance rush), make love regularly (to release oxytocin and sexually bond), cut themselves off from cheating opportunities, and, in general, make sure their partners are "continually thrilling" enough to keep all three drives humming.

"Wow, that's a lot to ask of two people," I tell her.

"Yes, and even then you still may want to sleep with other people on the side," Fisher retorts. "So if you're gonna cheat, for god's sake, don't get caught."

That's it, then: Helen Fisher, the world's leading expert on mating, has given me permission to cheat. I'm shocked that this is the prevailing scientific consensus on relationships. I've been working so hard to accept the premise that my desire for other women is a lifelong disease and only faith in a higher power can put it in remission. But perhaps it's not enmeshment or trauma or sex addiction that makes the notion of lifelong monogamy so unappealing. It's just, as I initially told Rick, part of our nature.

Even Sigmund Freud and Carl Jung, the fathers of modern psychotherapy, appear to have had affairs: the former with his wife's sister, the latter with a patient. "The prerequisite for a good marriage, it seems to me, is the license to be unfaithful," Jung wrote in a letter to Freud. And Bill W., the co-founder of Alcoholics Anonymous, was so notorious for cheating on his wife with attractive women who attended sobriety meetings that his colleagues later started calling this type of lechery the thirteenth step.

By Carnes's standards, they'd be addicts. By Fisher's, they'd be successful *Homo sapiens*. By society's, they'd be creeps. It's all very confusing.

Over the next few days, I dive deeper into the science of mating. But I'm unable to find a single credible item in the entire canon of evolutionary and anthropological literature that supports the contention that human beings are supposed to pick one partner and then remain faithfully and exclusively with that person for life.

On top of everything, I'd been feeling so guilty for avoiding intimacy with Ingrid by fantasizing. But, it turns out, a study on sexual fantasies conducted by researchers at the University of Vermont concluded that 98 percent of men (and 80 percent of women) report having sexual fantasies about people other than their partners.

So of course it's a struggle to focus 100 percent of my sexual attention and desire on Ingrid. I'm fucking normal. There's something liberating about that thought. Because I'm tired of beating myself up every day.

Even when I finally manage to find a group of researchers studying the benefits of monogamy to society—historically, it's increased the number of available women and reduced the number of single men, leading to less competition for partners and reduced crime and violence—they admit that not only does their definition of monogamy not preclude cheating, but they don't believe that monogamy is natural either.

"If it were all genetic, if humans just by nature mated for life and there were a very tight pair-bond," Professor Peter J. Richerson explains, "then we wouldn't need all these marriage customs."

As for marriage itself, historian Stephanie Coontz, the author of *Marriage, a History*, tells me that the tradition was never even supposed to be about intimacy. For the majority of its history, marriage was an economic and political institution, mostly about merging resources, forming alliances, or creating a bloodline for inheritance, she explains. Not until the late eighteenth century did people marry for love. And it took until the late twentieth century for marriage to start becoming an intimate partnership rather than a patriarchal institution.

Today, Coontz believes that the tradition is changing yet again. "People want to be monogamous or promiscuous, they want kids or they don't want kids, they want this or they want that," she says. "For centuries, they had to hide those preferences and take everything as a package deal. Now you don't have to: It's literally pick and choose. Cut and paste the kind of life you want. Family life and love relationships are essentially becoming a build-your-own model."

Perhaps Calvin was right, I think as I leave Coontz's house that evening. Maybe we have been brainwashed. Either that or we're living in a twenty-first century culture that's moving quickly, but stuck in twentieth century institutions that change too slowly.

Then again, no matter what your point of view may be, you can always find someone with a Ph.D to support it.

12

And so I find myself, nearly a year after returning from rehab, caught between one school of thought telling me I have an incurable psychosexual disease I need to treat daily, and another making a very convincing argument that over two hundred thousand years of human culture and evolution support my behavior as perfectly natural.

In the meantime, my relationship with Ingrid has become a roller coaster. One minute we're laughing together and staring lovingly into each other's eyes, the next we're either arguing or not speaking. Most nights, I end up sleeping on the couch. Meanwhile, Hercules has somehow gone from sleeping on the floor next to the bed to sleeping on the comforter at the bottom of the bed to sleeping on a pillow at the head of the bed to spooning with Ingrid.

One afternoon, for a *Rolling Stone* article I'm writing, the British singer Ellie Goulding meets me in Malibu to play some music she's been working on. We paddleboard in the ocean, and discuss her art and her life. When Ingrid comes home from work with Hercules in tow, I fill her in on the day.

"We talked a lot about abandonment, because her dad walked out on her and her mom," I recap. "One day she was feeling really sad, so she texted him and asked, 'Do you still love me?' But her father's new wife texted back and said to leave him alone and stop bothering him. It's so cruel. We were both practically crying."

Ingrid stiffens and says dryly, "Oh, so you both cried together?"

It's a tone of voice I've heard before—like a clap of thunder on a sunny day, bringing with it a storm. She walks angrily out of the room, then returns seconds later, bombarding me with questions: "Why did you exchange numbers with her?" "What made you invite her here?" "And why did she come while I was at work?"

Ingrid's certain I had ulterior motives, which in this rare case I didn't. She listens testily as I explain this, then she utters the four words that are the kiss of death to any relationship: "Show me your phone."

While Ingrid analyzes every word of my exchanges with Goulding, I look at Hercules, who's sleeping on his back on the bed. His shriveled little organ hangs there, robbed of its function and purpose so he can be a servant whose sole job is giving affection and unconditional acceptance to his mistress. It seems wrong to rob any living thing of the joy of sex.

When Ingrid finishes going through my phone, we spend half an hour bickering about Goulding. This is the first time she's accused me of something I haven't actually done and refused to believe the truth. And it feels horrible: Not only is this a direct consequence of all the times I have broken trust, but it can't be easy dating someone who has to work so hard not to cheat on her.

No woman wants a sex addict as a partner, except maybe a love addict.

Eventually Ingrid collapses on the bed next to Hercules and lapses into sullen, tearful silence. For the first year of our relationship, she was always smiling, laughing, and busy with creative projects. One of the reasons I fell in love with her was that she cast a ray of sunshine that penetrated even the darkest corners of my thoughts. But now her light and creativity seem to have extinguished completely. She doesn't even speak to her friends anymore because they don't approve of her dating me.

As I look at the tear-wrecked mascara around Ingrid's eyes, the deep frown on her face, and the tragic fetal ball she forms around Hercules, my mother's warning echoes in my head: "Never grow up to make anyone as miserable as your father makes me."

STAGE IV

Love Avoidant:
Leaves Relationship and
Repeats Cycle with New Partner

Love Addict:
Returns to Fantasy About Partner or
Repeats Cycle with New Partner

13

When she steps into the car, wearing a red dress with her ever-present black boots, I'm relieved to see her. Of all the professionals I've met, she's the only one who truly seems to see the tangled invisible strings that guide human behavior.

And the first words out of Lorraine's mouth not only shock me, but they're exactly what I need to hear right now. "We had a discussion when you left rehab," she says. "And we don't think you're a sex addict."

"Really?"

"You have a sexual compulsivity and it's one of many symptoms of your upbringing."

"Thank you."

I'm not sure what the exact difference is between an addiction and a compulsion, and I don't care. Her words are the final bolt sliding open and setting me free from all the shame, repression, and struggle of the last year. It's the best compliment anyone's given me since I started this whole process.

After my argument with Ingrid, I emailed Lorraine, who probably knows me on a deeper level than anyone, to ask whether breaking up would be a healthy decision for Ingrid and me or a mistake we'll regret for the rest of our lives. She replied that she was coming to town soon to run a workshop in Orange County and we could discuss it in person then. So I invited her to dinner with Rick and me.

When we enter the Italian restaurant Giorgio Baldi, we spot Rick sitting alone in a white T-shirt. I've rarely seen him wear anything else. He smiles and nods his head in gentle greeting as I introduce him to Lorraine.

After we order, I let Rick know that I'm ready to throw in the towel on this whole accept-everything-a-sex-addiction-expert-says idea. "It's been a year and I'm still not happy. I've followed everything to the letter and I've learned a lot. But not only is my relationship hanging by a thread right now, what hasn't budged is my desire to be with other people and my belief that I should."

I study Rick's face for a reaction. He takes it in and closes his eyes lightly as if arriving at a thought—or, more accurately, letting a thought arrive to him.

But before he can respond, Lorraine asks me, "Is that outside your value system?"

"No."

"Then I don't see what's wrong with it. After my husband died, I decided I didn't want to live with anyone again. I live alone and I'm happy, and I wouldn't want anyone in that space. And that's what's right for me. What's great about today is that there are many different options and you can choose any one that's true to you."

I'm surprised to find her so open-minded. It sounds like she's changed her beliefs since rehab, so I ask her about it.

"Everything I told you during your chair work was true," she says. "However, Joan is the program director, and she has very strict guidelines about condoning any sexual behavior outside of a committed monogamous relationship, so I can't always say everything that I think there."

"So you actually *do* believe it's possible to have intimacy outside of monogamy?" I press, just to make sure I'm understanding her correctly.

"There are some couples who have a lifelong relationship and children, and they agree to have an open marriage. As long as both people are truthful and intimate and operating with integrity, I'm not going to judge them."

I look at the powder-dabbed wrinkles on her face, the folds of skin threatening to pull down her neck, and the earned intelligence in her eyes. And I think, Thank you for understanding.

I'm surprised by how much her approval means to me. Maybe it's because my permission to be a sexual being was taken away from me in rehab. It was my punishment for abusing that right in my relationship, for harming someone innocent with it. And now, after a year of probation, I'm finally being granted provisional custody of it again.

"I feel like I'm ready to explore other relationship styles, but I'm a little scared," I tell Lorraine. "I've been waking up every morning this week full of anxiety about losing Ingrid. I'm worried I won't be able to find this quality of love again and I'm ruining what may be my only chance for a happy future and family."

I'm so bad at commitment, I can't even commit to being uncommitted.

Ambivalence. That's my higher power. All hail Ambivalence, destroyer of relationships.

Meanwhile, Rick sits in silence, listening to the conversation, nodding and collecting thoughts.

"Have you asked Ingrid if she's open to another type of relationship?" Lorraine suggests as the food arrives.

"That would be the perfect solution. I just don't think she'd be into it, though."

"You may be surprised," she says.

Just as we have a family of origin that we're stuck with, we can create a family of choice that we freely select. And in some ways, it feels like I'm sitting with the functional mother and father I've chosen.

This is when Rick finally opens his mouth to speak. "What I wish for you," he begins, measuring each word to make sure it lands as powerfully as possible, "is that you commit all the way to living this adventurous lifestyle you want, without any other option. Because you need to get to the place where you have all the women you desire and find out it doesn't solve your loneliness or your need for connection or your pain."

I'm shocked by the severity of his words. I thought we had an agreement that I would try each path without judgment. "That wasn't the way you put it when we first discussed it."

"Well, I had a little more hope for you then. But this seems to be what you wanted all along."

Lorraine watches him speak. I feel a mounting sense of anxiety that she's going to agree with him. "If you're indeed going to follow through with your decision," she eventually says, arbitrating, "I'm going to ask you to solve a mystery."

"What's the mystery?"

"The mystery is whether the path you're embarking on is authentic or you're operating out of a wound."

"How will I know the difference?"

"Wounds bring drama and trauma. They don't bring comfort." She pauses to make sure I understand, then elaborates. "We all have six core needs: emotional, social, intellectual, physical, sexual, and spiritual. And if they're being attended to and enhanced, then you're doing the right thing."

"If this choice is coming from a healthy place, then you'll find that it leads to lasting happiness," Rick adds. It seems less like he's backing down and more like he's decided to let me learn for myself where this path will lead.

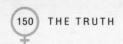

"I hope it does," I tell them. "Maybe I'll be able to find someone who shares my beliefs and values."

As the words leave my lips, I worry that I'll end up with the fate I deserve: a woman who's just like me.

"Remember," Lorraine urges, as if reading my thoughts, "anything that doesn't bring you alive is too small for you."

"And whatever you do," Rick adds ominously, "I hope you do it cleanly and honestly, with no baggage."

14

"This is the best relationship I've ever had," I tell her. "I've never loved anyone so much."

We are lying in our spare bedroom, which Ingrid decorated and named the Spaceship Room. There are four mattresses pushed together on the floor and black sheets covering the ceiling and windows. A projector plays videos of galaxies on the wall, another beams constellations onto the ceiling, and a light-up toy moon hangs over our heads. The room itself is a testament to Ingrid's playful creativity, and another reason I admire her. Yet, nonetheless, I am about to break her heart. And mine.

"And that's the problem," I continue.

"The problem?"

I start to stutter. It's hard for me to spit out the words that come next. Tears well in her eyes. She knows what's coming.

"I don't want to lose you," she says. Yet she knows she will.

We sit in silence for a moment, then she continues. "I feel like all our problems lately have been my fault because I haven't felt safe and that's made me distant and suspicious."

I want to let her believe that, but it's not the truth.

"No, it's me," I tell her. I feel horrible, I feel selfish, I feel guilty, I feel defective. "I don't know, but maybe we can try as an experiment a less traditional type of relationship, just for a little while, to get things out of my system."

Who am I kidding? These things will never leave my system. I've tried.

"To get what out of your system?"

I take a deep breath. I start to shake. I'm nervous to say what comes next. "I don't think I'll ever be able to earn back your trust." Long pause. "Because I don't think it will ever feel right for me not to be with anyone else. For the rest of my life."

There. I said it. I look at her prismatic eyes, her high cheekbones, the delicate double V of her neck and shoulder blades, and that intangible quality of her soul that is more beautiful and enduring than all of it. I don't want her to have a body like that woman on the plane or to leave me alone when she comes home from work or to stop reading over my shoulder. I'm embarrassed that I ever had those thoughts. And I wonder: Why is she not enough? Why can't I just be happy with her? And my eyes start to water.

She doesn't get angry. She doesn't break down crying. She looks me in the eyes and says, tenderly, "Maybe you want to sleep with other people, but I don't want to do that. I can't imagine having sex with someone I don't care about."

"Maybe we could just take three months off and use the time to decide what's right in our heart." As I'm making the suggestion, I know she'll never agree to it.

"If we stop, if we take a break, that's it. We're done. I will never see you or talk to you again." Her words are loving but firm, not the dithering of an ambivalent.

This is it, then: I must make a decision. A lifetime of monogamy with the woman I love. Or a lifetime of dating who I want, of doing what I want, of having complete and total freedom. It doesn't mean I'll never have a girlfriend or a child or a family. It just means I'll have them on my terms, not those of this repressive society that expects you to cut off your balls as soon as you say "I do."

I'm silent. I can't do it. This is what I've been saying is so natural, yet now I can't bring myself to let go. We have a trip scheduled to Machu Picchu in a couple of months, and countless other adventures we've planned and imagined. I've spent my whole life dreaming of being with someone like Ingrid: someone who I respect, who I trust, who I laugh with constantly, who I wake up next to and look at and just smile, grateful to the universe for bringing someone so lovely and loving into my life. But . . .

The silence is more painful than words for her. The tears come now, slowly. "You need to go on your quest," she says. "And it's one I can't go on with you. You have to go alone."

"I don't know. Is this ridiculous? We love each other so much. Are we making a mistake?"

"No," she says. "You have to do this . . . for you to be happy." Fortunately, one of us is strong.

"Do *you* want to break up?"

"No. I'm doing this for you."

And that's when I lose it. I hug her, tears drenching our faces. "Thank you for teaching me how to love and for teaching me what love is," she says. "You have the biggest heart of anyone I know." I don't believe those words or even see how she can believe them. Yet she does.

We cling to each other in silence, until she says softly, "I wanted to have babies with you."

On the ceiling and walls, galaxies are in motion, tiny replicas of planets and stars moving in their own orbits. And I think, We're changing the universe right now. This little decision is going to mean those kids aren't going to be born into this world. And we won't be the parents of cute little sunshine Ingrids and neurotic Neils.

A rumbling noise shakes the window, like an earthquake tremor or a violent gust of wind, and I wonder if it's a sign from the universe that we're making a mistake. Or maybe it's Mexican *sicarios* driving up to kill me for working on that book about the drug war. Rick Rubin once told me that on their deathbeds, people don't think about their work or their life experiences or the items remaining on their to-do list. They think about love and family. And I'm throwing it away. I may genuinely be turning that nightmare I had when I was a kid—of being a lazy, broke, unloved deadbeat sleeping on the couch in my brother's perfect suburban family home—into a reality this time.

But do I actually want that dream: a house in the suburbs, a domestic routine that never changes, a lifestyle where going out to a movie is some sort of grand adventure, ungrateful kids like me who blame all their problems on their parents? Maybe my heart isn't as big as Ingrid says it is. Or maybe it's big, but only because it's hungry and constantly trying to consume more so it doesn't starve.

I'm on the threshold of the freedom I've been fantasizing about for the last year, yet now it feels like plunging off the edge of that rooftop bar.

Ingrid strokes my head reassuringly and says, "I feel like I caught a beautiful bird in the wild and put it in a cage, just for me to look at."

I listen. She knows. She understands me.

"The cage is near the window, and the bird keeps looking outside and thinking about life out there. And I need to open the cage and let it go, because it belongs in the wild."

Then her face falls, her eyes redden, and the tears start coming faster. I can't let go, but she can. Between sobs, she sputters her last thought, the six words that will haunt me forever after: "But birds die in the wild."

Door

3

ALTERNATIVES

STAGE I
▪ Polyamory ▪

YOU EXPECTED *NOT* TO DESIRE
ANY OTHER MEN AFTER MARRIAGE.
AND YOU EXPECTED YOUR HUSBAND
NOT TO DESIRE ANY OTHER WOMEN.
THEN THE DESIRES CAME AND YOU WERE
THROWN INTO A PANIC OF SELF-HATRED...
DID ANYONE EVER TELL YOU THAT MAYBE
IT HAD NOTHING WHATEVER TO DO
WITH YOUR HUSBAND?

—ERICA JONG
Fear of Flying

1

I'm free.

I can go wild. I can date any woman I want. I can text anyone anything at any time. I can start searching for the ultimate free relationship.

But for some reason, that's not what I'm doing. Instead, I'm relaxing in solitude. I didn't even know I'd missed myself.

I finished a book last night and I'm deep into another one this morning. I haven't read this much in years, or enjoyed it quite so much. The bed feels clean and spacious, the sun warm and comforting, the Cinnamon Toast Crunch soulful and decadent.

Rick says I'm going to eventually become one of those lonely old men who yell at happy children. But I have my books to read. I have my warm bed. And I have my breakfast cereals. As long as I have these, I will never be alone.

Ingrid left with everything she owned in garbage bags two nights ago. It was painful: Neither of us could stop crying. She left behind only a ficus plant and a note:

> *Thank you for letting me see your heart. You always said it was full of darkness, but what I saw was bright and warm, full of life. It's the most beautiful thing, kind of like walking inside of a cave with a candle and finding this amazing hidden treasure. I think that's why you have the treasure map engraved on you. You told me that your mom gave away your goldfish when you were young because she said you couldn't take care of things. So I'm leaving my plant with you. I call it the Survivor because when I got it, it went for months without water and still kept growing. So now it's yours, full of life, to prove you can take care of things.*

Her words pierce my most vulnerable organs: my heart and my shame core, which I'm starting to think may be one and the same. Love is so hard to find as it is, it's insane to tell someone to stop loving you—for possibly no good reason. Especially someone as genuine and caring as Ingrid. But that's what I did.

I feel loneliness at times, sadness occasionally, and a hovering sense of doom without Ingrid, as well as guilt for subjecting her to all my doubt, resentment, and struggle for nothing. But, still, I'm happier alone. Just me and the Survivor. At least the Survivor will let me water other plants.

I flip the card over to find a postscript: "Please do not reply to this and do not call me. I will be trying to heal. If you ever need to reach me in an emergency, your code word is 'Freeeeeeedom!' You may only use it once and I will be there for you."

I wander into the kitchen to drop my dirty cereal bowl in the sink. I don't clean it. I don't brush my teeth. I didn't even shower or wash my face this morning.

I load a surfboard into my Durango and drive to the beach. The sun is blazing, the mountain view is majestic, and the waves are clean. I feel guilty for enjoying it all. Perhaps the people who hurt you the most when they leave are the ones you shouldn't have been with anyway, because they do it without compassion. Ingrid left with nothing but compassion.

When I return home, I change into jeans and a thin hoodie. On the kitchen counter, I see *Silently Seduced* staring me in the face. I flip through it and read some of the passages I underlined: "Make a full commitment to stay in your relationship if you judge it to be good for you," Adams writes. "Separate the insatiable needs of the inner child from the realistic intimacy needs of the adult. Regrettably, all the developmental needs lost to the incestuous relationship will not be met fully in any one partnership."

I panic for a moment, worried that I've made a horrible mistake, that my grounded adolescent has broken up with Ingrid's abandoned child. But then I think that if my needs can't ever be met by one partnership anyway, then I'm definitely doing the right thing by trying to get them met through multiple partnerships. Maybe the damage is irreparable and I just need to find a way to live with it, to make friends with it, to embrace the shadow rather than fighting it.

When the sun sets, I drive to the market to pick up a quarter pound of pulled pork and some coleslaw. As I sit at home, eating out of the plastic containers and watching movie trailers online, I feel a sense of inner peace I can't remember having had in a long time. I can move in any direction I want without anyone stopping me, holding me back, being hurt by it, or even just asking where I'm going or to wait for her.

I thought for sure by now I'd be calling someone to spend the night with, just so I could feel a new body pressed against mine and extinguish the solitude. But instead I'm enjoying being me again. Either I'd lost myself and wasn't really taking care of my needs in the relationship as I thought I was. Or it's not actually Ingrid I feel freed from, but the incessant guilt and repression of the sex addiction world.

As I lie in bed that night reading *Zorba the Greek* ("the backside of the miller's wife, that's human reason," the eponymous character remarks), my mind keeps turning to Ingrid and replaying things she used to say and do. Like the way she used to pull down my pants and yell "Freedom!" and try to push me out the door. Or the way she'd buy ridiculously flavored drinks like bacon soda or sweet corn soda, and present them to me like a ring announcer introducing boxers. Or the way she'd try to keep me from entering our bedroom, claiming to be a bouncer and demanding to see my VIP pass. I miss my best friend.

I once asked Dave Navarro, a rock guitarist I wrote a book with, why he was sabotaging his marriage to Carmen Electra, who at the time was one of the world's biggest sex symbols. "It's like living with my best friend," he complained. And I responded, "That sounds great. Who wouldn't want to live with their best friend all their life?" Now I know the answer: When you live with your best friend, your dick gets lonely.

Linda, a girl I dated in the past, calls. It's as if she has a radar or, more likely, is stalking me online. I was Linda's first, and whenever we're between relationships—and occasionally when we're not—we hook up. When I tell her that I broke up with Ingrid, she replies kittenishly, "Good, now you can have a baby with me."

"Maybe we can do that someday. But I don't want to be monogamous."

I wonder why I feel like I can't handle marriage, but I can handle fatherhood. I think this is because it's not the responsibility I mind, it's the exclusivity. You can raise a child and still have one or two or ten other children. And growing apart and separating is the nature of that relationship, so over time everyone gains more freedom.

Linda and I talk about how the arrangement would work in a way that's healthy for the child, but ultimately it's just a role-playing fantasy. Especially since she has a boyfriend, so I have no idea why she's calling me. All I know is that I don't have to feel guilty for taking the call.

I close my eyes and sink back into the comfort of my bed, ready to wake to another limitless day, free to spread out in whatever direction I choose.

Any reality can be mine. I can have a baby with someone like Linda. I can create a free-love commune like Father Yod. I can find a relationship that's boundless and limitless. I can be true to myself.

And perhaps this is freedom: standing in a circular room surrounded by open doors, knowing that I can walk through any of them, and anticipating the new adventure that lies beyond each one.

I may miss Ingrid, but I'm ready.

Entry from Ingrid's Journal

DAY 1

1:00 p.m.

Hercules and I went to the dog park together. I feel weird and strange, sort of shy when talking to guys who approach me. I feel like I'm in a brand-new world. So far I haven't really thought much about Neil. Waiting for the night to come. It's the night that scares me.

Everyone at the dog park thinks Hercules is a sweetie pie. He mostly keeps to himself and likes to smell the grass.

I feel very sensitive. I don't want people to approach me or talk to me. I want to be alone. I feel lonely and sad.

9:00 p.m.

Waiting outside [my friend] Melissa's house. Meeting her for a drink. I need to ask her how she got over her breakup. On my way back to the office from the dog park, I stopped at Rocket Fizz for some fun flavored sodas. But every flavor reminded me of Neil because we tried practically every soda there. I found a few new flavors, but then I thought, Hmm, if it's good, I'd want to share it with him. So I just left without buying anything.

I miss my best friend. My family. My everything.

Can I do this?

When is Melissa coming out? Gad! Been out here for more than thirty minutes.

The moon is shining bright tonight. The moon is caressing me with its gentle light. I hope Neil is outside so the moon can touch us both and connect us with its light.

I love him. No doubt.

At a bar with Melissa now. She's talking to some guy she knows. He wants to introduce me to the bartender.

3

Charles is upset because his wife got mad at him all over again, locked him out of the house, and told his family that he'd cheated on her with prostitutes. Adam has stopped playing football, yet his wife still isn't thawing. A haggard rock guitarist named Rod confesses that he's been going to Asian massage parlors behind his wife's back.

And everyone is yelling at me.

This is my last group therapy session, and Sheila wants them to "process" my departure. The previous week, they did the same with Calvin, who left the group after deciding to bring Mariana and his son to Los Angeles for a long stay to see if they could make it as a family together.

"So what are you going to do now?" Charles asks me, as if life without sex addiction treatment is inconceivable.

"What I want to do is take some time to explore different alternative relationships, so I can find the one that's right for me."

"What do you mean by alternative relationships?" Adam asks, perplexed. He seems to have no idea that there are options in life besides monogamous marriage.

"I wrote down some criteria for the type of relationship I'm looking for." I pull out my phone and read a note I jotted the night before:

1. It can't be sexually exclusive, which rules out monogamy.

2. It has to be honest, which rules out adultery.

3. It has to be capable of developing romantic and emotional attachment, which rules out being a permanent bachelor.

4. It has to be capable of evolving into a family with healthy, well-adjusted children, which rules out unstable partners and lifestyles.

There's an awkward silence when I finish. Finally, Charles speaks: "I had hope that you'd be the two-cars-in-the-garage addict, who gets treatment and recovers before he's lost everything." He shakes his head in disappointment. His Alfred Nobel has turned out to be a Robert Oppenheimer. "But now it looks like you're going to have to hit bottom."

"You have a sickness in your brain!" a construction manager in the group yells, like a priest from the Middle Ages telling me I'm possessed by the devil. He's here because his wife caught him draining their bank account to pay for time with webcam girls. "You're not capable of deciding anything for yourself. Your head got you into this mess, so how do you think that same head is gonna get you out of it?"

I start to defend myself, but Sheila raises a hand to shush me. "Listen to everyone's feedback first," she instructs.

Rod is up next. "Some of my friends have tried open relationships," he begins. "And they don't work. It's natural for you to want one because you're a male and you're an addict. But no normal woman is going to date you if you tell her you can't be faithful, except someone who's so weak she'll accept that."

But who decides what's natural and normal, I wonder? What if it's simply the cultural pressure women constantly receive about being a good girl, saving their virginity, and finding *the one,* combined with a preponderance of abandoning fathers creating clingy love addicts, that people misinterpret as an inherent female disposition toward happily-ever-after monogamy? I'm starting to believe that the whole notion of classifying certain behaviors as normal and abnormal hurts people more than it helps them.

When everyone's finished condemning me, Sheila takes a few deep breaths, her upturned palms rising and falling with each aspiration, until she's slowed the energy in the room. Then, in as loving a voice as she can muster, she condemns me: "You're in relapse right now. What you're doing is making plans to avoid the emotional pain of the breakup and the pain of knowing you can't give Ingrid what she needs in a relationship."

I sit there trying to make sense of what she's saying, but it appears to be complete nonsense. Fortunately, Adam, who seems to be grasping the concept of an alternative relationship, comes to the rescue, "Let's face it: What Neil wanted is not what Ingrid's about. He was honest with her and that's a huge step forward. I don't know if any of us has been that honest with our wives. At least he's figuring all this out before he gets married."

"Can't you see, Adam, that this is his eroticized rage?" Sheila admonishes him.

I want to say that using the term *eroticized rage* as a blanket condemnation of all nonmonogamy and casual sex is an act of rage in itself, an attempt to shame anyone who doesn't share her personal views and morals. She could just as easily pathologize my writing, dismiss it as a trauma reaction to feeling misunderstood as a child, and tell me that to be intimate I need to have two-way communication and go through a twelve-step program to stop this solitary form of conversational masturbation.

But I keep my mouth shut—until Sheila gives me permission to respond and say farewell at the end of the session. At first I want to ask why no one's coming down on Rod for going to massage parlors, but when I look at him slumped pathetically in his chair, I understand the answer: He admits he has a sickness he's powerless over, whereas I still don't believe the sickness exists for most of us and am about to set off on an exploration of extra-relational sex. So if I don't end up either dead or in some way destroyed, that would threaten everyone's belief in this quasi-religion and thus their tenuous control over their desires.

So I fight back my rebuttal, which would only validate Sheila's rage accusation, and simply thank them and tell them to stay in touch. But when she gives me her sad-Sheila look and says she's hurting for me, it gets a little harder to stick to the high road. "Don't worry about me," I tell her. "That's your own pain and sadness you're feeling, not mine. I'm fine."

Fucked up, insecure, neurotic, and . . . enlightened. Because I'm done sitting here with these spineless men, most of whom don't even enjoy the marriages they're struggling so hard to save.

We've been living in the dark ages of relationships. It was the Catholic Church that began a relentless campaign to make monogamy and lifelong marriages inviolable institutions in the ninth century. It's time to enter an enlightened age of love, sexuality, and attachment. Someone has to undo the padlock that society has put on our genitals—even if it means getting burned at the stake by Sheila, Charles, Joan, Patrick Carnes, and millions of others who are terrified of change, freedom, and, ultimately, pleasure.

So goodbye sex addiction group, hello group sex.

Entry from Ingrid's Journal

DAY 4

I always get emotionally abandoned. My dad left and so does every man in my life. I thought earlier, Guys are jerks. Then I corrected myself and thought, Well, I pick them, so I'm a jerk.

I don't want to be a jerk anymore. I'm so hurt my heart is numb. Neil doesn't want me and he's probably happy he's not with me.

I try to forget so it doesn't hurt. One day at a time. Tomorrow is another day with a little less pain. I'll be okay. There's a light that follows me and makes sure I'm okay.

Neil forgot me this soon? I haven't forgotten him.

I don't want him to know he hurt me. He let me go.

I told you I was the villain in this story.

Beer cans and plastic bags crunch under the tires as I park near the address Shama Helena gave me. Rows of small mismatched homes line the street, each with its own dying lawn. The more affluent residents are distinguishable by low metal gates separating their property from their neighbors'.

The house I'm looking for is a one-story yellow stucco affair. Behind it, there's a garage and a garden shed, each leased as an apartment. I am here to see the tenant living in the garage.

It's not the best neighborhood in the Valley. And I'm not sure if I'm doing the right thing by coming here. But I have to start somewhere. So why not with Shama Helena?

The first place I started looking for monogamy alternatives after my last group therapy session was the online polyamory community. Where polygamy historically refers to someone married to multiple people simultaneously—polyandry if it's a woman with multiple men, polygyny if it's a man with multiple women—polyamory is a more recent and much more broad term meaning "many loves." It was coined in the early nineties by Morning Glory Zell-Ravenheart, a New Age writer whose name pretty much embodies the post-hippieness of the original poly community. Her neologism spread quickly because, among other reasons, it's far more graceful than saying "pluralistic relationships" or "multiple-partner relating."

While searching online for local polyamory meet-up groups, I stumbled across Shama Helena's name. In addition to leading one of the groups, she also self-published a book called *Polyamory 101* and coaches newcomers to the alternative relationship world. So I contacted her to discuss my options and the best places to find open-minded partners.

I knock softly on the door of Shama Helena's garage, excited to begin my journey into the world of alternative relationships and find my nonmonogamous one—or ones. Evidently, judging by her place of business, teaching people to have more lovers doesn't pay as well as teaching them to have fewer.

Shama Helena greets me in loose-fitting drawstring pants and a tank top with massive cleavage thrusting out of it. She appears to be in her fifties, with auburn hair, long bangs, and a compellingly witchy face, but with a nose that's broad rather than sharp. Common sense tells me to leave; curiosity drives me forward.

The garage has been converted into two rooms. The busty witch of the Central Valley leads me to the back one, in which a bed has been squeezed lengthwise between the walls. She sits cross-legged at the head of the mattress. This is her office.

Apparently I'm supposed to sit opposite her at the foot of the bed. I wonder what kind of woman would let a stranger, who contacted her off the Internet, into her home and onto her bed within seconds. Then I realize that's exactly the kind of woman I've come here looking for.

Centuries ago, a woman like Shama Helena would probably have been burned at the stake—not necessarily because of the way she looks or the candles, incense, and red draperies strewn throughout the house, but because women who were overtly sexual were thought to be witches in league with the devil. We've come a long way as a culture in five hundred years. Now, instead of calling them witches and killing them, we call them sluts and kill their reputations.

Men have a conflicted relationship with female sexuality: When a man is single, he wants women to be as easy and undiscerning as porn stars. But at the same time he's terrified by this behavior, because he thinks if a woman sleeps with *him* so easily, then clearly she'll sleep with *anybody* and thus won't be faithful in a relationship. We have so many contradictory, repressive, self-limiting beliefs about sexuality—and almost every one of them stems from a pathological need to dictate to someone else what they are and aren't allowed to do with their body and heart.

"So what can I help you with?" Shama Helena asks.

I start to tell her my story, but as I'm talking, something starts to collapse inside me. I pause and close my eyes to strengthen the walls of my heart, and Shama Helena the all-seeing catches me.

"What's wrong?" she asks.

I suck in a lungful of incense-laden air. "I was thinking about Ingrid, my ex." It feels weird to call her my ex, as if she's been crossed out of my life. "We booked this trip to Machu Picchu together, and I just got sad thinking of going without her."

In a slow voice that's a little too breathy, as if she's studied Marilyn Monroe singing "Happy Birthday" to John F. Kennedy, she tells me that she believes there are three types of men: til-death-do-us-part guys who want to be with one person for the rest of their lives; Peter Pan types who never want to grow up and just want to accumulate notches on their belt; and mature men who want to have intimate relationships with multiple partners.

As I listen to her, feeling like a combination of all three types, I start imagining what her sex life must be like. I see her naked, wrinkles everywhere, tits hanging down her chest, and with a huge radiant smile, being groped by guys with gray chest hair and with torsos like an expanse of hills. For some reason, the scene isn't disgusting; it seems joyful.

Shama Helena rises and walks to a hot plate on a shelf a few feet away—presumably her kitchen—to pour a cup of tea for herself. She offers me some, but I worry that it might have an aphrodisiac in it, so I pass.

When she returns to the bed—presumably her dining table as well—I ask about the most common types of polyamory. From her long response, I manage to piece together these three relationship structures:

1. Having a primary partner, with each person free to negotiate or enter into separate secondary and tertiary relationships.

2. Creating a triad, in which three people are romantically involved. This can take the form of three people in an equal relationship (a "triangle"); one person simultaneously dating two others who are not as close to each other (a "V"); or a couple sharing the same secondary (which she doesn't name but I suppose would be a "T").

3. Forming a group relationship of four or more people.

"Where would swinging fall into this?" I ask.

She grimaces like she's just tongued down a bleeding hemorrhoid. "The swinger lifestyle is just 'let's fuck.' The poly lifestyle is 'I'd like to get to know you.'"

I suppose if polyamory were all about sex, it would be called polycoitus instead. In the lecture that follows, Shama Helena explains that to most people, polyamory means having multiple loving romantic relationships in which all the partners know about one another. The key word here is *loving*. A relationship that permits only casual sex on the side wouldn't technically qualify. The other distinction is honesty. Having a secret mistress or being in a "don't ask, don't tell" relationship wouldn't truly be polyamorous either. And poly doesn't necessarily come with freedom. Many relationships, Shama Helena explains, require sexual exclusivity to some or all members of the group—or, as it's called, *polyfidelity*.

"Whatever the situation may be, what you want is a bonded partnership that gives you a foundation to fly," she tells me. "There's a concept called *compersion*. And that means if your partner has another lover, rather than being jealous, you're happy for her because she's happy."

Suddenly, reality sinks in. If I can do what I want, then of course whoever I date should likewise be free to do what she wants. And how am I going to feel if I'm home alone working while she's spending the night at some lover's house—or a long weekend at a five-star tropical resort with some dashing Romeo trained in the arts of the Kama Sutra?

Traditionally, adultery has been a privilege chiefly reserved for men. Anthropologist Gwen Broude researched 112 different societies and found that 56 percent permitted extramarital sex for husbands, whereas only 12 percent allowed it for women. Even in the Bible, and in societies today where they bury people up to their necks and stone them to death, it's typically adulterous women (and often their lovers) who are are punished, rarely married men who cheat with single women.

However, liberation for only one person in a relationship isn't truly freedom; it's totalitarianism. So I'll have to learn to let go and suck it up.

"What if compersion isn't an emotion that comes naturally to me?"

"Like anything, it takes work," Shama Helena responds, arching her back. Despite her witchiness, the display arouses me. The incense must be going to my head. Good thing I didn't drink the tea. "In order to truly be polyamorous, you're going to have to go through the path of uncomfortability. Just know that you're going to experience jealousy, and know that it's about you, not her. So allow yourself to be vulnerable. Don't be afraid to show your feelings and needs, and work through them. In the end, you'll find that true love is wanting your partner to have whatever she wants—whether or not you approve of it."

I inhale cautiously. It's excellent advice. And I think I can do this. I imagine Ingrid having sex with someone else, and I guess as long as I knew I was her primary, I could eventually learn to deal with whatever feelings came up. Maybe it would even inspire me to be better in bed instead of being lazy and fantasizing about other women.

There are just a few minutes left in the session. And I have two burning questions I still need help with. In my most challenging times with Ingrid, an image kept coming back to me: the picture of Father Yod living with all his happy hippie lovers.

So I ask: "What if I want to create a community of people living together in a single open relationship?"

I win big points with Shama Helena for this question. It's her dream also. She says she wants to get some property and have everyone in her "tribe" live there in different houses. I try to imagine her renting all the garages in the neighborhood.

Question two: "How do I know which type of relationship is right for me?"

She recommends dipping my toe in the water by going to the annual World Polyamory Association Conference, which she describes as the biggest and most established event in the community. "Take your time before deciding what relationship style is right for you," she adds. "Explore the different options this world has to offer first. See some good modeling and see some bad modeling. Stay on the outside and be in a place of inquiry, but notice what you gravitate toward."

As we wrap up our session, I feel energized and optimistic, with a better grasp on how to move forward and what to look for.

However, as I slide off the bed and make my way out of her lair, Shama Helena slowly raises her hand and points a crooked finger at me: "One more thing." The breathiness is gone. Her voice is stern. I worry for a moment that she's going to turn me into a toad or a dildo or something. "You need to be upfront with everyone you meet. Because if you date a monogamous woman, she's going to want to be in a monogamous relationship. It's not fair to her. So if you're serious about this, I want you to promise me you won't have any monogamous partners."

That massively narrows the playing field. It would rule out all of my past partners, not to mention most of the population of North America. However, if that crazy cannibal in Germany could find someone willing to be eaten alive, I can at least find a few women who will let me date other people. So . . .

"I promise."

"Good. You need to find someone in the paradigm. For example, I'm a Tantrika and I don't date anyone who's not Tantric."

So she *is* a witch, I think as I give her fifty dollars for, as she puts it, "an offering." I've never trusted people who mix spirituality with business, and I'm not sure if Shama Helena is an exception to that rule. But for my first small venture into the world of polyamory, it wasn't too bad. I'm looking forward to taking her advice and, for starters, searching the World Polyamory Association Conference for potential new partners.

As I walk out and make my way back down the path, Shama Helena asks when I'm going to Machu Picchu. "Next month," I tell her, imagining all the fit poly yoga women I'll be meeting at the conference. Younger versions of Shama Helena.

But then she calls out after me: "Let me know if you have any ET experiences in Peru!"

And something inside me plummets. I think it's hope. Perhaps Rod's right: Expecting to find sane women in this community may be unrealistic. They're like benevolent extraterrestrials, guardian angels, and Norse

gods—imaginary creatures, products of fantasy, symptoms of a longing not to be alone in the universe.

Entry from Ingrid's Journal

DAY 7

I feel much better.

At home the next day, I register for the World Polyamory Association Conference, which falls on the same dates I was supposed to be in Peru, so I push the trip back. Then I order a stack of books from Amazon, the classics in the field of consensual nonmonogamy—*The Ethical Slut, Opening Up, Sex at Dawn, Polyamory: The New Love Without Limits*—as well as a lesser-known book from a more therapeutic perspective, *Love in Abundance: A Counselor's Advice on Open Relationships,* by Kathy Labriola. I speak with her briefly, and she explains that she believes "multiple-partner relating is as fixed a sexual orientation as being straight or gay."

Since I have a month until the polyamory conference, I do something that I've been repressing for the last year. I re-engage with the women who were texting and emailing during my relationship with Ingrid. Even though Ingrid and I are no longer dating, I still feel like I'm somehow betraying her.

Unfortunately, my first dating experiences go *too* well. I take a trip to spend time with Raidne, the augmented Las Vegan who emailed me after I returned from rehab. But after just two nights together, she asks, "Are you sleeping with anyone else?" It's evident from her tone of voice that this is not an innocent question but an ultimatum.

So I very clearly and compassionately explain to her, "When I hear your question, it sounds like you believe that an experience with someone else would detract from whatever we're developing together. But wouldn't it be better to just allow this relationship to set its own course without trying to control it or limit each other? Sexual exclusivity shouldn't be a criteria for deciding whether to care about someone or not."

Raidne listens closely, blinking her false eyelashes, taking in every word and weighing its meaning carefully. Then she responds bluntly: "I'm not that kind of girl."

Bright monogamous apple, wrong orchard.

A week later, Elizabeth, the entrepreneur who wanted to distract me on Skype when I was dating Ingrid, invites me to a business dinner she's having with investors. Afterward, we end up making out in her apartment. She sucks my finger into her mouth, then reaches down my pants. Suddenly, however, she disentangles herself and says, "I'm so attracted to you. But I have a son. And if I have sex with you, you have to marry me."

Her words shock me: as if sex is something to barter with in exchange for commitment, as if love is a business agreement to be negotiated and notarized, as if her pussy is a fucking startup and my dick is the angel investor who's going to fund it. Even more shocking, she's already in a long-term relationship with a high-profile lawyer. Maybe she's planning to jump ship. There's a term called hypergamy, which is when people marry someone of higher status, so I suppose this would be hypogamy.

As I drive home, dispirited, I realize I've already made my first mistakes. Monogamous relationships are waiting in the shallow end of the dating world like fishing nets. Just one wrong move, and I'll get tangled up again. And to break up with Ingrid just to end up in another exclusive relationship would not only be a travesty, but neither Elizabeth nor Raidne, despite all their positive attributes, has even a fraction of the quality of heart, sense of humor, or joy of life that Ingrid has. Shama Helena was right. You can't just date people randomly and then hope to slowly ease them into a non-monogamous relationship. You have to be upfront from the beginning.

I spend the rest of the week looking through my options and eliminating everyone who's monogamous, already dating someone, or clearly not relationship material, leaving three strong possibilities. There's Violet, a bisexual writer with whom I've had many sexual adventures; but when I call her, she tells me she's currently experimenting with monogamy.

There's Anne, the French woman who emailed nude photos while I was with Ingrid. She's a healer and acupuncturist, and her social media posts suggest an alternative lifestyle. So I start talking to her and eventually make plans to visit after the polyamory conference.

And then there's Belle, the Australian coquette who kept texting while I was with Ingrid. When I met Belle, I brought her and a cute skater girl back to my hotel room to spend the night, so she's clearly nonmonogamous.

"Remember that night?" I ask when I call her. She giggles; she remembers. After a little small talk, I continue: "I don't know if you're familiar with polyamory, but it's the idea that love is not some kind of scarce resource that can flow only into a single person."

I pause and wait for a well-reasoned objection or verbal tirade. When she says nothing, I elaborate, babbling nervously. "Just as a person can love parents, children, pets, and all kinds of songs and movies at the same time, so too can they love different partners without the emotions for one detracting from the emotions for the other. So I'm—"

Finally she speaks, mercifully interrupting me. "You want to put together a harem, don't you, Mr. Strauss?"

I hadn't quite thought of it that way. I think Father Yod lived with men and women, each with their own husbands and wives. But who doesn't want a harem? And there's a lilt to Belle's voice. It's flirtatious and she hasn't hung up or said I'm a monster. These are good signs.

The last thing I want, however, is some kind of cult or patriarchal Mormon household. So I explain, "A harem, to me, is a bunch of women controlled by a guy. I'd rather live in a group atmosphere of learning and growth where everyone's equal and free."

"Who are these other women you want to live with?" Suddenly the lilt changes to a sharp, suspicious minor key. Behind every *yes*, there's always a *no* waiting to ruin all the fun.

"I don't know yet. But if you were interested in maybe joining me on this exploration, I'll make sure they're cool people we'd both get along with."

Somehow the word *exploration* seems safer than *relationship*. Less commitment, easier for her to back out of. And we don't really know each other all that well yet. But at least I'm being upfront this time.

"I'm not sure what you're up to, Mr. Strauss, but I trust it will be interesting." The lilt is back. That wasn't too difficult. If I can just get a few more women to say yes, I'm going to be living a fantasy that as an adolescent I didn't even dream was possible. I thought it would take years to put together something like Father Yod's group relationship.

"How soon can you get here?" I ask.

"I have some time off in three months."

"I'll see you then."

Now I'm committed.

And in over my head already.

Fortunately, I have time to learn to swim. The World Polyamory Association Conference is happening soon. And there I can find not just the tools to make this work, but like-minded people with knowledge, experience, and, hopefully, an interest in joining me. Because if monogamy isn't natural and cheating isn't moral, then the people there must be the bravest, most ethical, and most enlightened beings in the relationship world.

9

"My name is Sasha," he says.

Then he strips naked and runs around the interior of a circle of men. Afterward, the guys standing there—most of them gray-haired, loose-skinned, and pale—strip off their ill-fitting clothing and traipse into the center. There are man-tits, saggy asses, and swinging penises everywhere.

The only person still wearing clothes, holding fast as the last representative of the collapsed circle, is me. I thought the World Polyamory Association Conference was going to be a well-organized networking, lecture, and workshop event that would teach me about managing nonmonogamous relationships and living with multiple partners. Instead, I'm in a latter-day-hippie nudist resort called Harbin Hot Springs, surrounded by excessively happy naked men whom I can't imagine functioning effectively in the outside world. That said, at least they're free. Really, really free.

To kick off the conference, we separated into a men's circle and a women's circle. Then each attendee was asked to introduce himself and make a gesture for everyone else to imitate. One guy twirled. Another waved. I bowed. And good old Sasha—an energetic seventy-year-old with an infectious grin and deep-set smile lines—just had to strip naked.

Sasha also happens to be one of the founders of the World Polyamory Association along with his wife, Janet, who later explains that polyamory was a gift given to our civilization by aliens from the planet Nibiru. I'm reminded, fretfully, of Shama Helena's parting words. Is the idea of polyamory so far out that only people who believe in aliens can grok it?

Perhaps the connection comes from the classic science fiction book *Stranger in a Strange Land*, in which a man born on Mars comes to earth and starts a free-love cult. "The code says, 'Thou shalt not covet thy neighbor's wife,'" author Robert A. Heinlein wrote in 1961. "The result? Reluctant chastity, adultery, jealousy, bitterness, blows and sometimes murder, broken homes, and twisted children. . . . There is no need for you to covet my wife— love her! There's no limit to her love."

After the welcome circle, a gray-haired woman with an extremely soft voice—they seem to think here that speaking quietly means being spiritual— leads the group through an exercise in which we create an energy field around ourselves and a partner tries to sense it and walk into it. So far, none of this appears to have anything to do with polyamory.

"Do you need a partner?" a voice booms.

I look up and see a tall naked bearded man hovering over me. He seems creepy. In fact, there's nothing a naked guy could say to me right now that wouldn't seem creepy. Especially when he looks like a pot-bellied Abraham Lincoln. I take a step back and tell him I'm passing on this one.

I find an inconspicuous spot against the wall and press myself against it. Nearby, a large middle-aged woman is lying on her stomach, gravity flattening her excess deposits against the carpet. An extremely pale manchild with curly hair, who appears to be twenty years her junior and a hundred twenty pounds her inferior, lies beside her in a toga, his package dangling outside the sheet as he massages the meat of her shoulders.

The polys end the morning session by performing a contact dance. They roll around the floor like logs—crossing, colliding, and touching, touching, touching. I'm not sure I'd want to do this even with people I was attracted to.

I broke up with Ingrid for this?

So far, the conference seems more like bisexual New Age softcore swinging than polyamory.

When Sasha announces a lunch break, I dash to the buffet. I figure if I'm first in the food line, no one's pubic hair will end up in my veggie burger. I load my plate, then find a seat at an outdoor picnic bench. Just next to it, there's a hot tub in which a smiling nude woman is floating on her back, rapturously exposing herself to the sun's rays.

Naked Abraham Lincoln sits next to me and strikes up a conversation. He tells me he was recently widowed. It seems odd that the first thing he does after she dies is go to a polyamory conference to play log jam with a bunch of strangers, but then again that's what I did as soon as Ingrid and I broke up. He is the future me.

We're soon joined by a couple who introduce themselves as Martin and Diana. Martin is a tan, muscular painter from France; his wife, Diana, is a Latin woman with enormous natural breasts. She says she wishes her husband wasn't poly, but she accepts it and has her own secondary. However, she adds, shooting him a look, "I'd give it all up in a second if my husband decided to be monogamous."

A shy couple from Sacramento sits next to them. The man wants to open up, but his wife has reservations. These relationships sound like the exact opposite of the marriages in rehab: Instead of a wife expecting monogamy from a husband who doesn't like it, the man is expecting nonmonogamy from a woman not comfortable with it. Perhaps the women here are simply less stubborn versions of Ingrid, the men more strong-minded versions of me. I wonder how a wife would cheat in this inverse relationship: by *not* sleeping with anyone else?

Lincoln tells me that this used to be a big conference with nearly two hundred attendees, but one of the main volunteers stepped down. She had three lovers and was in danger of losing custody of her children because of her lifestyle, so she had to start acting more monogamous.

His story is disheartening: If anyone who has more than one partner is seen by the government as immoral and unsuitable as a parent, then this revolution has much bigger enemies to fight than the sex addiction industry.

We're interrupted by a naked rabbi who lives on a poly kibbutz in Israel and is in some way dating the woman who's either sleeping, dead, or meditating in the hot tub. He stands up, pours a glass of wine, and sings a prayer over it in a deep, beautiful voice as his dick swings in the air like a metronome.

It is in these moments that I miss Ingrid most. Loneliness is holding in a joke because you have no one to share it with.

After lunch, we return to the conference area. A few more attendees have arrived and I scan them, hoping to find a woman I'm attracted to. But even with my low standards, I see only one person: a short, curvy blond nerd with thick black glasses.

The next speaker, a relationship coach with long silver hair named Scott Catamas, teaches something called *the four adjustments*. To make relationships healthy and harmonious, he tells the assembled polys, it's necessary to:

1. Turn judgment into compassion and acceptance.

2. Transform shame into reassurance.

3. Change criticism to appreciation.

4. Replace blame with understanding.

It's the first piece of useful information I've gotten here so far, and reminiscent of the principles of functional adult behavior that Lorraine taught in rehab. Later, I notice a group of polys sitting in a circle and passing a talking stick, discussing being their authentic selves and yelling "Aho!" Maybe all these people are also sex addiction rehab refugees.

Just when I'm about to dismiss the conference as a waste of time, a pack of eight people bursts through the door. They're comparatively young, they're generally fit, they're reasonably attractive, and they're clustered around a rail-thin woman like she's their Father Yod. She has an angular face and a bob haircut. From one vantage point, she looks cute; from another, she looks severe; from yet another, she looks like a man.

"Who's that?" I ask Honest Abe.

"That's Kamala Devi. She's really big. She has a four-thousand-person mailing list," he says with awe.

Kamala walks to the front of the room and greets the admiring throng with a "Namaste," pressing her palms together and holding them over her head and then her heart as her admiring pod gathers around her. Everyone I've met so far came here either alone or as a couple. This group of men without shirts and women in half-tops and yoga pants is actually the first poly constellation I've seen so far—and, unlike the couples I had lunch with, the woman is in charge and clearly into it.

Kamala stands with perfect yoga poise in front of the room, her hair parted high off her forehead, her skin so taut that every contour of her skull seems visible. She begins her talk by leading conference attendees in a chant of *om*. Afterward, she introduces herself as a "goddess" and presents her "poly family," which appears to consist of her husband, her female lover, another married couple, the male lover of the woman in the married couple, and two floating fringe lovers. It's hard to follow. Serial monogamy alone has given us a complicated landscape of fractured and blended families; a world of poly families expanding and splintering would be a bureaucratic nightmare. Maybe that's one reason polygamy's illegal: Otherwise, some enterprising rogue could marry hordes of foreign women, get them U.S. citizenships, and claim thousands of tax exemptions.

As Kamala speaks, her pod sits intertwined with her and one another in a massive display of poly PDA. Minus the freaky New Age talk, their lifestyle looks like a lot of fun.

In concluding her lecture, Kamala says that in order to make a group this large work, she has to be a "benevolent dictator" and, at times, a "controlling bitch." I wonder if that's the secret to polyamory: a yin-yang of wimpy spirituality and repressive fascism. I hope not.

Shama Helena advised me to observe from the outside and notice what I gravitate toward. So that night, I gravitate toward Kamala's pod, scouring the retreat until I find three of her menfolk sitting in the resort's nudity-mandatory hot tub with the nerdy girl. One is Kamala's husband, Michael; another is one of her married lovers, Tahl; and the third is one of their orbiting lovers. "We're having a special party in our room later," the orbiter tells the nerdy girl. "You can come watch—or participate, if you want."

I slip into the hot tub and strike up a conversation with them. Michael tells me that he originally met Kamala at a *puja* in San Diego over a decade ago. A puja is a Hindu ritual in which worshippers honor and commune with a deity. And from what I gather, the polys have turned it into an erotic guided meditation and dance party.

Tahl tells me his wife initially had no interest in polyamory. So in order to open the marriage, he encouraged her to date other people while he remained faithful. After letting her enjoy this freedom for a year or so, he gradually started dating as well—which is when he met Kamala, who convinced the couple to move in with her.

His words are a revelation. When I was with Ingrid, I was hoping for my sexual liberation. But a far better way to encourage a partner to open a relationship is to start by giving her the freedom that you want for yourself.

I ask the orbiter what his story is. Squeezing Tahl on the shoulder, he answers, "We dated each other, but we're not gay."

"How is that possible?" I ask.

"The new young poly scene is largely bisexual," Michael explains. "Everyone in our pod is bi, except for me. I'm just bi-*sensual*."

This is the future of free love: no barriers whatsoever to sexuality, including age, body type, and gender.

As the podmates talk about a reality show they're working on and a polyamory hotel they want to build, a voice suddenly bellows over the water, "You guys ready?"

I look up and see a yoga stud from Kamala's pod.

"Have you rounded up any more girls?" the orbiter asks him.

Kamala Devi and Shama Helena said polyamory was about loving relationships, not casual sex. But these guys seem more like next-level pickup artists, coming to these conferences with the intention of sucking any available women into their powerful reality.

Although I suppose if you're a spiritually evolved super-being, you exist in a constant state of love, so there's no such thing as casual sex. If you love everyone, all sex is polyamory.

"No, but you're going to miss the birthday spanking if you don't hurry up! Kamala's waiting."

The guys leave the tub, taking the nerdy girl with them. "If you want to really learn more, you should come to this event we're putting on called Tantra-Palooza," Michael says on the way out, offering me a consolation prize. "It's sex everywhere with everyone."

I watch them leave, impressed that they've created not just their own alternative relationship, but their own alternative reality. They're taking dating to a whole new level: Why go to bars or comb online profiles to meet women? Just put together sexually themed hotels and festivals, and they'll flock to you in the hundreds.

If you build it, they will cum.

10

The following night, three dozen men and women with body parts falling out of colorful sarongs, shawls, togas, and wraps gather in the conference room, anxious for what's about to transpire.

This will be my first puja.

"I have an announcement to make," a gray-haired woman named Evalena Rose says beforehand. The brochures on the welcome table identify her as a practitioner of multidimensional healing, soul retrieval, and addiction recovery. "Some of the women have complained that in the pujas, the gentlemen were getting competitive and aggressive for the ladies. Please respect appropriate boundaries in the pujas."

She hands the microphone to Catamas, who begins by urging everyone to dance freely and let go of their inhibitions. From what I've seen, I'm not sure what inhibitions he could possibly be referring to.

He then instructs us to sit in a circle and make eye contact with one another. I look into old eyes that are sad, joyful, restless, scared, and scary, and into the uniformly youthful and bright eyes of everyone in Kamala's pod.

"Feel Mother Earth below you and Father Sky above, and allow them to meet in your heart and flow love through your veins," Catamas continues.

When he asks us to touch our hearts and rock back and forth, breathing deeply to inhale the light, I start to lose myself in the moment, to relax and suspend judgment, to feel connected to everyone else breathing and swaying in the room. Then suddenly I hear Kamala Devi's unmistakable voice on the microphone: "Remember that you're just three breaths away from orgasm."

And, unexpectedly, I start laughing. Her words are a complete non sequitur, awkwardly thrown in to remind everyone that sex is still on tonight's menu. Evalena Rose shoots me a nasty look like I'm ruining the puja. So I shut my mouth to contain the laughter and it starts to escape through my nose. Just as I'm beginning to get a grip on myself again, Kamala declares that she's stepping in as the "priestess" of the room and I lose it again. I suppose laughter is just my way of managing the discomfort I'm feeling.

"I'd like you to now touch the source of your sacred energy and make a connection with it," Kamala intones. I place my palm over my heart, but everyone else lays a hand over their junk. Clearly they know something I don't.

I move my hand to my sacred crotch and look at the diverse polys, their hunger for one another growing through this spiritual foreplay. And my crotch tells me, "Please, Neil, don't do this to me. I don't want any of these people touching me."

So I tell my crotch, "Listen, you're the one who wanted free love. You're the one who thought the image of Shama Helena frolicking naked was beautiful. Well, this is it. You've arrived. It's no time to start acting like a snob caught up with superficial things. We've left that world. We must love all people."

"Like that wart-covered Amazon over there?" my crotch responds fearfully. "And that sweet wrinkly septuagenarian from the planet Nibiru? And even that naked widowed Abraham Lincoln?"

Sigh. My crotch and I are out.

I slip away from the circle, sit in my safe spot against the wall, and try to make myself inconspicuous as Kamala plucks the unspoken desire out of the air and continues transitioning a roomful of strangers into a roomful of fornicators.

One minute, everyone's on the floor doing the log jam. The next, the men are hugging one another bisensually. Soon a very randy black-haired, pear-shaped fifty-something Tantrika is throwing her arms into the air and moaning loudly.

My stomach rumbles hungrily. I was so concerned about making sure I saw the puja tonight that I didn't have dinner.

"Now walk around the room, and allow yourself to gaze at and appreciate the feet you see," Kamala instructs. "If you want, you may ask for permission to touch your foot to someone else's."

She goes on, telling them to look at and touch a succession of increasingly intimate body parts, like a naughty hokey pokey. From the safety of the wall, it's an enjoyable show. As Tahl takes the black-haired Tantrika's hand in his and spins her around in a blissful ballroom dance, I wish I could be as free as he is, able to celebrate the joy and beauty that's in everyone. But even if everyone in the room looked like a supermodel, I'd still be too weirded out to join in. I need to take this opportunity to figure out why that is.

I tiptoe to the buffet table to forage for food, but all that remains is a bag of organic olive-oil popcorn. Technically, popcorn is an air-infused vegetable and olives are a fruit, so it's not all that unhealthy a meal. And the package does say *organic*. So I grab it and return to my perch.

"Now gaze downward at each other's lingams and yonis," Kamala is saying.

The men and women wander through the room, staring lovingly at one another's crotches as Kamala reminds them, "Appreciate the beauty of her sacred cathedral." The oldest men start to cluster hungrily near the youngest women as if it's a game of musical chairs, and when Kamala stops talking, they'll get to feel up the closest body.

So far, pujas seem like the ultimate form of intimacy for intimacy avoidants. For some of these men, it's a way to experience love and connection without attachment or commitment; for some of the women, a way to have random sexual encounters without feeling dirty, used, or unsafe.

In theory, this should be paradise for the sex addict that Rick thinks I am. So why am I so uncomfortable? Why is the guy who wanted sexual freedom so badly sitting against the wall feeling so . . . limited?

I reach into the popcorn bag and grab a handful of dinner. The crinkle of the packaging reaches Kamala's ears and she focuses in on the sound like a cat. She slinks toward me, crouches until her face is just inches from mine, and hisses, "This is a temple. We don't eat in the temple."

"Sorry, I didn't know this was a temple." I try to say it sincerely, but it comes out sarcastically. And maybe that's because I'm totally confused.

When exactly did they turn this generic conference room into a holy sanctuary? And if it's just make-believe time, then why can't my popcorn be the temple's equivalent of a Communion wafer? And how does she know it's not sacred popcorn, anointed in the oil of a virgin olive?

But I say nothing. I kiss the bag tenderly, and quietly place it at the feet of the benevolent priestess. Goodbye, popcorn, our puja together has ended. We were just three kernels away from orgasm.

Kamala walks away and instructs the polys to form groups of four, select a person to be spoiled, and give him or her a three-way massage.

I still have a few pieces of popcorn in my fist, so I put them where they belong: in my mouth. It is not a dietary necessity, but a minor act of rebellion, the vestige of a male ego that doesn't really belong here. I am a food thief in the temple.

In a flash, Kamala is crouching in front of me again, her face a little too close to mine. "I told you once not to eat here," she whispers staccato, the veins on her thin neck bulging angrily. "You need to take that food out of here and eat it in the kitchen."

I stand up grudgingly and she watches as I return the popcorn to its rightful resting place on the buffet altar. I grab another handful to satiate my hunger and—

Who am I kidding? I'm not taking the food because I'm hungry. I'm taking it because I hate irrational, restrictive, unnecessary rules. That's the reason I left Ingrid and the world of monogamy in the first place. And now I'm in a world where the rules are even more irrational and more ridiculous. Kamala is not a good priestess for enmeshed men.

I hear her voice ringing through the metaphorical temple: "If you like someone's wand and want to touch it, don't be shy."

When I return from the kitchen, nearly everyone's wraps have dropped to the ground. Flaccid wands and hairy cathedrals are everywhere. All this talk of priestesses, temples, and lingams seems like just a fancy excuse to have casual sex—by pretending like it's serious business.

Perhaps just as there are cults around religion, so too are there cults around intimacy. But instead of monotheists, pantheists, and atheists, there are monogamists, polyamorists, and celibates. Each belief system comes with its own rituals, whether they be twelve steps, pujas, exclusivity, adultery, or arguing about money every night. And people like Patrick Carnes, Helen Fisher, and Kamala Devi are zealots who believe they've found the one true intimacy.

I try to stop my critical thinking, to use the four adjustments and turn judgment into compassion, to recognize the beauty of all these shame-free sexual revolutionaries connecting and turning an ordinary space into something sacred. Perhaps a puja is no different—and much healthier—than drinking alcohol on a date. It's a way for people to lower their inhibitions and let go a little with one another.

And that's when I get what this is all about: Thank you, Scott Catamas. There's a disparity between the masculine desire for sex, which tends to be carnal and ego based, and the feminine desire for sex, which can be more emotional and spiritual. So if swinging is for horny men, then this scene is for sensual women. Orgies are for ethical sluts; pujas are for goddesses.

Same destination, different ritual.

I look down and notice a few pieces of popcorn on the ground. I can't leave these sacrilegious foodstuffs on a sanctified floor. They're virgins. They don't belong here.

I pick them up and look for somewhere to throw them out, but I don't want to disturb the puja again. I could just eat them, though I don't want Abraham Lincoln's toe fungus in my digestive system. I glance at him and his mouth is hinged open, moaning appreciatively as the old Tantrika massages him.

I conceal the offending popcorn in my pocket, and instantly the dictator returns. However, she's forgotten to bring the benevolence. "I told you not to eat here!" Her eyes bug out of her skull and bore into mine with what appears to be hatred. She has shape-shifted from priestess to demon. *Devi*, I realize, is just one letter away from *Devil*. "You're not respecting my puja! Your energy is interfering with my experience and the energy in the room, so I'm going to have to ask you to leave."

"I was just cleaning the temple floor." I hold her gaze. "And what's wrong with my energy? It's not like I can control it." I've never had anyone insult my energy before. I actually think it's worse than being called ugly. After all, you can't hide your energy or go on an energy diet or get your energy surgically altered. Even in a room full of blind people, you're still a monster.

"We can discuss this tomorrow. But right now, you need to leave!"

I want to stay and see what happens next, but I heave a sigh and rise to my feet. She's right. These people need to feel comfortable getting naked and weird together without some overly clothed journalist eating junk food in the corner and silently mocking them.

This is truly the blackest day of my life: I've been kicked out of an orgy for eating popcorn.

I rise to my feet and walk out to the picnic tables on the patio. Fortunately, there are big glass windows. I can't hear the people inside, but at least I can see them. So I sit forlorn on top of a table and watch, the cool night air biting my face. I'm a grounded teenager again, sent to my room without dinner and forbidden from playing with girls.

Gradually the massages become more erotic. Kamala starts twirling and dancing through the writhing foursomes ecstatically, her arms outstretched like she's Julie Andrews in *The Sound of Music*. For a moment, the spectacle looks otherworldly and transcendent. But when the orbiter I met in the hot tub whips out his dick and masturbates above Diana, one of the reluctant poly wives, until he comes all over her enormous breasts, the entire façade of sacredness comes toppling down for me. It looks more like a scene from a gonzo porn film.

If this is polyamory, then it's not for me. Not only would I prefer monogamy with Ingrid to doing the sexual hokey pokey with a bunch of self-appointed deities every night, but I'd probably be banned from the scene entirely after a few more pujas. Because I've done some desperate things in my life to get laid, but I've never faked a spiritual belief.

11

"You should have talked to me first," Lawrence says. "I would have warned you to stay away from the World Polyamory Association or any of those kinds of events. They're organized by these New Age people from Maui, and the batshit-crazy types leech onto them."

Lawrence is a meditation and sexuality teacher. He's tall with a shaved head, and is so healthy his face glows as if he's swallowed a lightbulb. I'd met him once before at a party, where I introduced him to my friend Leah, a girl-next-door type with a wholesome face you could gaze at for hours. Leah called me afterward and said that on her first date with him, she had the best night of orgasms of her life. I haven't seen either of them since, but evidently those orgasms produced so much oxytocin that, four years later, they're still dating.

"It's my first open relationship," Leah tells me, beaming. I ask them how it developed, and it turns out that just like Tahl with his wife, Lawrence initially gave—and continues to give—Leah more freedom than he takes himself so he can teach her a lack of fear and possessiveness by example.

We're sitting on the patio of a pizza restaurant in Los Angeles, where I'm attending my first polyamory meet-up group. I returned home from the conference disappointed and discouraged, but after digging deeper found that there's more to the polyamory scene than pujas and priestesses.

And at this meet-up, that's certainly the case. More than half the attendees are from a completely different poly offshoot: the BDSM scene (bondage & discipline, dominance & submission, and sadism & masochism). Like the conference attendees, most of the people here are over forty. But instead of wearing togas and sarongs, they're clad in vinyl and leather. Instead of goddesses and priestesses, they're masters and mistresses. Instead of worshipping the light, they worship the darkness.

To my surprise, among them are Lawrence and Leah, who came to meet one of Lawrence's students. So I've been asking them about the polyamory conference, trying to get some perspective on what planet I was on.

"I don't understand what pujas have to do with polyamory," I tell

Lawrence. "It doesn't even matter whether the participants are in relationships or not."

"At the end of the day, what you saw there is a specific type of polyamory," he explains. "Tantra polyamory."

Before the conference, I thought Tantra was the practice of holding out on having an orgasm during sex in hope of a bigger, better, longer high. Since the conference, I have no clue what it is. Kamala Devi defined Tantra as "life itself." And the orbiter definitely wasn't denying himself release when he shot all over that woman's breasts.

"So in a nutshell, what is Tantra to these people?"

"What they call Tantra is basically an American phenomenon, invented as a way of talking about sex without using the word *sex*." So far, Lawrence is the first person I've met in this world who I feel like I can relate to, who doesn't start conversations with "namaste" and end them by asking about ETs. "Because of all the immoral connotations of sex, they make it into something divine and polite instead of physical and passionate. I think this is because a lot of the gurus know that most women need an emotional connection to have sex, and spirituality is the quickest, deepest way there."

"Unfortunately," Leah adds, "some of the women are just replacing one type of predator with another. Lawrence used to work with this one Tantric sex guru who told women his dick was the Godhead, and they had to open up and receive it to be awakened. He called his sperm the nectar of the gods. Afterward, a lot of the women felt deceived and used."

Since the conference, I'd been feeling guilty for just dipping my toe in the water of the scene rather than immersing myself before forming a conclusion. After all, pujas are the closest thing I've seen to free love in my life. But after talking to Leah and Lawrence, it's clear that what I saw didn't actually represent polyamory, just one of its many branches. But at least I learned that there are accessible communities where sex and love are seen as free and joyous, not possessive and pathological.

As we're speaking, a heavyset, deep-voiced African American man standing nearby extends a thick hand and introduces himself as Orpheus Black. He's with three women: one he introduces as his slave, another as his partner, and a third as one of his three wives. He tells me that since marrying multiple people can come with a one-year prison sentence in California, he committed to two of those wives in a pagan ritual known as a handfasting ceremony.

With his wives, girlfriends, and submissives, Orpheus comes across like a Master Yod. So I respectfully blitz him with questions, hoping to learn what I'd wanted to at the conference. "I'm trying to put together a house like yours," I explain. "Do you have any advice on how to make it work?"

He lets out a long, low chuckle, then leans in conspiratorially. "It's a full-time job. You have to be the leader. You can't show any weakness or doubt, or you'll get eaten alive."

That doesn't sound like much fun. "But if you can't show vulnerability, then you don't really have any intimacy," I respond, sounding a little too much like Joan. "What if, instead of a master/slave thing, I want everyone to be equals?"

"No matter how you do it, all the women need to be equals on some level," Orpheus responds. "The key is to make sure you don't have more feelings for one than the other. The other key is to sell them on the concept of the future but ground them in reality."

"So what is the future?"

"Family." He says the word powerfully, then crosses his arms over his chest and nods with deep assurance. "You have to make sure they all know you're a family and nothing ever supersedes the family. The mantra should be doing what's best for the community, not for the individual."

The relationship he's describing seems even more restrictive than a monogamous one. Perhaps that's because restraints, rules, punishments, and power are integral to the BDSM community. And while hog-tying people, whipping them, and taking them for walks on a collar and leash may be fun for variety, they're not my kink. I'm not a top or a bottom. I'm a middle.

Why is it that in order to escape monogamy, I have to look so far out on the fringes? Or are there many more people doing this, but hiding in shame, scared of the consequences to their career, family, or reputation if they're outed?

I drive home discouraged, worried that I'm never going to find what I'm looking for or a place where I fit in or more people for my pod with Belle.

That night, I dream I'm in the back row at a magic show with Rick Rubin. Ingrid is there, but she's in the front row. Afterward, I sit in my car, waiting for Ingrid to arrive so we can talk about the performance. But she never appears.

I wake up covered in sweat and filled with dread that I made a bad decision, that I've lost Ingrid forever. All the pain I never felt after Ingrid moved out suddenly overwhelms me. I look at the Survivor, surviving on my ledge as proof that I do have a heart, and sink into a deep melancholy.

I've officially tipped to the other side of ambivalence: Instead of wondering whether to leave Ingrid, now I'm wondering if I should have stayed. I consider reaching out and telling her I want to forget this whole search and just be with her, that the security of the cage is better than the freedom of the wild. But I've learned enough to know that these are just the thoughts of an ambivalent, manifestations of fear and loneliness from my failure so far to find what I left to look for. All that would happen is we'd begin the love avoidance cycle all over again.

For most men, what's tougher than breaking up is the moment when their ex finally falls out of love with them and lets go, perhaps because it triggers a childhood fear—a psychological terror—of losing the first woman whose love they needed: their mother. And so, as Sheila would recommend, I let myself feel the pain, the loneliness, and the fear, using all my strength as the days pass to keep from giving in and reaching out to Ingrid.

In the meantime, I continue to attend occasional polyamory and sex-positive events, but without much luck or any adventure I'd actually want to take part in. As the pain turns to mourning and the mourning turns to acceptance, I decide to stop going to them altogether.

And that's when I finally find the scene I'm looking for: not at a polyamory meet-up, but in the laundry room of Seth MacFarlane's house.

12

Entry from Ingrid's Journal

UNSENT LETTER

Dear Neil,

I was hoping that we'd meet each other at the end of this hard road. But as the days pass, I see that our roads won't meet again. I've been scared, hoping you could save me and take me away from this road onto yours. But it hasn't happened.

I didn't think this was something that was going to come up, but I have met someone. Meeting this new person was a complete accident. I don't know what it is, but I really like him. At first I thought I could have some fun with him and nothing would come of it. Maybe I'll get tired of him and stop answering his calls. But as I'm spending time with him, I realize this is a person I cannot just use like a rag doll. I can tell he likes me a lot. Seems too soon to know, but my intuition is very strong. I would like to give him a chance.

To be honest, I'm completely terrified. I don't want to be in another relationship for a while. But at the same time, it feels right for some reason.

Sometimes I wish you would come and take me away, but as the hours go by, I look back and see you so far away, almost like a blur in the distance.

I'm sorry we've gone through this. I really wish you the best in life and I hope you will find someone who can make you as happy as you made me. And I do mean it. With you I was the happiest I ever was.

Goodbye,
Ingrid

STAGE II
▪ Swapping ▪

VERY TOTALITARIAN SOCIETY,
NO MATTER HOW STRICT, HAS HAD
ITS UNDERGROUND. IN FACT, TWO
UNDERGROUNDS. THERE'S THE UNDERGROUND
INVOLVED IN POLITICAL RESISTANCE AND
THE UNDERGROUND INVOLVED IN PRESERVING
BEAUTY AND FUN—WHICH IS TO SAY,
PRESERVING THE HUMAN SPIRIT.

—TOM ROBBINS
Still Life With Woodpecker

13

Nicole reminds me of a shorter, more conservative, even skinnier version of Ingrid. She's five foot four and wearing what looks like a blue prom dress, her shoulder blades jutting over the top like the frame of a kite. She's a lawyer visiting from San Francisco. The kind of girl you marry and take home to Mom—unless your mom is like mine.

And I've known her for only half an hour. We're at a Japanese restaurant with a mutual friend, a film producer named Randy. He and his wife have invited us to join them for dinner, followed by a party at the Hollywood Hills home of Seth MacFarlane, the creator of *Family Guy*. Randy's wife, Jessica, is naturally full lipped and voluptuous. *Smoldering* would be a word to describe her. *Uptight* would be another.

When I tell them that I'm looking for an open-minded partner, she scowls and interjects, "I would never have a threesome."

"Why?" Her vehemence takes me by surprise.

"It's just that Randy and I love each other very much, and our love is real. And those are not the kinds of things you do when you're married."

Her words send a chill up my spine. She's verbalized my fear: that marriage means the end of fun, that the things a woman will do with a random guy she meets in Cabo are actually more fun than the things she'll do with the man spending the rest of his life with her. My head drops into my hand before I can stop it. Randy looks as disappointed as I do, but conceals it slightly better.

"What's wrong?" she asks.

"Look at Randy. He's dying inside. No one wants to hear that his sex life with you would be better if he hadn't married you." Randy avoids eye contact with her—and the fight that will occur later if he agrees with me. "So if you weren't married, would you—if the circumstances were right and it just happened—ever have a threesome?"

She doesn't say anything, but a smile flickers across her lips. "You would!" I exclaim. Something in me is trying to prove a point. "So let me ask you, then: If a man's need for sexual variety isn't met in wedlock, what needs of yours aren't fulfilled in your relationship?" Even the word *wedlock* sounds more like a prison sentence than a free choice motivated by love.

"I'd say the needs that most women don't get fulfilled are for emotional connection and emotional support. But I don't look to get those needs fulfilled entirely by Randy."

"See, and that's where I'm having a problem! At least you can get those needs met by having emotional connections with family and friends outside your relationship. But with sexual needs, you're stuck trying to get them all met by just one person. And if you try to get them from anyone else, you're pond scum."

That's when Nicole turns slowly, gazes at me with soft blue eyes, and says quietly, "I couldn't agree more."

"Really?"

"I just look like a good girl on the outside," she tells me.

"It would be great if you could talk my wife into a threesome," Randy whispers as we wander around MacFarlane's backyard an hour later. It is not a small party: There are ice sculptures, porta-potties, a full orchestra, and lots of thin, awkward, six-foot-tall women.

Nicole stays close to me the whole time. And gradually the air around us charges: She makes a little more eye contact than she needs to and laughs at even the bad jokes I make. These are known in the game as indicators of interest. And for the first time since I broke up with Ingrid, they're coming from a woman who just may be open to . . . being open.

I take her hand and lead her to an outdoor couch as MacFarlane croons "Luck Be a Lady" in front of the orchestra. For some reason, Randy follows us and sits next to Nicole. I'm not sure if he's there to protect her or if he's just completely oblivious. While whispering in Nicole's ear, I poke Randy's leg with my hand to signal him to make an exit. He sits there unreactive, as if absorbed by something he's thinking.

"Do you think he's going to leave so we can kiss?" I ask Nicole.

"I don't think he'd leave if we started fucking," she replies.

What's rare about Nicole is that she doesn't seem to have any hang-ups about sex. And that's the kind of woman I've been hoping to find: one who's free of the sexual shame that parents heap on their daughters as soon as they're old enough to ask why boys look different down there.

I remember one night I was sitting in a hot tub with a divorced man who was complaining about his dating difficulties as his two preteen daughters splashed around him. "Boys are weird," his eldest said in response to a comment he made. He looked at her approvingly and told me, "They're not dating anyone until they're thirty." His youngest daughter responded, "I'm going to be a single pug lady!" And that's when I realized that guys bring their dating problems on themselves. They program their daughter with an aversion to men and sex for fear that she'll meet someone just like her father, then they meet someone else's daughter and expect her to just jump into bed without anxiety or reservation.

I run my hand through Nicole's hair and we start making out. As the kissing intensifies and hands begin wandering, Randy sits still next to us like some sort of Rodin sculpture: The Voyeur.

I pry my lips off Nicole's and tell Randy, "We're gonna take a lap, then let's all leave."

Inside MacFarlane's house, Nicole and I try the handles of various rooms, but they're all locked. This is clearly not his first party. Then I spot a glass window and, through it, a laundry room. Fortunately the door's unlocked.

We slip inside and close the door behind us. I switch the light off so no one can see through the window. Then I throw Nicole against the door, reach under her dress, and massage her through her panties. She arches her back and moans, then starts fiddling with the buttons of my pants. Compared to the sacred sex at the World Polyamory Association Conference, dirty, furtive, and spontaneous sex feels a lot more meaningful.

Many women think that if they put out too quickly, their partner won't respect them. This is not the case. It's not about waiting for a certain quantity of time before having sex, it's about waiting for a certain quality of connection. And I already like Nicole enough to hope she'll consider being my consensually nonmonogamous polyamorous pluralistic multiple-relating primary partner. Maybe she'll be interested in moving into the free-love house with Belle and me.

As she kneels and goes down on me, I reach into my back pocket and pull out a condom. And that's when it happens.

She removes her lips, gazes up at me innocently, and says, "I can't have sex with you unless my boyfriend's here."

It takes a moment for the meaning of the words to register in my brain.

It's not a sentence I've heard before. I'm more used to someone saying, "I can't have sex with you *because* I have a boyfriend."

I repeat the word like a cry of pain: "Boyfriend?!" Someone else is already living my dream with her.

"We're in an open relationship. But I'm not allowed to fuck anyone without him there." The disappointment on my face must be clear, because she adds, "But when we do fuck, it's going to be very, very good."

She slides her mouth around me again. "Is it okay if I come?" I ask. I'm not sure why I'm checking for permission. Maybe I need to call her boyfriend and make sure it's okay with him too.

"Of course," she replies. Good answer.

I watch her work, but I'm so confused and let down that it's hard to stay in the moment. I remember watching the documentary *Anatomy of Sex*. It explains that when the penis is limp, that's when it's actually tense. The muscles are constricted. When it gets aroused, the penis relaxes. And this allows blood to enter, which expands the spongy tissue and creates the erection. So you need to be relaxed to get hard. You can't get hard when you're tense. And I'm tense, because I finally found someone open-minded who I can see myself dating—and she's taken.

Unable to perform, I zip up.

"I think I was meant to meet you," I tell her as we sneak out of the room. "I've been thinking a lot about open relationships lately."

"Are you in the Lifestyle?" she asks, speaking the words cautiously, probingly.

"What do you mean by the Lifestyle?"

"I hate that name. It's swinging."

"Wouldn't I need a girlfriend to swing?"

"Not necessarily. Do you know about the Lifestyle Lounge?"

"No."

"It's a website my boyfriend and I belong to. You can find someone there."

"Is that where all the sane ones have been hiding?"

"They're actually hiding at Bliss. And they're really hot. We're going in a couple of weeks. You should come with us."

"Will there be pujas there?" I ask, just to make sure.

"What are pujas?"

"Great, I'm in."

14

"Thank you again for last night and for respecting my boundaries," Nicole texts as she boards a plane home to San Francisco the following day. "I'm looking forward to getting together again, this time with James."

I had hoped to be on the other side of the relationship—and I'm not sure I'm comfortable with a guy in the room, even if he's just watching. Especially if he's watching. But Shama Helena did advise me to observe some relationships, and this may be a chance to do that.

Unfortunately, I get the chance sooner than I expected. Two hours later, Nicole texts and says we need to talk.

It's never a good sign when someone you just had sexual contact with *needs* to talk. The only thing I can imagine is that she has an STI she didn't tell me about.

I call and ask what's wrong. "I just had a discussion about trust with James, and I crossed some boundaries with you that I shouldn't have," she tells me, distraught.

"I thought you had an open relationship." Maybe their relationship isn't actually open but just ajar.

"Actually, our agreement was that I wasn't supposed to have sex *or* oral sex," she confesses. "I didn't think it would be that big of a problem for him, but when I started telling him what happened, he got really pissed. I honestly think this could be the end. Because he wasn't there, it wasn't okay. He says if I loved him, I wouldn't have done that. The fact that it started in the laundry room made it seem cheaper to him, and he's mad that I jeopardized the relationship in that way." She pauses. "And what makes it worse is that we're lawyers, so contracts are important."

An hour later, he texts: "Neil, James here. You shouldn't feel bad about anything you did." I don't. "I need to think through some things. Unconditional trust is vital when you live life the way we've chosen. Nicole violated my trust and that's something I need to process."

So far, it sounds like their open relationship has just as much drama as a closed relationship. And the drama is about the same thing: trust. Perhaps the reason friendships tend to last longer than relationships is that most of them don't come with rigid rules and exclusivity clauses.

A minute later, James texts again: "I'm not sure where this goes next (and I don't know where you want this to go). That's just something we all need to figure out together. I will text you once I've worked it through on my end."

The word *together* strikes me as oddly inclusive. It almost sounds as if I have the option of being involved in their relationship.

Whatever the case may be, I hope it hasn't ruined my chances of going to Bliss.

15

Swinging is a victim of its own success.

When most people think of a marriage with sexual freedom, *swinging* is the first word that comes to mind. However, the public relations campaign against swinging has been so complete and thorough that the word alone evokes derision rather than concupiscence. Even rock groupies have a better reputation.

The main strikes against swinging are, first of all, its apocryphal depiction as an activity mostly for old, out-of-shape, tastelessly attired, and otherwise dull suburban couples. And, second, the idea that swing clubs are crawling with diseases. Partly for these reasons, adherents have attempted to mitigate the stigma by renaming their scene *the Lifestyle* instead.

In swinging's defense, the judgment that only good-looking people are allowed to have pleasure is more a condemnation of the accuser than the accused. As for STIs, researchers say that HIV hasn't been any more prevalent among swingers than the general population. As one researcher put it: It's used as a moral argument, but it's not a scientific one.

If all parties were like Bliss, however, swingers would be envied instead of mocked.

Nicole sits at a Chinese restaurant in the Las Vegas Palms Casino next to a man who I presume is James. He makes strong eye contact and shakes my hand firmly. It's an overly masculine greeting, formal and slightly self-conscious. Evidently it is customary for strangers who've shared the same woman to greet each other like gunslingers before a shootout.

Though he's in his mid-thirties, James is dressed more like he's in his mid-twenties, with a garish fitted T-shirt and factory-faded jeans. He's tall, with close-cropped blond hair and a solid, broad frame, which seems to be more a result of genetics than the gym. So though he's big, he doesn't look like he'd last long in a fight—which is a good sign, since he may not be happy that Nicole and I have been texting constantly since we met. Out of respect, however, I've made sure to text him once for every five she and I send.

"I just want to let you know there's no bad blood between you and me at all," he says. "As a result of what happened, Nicole and I have actually improved our communication and strengthened our relationship."

Well, I'm glad that's resolved, so I can have sex with your girlfriend now.

We're soon joined by two couples, each with men who dress too young for their age and women who look like they stepped off the pages of *Maxim*. One is a sculpted, statuesque, raven-haired woman. The other is a living Barbie doll who introduces herself as Chelsea.

Chelsea is tanned bronze, dyed blond, and toned tight. She has had one surgery, bringing her to a D cup; the rest comes from hard work. I soon learn that she's the product of at least five hours a day of dedication to her appearance, 365 days a year, for the last fifteen years of her life. That's more than 27,375 hours of perfection and hundreds of thousands of dollars in makeup, manicures, clothing, shoes, doctors, hairdressers, aestheticians, and trainers.

Beauty like this is an addiction, catering to a masculine fantasy that only gets more impossible to match every decade as photo-painting, then airbrushing, then Photoshopping, then photo-editing apps keep raising the bar in the endless arms race of female perfection.

I'm clearly the weak link here—and, as a solo male, perhaps even persona non grata. Fortunately, Nicole flew an old friend of hers into town who, she says with a suggestive smile, can be my "special date."

As everyone settles in, James asks about my last relationship. It seems like he's testing me, trying to gauge what kind of person I am, determining if I'm someone worthy of sleeping with his girlfriend. I tell him the truth: that I wanted to open it up, but Ingrid had no interest.

"I think the mistake you made with her," Nicole jumps in, "is that you made it all about you wanting to be with other people. You should have made it instead about wanting to have sexual adventures together. This way, you can include her rather than making it seem like a failing on her part. That's what worked on me."

She's right: I was selfish with Ingrid. I just wanted my own pleasure, regardless of how much pain it would cause her. Perhaps if, instead, I'd wanted to do something that would have added to her life and to our relationship, she would have been more open to it. Or perhaps not. But it definitely would have been a better way to go about it.

Like many people in the Lifestyle, James and Nicole tell me they never thought they were going to be part of it. They grew up believing in the marriage myth: exclusive, happy, and 'til death. So, before ever meeting, they married other people, but found the reality of it more life draining than life affirming.

"Everyone at this table, and almost everyone I know in the Lifestyle, is either divorced or got out of a really long traditional relationship beforehand," Nicole says. "You kind of need to get that first marriage or big-deal relationship out of your system before you can come around to the truth that having sex with someone else has no effect on your love for each other. If anything, it can add to it."

She tells me she met James at the law office where they work. After they dated for a few months, he took her to a strip club for her birthday, which excited her enough to want to try swinging. At first they went to public swing clubs, but they had trouble finding couples they liked. Then they started exploring the swinger personals, where they found couples they enjoyed spending time in and out of bed with. And finally they discovered Bliss, which requires couples to submit photographs and an application for review before allowing them access to the members-only parties it throws at mansions, clubs, and resorts.

"No one we work with knows we do this," James tells me. "If anyone found my phone, they'd freak out if they saw the messages. Half of them are from guys in the Lifestyle talking about their girlfriend's menstrual cycle and saying they can't come out to party for a few days."

When a waitress arrives to take our order, James asks, "Should we just share everything?"

"I'm not in a sharing mood," the raven-haired woman says as her boyfriend sits sulking beside her. It's the first time she's spoken since I arrived. "Put the two of us on a separate check."

James leans in and whispers to me: "They've been arguing all day, so we can't take them out with us tonight. In the swinger community, you'll see couples fighting, throwing drinks at each other, or running off blindly into the street. The thing about swinging is that it strengthens good relationships and destroys bad ones."

Chelsea and her fiancé, Tommy, a spiky-haired jock wearing an untucked burgundy dress shirt, seem more ready for the night's adventure. "We're new to the Lifestyle, but we don't go to vanilla clubs or parties anymore," Chelsea tells me as Tommy gazes hungrily at her, apparently committing covert sexualized violence. "At Lifestyle events, everyone's cooler and more fun and more comfortable with themselves. And the girls aren't catty and jealous of each other, like in the vanilla world."

That word *vanilla* comes up often in the conversation, always with disdain. The term refers to people who are not in the Lifestyle. When it's mentioned, I laugh and joke back about those lame vanillas who ruin everything. But inside I wonder: Am I vanilla?

I think about Belle, the Australian woman who's coming to stay with me. I could probably share her. And I'm going to meet Anne the nudist in Paris in a couple of weeks. I could swap her for Chelsea. But sitting here, looking at James and Tommy, I just can't imagine feeling compersion while watching them violate Ingrid's every orifice as she gushes with orgasm after orgasm.

I think back to my conversation with Shama Helena: If I want true freedom, I need to accept that the path leading there is going to be one of discomfort and vulnerability.

"So where's my date?" I ask Nicole.

"She's coming. You'll see."

The anticipation is killing me. Blind dates are awkward enough, but blind swinger dates are even more stressful. I wonder how I'm supposed to greet her: "I'm looking forward to sharing you tonight"?

As we move through the lobby after dinner, Nicole and James greet various porn-star-looking women—all of them Bliss members, walking with a deadly confident swagger that actually does make the tourists around them seem vanilla. Some non-Lifestyle clubgoers are wearing equally revealing outfits, but the Bliss people seem to be owning their sexuality rather than just trying it on for the night.

The pariah couple break away to deal with their drama as we take the elevator to Chelsea's suite so the women can change. I can't imagine how they could possibly get any sexier—until I see the room, which looks like a Victoria's Secret store. There's lingerie, makeup, perfume, shoes, and lotions everywhere. Tommy is in the sex-toy business, so his contributions to the tableau are duffel bags and briefcases full of his merchandise, plus a camera on a tripod with professional lighting equipment next to it. Everything shamed in rehab is here in full splendor.

"It looks like a porn set," I tell James.

"What you're going to see tonight is better than that," he replies. "You'll never want to watch porn again."

Chelsea gives Nicole a Victoria's Secret gift bag while Tommy pops open the champagne. This is swinger foreplay. Though Tommy seems a bit fanatical, I'm much more comfortable in this scene than at the puja. Instead of dressing sex up in worship and religion, they're dressing it up in lingerie and champagne.

Suddenly, there's a knock on the door.

"That's her," Nicole says in a singsong voice.

My heart leaps into my throat. What if she isn't attracted to me? What if I'm not attracted to her? What if no one is attracted to us? What if, what if, what if . . .

"Don't worry," Nicole adds intuitively. "It's her first time at one of these parties too."

Instantly I feel better.

The door opens, revealing a tall woman with metallic red hair who looks like she belongs on the cover of a fashion magazine. She has pixielike features with an almost imperceptible dusting of freckles, smoky black eyeshadow, and full sensuous lips. Her hair is cut short and swept just above her right eye. It's a powerful beauty that's simultaneously mainstream and alternative, masculine and feminine, young and old. Most strikingly of all, I know her.

"Sage?" I ask. I'd seen her only once before, but I never forgot her. I was interviewing a band in New York for *Rolling Stone,* and she was hanging out with them. We barely spoke a word to each other, but she had an angelic glow to her, like a patron saint of alcoholic rock stars, that haunted me long afterward.

She squeals in delight, wraps her arms around my neck, and presses her body against mine. Either she remembers me too or she's just really friendly. I breathe in her heat, her moisturizer, her hair pomade. This is going to be a good night.

16

As Chelsea, Sage, and Nicole parade to the casino's club in their high heels and microskirts, every head turns—even the dealers crane their necks to catch a glimpse. It's unclear whether they're looking because they think the women are attractive or prostitutes or both, but it doesn't matter. In this moment, we are Vegas.

I trail behind them with James and Tommy, who are enjoying the wake their partners are creating. "God, look at her," Tommy says, lusting after Chelsea. He runs a hand through his obsidian-black hair, which is so gelled I can practically hear it crinkle. "I'm going to marry her. I can't believe how lucky I am."

A freakishly tall man and his dolled-up wife fall into step with us. "My girl and I married sixteen years ago and we've been in the Lifestyle the whole time," he tells us proudly. "Check out her body. What a great body!"

Swinging is definitely a step closer to the solution I'm looking for. Instead of lusting after other women, these guys still lust after the one they're with. And rather than letting themselves go, the couples stay in shape because they know they're going be naked in front of strangers. Perhaps swinging is the fountain of youth: a formula for escaping the monotony of growing older together and the loss of sexuality that comes with work, parenting, familiarity, and increasing responsibilities. Because despite the odds, after years together, these couples seem to have all three of Helen Fisher's drives—for sex, romantic love, and deep attachment—still running strong with each other.

Soon, we arrive at our destination: a dance club with a long line outside. As a beautiful Bliss promoter whisks us past the velvet ropes, the tall swinger who joined us pleads with his wife, "Honey, those two girls I told you about are already inside. Can I fuck them tonight?"

Okay, maybe they do still lust after other women. But at least they get permission first.

Couples in the Lifestyle don't merely go to clubs and hotels. Instead, they stage what they call *takeovers*. This involves invading a public space with rampant sexual energy and shocking the vanillas. While they don't swap there, they make plans and secure invitations for hook-ups afterward—and get to feel cool and one up in the meantime. The real swinging tonight, James tells me as we join a huge coterie of Bliss members inside, will be taking place at private parties in select hotel rooms later.

On the dance floor, a blonde in a tight, sequined silver dress is undulating so suggestively that my heart rate instantly spikes. Take the richest, most confident, most famous man in the world—and he's no match for a beautiful woman in the throes of a dance that oozes sexual energy. This is why fortunes are lost, families are torn apart, and wars are fought.

"I feel comfortable here," James says. "These are my kind of people."

Within moments, our dates have joined the enchantress on the dance floor. Conventional femininity seems amplified here, while conventional masculinity is tempered. Among their fellow swingers, the women feel safer being sexual—and being appreciated for it—than at vanilla events: Guys aren't ogling or groping or chasing or hitting on them. And, as Chelsea said, women aren't scowling at them as if they're competition.

My eyes lock on Sage, who's dancing with her legs splayed and her hips possessed, as if inviting lust to enter without knocking. Moments later, she walks over with the enchantress from the dance floor in tow. "Oh my god, your girl is so sexy," the blonde says. Her hands are all over Sage. She points to a short woman in a bridal veil who's standing nearby with an even shorter man in a tuxedo. "See my friends over there? They're getting married tomorrow. Can you fuck her hard tonight? She needs to get fucked."

"We'll see what the night brings," I respond, certain that I've died and gone to relationship heaven. Sadly, I wouldn't be the only guy in Vegas to have fucked a bachelorette the night before her wedding.

As the blonde sashays away, Sage leans in close, until her cheek is grazing mine. "If I'm dating someone," she says, "I don't want to be with other guys."

"Really?" I'm shocked. I hope she's not another monogamous one.

"If someone I'm with were to allow that to happen, I'd consider it unmanly."

"Then why did you come here?"

"I just got out of a relationship, and I haven't seen Nicole in forever. So she brought me out here to have some fun and see the scene."

"I actually just broke up too."

Her tongue flits alluringly between her lips and she tells me about her last relationship. She dated a guy who was trying to create what he called a circle—a group relationship consisting of himself, Sage, and two other women. It sounds very Father Yod–like. However, he eventually became obsessed with one of the women, broke up with everyone else, started dating her exclusively, and recently married her. Evidently a line was preferable to a circle for him.

I'm relieved that Sage is actually open to alternative relationships. Suddenly, the world of Joan's office seems very far away. Here, there is a different kind of normal, where it's Joan who would be shamed—for being so aggressively vanilla, a counter-sexual-revolutionary.

I lead Sage to a couch so we can get to know each other better. I tell her about cheating on Ingrid and going to rehab, and she tells me about cheating on her poly boyfriend. When he found out, he said there was only one way she could make it up to him: to arrange to meet the other guy at a bar, go down on her boyfriend in the bathroom first, and then, when she met the guy, kiss him, spit her boyfriend's sperm into the guy's mouth, and tell him what it was.

"I still feel really bad that I did it," she says. "But at the time, I felt so guilty about cheating, I would have done anything to make it up to him."

"I get it. I felt the same way."

Whether or not swinging is for me, at least I've found a world of people I'm comfortable with, who appear to have both intimacy and openness. Plus I've found Nicole, Chelsea, and Sage—and I don't have to choose between them, which is ideal for an ambivalent. Nor do I have to keep my distance from someone I'm attracted to just because she happens to be in a relationship at the moment. Though the cheating is a little worrisome, who am I to judge? At least this scene is more sensible than life after sex rehab, when women were triggers to be avoided rather than people to be enjoyed.

As we're speaking, James rushes over and tells us the group is leaving to go to an invitation-only after-party with an *Eyes Wide Shut* theme. "But first," he announces, "I brought some party favors."

We stop by his room, where he unzips a toiletries bag and pulls out a bottle of GHB. I've never done GHB, though I recall reading a disturbing article about a woman who was slipped some as a date rape drug on a cruise ship. Her system slowed down so much that she passed out, stopped breathing, and died.

"How do I know what dose to take?" I ask James.

He slices the air in an X pattern with an eyedropper like a wimpy Zorro. "Don't worry: You're in good hands."

"Then make mine half the dose you're thinking of giving me." GHB is odorless and tasteless: If he wants revenge for the laundry room incident with Nicole, now would be the perfect opportunity.

"You'll enjoy it. It's like being drunk, but without the sloppiness."

"I'm sold." Nervous but sold. In rehab, Troy and Adam asked me if I had any substance abuse problems, and I told them I wasn't into drinking or drugs. "If I lose control, I feel like the person who comes out is unlikable, so I try to stay in control," I explained. And Troy slapped Adam on the back and proclaimed, "See, I told you. He's definitely a sexaholic."

I wasn't sure whether he was referring to my self-control or my self-esteem, but perhaps allowing myself to let go a bit would be good for me.

James sucks a little GHB into the eyedropper, squeezes it into the bottle cap, and gives it to me to drink in some sort of erotic swinger's rite. After fifteen minutes, I feel a gentle wooziness. And then I remember something I'd meant to ask.

"As a guy, is this going to affect my, you know, performance?"

"Come with me," James replies.

I follow him to a table where there's a small medicine bottle filled with a thin syrup. "This is liquid Viagra," he explains. "It's only approved for testing on animals right now, but I got some online and it's great because you can measure out the exact dosage. Want some?"

"And there's nothing else in it? It's not going to make me trip or anything?" I wonder why animals would want longer erections.

"It's just going to help you have a really fun night."

"Okay, but don't give me too much. I don't want to hurt anybody."

He drops the Viagra into my mouth, and it tastes vile. We are ready to swing. Basically, these guys are ravers but with sex instead of music.

I wonder what I'm doing to myself. I suppose back in the late sixties, free love typically carried with it the implication of free drugs. And at least this is much more fun than hanging out with the Tantra polys. Perhaps all these subcultures, going back before drunken Roman Bacchanalia, have their own pre-sex ritual, conceived as a way of loosening inhibitions. I wonder why I was so resistant to the sacred rites of the poly people, but I'm so open to the illicit chemical concoctions the swingers are giving me. It's definitely a moral failing on my part.

We float into the hallway in a semi-euphoria and stop by a few very unswinging parties until, finally, with the effect of the GHB already fading, we cross to the Fantasy Tower of the hotel for the *Eyes Wide Shut* party.

Inside the two-bedroom suite, there's a DJ, a stripper pole, and, in the center of the room, a conspicuous round table with a white sheet over it. Milling around are nearly three dozen shirtless men and women wearing elaborate Mardi Gras masks. I've never seen more fake breasts in my life, even in a porn film. Oddly, no one is having sex.

Near the entrance of the room, there's a large cardboard box full of costumes. Sage selects a black eye mask with colorful peacock feathers protruding from the corners. I grab a white mask with a long *Clockwork Orange* nose and a jester cap on top.

"Let's top off," James says. He measures out a cap of GHB for each of us. And then we wait. For something to happen. It seems like everyone's waiting. There's an unacknowledged awkwardness in the room, like a high school prom with no one on the dance floor.

Suddenly I hear a pinched, gravelly male voice. "Hey, man, it's Neil Strauss."

I turn around to see an unmistakable figure in a red bathrobe and a white mask. I can tell from his slinking posture and the stubbly, well-shaped jawline beneath the mask that it's Corey Feldman. "What are you doing at my party?"

"This is *your* party?"

I haven't seen Corey, best known as the teen actor in *Stand by Me* and *The Lost Boys,* in at least seven years. I first met him while I was writing a book with Marilyn Manson, who had a minor obsession with Feldman that mostly involved mocking him.

"What are you doing here?" he asks, equally shocked.

As I tell him I'm new to the scene, in my peripheral vision, I see the blond enchantress from the club. She's completely naked except for a *Lone Ranger* mask. She walks to the round table, turns around, sits on it, and spreads her legs wide. She then scoots backward and puts her feet up on the edge of the table, ratcheting her legs even wider. She freezes there alone, as if preparing to suck the entire room into her vagina.

"So are you just in it for the numbers?" Corey asks.

It's a trick question. Men, it seems, like to test other men in this scene to make sure they're in it for the right reasons, whatever those may be.

Fortunately I'm not here to accumulate notches on my belt. "I'm in it to find another way to live besides conventional monogamy," I answer.

"Then this is the ultimate extreme," Corey replies enthusiastically. Evidently I passed. In my peripheral vision, I notice a man approach the table, drop to his knees, and bury his face reverently between the blonde's legs.

"Why is that?"

"Because seeing the person you love with someone else is the height of passion."

"Yeah, but usually the passion it ignites in people is murderous."

"That's the point: It's something that's hard to deal with. And normally you would feel jealousy and anger. But if you can control it"—he presses his hand palm-down from his heart to his crotch as if resisting a huge weight—"and turn it into passion, it becomes a very connecting experience."

A chorus of grunts and groans fills the room, and I look up to see three couples around the circular table. Two of the women are bending over the tabletop as guys slam them from behind. Everyone must have been waiting for someone with the courage to get the party started. However, it doesn't look like a giant swap meet or sex pile, just couples having sex around other couples having sex. There was actually more swapping at the puja. Perhaps the high of swinging for some is just being in an atmosphere of sexual decadence.

Suddenly the second dose of GHB hits me. It's not a gentle wooziness like earlier but a more aggressive takeover of my system. I'm light-headed, dizzy, and almost happy enough to actually want to do a puja.

"I put that table there on purpose," Corey says proudly, gesturing to the couples copulating against it. "There was a glass one, but we had them move it out and bring this one instead."

I try to focus my brain and stop my eyeballs from spinning long enough to respond, "That was, um, very thoughtful." But for the life of me, I can't understand why a circular table is the key to an orgy.

"I know what I'm doing," he replies immodestly. "I don't do drugs, but I make up for it with sex. Last night, I had sex with six different women."

Thinking back on my interviews with Feldman, he was also enmeshed by his mom. In addition to making him rub her feet, comb her hair, and draw her baths when he was a child, she used him to fulfill her own ambitions for fame—going so far as to put him on diet pills when he was fourteen.

Rick would tell me that I'm in a sexual crack house right now. The three signs of addiction, according to Joan, are that it's chronic, it's progressive, and it has life-damaging consequences. I don't think this is chronic for me yet, but it's definitely progressive. As for life-damaging consequences, the night is still young.

A shirtless man sits next to us. His partner, a heavyset blonde with the fake breasts that are evidently requisite here, unzips his pants and starts giving him a blow job.

"Am I keeping you from joining in?" I ask Corey through the haze, hoping to make my escape.

"No, I'm really picky," Corey replies. He proceeds to tell me about a night he and a girlfriend spent in Pamela Anderson's hotel room, unsuccessfully trying to seduce her. "Pamela Anderson has never even made out with a girl before," he continues. "Can you believe that? And she told me that when she was on coke, so it must be true."

My swinger pod appears next to us, and they seem antsy and ready to do something crazy. "Don't worry about me," Corey says. "Go have fun."

I mumble an awkward "nice seeing you again" and rejoin the group. I instantly feel better now that I don't have to hide the fact that I'm so fucking high.

It's time: This is an orgy I actually want to take part in, especially now that I have a partner I'm comfortable with. And I can't see myself getting kicked out—especially since I know the host and there's no popcorn in sight.

I lean in to kiss Sage, but the nose on my mask pokes her in the face. I'm not sure if it's just the design of the mask or my dizziness. She giggles and cocks her head to the side to avoid the obstacle. As her lips approach mine, the feathers on her mask tickle my nose. I want to lose myself in our first kiss, but I feel like I'm going to sneeze.

I pull back and the pointy extensions on my jester hat poke James in the eyes. In the meantime, his mask is so elaborate that he can't kiss anyone. Sage and Chelsea start making out with each other, but their masks jab Tommy and me, so we back away.

In *Eyes Wide Shut* and every other movie with a decadent masked ball, the guests intermingle with grace, fluidity, and sensuality. But in actuality, it's impossible to kiss anyone without multiple noses, feathers, horns, and bells poking, tickling, and obstructing. The result is more like a slapstick comedy.

"Let's just take these stupid masks off," Nicole finally says.

Real life is never like the movies.

17

As I start to remove my mask, Sage whispers to me, "Leave it on." I'm not sure whether I should take it as an insult or a compliment—probably an insult—but I comply.

Sage grabs my crotch and starts rubbing me through my pants, so I reach under her skirt. I hook my index finger inside her and, within minutes, a hissing sound escapes from between her legs along with a stream of fluid.

"She's a squirter," Chelsea exclaims. And suddenly everyone has their hands on my date.

"I'm going to scout for a more comfortable place," James offers.

As the GHB intensifies, I look up and see couples fucking everywhere. Most of the masks are off now for practical reasons. As the swingettes go down on the guys they're with or sit on top of them, they're doing more than just having sex, they're performing for everyone else in the room.

James was right: This is much better than porn.

"I found a free bed," James says. We make our way into one of the suite's bedrooms. I don't know what's about to happen, but between the GHB, the champagne, the liquid Viagra, the copulating couples everywhere, Nicole's legs, Chelsea's breasts, and Sage's orgasms, I couldn't be any more turned on. I just wish there were some way to get rid of the two guys. I don't know what their expectations are.

I drop onto the bed, grateful for the softness. It soothes the dizziness. Sage climbs on top of me and starts grinding against me, while Chelsea strips down to just underwear and heart-shaped pasties.

Tommy and James are stuck standing awkwardly on the side of the bed, so I slide over to make room for them. I don't know why. I'm in the middle of three scantily clad, ready-to-go nonmonogamous women. Why the fuck should I care about these guys' comfort? I would've paid every penny in the bank for this experience ten years ago—if I'd known it was even possible. Now, instead of enjoying it, I'm turning into a theater usher.

Chelsea lies on the bed, petite and golden with sculpted abs, her pasties thrust toward the ceiling. "Take care of her for me," Tommy tells me.

"Define *take care*." This is my first real swinger party, so I'm unsure of the etiquette. I don't want to start fucking her, then find out he just meant to get her a pillow.

"Do whatever you want," James explains. "You're the lead sled dog here."

"Just be safe, okay?" Tommy whispers in my ear.

They're literally offering their girls to me. When I was learning the game, I worked so hard for an opportunity with just one woman like this. Now there are three, and no stupid games and will-you-still-respect-me-in-the-morning fears. I'm so intoxicated by all the possibilities that I feel like I'm going to explode with excitement, desire, gratitude, lust. Or maybe it's just the GHB and Viagra. I don't know. I don't care. It's the closest thing to heaven I've ever experienced.

"Wake up!" a male voice is yelling in my year. I think it's James.

"I'm not sleeping," I hear my voice say. "I'm not sleeping."

I look up. My head feels like it's stuffed with wet toilet paper. Fuck, I think I passed out. Sage is sitting on top of me. Chelsea is on my side. She whispers sensuously in my ear, "Can I help you with anything?"

That's so hospitable of her. She's like a Hooters waitress. "Do they have food here?"

She leans in closer, her breasts rubbing against my chest, and says even more sensuously, "Whatever you want."

"Actually, just some water would be nice." I smile gratefully.

She doesn't go anywhere or even make a motion to get any water, because clearly (at least to anyone not drugged up) she wants to help me with something else. In the dimness of my mind, a brain cell starts to illuminate: "Pasties," I tell her. The word seems to expel from my mouth in slow motion. She looks at me confused. "Those are nice pasties. Where did you get them?"

Why am I making small talk? I should tell her I need help with my dick or something. The regulator has come off my brain. This is why I don't like drugs. They make everyone cool but me. At least Sage is unzipping my pants right now. That's a reassuring—

"Wake up!" It's that voice again, drilling into my ear.

"Why do you keep saying that?" I ask. My eyes focus in the direction of the noise, revealing James again. I look up and Sage is still on top of me, but she's laughing.

"You fell asleep on her," James tells me. "You were snoring."

"You should be ashamed of yourself, falling asleep on a beautiful woman like that," Tommy chides.

"Are you joking?"

"No," Sage confirms. "I was going down on you, and you fell asleep and started snoring."

I have absolutely no memory of falling asleep. That's terrifying. Now I see why this is a date rape drug. I want to ask how loudly I was snoring, but I'm afraid of the answer. Instead, I stupidly ask her, "Did I stay hard?"

"Yes."

"Wow, that Viagra really works."

I notice a line of guys standing against the wall in front of the bed, just watching us. Not only didn't I notice them before, but I haven't seen any other people being blatantly stared at here.

I peel myself off the bed and nod my head, trying to clear out the toilet paper, which is whirling faster inside. I notice that my mask isn't on. I wonder where it went. James mumbles something I can't understand, but I can see he's handing me a folded breath strip. Maybe my breath reeks.

He starts to place it in my mouth, but it feels a little too intimate. "I can do it myself," I insist, taking it from him.

"Careful." He guides my hands toward my mouth so I don't drop it.

That's two orgies ending in disaster. I'm like the orgy ruiner. The saddest thing is, I got more action here asleep than I did awake. I remember now another part of that article on GHB: The writer warned not to mix it with alcohol.

As we start to leave, one of the guys who was watching earlier introduces himself. "I run the Bliss parties," he says. "I'm familiar with your work. I think you'll find this community very interesting."

He points out another guy who was watching. "He's actually here because of your books."

And I realize, that whole line of people against the wall—not only were they watching me humiliate myself, but they know who I am. I tell myself that maybe it's cool to pass out at an orgy. Like I've been to so many in my lifetime, they bore me.

The promoter starts talking to me about how he scouts talent for these parties: He'll go to clubs, watch couples and their dynamic together, then selectively recruit them. "The formula is hot girls," he explains. "And as long as the guy isn't a toad and doesn't have a jealousy switch, he's fine."

Perhaps this is my scene, I think as James pulls me away. Just being able to go on a sexually decadent vacation like this a couple of weekends a year would probably be enough to make monogamy bearable the rest of the time. Kind of like the cheat day in a diet. This was supposedly one of the functions of ancient ritualistic orgies as well: to serve as a psychological release valve alleviating the pain of human separateness.

"Should we go check out some other parties?" James asks.

"I think I'm done for the night," I tell him.

"How are you going to get to sleep on E?"

"I'm just not gonna do any."

"Too late for that."

"What do you mean?"

"You just took some."

"What?" How could I have possibly taken ecstasy? Unless when I was passed out . . . But that would be fucked up, to dose me while I'm sleeping.

"In the breath strip. I thought you knew."

"I thought it was for my breath."

"Don't worry. It's really pure. The only problem is that while you're on it, you can't get it up. And it's dangerous to mix with too much Viagra."

"Then why are we doing this?!" I'm starting to think James may be completely crazy, like the Joker in *Batman* comics. This makes no sense. "Doesn't that ruin the whole point of being here?"

"No, because the girls like it and they can still get turned on."

"So how long is this gonna last?"

"Probably five hours."

Oh god, what have I done?

18

We leave the room, take the elevator downstairs, and get on a moving walkway. As soon as we step off, I feel it. I'm rolling.

I touch Sage's back, then my hand moves up to her shoulder and starts squeezing. I need to touch something solid. She seems irritated.

"What's wrong?" she asks, shrugging my hand off.

Instantly my hand returns to her shoulder. Must squeeze. "I'm totally rolling. Do you feel anything?"

"No."

"Did you take any?"

"Yeah, but I've done a lot before."

"How much is a lot?"

"Let's just say I've done it rectally."

We return to the central hotel and wander the halls looking for another party James wants to check out. The carpet unrolls in front of my eyes. I flash back to all the other times I've been fucked up in Vegas, and my only memory is these hotel carpets. They stretch on forever in the same repetitive patterns. Forever and ever. Endless. Carpet.

We arrive at a door. A shirtless guy opens it. There are glow sticks everywhere, including two being spun by a short blonde with gargantuan fake breasts.

"Take that jacket off," the guy says. "You're all wearing too many clothes."

We stand still, taking in the scene. There are glowing stickers affixed to the walls, the stereo, the refrigerator, everywhere. In a bedroom just beyond the entryway, there's porn playing on TV. "Why do they have porn at these things?" I ask Nicole. "It makes it unsexy. Like porn is fake and this is real."

"I don't know why. It's not classy."

"They should play, like, CNN," I go on. "That would be sexy. Because we'd look at the TV and think, Look at those boring people. We're having so much more fun than them. They're all dying and shit, and we're, like, fucking each other's wives."

When some people get fucked up, they become the life of the party. Others get aggressive or promiscuous or overemotional. I just get neurotic and nerdy. Especially on psychoactive drugs, when all the filters come off. This is who I am. I need to accept it, even if no one else can.

"Do you want to walk around?" Sage asks.

I clutch her arm. "Stay with me!" With my other hand I'm hanging onto the edge of a table for dear life. "I don't want to go in there. There's porn!"

"Then what do you want to do?"

I'm losing it. I need more anchoring. "Can you put your hands on my head and, like, do something?"

She cups my bald head in her hands like it's a fragile egg.

"No, like, *knead* it."

She starts kneading it. I feel more anchored.

"Don't stop doing that," I order her. And as her warm hand massages my scalp, I wonder if I've already found it: my nonmonogamate. From the moment Nicole introduced us, it felt like I'd already known her. Actually, I *had* already known her. But the point is, we've been floating through this experience together like a couple that's already in a comfortable relationship. And she hasn't been possessive around Chelsea and Nicole at all. Maybe I'll ask her to move in with Belle and me. She already has experience. This is perfect. She's perfect.

Maybe this is just the ecstasy talking. I have to get a grip on myself. Need to make sure I don't get carried away, profess my undying love for her, and scare her off. It's too soon. I'm probably rebounding. She's probably rebounding. Everything is rebounding.

I notice a portly guy in an undersized T-shirt passed out on the couch—missing out on everything and oblivious to it all.

"You have to be pretty high to pass out during an orgy," I tell Sage. "What an idiot."

She looks at me like I'm crazy. And I am. I'm way too high.

James says we're leaving. I have no idea why we're going, but I know it's the right thing to do.

We walk out with Sage still kneading my head. I don't know why we're still looking for after-parties. We are six ecstasy-breath-strip eaters in the prime of our sexual lives. We are the party. I tell them that.

"I'm totally feeling it," I tell Nicole as Sage continues to knead my head.

"I know," she says.

I wonder how she knows. Is it that obvious? "Why isn't anyone else this high?"

Nicole smiles at me sympathetically.

"Fuck, I'm that guy, aren't I? I'm such an amateur." Another wan smile. "Hey, if you aren't doing anything, can you knead my head? It's important right now."

As we continue through the hall, I don't want these two women to remove their hands from my head. I can't feel my teeth. The ecstasy is getting stronger. I tell them.

"It's kicking to another level."

"It's okay," Nicole says soothingly, as if to a child afraid of thunder.

And so we follow the carpet in silence. Always the carpet. Unrolling into infinite corridors. No beginning. No ending. No escape.

Finally, a door appears. It opens. A wooden floor inside. Yes.

We enter. I am still being kneaded. This is good, because my body is feeling less and less substantial.

I see a couch across the room. It is soft. It is beckoning. It wants me.

"Should we go to the couch?" I ask my head-kneaders.

Then I worry that maybe they think I'm trying to get them into some sort of sexual situation there. "No, no, that would be bad," I add quickly. "Maybe we should stay here."

Then I remember that getting into sexual situations is the whole reason we're here. "No, no, okay. Let's go to the couch."

We walk to the couch and sit down. Much better. We're lounging comfortably now. It would make a nice photo. "Maybe we should take a picture," I suggest. "Where's the camera?"

"I'll get the tripod," Tommy offers a little too eagerly.

Suddenly, a scenario of him snapping away while we all have group sex flashes through my head. That's the last thing I need on the Internet. Even if he just posts it on his social networking profile, if it's embarrassing enough, other people will share it, blogs will pick it up, and it will spread far and wide until it's my top Google hit.

In a world in which everything is connected and archived, your mistakes live longer than you do.

"No, no," I say. "Never mind."

"Let's all have some chocolate, then," Tommy suggests. "You'll love it. It'll be the most sensuous experience you've ever had."

He breaks squares off an exotic chocolate bar and gives one to each person. A hot chocolate experience is what I need right now, to ground me. But when I put it in my mouth, it feels wrong. I don't have a body, so eating something that's supposed to go through my digestive system makes no sense. I just feel it floating uselessly in my mouth, like an X-ray in which you see a coin in someone's stomach.

"This isn't working for me," I say, spitting it into Sage's free hand without warning her. "I can't eat. My body can't process food right now."

She looks at me, then looks at her hand, and says nothing. I think this was the last straw for her. I was starting to think that I no longer had to take this journey alone, that I'd have Sage at my side as a primary—coming with me to meet Anne in Paris, planning the Father Yod house with Belle and me, and going to dinner with Rod and Charles to show them that happiness can be found outside the socially accepted norm. But I just spit partially masticated, mostly melted, saliva-filled brown goo into her hand.

"We should drink orange juice," I suggest. "The vitamin C intensifies the high." That's the last thing I want to do. I have no idea why I mentioned it. Either I'm trying to fit in or my prefrontal cortex is even more jacked up than Daniel Amen thought. Maybe I need to go through chair work again. No, I definitely need to. Whatever I'm doing, I don't think it's healthy. Unless this *is* my authentic self. That would be pathetic.

Chelsea and Tommy are talking about their honeymoon. They're inviting Sage and me to come along on it, like we're a couple.

"You should totally use my place in St. Kitts," I tell them. The country gives citizenships to people who purchase certain properties, so I spent an entire book advance buying an apartment there for some paranoid reason I can't connect to right now. "And I'm not just saying that because I'm on ecstasy. I really mean it."

They laugh. They don't believe me.

"Really," I insist. "I'll send you an email tomorrow confirming it."

There's an awkward silence. I *am* that guy. My words echo in the room, loud and shrill. Everyone just wants to have sex and all I hear is my voice saying, "I'm such a lightweight."

"Am I being funny or annoying?" I ask Sage. I don't really want the answer. I just want reassurance that she still likes me and I'm not making a total ass of myself. Sage looks at me as if she's too scared to reply.

"Or a bit of both?" I offer, to make it easier for her to respond.

"Yes," she says, smiling wanly. "A bit of both."

The words cut me like a knife. Yeah, I think, I guess I am a fucking awkward loser deep down. So I'm going to cover up for that fact by making out with these two girls sitting next to me.

That thought pretty much summarizes the last decade of my life.

I make out with Sage. I make out with Nicole. I feel a stirring in my pants. I turn and tell James, "That thing you said about ecstasy—fortunately it's not true."

"What are you talking about?" he asks.

"That's okay." Fuck, everyone's annoyed with me. I'm the worst guy to ever bring to an orgy. I'm about to get kicked out of this one too.

"I'm tired," Sage says. She stops massaging my head and slouches into the sofa. I can't let this happen. If she sleeps, we'll disconnect. I won't have her as my safety. She must stay awake.

There's only one way to save her. I start rubbing her through her panties.

"Your fingernail is digging into me," she complains.

Why's she being so moody and oversensitive? I've been nothing but nice to her—if anything, too nice. And then I realize that I'm on ecstasy, completely oblivious to reality, and my finger probably *is* digging into her. I stop instantly.

"Wanna see Chelsea ride the Sybian?" Tommy asks.

"Sure." Who doesn't want to see a beautiful woman have an earth-shaking orgasm on top of a mechanical saddle?

Tommy starts unpacking his bags of toys. He's equal parts traveling salesman and sexual Santa Claus, pulling out dildos, lubrication, and attachments. Something exciting is going to take place and I have a front-row seat.

There's only one problem: my head. It needs attention and reassurance.

"Can you just knead my head again while we watch?" I ask Sage.

"I should really go," she responds.

Fuck, I completely ruined this. Me and my stupid head. We're scaring away the nonmonogamous love of my life. But we can salvage this: "I'll walk you to your room."

"No, it's okay. I can get there by myself."

Or maybe we can't.

She seems to have turned on a dime tonight, from sexual and fun-loving to cold and cranky. It really takes a special talent to be capable of making someone who's on ecstasy, the love and empathy drug, be repulsed by you. I feel vanilla. So fucking vanilla.

I had it all tonight. And I lost it.

"I'm gonna go back to my room too," I announce.

"You sure you don't want to stay and watch?" Tommy asks. He seems more disappointed that I'm leaving than he was when Sage said she had to go.

"I should go to bed before the sun comes up." I turn to Nicole, who not only made this adventure happen but has been so patient with me, and tell her, "You've been a really great host and guide through all this. And I'm not just saying that because I'm on ecstasy right now."

"Thank you."

She sounds dismissive. Maybe she doesn't believe me. How can I convince her that it's not the drug talking, it's me? I know.

"Really. I'll send you an email tomorrow confirming it."

As I try to get to sleep that night, I wonder if James purposely dosed me as revenge for the laundry room incident. Maybe he intentionally planned to humiliate me in front of his girlfriend and everyone else.

When I wake up, I get my answer. On my phone, there's a text from him. It was sent at 5:13 A.M., after I left. "Dude," he writes, "wish you were in our bed right now. Next time we need some time with just the three of us."

Evidently, all is forgiven. And he didn't intentionally humiliate me. I did it to myself.

"Now when you go to hell, you know what it's going to be like," Rick says when I conclude my story about Bliss.

We're sitting on the porch of his house, drinking ginger tea. Like Rick himself, the environment is still, peaceful, serene. It is everything Las Vegas isn't. "But there's a positive side to it," I tell him. "These people have figured out a way to have their cake and eat it too. They're in intimate, loving relationships, but instead of having affairs and compartmentalizing, they've chosen to have their sexual adventures together."

"They don't know what their cake is! They're operating purely out of addiction, habit, and trying to fill a void. Only a very sick person would go to Vegas in a-hundred-and-ten-degree heat. It's a desperate place to begin with, and this sounds like a low-self-esteem convention."

Rick is like my conscience. And right now a conscience is the last thing I need. Whenever I close my eyes, I see flashes of the carnival of sexuality I glimpsed, and it gives me hope. Hope that the skeptics are wrong and there are plenty of nonmonogamous functional adults in the world, women who I'm emotionally and physically and intellectually attracted to, women who don't call themselves priestesses and talk to aliens, women as cool as Sage.

As soon as I returned home from Bliss, I emailed Chelsea to confirm the offer to honeymoon in St. Kitts and I emailed Nicole to confirm that she was a good hostess—just to prove I really meant it. And Nicole, hostess that she is, said she wanted to throw me a dinner party in San Francisco to introduce me to more friends of hers in the scene.

"Don't forget that the goal was to see which path leads to happiness," I protest to Rick. "Whether or not this scene is right for me, at least it's leading me in a happier direction. I don't feel constantly guilty anymore. And I'm not hurting anyone."

"Except yourself," Rick responds. "You're doing drugs that aren't good for you, that you don't even like. And look closer at what happened. A root problem surfaced while you were high: You discovered that you live in a reality where you don't feel good about yourself. And sex, for you, is a drug to temporarily escape from that feeling."

"You may be right. But sex addiction treatment didn't solve anything. I feel like these experiences are bringing me closer to something true and honest. So I'm going to just keep following my bliss and seeing where it takes me. This is all completely new and it's only been a couple of months, so of course I'm going to make mistakes."

Rick shakes his head. "I think you should have stayed in rehab."

After leaving Rick's, I call Adam to check in. Though I don't miss group therapy, I do miss some of the guys in it.

Adam tells me that his marriage has gotten worse. "I'm like a whipping boy. I'm pretending I'm happy, but I'm really not happy at all. It always seems like she doesn't want to be with me. I asked her when was the last time she asked how I was, and she couldn't even remember."

What's incredible is not that Adam had an affair, but that he hasn't had another one.

When your wife is tired of making the effort to understand you, when she's fed up with hearing the same stories coming out of your mouth, when she holds so much resentment that it poisons every conversation, when she's nicer to telemarketers than she is to you, when the only time she's passionate anymore is when she's criticizing you—that's when you want a mistress. Someone whose eyes glisten with attraction when she looks at you, whose ears perk up when you speak, whose hands crave the feel of your skin, whose thighs moisten when you kiss her—someone who actually appreciates your presence and treats it like a gift instead of a punishment. Someone who will see you the way your wife once saw you before she grew so fucking sick of the sight of you.

As Troy put it when I asked him why he, of all people, cheated: An affair fills you back up when the marriage empties you.

"Doesn't she realize she's setting up the exact scenario that led you to cheat in the first place?" I ask Adam.

"I know," he sighs. "I could live without the sex, but you need to at least feel like someone likes you. It's been over a year and she won't even come to church with me. She's still making me go over every detail of the affair. And, you know, whenever I check my email, everything's in the *read* folder because she's already gone through it all."

"That's a horrible way to live—for you *and* for her. You know what Lorraine calls it?"

"No."

"Pain shopping. She's not getting healed by that. She's just getting retraumatized."

"That's exactly what she's doing. Even my dad's upset. He says he feels sorry for me. He can't believe I've stuck around this long in the marriage."

"So why don't you leave?"

The frustration in his voice fades to resignation. "There's a part of me that just can't do it, you know. I will sit here and take a beating for the rest of my life rather than divorce. Because of the kids." They're fourteen and sixteen years old. "I'm here to serve them. Maybe that's what it comes down to."

This can't be what marriage is like for most people: two aging individuals chained together in escalating resentment and indifference. If human beings are the culmination of some sort of plan—be it evolution, a divine spark, or an alien polyamory experiment—then why weren't we built to get along better with those we choose to create a family and perpetuate the species with? Unless we're doing it wrong.

"But do you really think you're serving your kids by staying together in an unhappy marriage?" I challenge Adam. "What kind of relationship are you modeling for them?"

As he dances around the question, I start to understand why Adam's story gets me so emotionally worked up: because I *am* his kids. I was raised by parents who rarely got along and who brought out the worst in each other. Yet for some reason, they never divorced. So I grew up hoping they'd separate and find partners who made them happier. Perhaps I'm trying to get closure by encouraging Adam to do what my father never could.

"So what am I missing in group?" I change the subject. "Any interesting updates from the other guys?"

"I'm not supposed to say anything, but you should really call Charles."

20

Gathered around the table at a Mexican restaurant in the Mission are not just couples in the Lifestyle, but also leather families and other non–New Age poly people who Nicole and James want me to meet. I've been trying to call Charles all week to no avail, so in the back of my mind I've been playing out horrific scenarios of what could have happened to him.

The moment I arrive, Chelsea greets me with a powerful kiss on the lips. Shorn of her Vegas club wear, she looks prim and domestic. Stiletto heels, a tight dress, false eyelashes, and well-applied makeup are perhaps the closest thing to true magic in this day and age, able not just to transform a woman but every man around her—regardless of her looks, because ultimately men are more attracted to sexual availability than they are to beauty.

Tommy, with his spiky hair and untucked, fitted dress shirt, looks the exact same as he did in Vegas. In fact, he may be wearing the same clothes. Seated next to him is a large, charismatic gentleman named Stefanos, who's dressed like a Prohibition-era gangster. Nicole tells me that he films weekly fetish parties at the San Francisco Armory, which was bought by a porn mogul and turned into a huge labyrinth of film sets for a kink website.

As I look around the gathering, I feel like I've arrived at the threshold of something big, something I've been looking for my whole life.

"Have you talked to Sage at all?" Nicole asks me.

"No, have you?" She never even gave me her phone number.

"I haven't heard from her since Vegas."

She must have had a horrible time. And I was really falling for her too.

Though, of course, I was on ecstasy, so I could have just as easily fallen in love with a particularly shiny doorknob.

I choose the sole empty seat, which is next to James, and ask him about the text he sent at the end of that night. I'm still not sure whether he was hitting on me or offering Nicole to me, but I soon find out that it was the latter: "I was abandoned by my father, so I want the approval of other males and I do it by sharing my hot girlfriends with them."

His words surprise me, and I realize there's more to swinging than anything I've read about it before. I always thought that, for men, the Lifestyle was about fucking other women. But for guys like James, it's also about showing off the woman they love: *Look what I got. And she loves me, so I must have value. And if you treat me with enough respect and admiration, I will share her with you—but not too much, because I don't want to lose control of her. That would cause me to feel pain and question my fragile sense of self-worth.*

Maybe Rick was right, I think as James continues to hold court.

"If I were gay, I'd be so fucking happy," he's saying, "because all I want is the love of other males. When Nicole and I dated another girl for a while, the best part wasn't the threesomes, it was walking into a club with two hot women and getting the male admiration."

Suddenly, the way the guys thrust their girlfriends on me at Bliss makes a lot more sense. Swapping is the ultimate in male bonding.

I tell them I'm going to Paris next week and ask if they have any connections in the Lifestyle there.

"They take it to a whole new level in Paris," James tells me. "Our friends call it switching, and it's not really a couples thing. It's more open than that. There's a girl in the scene we'll hook you up with. She's a writer, too, and she's gorgeous."

"That would be fantastic," I tell him. As I do, I notice Tommy and Chelsea staring at me and whispering to each other.

"Don't get fixated on the idea that swinging is your only option just because it's all you've experienced," a quiet, authoritative voice warns from the end of the table. I turn to see the only dinner guest I haven't spoken to: a sharp pale creature with long black hair, a black choker, and soft, vacant eyes.

He introduces himself as Pepper and identifies himself as a queer-friendly Goth who's into poly and S&M. Just as it did in rehab, one diagnostic label seems to work like a magnet, attracting others until people can't introduce themselves without sounding like they're reading a grocery list.

Pepper tells me his parents were in an open relationship. After unsuccessfully trying monogamy, he followed in their footsteps. Today he lives with his primary of eight years, has two secondary girlfriends of four years each, and is dating four tertiary lovers. His primary girlfriend has just one other lover, who she wants to move into the house, and Pepper is cool with that.

This is love in the era of having it all.

"So are there any specific rules that help things work for you?" I ask.

"People who have been doing poly or any kind of nonmonogamy for years tend to have intents rather than rules," he replies. The distinction resonates well with my punished inner adolescent. "For me, the intent is to be respectful to my partner's partners and not to do something that might trigger my partner's jealousy."

"How do you handle jealousy when it does come up?"

"Once fear of loss is taken away, you get past jealousy." He speaks in an almost academic monotone, with very little feeling. Maybe the reason jealousy isn't a problem for him is that he wasn't born with a full emotional range. "For example, if someone breaks up with me, I know it's because the relationship is no longer working between me and them. It's never because they found somebody better, since the monogamous contract has been replaced by a new contract that doesn't involve someone having to make a choice between two people. They can have them both."

"I like that way of thinking," I tell him. "But for people who didn't grow up in an environment like yours, I think the old contract is hard to change. Some of my married friends would find it easier to cheat than to openly sleep with someone else, because if their wife knew what they were doing, they'd feel like they were hurting her."

"It actually takes most people a couple of years to work through those powerful feelings of guilt and disloyalty," Pepper responds. "So I'd say the most important thing for you as you expand your relationships will be open and honest communication with your partners."

Like when I first met Lorraine, I trust Pepper as an authority—even after I learn that his last name is Mint. He's a walking glossary of terms that I've never heard before. He tells me about the *burning period,* which is the length of time (usually two years) it takes couples who open up to deal with the issues and challenges that occur as a result. I learn about *the joys of theoretical nonmonogamy,* which is when two people say they're in an open relationship—but instead of actually sleeping with other people, they just get to feel free knowing they have the option to do so. There's *the jealousy test,* which you pass if you're able to have a serious relationship with someone who's sleeping with other people or in love with someone else. Then there's *fluid bonded,* which refers to partners who feel safe having unprotected sex with one another, and *veto power,* which means that one partner can ask another to end an outside relationship—an agreement that Pepper feels can cause more problems than it solves. Finally, there are the wearisome *cowboys*

and *cowgirls* who get into the poly scene, date someone's partner, and then try to rope that person into a monogamous relationship.

I learn more in a half-hour conversation with Pepper than I did at the entire polyamory conference. After dinner, I thank him for the advice and make sure to get his phone number.

"It's a shame," Tommy remarks as the dinner party breaks up. "We barely had time to catch up."

"I know, but I'll be back soon."

"What are you doing later tonight? We thought we'd give you a chance to watch Chelsea ride the Sybian, since you missed out in Vegas." He delivers the invitation casually, as if offering a breath strip laced with ecstasy.

As attractive as Chelsea is, there's something about Tommy that makes me uncomfortable. Maybe it's because he's been trying to push his fiancée on me since the night we met. It's the equivalent of someone constantly pestering you because he wants to give you free money: After a while, you start to feel he has a hidden agenda. Then again, I'm here to observe alternative relationships, and this is definitely an opportunity to do so up close.

"I have to drive home early tomorrow," I respond. "Let's see what happens."

What happens is that Tommy invites himself back to the apartment I'm renting for the weekend. And I don't protest.

21

Tommy and Chelsea arrive outside the apartment in a mostly windowless white serial-killer van. After parking, he hauls out the briefcases and bags I saw in his room in Vegas. He opens one briefcase to display a collection of dildos that range from medium pink to ginormous black. There's something sinister about two men standing in the street at night and staring into a box of phalluses.

"Are those the toys you sell?" I ask to break the awkward silence.

"Rent," he corrects me.

"You *rent* sex toys?"

It's quite possibly the worst business idea I've ever heard. You'd have to be a pretty fearless swinger to want a used sex toy that's had someone's possibly diseased juices all over it.

"We clean and disinfect them after each use, of course."

"Of course."

As Tommy explains his business, I start to understand that he's not in it for the money. The real payoff is that he's constantly hired to attend sex parties, where he sets up shop like a medicine show, encouraging women to test the toys until the room turns into a XXX-rated Tupperware party. His used sex toys, as disgusting as they sound, are the equivalent of Kamala's pujas: the spark to the gas of anticipation.

After hauling his gear into the living room, Tommy tells me that everything's ready. And that's when I realize: I don't know this guy at all. I don't even know how well Nicole and James know him. In Vegas, Chelsea did say that they were new to the scene.

He opens a bag filled with extraordinarily unsexy gadgets that look like they were stolen from a 1950s research lab. Their sole purpose, he explains, is to give varying degrees of electric shocks to masochists looking for a new type of pain. He also has a duffel bag filled with varying lengths of thick black nylon rope. The whole array is like something out of a horror film. For all I know, I may have just invited serial killers into the house. Swinging psychopaths.

The crown jewel of his collection is the Sybian. Priced at more than thirteen hundred dollars, it's the Cadillac of sex toys. He spreads a blanket on the floor as if we're about to have a picnic or roll up my dead body in it. He carefully places his Sybian on it, then tops the saddle with a small rubber-ridged pad that has what looks like a large pencil eraser sticking out of it.

From another briefcase, he removes several meticulously folded squares of plastic wrap, opens one, and places it on top of the pad. I have no idea if plastic wrap is an effective barrier against pathogens, but fortunately I won't be sitting on it.

Chelsea hikes her skirt and straddles the Sybian.

"Look at that ass!" Tommy urges me.

Thanks to my dinner conversation with James, I understand that this is my cue to give him the male approval he needs. "A work of art," I tell him.

"You control it." He gestures to a small square box with a dial that goes from zero to a hundred. It sits on the floor, attached to the Sybian by a black cord.

I slowly bring the vibration level up to twenty-five and, as the pad moves in faster and smaller motions than anything the male finger is capable of, Chelsea starts moaning. The sound is an intoxicant. Instantly, blood rushes from my head, where all common sense and caution reside, to my loins, where nothing but instinct and the moment live.

As I slowly bring the dial to thirty, her body flushes and she tilts her head skyward as if seeing the face of God. Whatever she's feeling, I'm jealous of it. I don't think I'm biologically capable of experiencing that kind of pleasure—unless there's a Sybian equivalent for men, perhaps some sort of jelly-filled, soft-walled vacuum cleaner that keeps saying you're the biggest and best it's ever been with.

Tommy kneels behind Chelsea and massages her back and shoulders, occasionally adding a resounding slap on her ass. "Why don't we switch places?" he turns to me and suggests after a few minutes.

This appears to be a routine they're running. They know exactly where the night's going—and I hope it isn't anywhere that involves tying me up and using the dildo collection. I'm sure these two could get just about anyone alone and vulnerable with their whole "Wanna see my girlfriend use an expensive sex toy?" routine.

I give Tommy the controls and watch as he brings it up to fifty. It's violently fast, and Chelsea is thrown into an altered state of pleasure.

"You can touch her if you want."

I cautiously rub her back and arm through her blouse. She grabs my hands and smashes them onto her breasts as the Sybian takes her higher.

Tommy lowers the speed so that Chelsea can remove her shirt and bra, then dials it up until it's at a hundred and Chelsea's fake breasts are firing like pistons. I can't tell anymore whether she's moaning from pleasure or pain. But when Tommy starts cycling it down again, the word "more" escapes from Chelsea's gorgeously open mouth. The skin on her face and chest bursts with every shade of pink. Suddenly her hand lunges like a cobra and grabs my crotch through my jeans.

I glance at Tommy for permission so he knows that whatever is going on, it's being done with respect for him. "She's too much for me," he responds, nodding like we're bros in this adventure together. "She once came fourteen times in one night. That's why I appreciate what you're doing."

Despite all the Vegas decadence, I've never had sex with another man's girlfriend in front of him. This is about to be my first actual swing—or half-swing.

After a few more minutes, Chelsea dismounts and lies on the bed. Tommy grabs a length of rope from one of his bags. I back away just to be safe and watch as he ties Chelsea's hands together over her head.

"Do you have any latex gloves?" Tommy asks afterward.

When I tell him I didn't happen to bring any, he gives me a condom and tells me to put it on my pointer finger so I can touch her. This is free love in the twenty-first century. It's hygienic, electronic, and sanitary.

After an old-fashioned manual orgasm, Chelsea asks softly, almost meekly, "Which one of you wants to enter me?"

"You didn't get to go last time, so it's your turn," Tommy says magnanimously, like she's a ride at an amusement park.

"That's okay." I shouldn't be doing this. It feels compulsive, impulsive, even slightly repulsive. All the pulsives.

I massage Chelsea's chest for a few minutes, stalling for time. As she grinds her hips and moans, I snap back into the moment: Fuck it. Why am I holding back again? He *wants* me to have sex with her. It would be a personal insult to both of them if I didn't. That's why they're here. Besides, I'm trying to have free relationships that don't hold anyone back from these types of adventures. This is exactly what I told everyone from Joan to Ingrid that I believed in: sex as an end in itself.

So I ask him for another condom.

"Is it okay if I film it?" Tommy asks.

"No!" I scream instinctively. That's the last thing I need leaking all over the Internet.

"Why?" he asks, as if my answer makes no logical sense whatsoever.

"Let's just savor the memories."

As I try to get myself back in the mood, I start to worry that he has a camera hidden somewhere. Technology gets smaller and easier to conceal every day.

"You haven't been filming, have you?" I double-check.

"No sir," he says. "But I have been recording audio."

I thought I was starting to understand the swing scene, but this makes absolutely no sense. What the fuck is he going to do with the audio recording? Play it in the car on long road trips?

"Can you turn it off?"

"Are you sure? Sometimes I like to listen back to the moans."

This guy is a freak. I absolutely should not fuck his Barbie doll girlfriend who's spread-eagled naked in front of me.

So I pull my pants down just low enough to get my dick out without showing too much ass and skin, in case there is a hidden camera somewhere, and enter her.

As I thrust inside, Tommy props a pillow against the wall and lounges there, watching. "Do you like the way it feels?" he asks her. "Do you like the way he's fucking you?"

"Mm-hmmm," she articulates.

I assume he's trying to stay involved and in control in some way. I try to tune out his voice, to shut his form out of my peripheral vision, to move faster and lose myself in Chelsea.

"Wow, look at you go!" he exclaims. "It's like a jackhammer."

Now he's commenting on the whole thing like a fucking sports announcer. I ignore him and start grinding my pubic bone against her clit to turn her on again.

"That's interesting," Tommy says. "I haven't seen that one before. Is that your style?"

This is a terrible time for a discussion about technique. "I don't know. Just improvising as I go." It's not easy fucking someone while trying to carry on a conversation with her fiancé. It's like trying to race a motorcycle while texting.

Tommy's silent for thirty blessed seconds or so, then he unties Chelsea and announces, "Condom check."

I'm worried he wants to feel it to make sure it's still on. So I reach down, confirm that it's completely snug, and tell him everything is in order.

"Show him that thing you do with your hips," he instructs Chelsea, who lifts said hips and starts moving rapidly up and down along my shaft.

When I flip her over, Mr. ESPN goes, "I like that. That's a good one."

He doesn't appear to be getting turned on by watching. He seems more like a detached observer studying gorilla mating habits. And every time I change positions, he makes a new comment as if he's on the verge of some evolutionary discovery. Hopefully this isn't narration for an audio recording.

It's time to pull the curtain on this show. I force myself to come, careful not to make a sound in case Tommy's recording.

Relieved that it's over, I pull out, remove the condom, drop it onto the floor, and lie next to Chelsea. As I stroke her hair and try to enjoy the after-glow, Tommy, of course, pipes up and ruins the moment. I can't make the words out exactly, but they sound like, "Let's see the juice."

"What do you mean?"

"I need to see the condom so I can make sure it caught everything."

I want to ask him how he's going to know whether or not it caught everything. Maybe he has a semen-measuring scale in his duffel bag that he uses to weigh the load.

I fish around the floor for the rubber and hold it up so he can see. I really don't want him touching my used condom.

"That's good," he approves. I put it back on the ground and silently pray he doesn't collect it before he leaves and put it in a formaldehyde jar in one of his briefcases.

Tommy returns to Chelsea's side, kisses her softly, and tells her, "I adore you, honey."

"You were incredible," I compliment her—for him.

As they lie there, I make swinger pillow talk and ask them how long they've been doing this. They've been dating for five years, they tell me. But a year and a half ago, they put an ad on Craigslist and selected a guy, then went to his house and she gave him a hand job. She gave the next guy a blow job. Finally they found a swinger couple on the Lifestyle Lounge, but Chelsea became sick with jealousy while watching Tommy ravish another woman. It took a dozen swings until Chelsea became comfortable enough to let Tommy interact with other women again.

Their story reminds me of Tahl's and Lawrence's. If you want to open your relationship, then proper etiquette is required: ladies first.

I bid them good night and invite them to crash on the pullout couch if they want.

As I lie in bed, I reflect on my experiences with Chelsea, Nicole, and their friends. Swinging is the best alternative I've seen so far. And I like the way some of the couples form long-term intimate relationships with other couples, becoming both best friends and lovers. But I'm not like Tommy or James or Corey Feldman. I don't get off on seeing other guys sweat on my girlfriend.

I'm sure there are just as many men who are in the Lifestyle simply for their own sexual gratification and variety, and willing to tolerate letting

their wife screw another man in exchange. But if sex becomes just a service to be traded, that's not freedom. It's commerce.

Ultimately swinging is a traditional relationship with an escape hatch, a way to experience Helen Fisher's dual reproductive strategy without deception. If monogamy is like only being allowed to eat at home, as I told Joan, then swinging is like being allowed to eat wherever you want on the condition that your partner approves of the restaurant and eats with you.

It's still a form of possession, only the chain is extended a few feet longer. In fact, if the way guys like Tommy talk about their girlfriends is any indication, partners are actually treated more like possessions than in monogamy.

Perhaps it's time to create the world I want rather than trying to fit into someone else's scene, to go in all the way on freedom, to finish building my free-love dream house. With luck I'll find the rest of the people I'm looking for in Paris. I'm running out of time: Belle is going to be here in just five weeks.

22

While driving back to Los Angeles, I try to reach Charles again. This time, he answers the phone.

"Are you okay?" I ask. "I've been worried about you."

"I'm sorry," he answers in a quiet, halting voice. "I've been out of town. My whole world turned upside down and I've been trying to make sense of it."

"What happened?"

"I found out my wife's been cheating on me." He raises his voice. "For the past twelve years!"

I'm so shocked I'm unable to form an articulate response. We were all so busy trying to earn back the trust of our partners in rehab, we never even considered questioning *their* integrity.

The story Charles goes on to tell is fragmented. But as best I can piece it together, he was looking at his wife's phone when a text arrived from a security guard at her office building. It read, "I gave you my heart for twelve years."

Just to make sure he was interpreting the message correctly, he texted back: "One thing's for sure, we definitely had great sex together."

"Yes," came the reply, "I miss it."

Digging for more, Charles texted: "Do you remember the first time we did it?"

"In your car."

Charles kept pain shopping: "That's right, I sucked your cock."

And the security guard responded, "You don't talk like that. Who is this?"

At this point, Charles was shaking with an emotion beyond pain. He let the conversation drop, and obsessively went through his wife's phone and emails. Soon, he pieced the backstory together: nearly every afternoon, his wife and the guard had been sneaking off for a lunchtime tryst—for more than half their marriage.

"Oh my god, how did you react?" I ask. I've known people—mostly love addicts—who would be less hurt if their spouses died than if they cheated. They'd even prefer the former, because at least they couldn't take it personally. But Charles's response is the last one I'd expect.

"The release was impossible to describe."

"Because you were so angry?"

"No, I was relieved!"

"You're kidding."

"Neil, all my shame and guilt just melted off me." He pauses. "When she found out I'd relapsed, she threw me under the bus, like she was so pristine and perfect. She told all our friends that I'd betrayed her again and I was this terrible sex addict. She locked me out of the house and threatened to take everything I had and turned my own family against me. And I've felt so bad about myself for so long." His voice begins trembling. "But what she was doing . . . I just don't understand how she could be so cruel."

I wonder how many other people go through years of sex addiction therapy and meetings trying to make amends, only to find out their partner has also been cheating. Or even worse, they never find out and go to the grave thinking they're a sinner and their partner's a saint. One of the unfortunate axioms of human behavior is that what others shame people for the most is usually what they're doing in secret themselves. After all, an accusation is much more powerful than a denial: It's a way to seem one up when you're really feeling one down.

"So are you going to stay in recovery?" I ask.

There's a long silence on the other end of the line. "Well, I went away for a few days with my sponsor to cool down and determine the right thing to do." A deep inhale. "And I'm going to get divorced." A long exhale. "And then I'm going to start fucking something every day."

This is not the Charles I've come to both pity and admire. It's a side of Charles I've never met. And so I get the chance to tell him a version of what he's been telling me for the last year: "That can't be what your sponsor recommended. It sounds more like your disease talking. Be careful."

"Neil, I'm a fifty-year-old man who's free of a twenty-two-year-old marriage, half of which was a total lie. I just want to . . . I don't know. I don't know what's true anymore." A heaving sob explodes into the phone, followed by the muffled sound of crying.

Some people live in an endless on-and-off relationship with control. Either they're trying to exert it over their lives—by getting obsessive about a diet, a belief system, a phobia, a hobby, a need for order, a twelve-step program—or they're completely out of control, making a mess of their lives. And it sounds like Charles is on the verge of a mess. The shadow he's been repressing has broken loose. And I can relate: So has mine. But as any good Jungian therapist will tell you, you're not supposed to repress the shadow in the first place. That's when bad things happen. The goal is to integrate it. And I hope that's the path we're both ultimately on.

I want to ask Charles if he still thinks he's a sex addict or if he thinks his wife is one—or if he thinks the disease was contagious and she caught it from him. But now is not the time to prove a point. "Whatever you decide to do," I tell him instead, "make sure you process it in group first."

"I will," Charles says, stifling his tears. "So how are you feeling without Ingrid in your life? Do you miss her?"

It's the one question no one's asked. And in the moments of decadence, connection, and extreme awkwardness with the swingers, I've managed not to think about her. But in every other moment, I've felt her presence somewhere—in my mind, my heart, my home, my conscience.

"Constantly," I tell him.

23

Everywhere I look while traveling to Paris, I see young couples pushing sleeping children in strollers, carrying blanket-wrapped babies in their arms, hurrying along superhero-backpacked toddlers. Each family makes me think of Ingrid and the future I ruined. I wonder what Ingrid's doing, who she's doing it with, and if she's happier living without my wandering eyes and ambivalent heart. One of the many hazards of breaking up is that it takes years not just to find love again but to discover if it's real, stable, and sustainable.

In Paris, however, everything will change. I will find the rest of my pod. And maybe, just like several little-t traumas add up to one big-T Trauma, several little-l loves can add up to one big-L Love.

First, there is Anne. She's waiting in the hotel room when I arrive. She's slender and toned, with dirty blond shoulder-length hair, minimal makeup, and boyish clothes. As I approach her, she looks deeply and mutely into me with quivering brown eyes. I take a step toward her, brush her hair aside, and we kiss.

We disrobe. Get in bed. Make love. Spoon. And then she says *salut*. It's the first word we've exchanged.

Then, there's James and Nicole's friend, Camille. "Hi Neil. I'm meeting my friend Laura, who's American just like you," she texts. "She wants to go to a great switch club and I promised I'd get in trouble with her. Do you want to come with us?"

"Is it okay if I'm with a date?"

"Dump the girl. There'll be plenty of dates for you there! And they all want to have sex :)"

This switch club sounds like a goldmine of open-minded single women. The only problem: I *want* to bring Anne.

"If you have to bring her, use the 'We'll just have a drink and watch' technique," Camille relents. "That's how my boyfriend got me there in the first place, and look at me now! The club is by Montmartre. Give me a call after dinner."

In my relationship this last year, my credo was to say *no*. Only by saying no to others could I protect Ingrid's heart. But now, I am saying *yes*—to everyone, to everything, to life. Because every *yes* is the gateway to an adventure. Whatever I am heading toward, it is a relationship that operates out of a place of *yes*.

At dinner that night, I do exactly as Camille instructed. Anne and I are with two women I met on a European press tour a few years earlier: a German fashion photographer and a Swedish designer. They spend most of the meal gossiping about people I don't know.

"We don't have to do anything," I explain to Anne. "Let's just plan on having a drink and watching, and we can leave right away if it's lame."

"I'm a little tired," she replies, her voice barely audible. Throughout the day, she's barely spoken. Instead, she's attached herself to me energetically, gazing at me almost constantly with big, vulnerable, barely blinking eyes. I get the sense that she wants something from me or may already be getting it from me. "Is it okay if I go back to the hotel?"

"Can we come?" the fashionistas interrupt.

"You can go with them if you want," Anne tells me softly.

It's hard to read Anne. I'm not sure if she's legitimately tired or just uncomfortable with the suggestion. "Are you sure it's all right for me to go?"

"I don't mind," she replies.

I study her face to make sure she's sincere, that it's not a test to see if I'll choose her. She appears placid and unconcerned. I ask three more times just to make sure.

"She said you could go!" the German photographer snaps at me.

Yes, it turns out, is not an easy principle to live by. I wonder why, after knowing Anne for just a day, I already feel like it's wrong to do this without her. Perhaps the problem is not that the people I date want to possess me, it's that after sex I give them ownership out of guilt. I'm replaying an enmeshment script, pathologically accommodating to monogamy. If I truly believed that sexual possession was wrong and acted accordingly, I wouldn't have agreed to an exclusive relationship with Ingrid in the first place and would have saved us both a lot of grief. In life, whoever has the strongest reality wins. Lose your moral certainty and lose the ground you stand on.

We drop Anne off at the hotel, and she gives me a deep kiss and walks off. It's a good sign: Letting your lover go to a sex club alone is actually a much more open-minded feat than going with him. As the taxi speeds away, the German photographer loops her arm in mine.

I'm determined not to wreck this orgy like all the others. My stomach is full, so I won't be snacking on popcorn. And I haven't touched a single mood-altering substance, nor do I plan to. I even clipped my nails.

We arrive at the club just after midnight. I spot Camille instantly. She has long brown hair worthy of a shampoo commercial and skin so smooth and flawless that a metaphor to an inanimate object, like a pearl, would hardly do it justice.

She's standing with two other women: Laura, her American friend, who looks like a burning candle—long and narrow, with a white pantsuit and a shock of short blond hair. And Veronika, a haughty beauty from Prague with lips like cylindrical sofa cushions, flowing brown hair, an overdeveloped nose, and a tall, thin, sensuous frame that reminds me of the actress Jane Birkin.

"Do we have to put on robes or towels when we go in?" I ask Camille, unsure what protocol is for places like this.

Camille looks at me like I'm crazy. "No, we just wear our clothes."

That's a relief. Despite my desire to be open, evolved, and shame free about sex, I'm still not totally comfortable with the sight of my own body. The first time I ever had sex, I was too embarrassed to remove my shirt. And the second and third times as well.

Behind us in line, there's a Frenchman with a shiny suit and slicked-back hair. He looks like a shady businessman who snorts a lot of cocaine. "Since you have so many girls, is it okay if I come in with you?" he asks.

The club has a rule that all males must enter with a female—and I'm standing there with five of them like a glutton. I suppose this is what I missed when I was dating Ingrid: options, variety, adventure, discovery, novelty, the unknown. As Lorraine would put it, intensity.

"I don't know," I tell him. "It's my first time here."

As we wait, Camille and Laura discuss sharing toys, by which they mean boys. "Is your boyfriend coming?" I ask Camille.

"No."

"Does he know you're here?" I'm asking not to judge her, but because I'm curious how their relationship works.

"No." She smiles guiltily. Clearly, having an open relationship is no cure for infidelity. First Nicole, then Sage's story about her ex-boyfriend, now Camille. Perhaps the problem with most relationships is that the rules start to become more important than the values they're supposed to be representing.

Eventually two of Camille's toys arrive, both in designer jackets and skinny ties. They introduce themselves as Bruno and Pascal. Bruno looks like a clean-cut college athlete, while Pascal, with thin-framed glasses, tight curls, and slow, well-mannered gestures, looks like an intellectual dandy.

Unlike the highly sexualized crowd at Bliss, the men and women here aren't divorced weekend warriors dressed like porn stars. Aside from the slick-haired businessman behind us, they're all young, hip, well dressed, and silicone free. They don't look much different than the crowd outside an exclusive nightclub. Evidently, after a night on the town, they come here for dessert. As the line starts moving, Laura takes pity on solo slick guy and invites him to come in with her.

"Do you know how I can tell these people are barbarians?" the German photographer says to her friend. "Look at their shoes. I wouldn't wish a single pair on my worst enemy."

It seems I make a critical mistake at every orgy, and the fashionistas may be this orgy's ruiners. But it's too late to slip away from them: We're being let inside.

When we enter, a hostess asks us to check our jackets (which for some reason leads to sniggers from the fashionistas), then gives me a card that she explains will serve as my tab for the night. Veronika removes her blazer to reveal a loose-fitting backless dress that, when her stride is long, would get her arrested. "She will be my first fuck tonight," Pascal tells me confidently as I stare mutely at the tan expanse of Veronika's back.

We walk downstairs to an empty, low-lit dance floor dotted with stripper poles. The twenty or so people in the room are clustered against a bar, drinking away their inhibitions. Katy Perry's "I Kissed a Girl" is playing. It seems so . . . obvious.

At the end of the anteroom, there's a black door that leads to the fun. After her friends have drifted into the rooms behind it, Camille takes my hand and offers to show me around. "What about my friends?" I ask.

"They'll be fine. Are you coming or not?"

I look over and they seem deep in snide conversation, concealing their discomfort by increasing their arrogance. I should invite them to join us, especially since I brought them here. The last thing I want to do, however, is walk around the orgy with them making obnoxiously loud comments about how everyone's sexual techniques are so last year.

I feel guilty leaving them behind, just as I left Anne behind. But I say, "Yes."

24

Behind the black door, Camille and I slowly wander through sunken living rooms and small porthole-fitted chambers, all in copious use, until we arrive at a space that consists of just an enormous bed and a narrow walkway along the front wall.

Most of the women on the mega-bed are completely naked while the men are still wearing dress shirts, ties, and pants. However, their pants are all unzipped or lowered and their junk is hanging out. Dicks are everywhere. Even the guys who aren't with women are walking around the room with expectant cocks dangling in the air in case someone has a need for them. I'm the only guy who's zipped up. Until Bliss, I'd rarely seen a guy naked before. And here, with more people in less space, it looks like a snake pit.

In the bottom right corner of the bed, Laura is on all fours with her dress up. Bruno pulls out of her and parks in Camille's mouth while Pascal, true to his word, fucks Veronika against the wall. She's standing up, facing frontward with one leg raised and her face flushed, in a pose that, if photographed, would incite a million sticky nights.

I don't know what to do, how to get involved, or what the rules are. At least James and Nicole explained what was happening at Bliss and made sure to include me. But here it's much more extreme: the closest to a free-for-all I've ever seen.

I sit in the empty space on the mattress in front of Laura, who's still posed on her hands and knees expectantly. "Thanks for letting me come here with you guys," I tell her, because I feel like I need to say something.

"Is this your first time at a switch club?" she asks astutely. This is probably the stupidest place I've tried to make small talk since the last orgy.

"Pretty much."

As we're talking, the creepy businessman from outside the club materializes behind Laura and rubs her pussy. Then he scoots under her like he's repairing a car and starts eating her out.

"Is that cool with you?" I ask her. "I can tell him to stop if you're not comfortable." Here I go again: taking care of everyone's needs but my own.

"That's so American of you to say," she laughs.

"What do you mean? How is that American?" I don't even understand the comment: She's American herself.

"No one's ever asked me that before."

"But I thought maybe—"

"I just want a cock in me."

This is the kind of woman I fantasized about as a teenager: an indiscriminate one. And more than even the pujas and Bliss, this seems like free sex—because there's no spiritual baggage, drug baggage, or even much relationship baggage around it. In fact, there's no baggage or encumbrances whatsoever, just randomly intersecting body parts. And now that I'm in the midst of it, I'm terrified. It's so shockingly . . . open.

It's not society that holds us back, it's ourselves. We just blame society because not only is it easier but it's a nearly impossible weight to move. This way, we don't actually have to change. I thought I was fighting the system, but all I've really been doing is fighting myself: first my compulsions, now my inhibitions.

Meanwhile, the slick-haired guy stops licking Laura and appears to be going for a home run.

"Can you make sure he puts on a condom?" she asks.

"Okay," I reply overenthusiastically, grateful for the opportunity.

I have a job to do now. A purpose. I am the condom police. I watch him carefully to make sure he puts the rubber on. Then I worry that I'm creeping him out. But I won't be swayed from my very important duty: no protection, no service. *That's right, sir, roll it on all the way. Otherwise I'm going to have to ask you to step out of the bed.*

"It's on," I tell her with an air of authority,

As he thrusts inside her, Laura's face swings closer to mine. Now's my chance, I think, and I start making out with her.

And that's when I realize: No one else here is making out. How many dicks has she had in that mouth tonight?

So I pull away. It's time to say *yes* and unzip. I kneel so that my crotch is level with her head. And sure enough, the power of the cock-right-there-in-front-of-the-face is too strong to deny. She takes it in her hands, guides it into her mouth, and starts sucking.

I realize this is very crude, but the story takes place in a sex club. What else am I supposed to describe? The chandeliers? There's nothing going on here but sex.

"What do you like?" Laura pauses to ask.

Good question. I like *this*. What's better than a blow job? Or does she want more specific instructions? Perhaps they have names for different blow jobs here—the spit-shine, the round-the-world, the confused American.

Like anything, I suppose sexual freedom is a learned art. I still need more experience to get comfortable.

Suddenly, I see Pascal's head appear over mine. He whispers in my ear, "Veronika wants you."

It's music to my ears, especially since things with Laura feel awkward. I know she has an any-cock-will-do attitude, but I have a sneaking suspicion that my cock isn't quite doing.

When the businessman finishes, Laura makes her escape. But instead of Veronika appearing, Camille kneels in front of me and takes Laura's place with more enthusiasm. I'm not fully present because I've been stuck in my upper head, so I look around the room and notice an exotic-looking woman lying in front of me. I take her hand and start massaging it, and she massages my hand back. I move my hand between her thighs and start playing with her. She's soaking wet. Good thing I clipped my nails.

I'm starting to get comfortable here. Finally, I'm actually part of an orgy—awake, accepted, alive. I rear up tall and look around. Everyone is fucking and sucking.

Perhaps my previous disasters in the swing and poly scenes have actually been necessary experiences to get comfortable at these things, learning lessons on the road to orgy mastery.

Suddenly I hear a guy's voice exclaim loudly, *"Tu es sur ma jambe."*

Nearly everyone on the megabed starts laughing.

Evidently I'm kneeling on some guy's leg. I slide out of his way and notice Veronika crawling toward me on the mattress. I drink in her unique amalgamation of devastating beauty and awkward innocence, and I instantly harden.

I make out with her passionately. I don't know why I keep touching people's filthy lips, but I crave the intimacy and connection more than the anonymous sex. Maybe I am polyamorous—because it's not just free sex I'm searching for, it's free romance, free connection, free relationships, free getting-naked-with-someone-you-enjoy-and-who-enjoys-you-and-then-getting-to-know-each-other-even-better-afterward.

I seriously need to gargle with Listerine when I leave this place.

Meanwhile, Bruno has appeared out of nowhere and started having sex with the exotic-looking woman.

I pull back and look at Veronika's face, and she bites her lower lip in response. There's so much heat between us and we've only just met. I hope it isn't because she was abandoned by her father.

I run a finger across her lips and she sucks it into her mouth and . . . oh god, I feel like I'm about to . . .

But I don't want this to end, so I pull out of Camille's mouth.

"Let me suck you!" she begs.

This is the best night of my life.

The scene on this bed is basically what Muslim martyrs are promised in the afterlife, except with virgins. But paradise is here. Now.

I've finally entered the world I've been reading about in porn magazines and watching in adult movies since puberty. Just as women are trained by the media and society to look for their Prince Charming, men are conditioned to look for their nasty slut. Not for a marriage, but just for an adventure. Both are fairy tales, but a Prince Charming is nearly impossible to find, because it's a lifetime illusion to sustain. It takes only a few minutes to play the role of nasty slut.

The only thing keeping me from fully enjoying this sexual paradise is the guilt: that Anne is in the hotel worrying, that the fashionistas are angry, and that because I'm liking this so much, it means I'm a sex addict, as is everyone else here. The counselors at rehab have really done a number on my head. I used to be worried just about sexually transmitted diseases, but they've turned sex itself into a disease. And now, any time I'm giving myself over to pleasure, I hear Joan's voice in the back of my head telling me I'm avoiding intimacy.

Just as I promised Rick I'd go all in on addiction treatment without doubt, I need to go all in on freedom without guilt. The answer will become clear over time: Either I'll hit bottom, as Charles predicted, or I'll find a solution that works for my life, as I hope. I need to get out of my head and be present for this experience. And to remember why I'm here: not to have a lot of sex, but to find my relationship orientation and like-minded partners.

As my eyes meet Veronika's again, I notice a dick hanging in my peripheral vision like a cloud covering the sun. Its owner says to me in a thick French accent, "All the girls here, they have been sucking your dick."

"I guess so."

"Do you like having your dick sucked?"

It seems like an obvious question, but I reply anyway, "Yes." I try not to make eye contact. This conversation definitely isn't helping my staying power.

"Would you like that I should suck your dick?"

"Oh, no thanks." I don't know why, but the situation seems to call for politeness. "I'm good."

I suppose if I technically wanted total freedom, I'd let him go to town. But, I realize, the goal isn't sexual anarchy. It's that I want the rules around my sexuality to be self-imposed, not externally imposed. That's the key difference—perhaps in everything.

The goal, then, is liberation: to be the master of my orgasm. I don't want my partner to own it, which would be monogamy, but I also don't want the orgasm to own me, which would be addiction.

My new admirer has inadvertently given me a gift. Though he doesn't say anything else, I keep seeing his dick—on my right side, then my left, then a foot above me—as if he's hoping that by just dangling it around me, at some point I'll decide to show my appreciation. That seems to be how things work here. Maybe this is where all the women hang out who actually like it when guys text photos of their dicks.

A Valkyrie with long blond hair and missile breasts clambers onto the bed with her boyfriend. I eye-fuck her to get back into the spirit of the orgy. She holds my gaze. But before I get a chance to do a thing about it, Bruno appears out of the blue and starts fucking her.

I don't know how he does it. This must be his tenth woman. Suddenly I remember that Camille has been down there sucking me for half an hour straight. I put on a condom, lie down, and move her on top of me.

Camille rides me as Veronika positions herself over my face. I am smothered in woman. If this is happening right now because my mother smothered me, then I owe her a serious thank-you.

Suddenly, a loud, condescending German voice fills the room: "Where is he?"

I tilt my head back and see an upside-down image of the fashionistas standing against the wall, staring into the mass of bodies.

"It's just like him to do this to us!"

I try to shield myself underneath the women so the fashionistas don't spot me.

"Let's just leave without him."

Their voices cut through the room, killing all sexuality in their path.

"So selfish."

For a millisecond, I consider stopping. I should probably get back to the hotel and check on Anne anyway.

Then I think, No. This is amazing. I don't want to stop this. So I'm selfish. Let me be selfish. They can leave and I'll deal with it later. I'm learning how to take care of my own needs for a change.

In moments like these, the true nature of one's soul is revealed.

"Let's switch," Veronika suggests. This is a switch club after all, so I slide out of Camille so she can swap places with Veronika. However, as soon as Camille's lower orifice is free, Bruno is in there. The guy never misses an opportunity. I'm sure he's a great businessman in the outside world.

Veronika slides her body over mine, her skin rubbing against my clothing, her back arched so we can see each other's faces. I switch condoms and slowly enter her. We move against each other sensuously. Time slows. We fall out of sync with the rest of the club and into each other.

I gaze deeply into the world in Veronika's eyes and she into mine—and it feels like love. Not the love that is a thought that comes with expectations of commitment and fears of abandonment, but the love that is an emotion that makes no demands and knows no fear. I've found, for a moment, love in a swing club.

Connected sex is a spiritual experience, but not in the way the Tantra polys describe it. It is spiritual because it's a release from ego, a merging with the other, a discorporation into the atoms vibrating around us, a connection to the universal energy that moves through all things without judgment or prejudice.

Thus, orgasm is the one spiritual practice that unites nearly everyone on the planet, and perhaps that is why there's so much fear and baggage around it. Because they were right both in rehab and at the puja: It *is* sacred.

And every orgasm. Is in itself an act of faith. An attempt to reach out. And just for a moment. Relieve our separateness. Escape from time. And touch eternity. And, yes!

As she drenches the mattress, I fill the condom.

Not only did I find love at an orgy, I think I found enlightenment.

25

"Should we go get a drink?" I ask Veronika as we slide off the bed. What we really should go get is a shower.

"I need a cigarette," Camille says, crawling away from Bruno, who quickly slips away, no doubt looking for another business opportunity.

Back in the lounge, I no longer feel guilt. Not about the experience, which was incredible. Not about Anne, who is responsible for her own decisions. Not about the fashionistas, who chose to remain separate from everyone and are probably back at their hotel talking shit about how the birthmark on my left ass cheek looks like a fake Gucci symbol or something.

We walk upstairs to a smoking room, and Veronika and I finally have a chance to talk. It's like the perfect date in reverse: first have sex, then get to know each other.

She's a lapsed visual-arts graduate student with a fiercely independent streak, a passion for learning new things, and a light melancholy worn under her skin for insulation. She speaks in a thick Czech accent, clipped and blunt. There's a coldness in it that probably comes from generations of ancestors who froze and starved and suffered and survived against all odds so that she could be here today, fucking a bunch of strangers in a trendy Paris club.

"It was my first time," she tells me. "I liked it."

"You mean you haven't been here before?"

"No. I'm visiting a guy in Paris. I told him I was only coming as a friend, but when I wouldn't have sex with him, he got angry. Camille lives next door, so she said she would take me out tonight without him."

"You don't want to sleep with him, but you had sex with all these random guys?"

"This is for the experience. That guy is too pushy. He threatened to kick me out when I wouldn't kiss him today."

"If you want, you can stay with me. I'm here for a few more days."

"I would like that," she says, unsmiling yet smiling. As we continue speaking, I'm reminded of a line from a classic sixties song: "I could be in love with almost everyone / I think that people are the greatest fun."

And this is what I'm discovering since leaving Ingrid. Whether it's Nicole or Sage, Anne or Veronika, each woman is a wonderful world unto herself.

And monogamy? It's like choosing to live in a single town and never traveling to experience the beauty, history, and enchantment of all the other unique, wonderful places in the world. Why does love have to limit us?

Perhaps it doesn't. Only fear is restrictive. Love is expansive. And I wonder, since fear of enmeshment impels us to avoid commitment and fear of abandonment makes us possessive, what type of evolved relationship can emerge once those wounds are healed?

For the first time, Ingrid is starting to recede in my mind, to become a beautiful memory, a heartrending casualty from my misguided attempt at monogamy. In front of me, a world of endless relational and sexual possibilities is opening up. Behind me, a struggle is ending. Even if someone is your perfect match, it's unlikely to work if your core values are different.

When Veronika mentions a documentary she recently saw called *The Workshop,* about a retreat in which participants get naked and have group sex to heal their shame and find enlightenment, I decide to tell her about the poly house I'm putting together.

"That sounds fun," she replies and rests her head on my shoulder. "I'd be interested in trying that with you, depending on when you do it." My heart races. If things work out after spending more time together, I just may have a V.

The rest of Camille's friends soon surface and we part ways outside the club, all exchanging numbers. When I return to the hotel, Anne embraces me—not with fear or relief or jealousy or worry, but with acceptance. She nuzzles happily into my shoulder and whispers, "I want to be an experienced woman."

And that's when I realize I've done it: I'm living in a world of liberated women and free sexuality. It's becoming my lifestyle. My reality. I am finding my tribe.

Now it's time not just to have sex with multiple partners, but to build intimate relationships with them also. Time to find out if this way of life is truly sustainable for me and can lead to a better kind of love, a stronger kind of family, and a fuller sense of happiness.

STAGE III

▪ Harem Life ▪

T HE PROPHET [MUHAMMAD]
USED TO VISIT ALL HIS WIVES IN A ROUND,
DURING THE DAY AND NIGHT AND THEY WERE
ELEVEN IN NUMBER. I ASKED ANAS, "HAD
THE PROPHET THE STRENGTH FOR IT?" ANAS
REPLIED, "WE USED TO SAY THAT THE PROPHET
WAS GIVEN THE STRENGTH OF THIRTY [MEN]."

—ABU QATADA

Sahih al-Bukhari, volume 1, book 5, number 268

26

Deep in our nature, we are foragers. And life is a process of gathering the resources we need from a large, connected planet. It's all out there: every color, shade, flavor, and mutation of life and experience. Whatever we are looking for, we will find—if it doesn't find us first. However, the result will not be what we're consciously looking for, but what we're unconsciously seeking.

And so what we want will never be anything like what we expect. It is the forager's law: You can find the berry bush, but you can't control its yield.

I leave Paris with plans to live with three lovers: Anne, who was overjoyed at the prospect of being together again so soon; Veronika, with whom I spent three blissful days in Paris after Anne left; and Belle, who has stayed in constant contact this whole time. I had met each of them under adventurous circumstances that went well, so it didn't take much for them to agree to continue the adventure.

I wonder what Shama Helena would call this relationship. It's one too many people for a V. I guess it would be a quad—or a one-legged W, maybe a tridactyl foot ↘. Whatever the case, I'm excited to finally turn the corner from observing nonmonogamous relationships to being in them.

Since I'm walking into the unknown, I do my best to prepare. I speak with the three women almost daily after returning to Los Angeles, getting to know them better. And with each text and call, the connection grows and blossoms. It has the feeling of a new romance, filled with hope and expectation, unsullied by reality. It's clearly premature to move in together, which is why we've agreed to try it for two weeks initially to see how it goes. It's a shame I ruined things with Sage, because she's the only woman I've been with so far who has experience in a group relationship like this.

Because the guesthouse I rent is too small for four people, I call the owner of the big, dilapidated tree house I looked at with Rick when I was dating Ingrid. Unfortunately, it's not available, so I scout for other options, sending the girls photos of my favorite places.

"Why don't you just do it here in San Francisco?" Nicole suggests when

I fill her in on my plans. "There's no place in the world more tolerant of alternative relationships. All those books on polyamory you've been reading—most of those authors live here. And I can get you into all the underground parties."

Nicole has been my Beatrice in this new paradigm and she hasn't let me down yet. I think she enjoys taking on the role of alt-relationship tour guide to fresh recruits. So I agree to try this new relationship somewhere new.

A few days before Belle, Anne, and Veronika are scheduled to arrive, I find a decently priced vacation rental near Fisherman's Wharf. It's a two-story apartment with three bedrooms, which will allow each of my sort-of girlfriends to have her own room, closet, and bathroom. Ideally the women will build corresponding relationships with one another and we'll all end up sleeping in the same bedroom. But in a worst-case scenario, I can just spend the night with each separately in a regular rotation, which is presumably how most polygamists do it.

Veronika is scheduled to arrive first; Belle's plane lands seven hours later; and the following afternoon, Anne gets into town.

So it's with equal parts astonishment and anxiety that I wait for Veronika at the airport, preparing to turn what seemed like an impossible relationship fantasy into a daily reality. Eventually, I see her emerge from customs. She's two inches taller than me and probably thirty pounds lighter, wearing high heels, skinny jeans, a tight yellow T-shirt, and the soulful sadness that never leaves her eyes. Her accent cuts strong and seductive through the crowd, with trilling r's that make me think of a Cold War spy.

Three hours later, we're lying in bed, content in the afternoon light of San Francisco, having a postcoital talk about body language. I try to take a snapshot of the moment in my heart so I can remember the exhilarating feeling of having gone from strangers to lovers to domestic partners in a matter of weeks. If I'd stayed with Ingrid, I never would have gotten to experience this.

My phone beeps with a text from Anne, who says she's packing and looking forward to holding me. I text her back and let her know that the girls and I are looking forward to holding her too—just to remind her that, as Orpheus put it, this is about family. A few minutes later, Belle texts to let me know she landed on an earlier flight and has "vajazzled" herself for me. I have no idea what that means, but I tell her it sounds hot and we'll come pick her up immediately.

When Belle responds that it'll be easier for her to take a cab to the apartment, Veronika sighs, exasperated. She gets out of bed, wraps a towel around her body, opens her suitcase, and starts hanging clothes in the closet. There is a light violence in the sound of each hanger hitting the brass bar.

"What's wrong?" I ask.

"Nothing."

"Nothing always means something. I'm open to talking about it."

"I'm fine, really." She unpacks her toiletries and brings them into the bathroom. A gentle frost accompanies the breeze of her every movement.

"Fine stands for fucked up, insecure, neurotic, and emotional."

She is unamused. "It's disrespectful to keep texting girls when you're with me," she snaps.

And I think: She's right. Then I think: I'm fucked. There's only one woman in the house right now and we're already having jealousy issues. The exhilarating feeling of domesticity disappears instantly. But this is what I'm here for: to be in reality about this lifestyle. It's easy to have sex with other people's wives and girlfriends, but learning to actually be relational (as Joan would put it) with multiple partners is far more challenging because it's not just body parts intersecting, it's feelings. Anything goes in a switch club between two strangers, but here in the real world as two lovers, everything now means something.

So I need to choose my next words carefully and with maturity if I want the experience to go well. Because it's not just about a couple of weeks, it's about my future. "I was texting to make arrangements with the girls who are coming to stay with us," I tell her. "But from now on, unless we're making plans for that day, let's all try to ignore the phone when we're together so we can be in the moment with each other."

She nods and smiles, content with the diplomacy. I used to think that a good relationship meant always getting along. But the secret, I realize, is that when one person shuts down or throws a fit, the other needs to stay in the adult ego state. If both people descend to the wounded child or adapted adolescent, that's when all the forces of relationship drama and destruction are unleashed. I share this with Veronika and teach her about the different ego states. Soon, we're connected again.

"I'm already learning things from being here, and that's why I came," she says happily.

An hour later, Belle arrives. She's pale and petite, wearing a plaid skirt, a navy blue cardigan, a white blouse, funky red glasses, and braided honey-blond pigtails. It's a schoolgirl look designed to drive men wild with both lust and guilt simultaneously.

"Is this your den of sin, Mr. Strauss?" she asks playfully as we embrace in the doorway.

I lead her to the living room to meet Veronika. Then I leave them alone for a few minutes and give them a chance to get acquainted without me. After a while, I hear laughter. A good sign. I return and Veronika tells me she's going to take a walk.

As soon as she leaves, Belle jumps in my lap and starts removing my clothes. I assume they worked out an arrangement between themselves. Already, the impossible is happening here.

Women like Chelsea put an extraordinary amount of effort into trying to look like the doctored photographs they see in magazines. But more exciting and more forbidden than that impossible feminine ideal is the nakedness of tender flesh that should not be uncovered, skin so pale and thin that it seems like exposure to light and air will damage it, flesh that seems to tremble all on its own simply from being looked at.

This is Belle's body.

It is marred only when I discover what she means by vajazzle: It's a bedazzled vagina, with brightly colored sequins stuck where pubic hair used to be. It's as pointless as it sounds.

Minutes after we get our clothes back on, Veronika returns. I watch her face and movements carefully. She doesn't seem upset.

We get ready for dinner, then walk downstairs to my Durango, balancing on a thread of unity. That thread threatens to snap as soon as we get to the car, where I encounter the first challenge of a group relationship.

Both women stand in front of the passenger door bristling with anxiety, waiting for me to make a decision.

"Since we didn't pick Belle up at the airport, she should sit in front," I tell Veronika. "Then you can have the front seat on the way home."

It's embarrassing to hear these words come out of my mouth. It sounds like something my father might have said to my brother and me when I was twelve. I don't remember anyone teaching multiple-partner seating arrangements at the World Polyamory Association Conference.

I get the sudden feeling that nothing about this experience is going to be like I expected. I am living under the forager's law.

27

Belle sits at dinner in her schoolgirl outfit, gawked at by every pervert in the restaurant.

"Oh my god," she's saying, throwing back her third drink of the night. "I went on a total lingerie shopping spree before I came here. I want to model it *all* for you tonight."

Normally, this would be ideal dinner conversation. However, there's a problem: She's looking only at me when she speaks. In fact, she's acting as if Veronika isn't even at the table. I can sense the frost beginning to coat Veronika's skin.

When Veronika goes to the bathroom, I remind Belle, "Make sure you include Veronika when you talk."

"I don't care about her," she responds. "I only care about you."

Her words floor me. "But that's not why we're in San Francisco. We discussed exploring polyamory here, and that means more than just the two of us are involved."

"I know." She sighs and stares at her drink, like a child disciplined for doing something she knew was wrong in the first place.

Bringing lovers together can evidently be like introducing cats. Everything must be done with care, thought, and precision, otherwise they'll never get along.

After dinner, I take them to a speakeasy in the Tenderloin called Wilson & Wilson, hoping a change of scenery will foster more camaraderie. But with every cocktail, Belle gets more talkative and Veronika gets more irritated, until she's looking at the table when Belle talks. And avoiding eye contact with people is worse than directly telling them they annoy you: It's your soul telling their soul that it annoys you.

This is already teetering on the brink of disaster, and Anne hasn't even arrived yet. Father Yod seemed to live in harmony with fourteen different wives at his peak, so surely I can make things work with just two.

I flash back to rehab. The guys in my group were all very different, but what enabled us to form deep connections quickly was discussing our timelines and childhoods. Maybe it's time to end the small talk and really get to know one another.

"I'm curious," I say to Belle, changing the subject. "What were your parents like when you were growing up?"

"They were perfect. They loved me very much." She takes a sip of her cocktail, then looks up at us, a big red smile covering the truth like a latex mask.

Whenever people idealize their caretakers, chances are pretty good that the opposite is true. Sometimes this illusion is created by the parents, who insist in godlike fashion that they're perfect and that the child owes them obedience because they're responsible for his or her existence. Other times the illusion is created by the child as a survival strategy, disconnecting from reality in order to avoid the pain of growing up in a toxic environment.

So I make an ill-advised attempt to break through Belle's walls. I explain this theory to her, concluding: "No parent is capable of being perfect. They're only capable of telling their children they are."

"And you can get good things from bad parents," Veronika adds, allowing herself to engage with Belle. She wants to help. We're growing closer already. "My father was never around when I was growing up and my mother always worked. So I was taking the bus alone around the city when I was only eight. That's why I'm so independent now."

I wonder if I give off an enmeshment pheromone that attracts abandoned women. Or if it's just that the majority of fathers are so shitty that most women have been abandoned by them in some way.

As we continue with our stories, Belle slams her drink onto the table and shouts so loudly that heads turn. "All right, my mom is a narcissistic, self-righteous bitch!" Then her face scrunches and tears pour out. "Don't go there anymore, okay? Just don't go there! You kept pushing—and now you're there."

And just like that, our moment of intimate connection has popped.

Or has it?

At least Belle broke through to reality. Now we know who she is. Just as some people have a drug or sex addiction, she has a word addiction. She builds a wall of words to protect herself from uncomfortable feelings. However, when someone is enmeshed with a parent of the same sex, this can make it difficult for them to form intimate friendships of the same gender. So that may be a big barrier for us as a quad.

On a more encouraging note, now that we've shared our vulnerabilities, Veronika's actually started looking into Belle's eyes again when she speaks.

Lesson of the day: The quickest route to poly-harmony—and life among the rest of the walking wounded—is truth and understanding.

As we leave, Veronika puts her arms around me and kisses the back of my neck. Then she moves my arm around Belle and we all walk out together. I kiss each of them on the lips. And for the first time that day, I have hope. We feel like a V.

When we return home, Veronika says she wants to take a shower. I step into one of the bathrooms to clean up and prepare myself for the culmination of our first night together.

But as I'm standing there, Belle walks in behind me, flicks my ear provocatively with her tongue, and whispers, "I want to fuck you. But I want you to turn around first and put your cock deep down my throat."

"I'd like to do that so badly," I tell her. "But we need to wait until Veronika's out of the shower."

I lead her into Veronika's room, and we lie on the bed and talk while waiting. But after a couple of minutes, Belle starts to fidget. Then she suddenly jumps up and runs through the house, laughing and giggling.

And my hope, once again, plummets. Belle seems to have gone haywire. I'm not sure if it's the alcohol, the jet lag, the nervousness, the mother wound we poked, petulance about having to wait for Veronika, or some kind of misguided flirtation meant to get me chasing her.

Veronika emerges from the bathroom and lies in bed next to me. The sound of Belle crashing into walls, laughing hysterically, then panting like she has asthma, fills the house.

"What's that girl doing now?" Veronika asks, her voice dripping with condescension.

"I honestly have no idea." When I met Belle, she was shy, cerebral, and good-humored. This is a side of her I've never seen. In fact, I've been around more drunk women than I'd care to admit and this is something I've never experienced or even imagined before. All I'm able to empathize with right now are the walls.

Life has a sick sense of humor: One of the reasons I felt so trapped with Ingrid was that I resented her for holding me back from sleeping with Belle. But now all I want is a break from her—and it hasn't even been twelve hours. Perhaps the secret to fidelity is knowing that the grass is crazier on the other side.

Belle runs back into the room, jumps into bed, and tries to kiss Veronika.

But Veronika turns her head away wordlessly. Belle freezes for a moment, then stands up and stumbles back out of the room. We hear her running manically through the house again, opening and closing closet doors, until finally she runs into her bathroom, shuts the door, and locks it.

"Maybe she's on a medication that reacts badly with alcohol," I apologize to Veronika.

"Maybe she is," she responds dispassionately, then rolls over and grabs her journal and a pen from the bedside table. I wonder what she's writing. I should probably ask everyone to keep a journal of her experience here so we can untangle it later.

I lie silently next to her, hoping that tonight is an aberration, that Belle just got too nervous and drank too much, that through some miracle Veronika will forgive and forget. This isn't supposed to be our honeymoon night, I remind myself, but simply the first date.

When I wake in the morning, Belle is back in bed and the three of us are spooning.

That's when I discover yet another challenge of polyamory: It's difficult to get up and go to the bathroom without disturbing anyone when you're sandwiched between two sleeping women.

But at least there's still hope for this group relationship. After all, things can't get any weirder than they did last night.

28

Excerpts from Veronika's Journal

I just arrived to the airport and I'm waiting to go through customs. I'm so happy he asked me to come here. Last time we saw each other, I loved him, at least for a few hours until my mind took over. I guess he has many girls like me. Just like I have my other potentials. For me it's not a problem. Let it be.

Since the day I was born, my life has been adventurous. I'm not sure how it was possible that so many things happened to me all the time. I guess I was silly and careless and extreme, and also there wasn't anyone to look after me. My father was most of the time drunk or at work or both, and my mom was always busy looking after the garden and the animals and she had some kind of job somewhere also.

• • •

What I've learned about relationships is that the most important thing is talking. If two or more people have a relationship, they must be able to talk with each other with no hesitation about their feelings. As an example, I was upset about his texting and didn't say anything. But he understood me and started to talk with me himself. I told him what I was feeling and ever since that moment, everything's been different. We changed our behavior and found a compromise. It was very surprising because it wasn't hard at all. I'm so glad that he did it.

• • •

Stretched-out cardigan, white shirt, plaid skirt, black high platform shoes, glasses, Pippi Longstocking pigtails, Aussie. Total schoolgirl outfit. Very porn. Cheap. But still interesting. And I guess men definitely love it. But he chose a girl like that to be part of this. Terrible!

I think I must have been okay with this idea only because I wanted to spend more time with him. I think I wasn't quite able to imagine how things were going to be here. I was silly, but I'm learning from it. And that's good.

• • •

I'm already sick of that girl. She talks so much! It feels like she's not going to stop ever.

And I don't look at him with the "I'm in love" look anymore. I feel like he's not able to feel sincere feelings. I feel like everything is mind games so he could make his idea come true. If he really cared about me, he wouldn't do this to me. Is he planning to fuck us all just one after another? What is he thinking? He feels that he can do everything. And at the same time, we gave him permission for it.

The difference between men and women is that we do things that we sometimes don't want to for something better. We gave him permission because of love. We hoped one day he would be ours. But maybe we actually just gave him away.

• • •

Now the Australian girl has become so desperate that she acts like a crazy person. She laughs all the time very loudly, but I guess deep inside she's crying. There's no logic in her behavior. She's really drunk and looking for him in closets. Seems like this situation makes us all act a little funny.

Tomorrow the third girl is coming. She's French. I hope she's going to be more normal, not like this one here.

29

In the morning, Veronika makes eggs-in-the-hole for the three of us and we sit around the breakfast table talking. Now that Belle is sober, there's actually a semblance of comfortable domesticity.

I'm not sure if Veronika will ever respect Belle after last night, but at least she's tolerating her. Hopefully Anne, with her quiet, centered energy, will be the connective tissue we're missing.

When we drive to the airport, Veronika gets the front seat since she made breakfast. I know, it's absurd.

As we arrive, I spot Anne standing expectantly outside the terminal, the missing toe of our tridactyl foot, looking so fragile that she'd blow over if a truck drove by too quickly. Her eyes, glowing like headlights, seem to take up a quarter of her face, the rest of which is obscured by strands of unkempt blond hair. When I jump out to greet her, she embraces me for a quiet, connecting minute. Then she climbs into the backseat and I take them on a mini-tour of the city.

"She's incredible," Veronika tells me when we return home. "I think there's a lot I can learn from her."

I breathe a sigh of relief. Maybe this is the dose of fresh air and peaceful energy we needed for balance. Perhaps this quad will actually work now.

That night, we join James and Nicole at Supperclub, followed by an after-party at Nicole's loft with six other swinger and BDSM couples, including the inescapable Chelsea and Tommy.

Her loft is the swinger version of a bachelor pad. There are scaffolding towers hung with lights and speakers, all remote-controlled from her computer; a stripper pole in the center of the room; even an inexplicable round table like the one in Corey Feldman's hotel suite.

Veronika and Anne sit on the couch and discuss the healing center in France where Anne does acupuncture for a living. I put an arm around them and join the conversation. Belle, who's snuck a couple of drinks in, sits on my other side and takes my free hand. For a moment, we are a functional relationship.

Then Belle sidles closer to me and tries to make out. It seems not like an act of spontaneous passion, but an attempt to prove to the others that she's the number-one girlfriend.

When I pull back, Belle storms away, then dances erotically on the stripper pole and makes out with Nicole. "She's just doing that to get your approval," Veronika remarks drily. "Can we go home soon?"

And now we are a dysfunctional relationship.

"Let me check with everyone else," I tell her. I'm starting to wonder if the more people there are in a relationship, the less freedom each person actually has.

I talk to Belle and, of course, she wants to stay.

I return to the couch and discuss it with Veronika as the swingers next to us stare at the circular table as if it's the monolith from *2001*. Suddenly, Anne rolls her head softly toward me, her eyes gentle and pleading, and asks, "Can I talk to you in private?"

I tell Veronika we'll be right back and walk with Anne to the entryway of the apartment. She's silent at first, as if too scared to speak, until finally the words come tumbling out. "I don't understand why you're always going like this with everybody," Anne says, agitated. To demonstrate, she grabs my left arm with surprising roughness and rubs her hands along it spastically. "In France, when people do that, it isn't just a friendly thing. It means something. So I don't understand it." She pauses and shakes her head as I try to grasp what she's saying. "At home, we just don't do this."

I stand there for a moment, mystified. When her point becomes clear, my last flicker of hope dies: She's already jealous. She thinks I'm hitting on Veronika and Belle.

"Everyone I'm touching, I've already slept with," I tell her. "Just like I have a relationship with you, I have a relationship with them. I explained that to you that before we came, remember?"

She nods yes, but she still seems displeased. It clearly wasn't the answer she was hoping for. And I'm in shock. I met Veronika at a switch club where she was fucking everyone in sight; Anne presumably knew where I went and what I was doing that night; and when I first slept with Belle, we had another woman in bed with us. I met each of them under nonmonogamous circumstances and clearly told them we'd be living with two other women in a group relationship.

And now every one of them, with the possible exception of Veronika, seems to want me to herself. Maybe what Randy's wife said at the dinner where I met Nicole *is* actually true for most people: Sexual experimentation is fun—until you're with someone you have feelings for.

It's these damn feelings. They're to blame. Why is it that as soon as they descend on someone, they bring ownership with them in the passenger seat? A piece of relationship advice Lorraine taught in rehab rings ominously in my head: "Unspoken expectations are premeditated resentments."

When we return to the party, Belle rushes to my side. "Nicole's so hot," she says. "I've been making out with her all night."

She hooks her arm in mine, and I worry that Anne will see it and get upset. "I don't know if we can do this in front of Anne," I tell her. "She needs some time to get comfortable with all the touching."

Belle wheels around and stomps off again, grabbing James's arm to spite me. I'm locked in a game of emotional chess that's far out of the depth of someone who's experienced nothing but monogamy all his life. If I touch anyone, someone will get upset. But if I don't touch anyone, someone else will get upset.

I feel not like a lover anymore, but a referee.

It looks like the party's about to get started here, but it's not one we can be part of. I gather my partners and leave, trying to figure out how to create the sense of family that Orpheus Black talked about. When Anne clambers into the front seat without checking with the other women, who exchange peevish glances, I console myself with the thought that maybe we're actually acting like a typical family.

Back at the house, I visit Veronika in her room and bid her good night. "Come back," she implores. I tell her I'll try.

Then I visit Belle. "This isn't working for me," she complains. "I want to be able to touch you when I want."

"We need to stick together as a team to make this work," I remind her.

"I'm a girl and I have emotions," she responds. "And though my head says we're a team, I still want to be with only you."

And then I visit Anne. But when she asks me to stay for a little while, I look at her lying there, starved for connection and reassurance after her long trip, and give in. It's only fair: I've already slept once with each of the others. As I remove her clothes, I'm excited to feel once more the runner's legs, swimmer's abs, and ballerina's breasts she keeps hidden beneath her formless clothes.

Still, I can't spend the night because that will hurt the other girls.

When I break the news a while later, Anne inquires, simply, "Have you ever felt true love before?"

It's an odd non sequitur, so I tell her, "I've been in love."

"But true love?"

"What's the difference?"

"True love is when you're a mother and your daughter is born. It's that much love and you feel it all the time."

"So it's feeling that way every second of every day forever?"

"Yes. You're so in love that you don't want to be with other people."

"I don't know," I reply. "Have you ever felt true love before?"

"Not before I met you."

My blood freezes. I thought this was just sweet pillow talk. I can't believe she's gotten that attached so quickly. I've invited an addict here: a love junkie, connecting in a fog of fantasy. "When you're a mother and your second child is born, you still feel just as much love as when your first child was born," I tell her. I speak as slowly as possible, so she'll understand. "It's not a sign of true love when you only want to feel it with one person who you just met and don't really know yet. That's more like obsession."

She's silent.

"Do you understand?"

"Yes," she says, kissing me tenderly. "I understand."

And I hope she does.

I walk upstairs and search the closets for extra blankets, but all I can find is a single spare sheet. I grab it and check the living room couch to see if it unfolds into a bed. Unfortunately it doesn't.

So I toss the back cushions onto the floor to make a little more room, lie on the narrow couch, and spread the sheet over myself.

It's cold, cramped, and uncomfortable. The only thing keeping me warm is my frustration. I'm living with three women I'm dating, and I'm spending the night alone on the couch. This is most definitely the last thing I thought I'd be doing in my Father Yod dream house.

30

As soon as I wake up, I place an emergency call to Pepper, explain the situation I'm in, and beg for advice.

"You're trying to run before you can walk," he responds.

"What do you mean?"

"How many people are in the house?"

"Four of us."

"So mathematically that's six relationships. And it's hard enough to make one relationship work."

I had thought of it as a single relationship, or three at most. But I do the math—the Gauss formula of polyamory*—and he's right.

"But there was this guy Father Yod," I protest, "who had fourteen wives and it worked for him . . . I think." I realize I don't know much about how Father Yod managed his relationships. In fact, I never actually read the book Rick showed me. I just looked at the pictures.

"Who's Father Yod?"

"He's like Charles Manson, but without the killing." Actually, that's not totally true. I recall reading online afterward that Father Yod was a judo expert who murdered two people with his bare hands in self-defense.

"What I can tell you is that a shared living situation is what we call an advanced skill," Pepper explains. "But trust me, it can work. I just went on a weeklong vacation to Hawaii with my partner and her boyfriend. And it was totally smooth because the three of us had spent so much time together."

"Right now, I can't see us ever getting to that point." I suppose after a few years, one can get used to anything.

"Do you want me to come by and talk to them?"

"Please!"

When Pepper arrives an hour later, we gather in the living room, desperate for a miracle. I dare not sit on the couch in case it looks like I'm favoring whichever woman drops down next to me, so I take an armchair instead. Veronika and Pepper sit in the other chairs while Belle and Anne share the couch.

---

*n(n-1)/2, with "n" being the number of lovers in a poly pod.

I introduce Pepper to the women and tell him about the previous night. He listens carefully, then responds as if telling preschoolers to play nicely with one another. Unlike with monogamy, our culture offers no schooling on how to make a group relationship work, no real role models to look up to, and few—if any—friends to turn to for advice. Even in movies, when couples decide to open their marriage, the results are usually disastrous and the moral of the story is to stick with what you've got.

"Here's your first lesson in going out together," he begins. His voice is so slow and measured that it's hard to imagine anything short of a machete-wielding maniac ruffling him. I wonder if he was always this calm and deliberate or if it's something he learned from years of managing multiple relationships. "You need to talk before you leave and have a plan for party protocol. If someone gets tired, do they take a cab home alone or do you all leave together? And if it's a sexual situation, decide ahead of time whether you want to watch or leave or join the sex pile." This makes perfect sense, yet it never occurred to me: The art of group relationships is logistics. "I want to encourage you to do little check-ins with one another constantly, with the knowledge that you don't know each other very well. This way you can start to build a team feeling together."

We nod in agreement. I suppose I was naïve to assume we would all just instantly become attached and live in relational utopia together. I've made mistakes in every monogamous relationship I've had, but I learned from them and that made the next relationship better. So it makes sense that my first multiple-partner relationship isn't going to be a runaway success. It takes experience and failure to get good at anything. This is my opportunity to learn.

"I want to add something that's important," Pepper continues. "You"—he points to me—"are the *fulcrum*. This is a long-known poly situation. The fulcrum is the only person in a relationship with each partner, but because of that, you end up torn in a lot of different directions. It's a very uncomfortable thing, because you're empowered and disempowered at the same time." He turns to the women. "So I would like to recommend that you all try to de-center Neil a little."

I heave a hopefully imperceptible sigh of relief. I watched several documentaries on poly pods before coming here, and many were led by people with a pathological need to be the focal point of everyone's love. They didn't seem to care whose feelings got hurt as long as the empty space in their own heart was kept filled. But for me, it's no fun being the center of attention when it results in collateral damage to other people's feelings.

"So how do we de-center me?" I ask Pepper.

"The three of you"—he gestures to the women—"should hang out without him and also start negotiating decisions that don't have to go through him first. The easy part of the situation is you and Neil, and you and Neil, and you and Neil"—here he points to each woman. "The hard part of the situation is your relationships with each other. I have a saying: Poly works or fails on trust between *metamours*."

"What's a metamour?" Veronika asks.

"A metamour is a partner's partner. So if Neil and I were both dating you, then Neil would be my metamour. And it succeeds between him and me, because we have the hard part but not the good stuff. So when you build trust among metamours, everything comes together and the group starts functioning. Does that make sense?"

We were in the dark before. This pale Goth guy is the light. He's a relationship pioneer, mapping new realms in interpersonal space.

"So what do I do if I want to spend time with Neil alone?" Belle asks. "Every time I try to do that, he says it's rude to someone else."

"Try not making the request to Neil. Make it to Anne and Veronika. And if they both say it's okay, then you can do whatever you want with Neil." The corners of Belle's mouth turn up in an unsuccessfully repressed smile. Pepper spots this and adds sagely, "But be willing to hear a no."

Veronika sighs and uncrosses her legs. "It's so hard to share a person," she says. "It would be easier if we didn't have strong feelings. But there's always going to be this mental fight to have him."

Although having three attractive women fighting over me may seem like an ego trip, in reality it's nerve shattering. Whatever interest they had in me before they arrived seems to have been exacerbated by the competition. According to a copy of O magazine I once read in Sheila's waiting room, polygamous men live nine years longer, on average, than monogamous men. But I wonder how Oprah could possibly be right. Because this is definitely not good for my blood pressure.

Pepper turns to me: "What you can do to get them past that point is reassure them. I've seen really jealous people and people with a lot of abandonment issues get past their shit once the fear of loss goes away. A good nonmonogamous group is like a flock of geese, which is to say it separates and comes back together."

Anne opens her mouth to speak. The words escape soft and unsure. Everyone leans in to make sure they catch them. "For me, I was really surprised last night because when everybody was touching, it was hurting me." She takes a pause so long it seems like an intermission. "I have a complicated family history, so maybe I get more possessive. But I understand now that we have to make things work so this can be a relationship."

Pepper's talk seems to be straightening everyone out. The metamours are remembering that they didn't come here to be in some *Bachelor*-like competition, but to live, learn, and grow in a mature relationship together. "I would recommend letting go of expectations and trying to get to a place of acceptance with everything," Pepper tells her. "If things get weird, let them be weird. If you can all get to a high communication level, and learn the process of negotiation and setting boundaries and talking through discomfort, this will start working much better for all of you."

Before Pepper leaves, the four of us agree to hold house meetings every day, during which each person will get a turn to speak uninterrupted—like in the talking-stick circle I made fun of in rehab.

As a sense of calm and understanding descends on the house afterward, Veronika makes egg salad sandwiches and we sit around the table, all on the same page for the first time. Then, with Anne taking the front seat of the car without incident, we visit Alcatraz. As we walk from the ferry to the island prison, Belle holds my left arm while Anne clutches the other. Veronika wanders behind, taking photos.

"I feel like I'm a third child whose mother doesn't have enough hands to hold," Veronika says as she catches up to us.

She takes Anne's hand in hers as a group of frat boys walks by and gives me a thumbs-up. For the first time, there's a group energy connecting us. Perhaps all of us just needed to let go of our expectations like Pepper recommended, adjust to being somewhere new, and allow the relationship to set its own course.

And that's when something unexpected happens: I'm overcome by a powerful sense of unworthiness. It doesn't seem fair that these women have to share me. Any one of them could easily have her pick of the guys here who keep looking at us. But instead they're settling for scraps of my affection—the crumbs of a crumb.

When I imagined living in a freewheeling love commune while I was dating Ingrid, I thought I'd be adrift in a blissful sea of pleasure, excitement, and feminine energy. But instead I feel embarrassed that I'm monopolizing three hearts.

I spent my childhood starved for my mother's and babysitter's love, feeling like most of their positivity went to my brother and their negativity to me. So being in a position where I'm actually getting so much positive female caring is a new experience. Maybe the real purpose of this quad relationship for me is to break through my walls and feel worthy of love—or whatever this is.

31

In the car on the way home, I tell the girls that Nicole and James invited us to a play party called Kinky Salon. Where a swinger party is generally for couples looking to swap, a play party is basically any hosted alt-sex event where people get together to throw down. And Kinky Salon is one of the most playful parties of them all: a cool, creative scene with beautiful women, costumed hipsters, and no creep factor.

"Is everyone comfortable going?" I ask.

"I'm going to stay home," Anne says.

It's the same thing she said in France. And, secretly, I'm grateful. Since Pepper's talk, she seems to have left her love-addiction haze and accepted our quad-ness. And now, finally, we are a flock of geese.

Even Veronika and Belle appear to be getting along. As soon as we get home, Belle asks her, "Can I dress you? You're so pretty and I have some clothes you'll love."

The compliment appears to be a sincere attempt to connect. And since women trying on one another's clothing is a universal sign of sisterhood, I leave them alone to bond. Maybe they just needed time—and Pepper's reassurance—to get comfortable with each other rather than feeling forced to be friends.

When they reemerge, Veronika is wearing a fitted pink-and-white-striped dress with a plunging neckline and a black leather corset. She looks stunning,

so Belle gets the front seat as a reward for her generosity. It's still ridiculous, I know.

Appropriately, Kinky Salon is throwing a harem-themed party. When we arrive at the warehouse apartment with James and Nicole, we see men wearing turbans and smoking hookahs while women in veils and gold lamé bras sit in their laps, fucking them as Arabic music pipes softly through the rooms. At every party I've been to so far, the women seem to be in control of when the action starts and with whom, but once things are underway, they tend to play submissive roles. I don't see any sultanesses, for example, worshipped by harem boys.

The back room is like a low-rent version of the French switch club. It's full of mattresses pushed together, but instead of a free-for-all, people are clustered in twosomes and threesomes.

As we sit and watch, Belle whispers to me, "Why don't you and Veronika have sex?"

"Do you want to join us if she's open to it?"

"I don't think she likes me that much. Go ahead. I'll get you later."

"Are you sure?" I can't believe this is happening. It's practically a miracle. In fact, I'll go out on a limb and say it *is* a miracle. The poly gods have smiled on us today.

"I'm sure."

Between Pepper's pep talk and the lack of alcohol in her bloodstream, Belle's another person tonight. I leave her with Nicole and James, then lead Veronika to the only unoccupied spot on the mattress pile, which is just a few feet away from a woman impaled on the lap of a man in a purple turban. Soon Veronika's on top of me, riding herself to orgasm after orgasm, her lips parted ecstatically, her back arched electrically, her hips pursuing perfect rhythm and pressure, and both of us once again enjoying the rapture we last experienced together in Paris.

When we rejoin the group, Belle rushes to my side and asks, "Can I spend the night with you tonight?"

"So that was your plan?" It seems reasonable, but then I think, What about Anne?

I check my phone and there's a text from her: "Need and would love to spend the night with you."

Now what?

I can't spend the night with Anne, because Belle will be upset. And I can't spend it with Belle, because Anne will be hurt. And I can't spend it with Veronika, because then both Belle and Anne will be angry. It is the polyamorist's paradox.

And anyway, didn't Pepper tell them they were supposed to negotiate this with one another, not with me?

I explain the situation privately to James and ask what he recommends doing. He shakes his head and grimaces. "There's no right answer. I tried dating another girl with Nicole and a similar thing happened. You want these multiple relationships, but you just end up hurting everybody. It's a lot of work. The amount of communication it takes is exhausting, and someone always feels left out."

I'm relieved to hear it's not just me who has these problems, that this would likely have happened with any women I chose to live with, unless they were very poly-experienced.

"I guess swinging works because all the women you're sleeping with are in other relationships, so they're not a threat to your partner."

"Exactly," he says, smiling. "It's polyamory light."

As we gather our partners and leave, James sizes me up for a moment, as if deciding whether I deserve whatever favor he's about to bestow. Then he puts his arm around me and whispers, "I want you to meet a friend of ours named Reid Mihalko. He's the Yoda of sex parties. If anyone can help these women loosen up and get on the same page, it's him."

Back at the apartment, I make the rounds. I tuck everybody in, discuss how they're feeling, and help them understand why I can't spend the night with them. Then I settle in for another uncomfortable night on the couch.

It was a good day. The best yet. But I'm still sleeping on the sofa. However, unlike the night before, this time I'm sleeping with hope. We made huge strides forward today. And if Reid Mihalko is even half as experienced and helpful as Pepper, this whole crazy idea just might actually work.

32

The next morning, the metamours follow more of Pepper's advice and have an adventure without me. Nicole picks them up and takes them shopping, then treats them to a fancy brunch. And just as Pepper predicted, they return brimming with positive energy and a surprising sense of camaraderie. I'm starting to become de-centered.

They also return with an extra body. He's a broad-shouldered, large-skulled gentle giant with sandy blond hair, wire-frame glasses, and large teeth. He's wearing jeans and a slightly undersized purple T-shirt stretched across his paunchy belly with the words SEX GEEK emblazoned on it.

"Meet Reid Mihalko," Nicole announces.

Reid, she explains, is one of the leading figures in San Francisco's sex-positive scene. He has slept with, by his own estimation, a thousand men and women. And he teaches courses on everything from kissing to pegging (when a woman puts on a strap-on and inserts it in a man).

"I've come here on a mission," he says. "James told me everything."

He speaks slowly and rakishly, with one corner of his mouth rising higher than the other. He's a cross between Clark Kent, John Malkovich, and someone recovering from a mild stroke. He says he wants to observe us checking in and then he has something important to discuss.

We take our seats in the living room. As usual, I choose a chair just to be safe.

For the first time, every check-in is positive. Belle says she had an epiphany last night at Kinky Salon that relationships are about giving, not getting. Anne explains that her mind and heart are starting to open to this experience. And even Veronika has warmed up.

"The vibe isn't so tense anymore," she says. "I feel like we're actually connected and can learn from each other now, so I'm very happy about that. I really liked last night and I would like to do it sometime more, yes?" She laughs.

When we're finished, Reid asks us to take a deep breath and exhale loudly. It reminds me of something Sheila would do. Then, in a very slow, didactic voice, he tells us, "Aside from doing cuddle parties, which are nonsexual workshops around touch and affection, I have been throwing play parties and creating spaces for adults to be able to frolic and explore their sexuality since 1999. And this evening I'm throwing a party for a friend who's staying with me and who hasn't had sex in a year. My objective is to get her laid. And we're having about thirty people come over to hang out and play, whatever that looks like for them.

"So I'm here to determine, one, if it's good for you all as a group. And, two, if it's a good idea for my community. I want to create a space that feels very safe and genuine because I specialize in those kinds of dynamics."

Once again, I'm in debt to James and Nicole: Where Pepper helped us negotiate the emotional boundaries, it seems that Reid is here to help us negotiate the physical ones.

Reid then asks each of us a series of questions designed to open us up to positive experiences that we've been denying ourselves:

"What are you afraid to ask other people for?"

"What don't you think you deserve?"

"If you could experience anything in your next few days together, what would it be?"

They are the right questions, and they allow each metamour to be heard and feel understood rather than judged. Soon Belle is talking about wanting to have sex with two men, and Veronika is saying she wants to be fucked by a girl with a strap-on. Even Anne, in her own way, says she wants to join in: "I want to feel free together without being hurt."

I suppose this is yet another female dilemma: to feel free to follow the cravings of one's heart and body without being hurt or shamed afterward. I've never met a man who didn't want to experience his sexual fantasies in real life, yet I've met many women who've said that they wouldn't be comfortable actually experiencing the scenarios they masturbate to.

"And what about you?" Reid asks me. "What are your intentions for the next few days?"

"All I want is for the three of us to laugh a lot, enjoy our days together, and then sleep in the same bed comfortably."

"Can you be more precise? Is there anything you'd like specifically to happen in that bed?"

"You know, it doesn't even matter. That's my hope for us. Probably more so now that I'm sleeping on the couch every night."

"Thank you." He looks each of us in the eyes appreciatively. It's difficult to tell whether he's genuinely connecting or performing a rehearsed gesture. But either way, it works. "My invitation for each of you is to spend more time asking for what *you* want rather than asking everyone else what *they* want," he concludes. "You will speed up your growth by being selfish. So imagine that the people you're looking at can actually take care of themselves. And if you ask for what you want and trust that the other person will say yes or no powerfully, it will make things very interesting."

Life is a learned skill, but instead of teaching it, our culture force-fills developing minds with long division and capital cities—until, at the end of the mandatory period of bondage that's hyperbolically called school, we're sent into the world knowing little about it. And so, left on our own to figure out the most important parts of life, we make mistakes for years until, by the time we've learned enough from our stumbling to be effective human beings, it's time for us to die.

In other words, if I hadn't met teachers like Pepper and Reid, who've at least excelled in one area of this short pilgrimage toward the grave, I would have given up on this quad and the possibility of one ever working. But I now see my responsibility for the problems we've been having. As usual, I've been trying to please everyone and sacrificing my own needs. And that's not what I broke up with Ingrid to do. In fact, in trying to take care of everybody, I ended up taking care of nobody.

I glance at Nicole and she nods back at me as if she's reading my mind. Reid takes a long breath and exhales enthusiastically. It's not a sigh so much as it is a display. "If I were to invite you all to come to the play party, raise your hand if you would like to go."

Everyone's hands go up. Even, ever so meekly, Anne's.

33

When we leave for Reid's house in Oakland several hours later, Anne clambers into the queen position in the car as if it's hers by right. I make a mental note to talk to her about it at the next house meeting. We then pick up Nicole, who went back to her apartment to shower and change.

"Is James coming?" I ask when she scoots into the backseat, wearing a black silk blouse and a tight gray skirt.

"No, he has to work," she says.

My quad has turned into a pentagram.

"Let's discuss party protocol," I suggest, taking Pepper's advice. The car is crawling through typical San Francisco traffic, so we have plenty of time to negotiate.

Nicole speaks first: "I can only watch, because James and I have a rule that we only play together." It seems their relationship has gotten more restrictive since she broke the rules in the laundry room. Trust is a chain that gets longer the less you pull on it.

"For me," Veronika says, "everyone can do whatever they want. I don't mind."

"Same here," Belle adds. "As long as Neil doesn't have sex with anyone in front of me."

When I met Belle, I had sex with another woman in front of her and she didn't mind. But that was when she thought she'd never see me again. According to evolutionary theory, it's supposed to be men who are wired to get more upset when a woman has sex with someone else because his genes won't be passed on if he raises children who aren't his; women have supposedly evolved to get more upset when a man has an emotional affair because of the fear of losing his support and protection. Of course, we have DNA testing and economic independence now, so evolution needs to catch up.

"You can all do whatever you want also," I tell them.

The only person who hasn't checked in is Anne, who's wearing polyester slacks, flat black shoes, a stiff button-down shirt, and a giant navy-blue shawl. She looks aggressively unsexy.

"What are your boundaries tonight?" I repeat the question for her.

She stares out the window for a minute as if she doesn't hear, then, without turning, responds, "I'm not comfortable."

"Not comfortable with what?"

She speaks so softly that the metamours in the backseat lean forward to hear. "With you having sex."

It takes a few seconds for the words to register. Then they hit me like a blackjack. "With Belle and Veronika? Or with the other people there?" Everything seemed to be going so well today.

"With anyone."

For chrissake. At the house meeting this afternoon, we told you where we were going and what we would be doing there. You raised your hand and said you wanted to go. And now you're changing the rules?

That's what I want to say.

Instead, I try not to react. Where there is reactivity, there is a wound. It seems they were right about everything in sex addiction therapy, except the sex part.

I scroll through my brain, searching for the right response. I try to follow Reid's advice—to speed up my growth by being selfish and see Anne as an adult who can take care of herself. My goal here is to be honest. To allow discomfort. To communicate openly. She needs to be prepared to accept a no.

"I can't promise you what will or won't happen tonight," I tell her. "I might just lie there and watch people and do nothing, or I might have sex with everyone. I have no idea."

Anne doesn't respond.

"Do you still want to go if that happens?"

Silence. Maybe she's scrolling through her brain for the right response. Or maybe she's shutting down.

She mumbles something.

"What?"

Mumble.

"Can you say that louder?" I'm fighting to stay in the functional adult.

Finally: "If it happens, then I want to go home."

"Back to the house?"

"Back to France."

I thought the French were open-minded, liberal, and tolerated affairs. I thought Anne knew what was happening when I went to those clubs. I clearly need to stop assuming that *anything* is true.

"Would you be more comfortable if I limited myself to just kissing or cuddling at the party?"

"No," she says.

The mood in the car dims as each of our fantasies for the night smash like a flock of geese against a picture window. This is beyond even my worst-case scenario for our free-love group relationship: Now I can't even hold someone's hand at a fucking orgy?

Irritation creeps into my voice. "Before you came here, I told you we'd be living with two other girlfriends and going to sex parties like the one I went to in Paris. So you have to understand that I can't just pretend like I'm only going to be with you."

And she's mute again.

I look at Nicole beseechingly, my eyes flashing a distress signal.

"There are many people who don't believe it's natural for them to be with one person for the rest of their lives," Nicole explains patiently. "They believe that their sexuality shouldn't be owned or controlled by someone else, and that if they have sex with another person it doesn't change the way they feel about their partner. These are the kind of people who are going to be at this party."

Anne doesn't react, so Nicole continues: "Think about it this way. When people have friends, they have different kinds of relationships with each of them. Even if they have a best friend, that doesn't mean they can't have other friends. And that's the way the people at this party think of sexual relationships."

After a long, uncomfortable silence, during which she appears to come to some sort of decision, Anne turns to face me. "In Paris, we connected on this level." She points to her head, her heart, and her crotch. "But this time my feelings for you are different. My body and mind are changing."

I don't exactly understand her point, but it sounds like she's breaking up with me in her own way, which is a relief. "I feel the same way," I tell her. "You're a beautiful person inside and outside. But we're very different and want different things. So maybe it's best if we're just friends."

When I say this, her face falls. Evidently I misunderstood. "What's wrong?" I ask.

"I said my feelings for you have changed."

"I know."

"They've gotten stronger."

And now my face falls.

34

"I gave up having sex at the party last night and today it's my turn," Belle vents as we approach Reid's loft. "I'm tired of everyone"—she searches for the word—"vag-blocking."

This is my chance to stop taking care of everyone else's needs and focus on my own. Anne and I never agreed to be exclusive. The deal was that we'd be in a group relationship. So she's the one breaking the rules. For the first time, I'm going to do exactly what I told the guys in rehab that we should do: train a partner to accept a relationship on our terms rather than us accepting it on theirs. And, most importantly, to do it honestly.

"Here's what I suggest," I tell Anne. "There's going to be a welcome circle where everyone talks about their expectations for the party. And I suggest leaving the room after the welcome circle. If you want to know later whether I did anything, you can ask me and I'll tell you the truth."

She nods in a direction that looks like yes. It's clear she's still not completely comfortable, but those are her emotions to worry about, not mine. I can't get enmeshed here.

We walk into Reid's loft. It's a large square space with a stage in the front, a huge carpet in the middle, a balcony that wraps around three of the walls, and a crowd best described as pansexual: straight men, gay men, bi men, bi women, butch lesbians, lipstick lesbians, and probably no completely straight woman, other than maybe Anne.

We settle in a corner next to a man who introduces himself as Reid's building superintendent. He's there with a woman he describes as his "mostly lesbian girlfriend" and her female lover. Only in the Bay Area would someone's maintenance man also be poly and into sex parties. Now I understand why Nicole encouraged me to rent a place here. We are in a free territory where the sexual revolution has already been fought and won.

As Nicole busily texts James, Reid runs the welcome circle. He lectures first on safe sex, then on how to ask for permission to touch someone, and finally on how to be comfortable saying no. He asks us to practice the following dialogue with our neighbors:

Orgy Participant 1: Can I _____ you?

Orgy Participant 2: No.

Orgy Participant 1: Thank you for taking care of yourself.

Supposedly no one is born with greatness. It takes, the theory goes, ten thousand hours of experience to master something. And Reid has clearly put in his ten thousand hours of orgies. By the time he finishes his lecture—which serves as foreplay in the same way deity worship did at the puja—everyone feels safe, comfortable, and ready to free their libidos from their socially strung corsets. Everyone, that is, except Anne—and Nicole.

"Do you know what time we're leaving?" Nicole asks.

"I don't know, really. We just got here."

"Because if it's going to be more than an hour, I'll have James come pick me up."

I don't understand why she came all the way here with us if she wanted to go home right away. "I doubt it will be longer than an hour, but I'm not sure. I don't even know what's about to happen." I'm getting overwhelmed. "Fuck. Why does it matter?"

"James is nervous that I'm here."

"Then why did you come?"

"He said it was okay as long as I didn't play with anyone."

"So then don't play with anyone."

"I know, but he's upset because he feels left out. So I just want to go home soon, okay?"

So far, not a single alternative relationship that I've closely observed appears to be free, intimate, and healthy. In the sex addiction community, they wanted us to control our bodies so our hearts could connect; in this community, they want us to control our hearts so our bodies can connect. But maybe expecting to have it all—the deepest intimacy and the most unrestrained lust—is an unrealistic quest, like expecting a human being to be perfect. All you can do is work to get as close as possible to the impossible.

After instructing the assemblage to take a deep breath, Reid concludes the welcome circle by asking his guests what they want to experience during the play party.

"I want to watch the couple next to me have sex."

"I want to make out with every woman here for seven minutes each."

"I want another woman to use a strap-on on me."

"I want to go down on my boyfriend with another guy."

Anne sits still next to me. She's not so much holding my hand as she's clutching onto it for dear life.

"Do you want to leave?" I ask her when the welcome circle ends.

Silence.

A woman in front of us removes her girlfriend's shirt and buries her face in breasts. A guy behind us takes off his pants. He's wearing tightie blackies and knee-high black socks. An avalanche is rolling toward Anne's psyche.

"You should really leave right now," I warn her.

Two women who are with knee-sock man begin removing their clothes. A sex pile is forming.

I call Reid over. He's the Yoda of orgies. He'll know what to do. "You always have to go with the person who has the least amount of comfort," he advises. "So if you have to sit here and just watch, then that's what you have to do."

I'm confused by his advice. It seems like the exact opposite of what he said at the house this afternoon about being selfish. Maybe he doesn't understand the situation. "But what's not fair is that she doesn't want anyone else to touch me or hold my hand, yet she does those things with me." I sound like I'm in kindergarten. "And she knew that she was coming here to be in a group relationship."

"If that's the case, then she needs to understand that you're not exclusive with her, and that you need to take care of yourself and she needs to take care of herself."

He did a total 180 again. Now I have no idea what's right. My moral compass has lost true north. I have to look inward for answers.

My functional adult says I should suck it up and do nothing so I don't hurt this wilting flower. But my inner child wants to play. He's tired of being held back by the emotions of the people around him.

I watch enviously as the guy with the knee-high socks enjoys his threesome. Their bodies, hands, and tongues artfully slide across one another in myriad shifting positions, each one natural, effortless, creative. This picture was what I'd hoped to step into with the house here. In his case, it's clear the women are more into each other than him—and maybe that's why it's working so well.

Meanwhile, Anne is desperately clinging to me like a stop sign for fun. Belle is whispering sexual enticements in my ear. Nicole is asking when we can go. And Veronika is sitting in a chair, either sulking or just being herself.

I feel like I'm wearing a spiked suit; any move I make is going to hurt someone.

This is the moment of poly truth: I need to man up and take charge. I need to be Orpheus Black. I need to channel Kamala Devi. I need to get Father Yod on them. My problem this whole time is that I've been trying to rule by consensus. And every large group relationship I've seen or even heard about has been run by, as Kamala put it, a benevolent dictator. These girls are looking for a daddy, so as loathsome as that whole dynamic is, maybe it's time to step up and be that daddy. Not the abandoning daddy or the enmeshing daddy, but the functional daddy with a sense of what's right. And what's not right is that Anne is violating the agreements she made and the rights of the other women in the group to also have a relationship with me.

"Nicole, take Anne to the car," I order.

"They can wait in my apartment if they want," the building superintendent offers.

"How much longer do you think you'll be?" Nicole asks me as he zips up his pants and leads them out.

"As long as it takes," I tell her.

Veronika remains seated in the chair. She had her turn last night. Fair is fair. I once spoke to Barbara Williamson, a cofounder of Sandstone Retreat, one of the most famous swinger meccas of the seventies, and she said that she was introduced to the Lifestyle shortly after her wedding, when her husband fucked another woman in front of her. Although it was painful in the moment, after she saw that it didn't affect the relationship in any way, she realized it wasn't such a big deal. Maybe I should have slept with each of the women in front of the others on the day Anne arrived, just to get the pain and possessiveness over with for everyone.

I take Belle's hand and we walk through the orgy, drinking in the spectacle. Unlike the parties I've been to so far, here the lights aren't even dimmed. There is no shame. And though the couples look more like the ones at the polyamory conference, the scene is as beautiful as the one at Bliss. That's when I understand that it's not physical beauty that makes these parties pretty or ugly—it's honest and open intentions. Hypocrisy is ugly.

Upstairs, there's a fucking machine. (Not a fucking *machine*, but a *fucking machine*—a dildo powered by a piston engine.) An Asian girl lies in front of it as a large hippie woman I recognize from the polyamory conference turns it on, then massages the girl's breasts as she gets robo-fucked.

Nearby, a couple is rolling around the room having sex in a large circular ball with stirrups and handgrips. Reid's loft is like an amusement park for horny adults. And, as exciting as it is, it's hard to focus. The longer we walk around, the guiltier I feel about Anne and Nicole. Even if they did renege on the plan, it was still inconsiderate of me to just banish them like some sort of orgy despot. People are allowed to change their minds.

A woman with black hair latches onto Belle and asks permission to kiss her. They start making out, but as soon as I get turned on, Belle breaks away and tells her, "Where's your boyfriend? You should go find him."

She wants me to herself even at an orgy.

Belle drags me to a spot along the balcony. Twenty feet away, Reid is fucking a cute indie-rocker woman.

Belle and I make out as I rub her to wetness. Then she unbuttons my pants and goes down on me. Once I'm hard, she stands up, turns away from me, and grips the railing of the loft balcony, her ass in the air. As I put on a condom, I start thinking about Anne again. I worry that she's suffering in the superintendent's apartment, picturing me in the middle of a sex pile. Next to her, Nicole's probably stressed out on the phone, getting yelled at by James for staying here without him. And I feel like a selfish prick. I can't believe I actually kicked them out of Reid's apartment just so they wouldn't get in the way of my fun. Last night, Veronika and I had permission. Tonight, Belle and I don't.

I notice a nearby couple watching. Even people downstairs seem to be looking up. It feels like their eyes are judging us, accusing us of violating poly protocol.

The chair Veronika was sitting in is empty. I scan the room for her, but she's not in sight. So either she decided to participate or she also got mad and left the loft. I feel drawn and quartered emotionally.

I shut my eyes, take a deep breath, and try to focus on the smooth, pale, shapely body part in front of me. I thrust once and imagine it penetrating Anne's heart like a dagger. I thrust a second time and her heart breaks. I thrust again and there's nothing left of her, just an empty shell. I thrust halfway and think that if Anne ever does chair work, this would be on her list of traumas.

I can't go on.

I pull out and it's completely soft. I stagger back into a desk chair and Belle tries to perform genital CPR. But it's dead.

"I feel too guilty," I tell her.

She doesn't speak. The look on her face says enough. It's not anger or sadness. It's the look of a child pouting, "It's not fair."

In a sudden flash of clarity, I see the truth: I made the wrong decision. When Reid said be selfish, he wasn't giving me permission to hurt people's feelings. He was giving me permission to ask for what I wanted. And it wasn't Anne who needed to be comfortable hearing a no, it was Belle and me, because the person in a relationship with the least amount of comfort *does* get to set the boundaries—even if she keeps changing the rules and putting on blinders to what's really happening. Anne heard what she wanted to hear so she could be here in San Francisco with me. And in the same way, I heard what I wanted to hear so I could have my free-love harem.

I'm just as bad as she is. Maybe we do belong together.

And so I sit surrounded by pleasure, descending into a giant shame spiral.

Guilt is about what you do with your dick. Shame is about being a dick.

"Let's just go," I groan, defeated.

"Fine!" Belle trails behind me resentfully.

When we reach the bottom of the stairs, Nicole runs up to us in a panic. "I've been trying to find you! Everyone's really upset."

"Everyone or Anne?"

"Everyone. And Anne is in a lot of pain."

"That's what I was afraid of." Being selfish and having a conscience are not a good combination. It's like having a gun with bullets that, no matter which direction they're fired in, always end up hitting you in the head.

"I should have just let James come get me," Nicole vents as she rushes us to the front door. "He's freaking out."

Leaving Reid's apartment, we see Veronika in the hallway walking briskly toward us. Her eyes lock on mine, then turn away in disgust. "I thought I was tough," she says bitterly. "But you really have no feelings."

Her words send me deeper into my shame spiral. When I take care of everyone else in the relationship, I'm miserable. When I take care of myself, I'm still miserable. I can't see any way to make this work.

This is the worst orgy of my life.

And maybe that's the problem: I shouldn't be dragging my quad around to play parties. That's exactly what a sex addict would do. I'm sure Father Yod didn't need to take his wives to sex parties. They had everything they needed at home. Even if I'm going in all the way, the point is to commit to a more open relationship, not to pleasing every carnal urge. At the very least, caring, understanding, and trust need to be established first.

Impatience is the enemy of intimacy.

Belle and I walk with Nicole and Veronika to the super's apartment like inmates to a courtroom. "Do I have to go inside?" Belle asks as we get close.

"Yes, you do. Maybe you should walk in ahead of me, though, so we're not arriving together and rubbing it in." A criticism Rick once gave me flashes through my mind: You create the image that you're a good person as opposed to actually being a good person.

I wait outside a few more seconds, then enter. The first thing I see is Anne sitting on the floor, wrapped deeply in her shawl. She looks like one of those children pulled by police from under a bed after having witnessed the brutal murder of her parents.

I apologize to her and she says nothing.

As we walk to the car, Belle darts ahead and positions herself in front of the passenger door. "Come on," I tell her, exasperated, showing too little consideration too late. "Be respectful of Anne and let her sit in the front."

The stupid fucking front seat. The modern automobile was clearly designed by monogamists.

Night has fallen, but it is not as dark as the mood in the car as we drive back to San Francisco. Pepper said that the goal was to de-center me, and I feel in this moment like I truly have lost my center. I have no idea what to say or how to navigate this.

"Does anyone want to check in?" I ask feebly.

No one says a word. Not even Nicole.

"I'll begin, then," I speak to the silence. "In short, I made the wrong decision here, and I—"

"You made the wrong decision?" Belle snaps. "Why?"

Fuck, now I've made it worse. Belle thinks I'm saying that I made a mistake by choosing to be with her. "Maybe there was no right decision," I continue. "All week we've managed to survive by making sure everyone was comfortable, even if that meant some of us not getting what we wanted. But Reid told us in the house that we should be selfish, that everyone will take care of themselves if you take care of yourself." I'm babbling now, making excuses. "And maybe I should have just gone with what I felt, but he seemed to know what he was saying, so it just really threw me off."

"You should maybe think for yourself instead of doing what other people tell you," Veronika pipes in icily.

She's absolutely right. Mean but right. I'm losing it: It's hard enough hurting one person in a monogamous relationship, but today I've hurt four people. Polyamory is not just about having room in one's heart for more love, it's also about having room for more pain and guilt. If love hurts, then polyamory kills.

"I don't think this works if people aren't considerate of others, and I violated that today. I really crossed a line." I sound like a murderer trying to talk a victim's family into feeling sorry for him. "I'm sorry, Anne, and also sorry, Belle. Sorry, everybody. That's my check-in." I heave a deep sigh.

"Same emotion," Belle says. "That's my check-in."

"Veronika, is there anything you want to say?" I ask, remembering how communication has saved us in the past.

"No." Her voice is flat and passionless. Even communication can't help us now.

"Anne?"

Silence.

The only woman still talking to me in the car is the GPS navigation system, who speaks for all of us when she says, "Recalculating."

"No more sex parties, okay? I don't even care if we have any more sex. How would you guys feel if we just spent the rest of this time trying to get to know each other better?" I ask.

No one replies. Anne stares through the passenger window silently, her senses registering nothing, flatlined, the embodiment of Henry from rehab's mysterious ninth emotion: the death feeling.

In that moment, I hate her. I hate her for not saying anything. I hate her for silently suffering, just like my mom. I hate her for not listening to a word we said at the house meeting before, or a thing I said when inviting her to live with us. I hate her for having completely unreasonable expectations of me. I hate her for not considering my feelings in any of this. I hate her for being wounded when I was trying to take care of my own needs for once. I hate her for loving me, for wanting to possess me, for embodying everything I'm trying to escape.

And, most of all, I hate her because I feel guilty. I've smashed someone's already fragile heart to bits.

35

Excerpt from Belle's Journal

This experience has been, to put it lightly, an emotional roller coaster.

When I arrived, I felt as though for the first time in my life I was free to be me, away from the judgment and potential disappointment of my family.

So on the second night, when I told Neil it wasn't working for me, it was a combination of feelings. I felt like I was disappointing him and not contributing the way he wanted me to, and it felt like he and the other girls didn't want me there. I was also fucking confused that there were different rules for different people, and it threw me: Why is he allowed to kiss others in front of me and not the reverse? I was disappointed that I wasn't getting to do what I wanted with him (fuck him senseless). After all, that's why I came.

Then the Anne drama happened tonight. I could understand where she was coming from, but it was frustrating! I could see she had some deep-rooted feelings for Neil. So why did she put herself in this situation?

After the conversation with Reid, Nicole and I tried to tell Anne not to come to the play party. We told her that she would get hurt if she came. I'm going to assume she was thinking: If I do this and go along with it, Neil will be happy with me and I will get what I want out of the situation. Basically, she decided to hurt herself and go against everything she believed in to get the guy.

The whole scenario just bloody confuses me, to be honest: How did she get those feelings for Neil and how the hell did he not see them?

That whole situation blew up and I was happy to leave—albeit somewhat begrudgingly. I could tell he wasn't into it and I still went along with it. He never needed me to make him hard before. Initially I thought maybe it was the situation of being surrounded by people. Then it got obvious: He was doing something he either wasn't enjoying or didn't want to do, which is okay.

I'll admit that I really didn't want to go into that room where Anne was afterward. God, nothing felt more daunting and emotionally fucked up than to go into that room. But he pleaded with me, so I went. And, yes, I did plant a fake smile on my face. I felt awkward and like a bully. I was the bad guy, and that is so against my nature. I don't go out of my way to hurt people or be selfish, and I did. I felt very, very scummy, especially in that car ride home. When no one was talking and I felt their anger, it was an *oh shit* moment.

Anne came and spoke to me back at the house afterward. I so didn't want to talk to her. I had uncomfortable emotions, and I felt I had knowingly and willingly hurt her. That was a tough conversation. She just wanted to keep talking and because I felt guilty, I listened and was there for her. She talked about being raped by her first boyfriend and I asked her if Neil knew. She said no. I said Neil wouldn't have put her in the situation if he knew, and that she needed to get professional help, and that hiding it and pretending it didn't happen was obviously not helping her life.

I'm in turn upset that I've not gotten what I wanted out of this—to jump his bones. But I gained other things and insight into myself. And I learned how sex is a massive part of who I am, most likely an addiction. And it causes me to do things or act a certain way to get it. I need to work on removing it from its pedestal and not let it be something that's all-powerful and consuming, as I believe that's an unhealthy place for it to be.

I'm not wishing I hadn't come and I guess I don't want to leave. I'm just attempting to accept that this situation is so very different from my expectations of it. Everything's so complicated: four different people with four different sets of needs and some people so unwilling to compromise. Everything is just a bit too much to handle all at once right now.

36

After dropping Nicole off, we drive home in silence. As we trudge up the stairs to the apartment, each in our own personal hell, I think about packing my bags, stuffing them in the car, driving away, and leaving the girls there. That would be a fucking funny end to this group relationship: just abandoning them.

Got a wife and two other wives in San Francisco, Jack / I went out for a ride and I never went back.

I used to fantasize when I was a teenage virgin about being the only man on earth and every woman wanting to sleep with me. But now I think it would be a nightmare: having all those people competing and manipulating and creating drama, then hurting so many feelings whenever you choose to sleep with just one or two. You'd be murdered before getting a chance to enjoy yourself.

Perhaps that's the price of making your fantasies a reality. You realize pretty quickly that they were more fun to imagine.

A friend of mine, Tina Jordan, used to date Hugh Hefner, who's well known for living with multiple women. On their first date, as he was courting her with champagne and strawberries in his bedroom, his other girlfriends got jealous, came to the door, and started pounding on it. Then they stormed in, yelling at Hefner and Jordan.

Throughout their relationship, Jordan says, even though he was technically polyamorous, Hefner often snuck around, cheated, broke the rules—and was almost always caught by his girlfriends. He seemed to enjoy the drama, she noted. Having women fight over him made him feel wanted. Maybe that's the type of guy who likes being the fulcrum.

"I need to talk to you," Anne says as the others disappear wordlessly to their rooms.

"Not right now, okay?" I respond, avoiding eye contact.

I walk to the bathroom, brush my teeth, and prepare for another night on the couch. None of us has had dinner, but I'm too emotionally exhausted to think about it. I just want to disconnect from everyone. Be alone with myself.

As I stand with my back to the open door, I brace myself for the kitchen knife in the spine or the hammer to the skull. Who needs to worry about Mexican cartels when you have jealous lovers around? They'll finish the job much quicker and with more enthusiasm.

As I write this, there's a story in the news about a Nigerian man with six wives. He was attacked with knives and sticks by five of them for paying too much attention to the sixth. According to the article, the five disgruntled wives demanded that he have sex with all of them, and then "raped him to death."

While washing my face, I sense Veronika's chilly presence behind me, casting an ominous shadow. Here it comes: the attack. "Can we talk?" she asks.

It's an emotional attack. The most dangerous kind. And right now I need time to myself before I say or do anything else I'll regret. "Not right now, okay?"

She pivots wordlessly, bristles past me, and runs a bath for herself while I retire to my quarantine area on the couch and grab my computer to take notes. For me, the best way to understand what actually transpired in any given situation is to write about it until the truth emerges.

As I'm typing, I hear the thud of Belle's heels on the floor behind me. I feel her drop down next to me. I sense her sitting there, falsely patient, waiting for me to look up. Irritation snakes through my body as I keep my head down. Now her hand is on my knee, sucking my heat, my energy, my soul, and leaving in their place just a cold dark void. After an interminable minute, she speaks: "I need to talk to you."

I feel like I'm in a horror movie, trapped in a house full of zombies. And every few steps I take, one's jumping out at me from around the corner. But instead of saying "brains," they're saying "I need to talk to you." And in a way it's the same desire: to consume my brain. Perhaps the latter is even worse. At least I can run away from zombies. There's no escaping from emotions. But I can try.

"Can we talk later? I need some time to myself right now."

"I guess rationally I understand that. Irrationally I don't. I will try not to let it hurt my feelings."

Her words are needles of nonsense poking my eardrums. "How's this hurting your feelings? I mean, when do I get any alone time? It's insane."

"Is it okay if I cuddle with you while you write, then?"

"From now on, I'm off limits," I snap. I imagine Anne coming upstairs and seeing us. "In fact, no one can touch me!"

I cross my hands in the air, forming an X for "off limits." What was supposed to be a wild poly pod has turned into a fucking nunnery.

She remains planted next to me stubbornly. So I stare at her with the full force of my irritation and anger, drilling it deep into her sockets, trying to drive her away. She came to get her feelings cared for and instead they're getting further demolished.

Everything about this situation reminds me of the final months of my relationship with Ingrid, when her every needy touch and expression made my skin crawl. Set free to make my wettest dreams come true, I'm right back in the same situation. Only it's three times worse.

"Can I just have one hug?" Belle persists. These zombies have a weapon greater than flesh-ripping strength: It's called guilt. And so I lift my arms and let them encircle her, though my nerves itch and my heart pounds and every cell in my body flees in the opposite direction. Despite this revolt, I try to give her the affection she needs. As I do, I realize I have no idea what the boundary is between taking care of my emotions, wants, and needs and taking care of the emotions, wants, and needs of others. It seems I'm always way off the mark in one direction or the other.

After the hug of death, Belle pads away, content. I make the mistake of thinking that the nightmare is over. But ten minutes later, like the scene after the end credits of a horror film, Veronika rises out of the water of the bath, hunts me down in the kitchen, and attacks: "Belle just ordered Chinese food, but only for herself. How am I going to eat?"

What the fuck: Am I responsible for everyone's diet and nutrition now? She figured out how to eat before she met me.

"You're a big girl. Figure it out for yourself!"

These women just don't stop going after one another.

She shakes her head and says, "That was mean."

Once again, she's right. Where there's reactivity, there's a wound. And I am overreacting to everything.

That's when I realize: This whole enterprise was doomed from the start. In my relationship with Ingrid, I felt trapped by her desires and needs. And so I absurdly deceived myself into thinking that somehow I'd feel more free in a house with additional women and additional needs. Polyamory—at least when I'm the fulcrum—is not the answer for a guy with enmeshment issues. Too many invisible nooses encircling me, tightening around me, choking me, killing my spirit.

Maybe I'm neither mono nor poly, but just solo.

I gather my strength, enter Belle's room, and ask her to add enough dishes to the order so everyone can eat. But five minutes later, she emerges and whines, "I can't connect to the Internet."

Now I'm technical support. Can't they figure anything out for themselves? "Give me the phone number and I'll call them!"

How did Father Yod survive fourteen wives? Or maybe he didn't—and that's why he died at age fifty-three. I should call one of his wives and ask how he made those 105 relationships (according to the Gauss-Pepper formula) work.

I get half an hour of alone time until the Chinese food comes. As I'm setting the table, Belle and Veronika walk in.

"We talked, and between us it's all good now," Belle says. "We decided that Anne needs to go back to Paris. And we came up with an idea together."

"What's that?"

"Veronika wants to have an experience with a guy and a girl with a strap-on. I'm going to be the girl with the strap-on. And if you want, you can be the guy."

I stand there with my jaw open. I'm completely speechless.

I thought I understood life. I thought I understood women. I thought I was at least starting to understand myself. Clearly I know nothing.

And then Belle asks Veronika, "Is it okay if I fuck you with a strap-on?"

And Veronika, in her sharp Czech accent, says, "I would prefer not."

Okay, that's more like it. One of the girls just poured cold water over the other's hopes and fantasies. Evidently I do understand how things work after all.

"Let Belle fuck you with a strap-on, for chrissake," I tell her. "In the spirit of communal living."

She's not amused.

The three of us finish dinner in silence. I've really outdone myself with this relationship: Rather than making one person miserable, like my father made my mother, I've made three women miserable.

Afterward, I hear Anne walking up the stairs. I hide in the bathroom. Emotionally, I'm eight years old right now. But I don't want to look at her. It's like staring into a vortex of guilt, which keeps howling, "You're hurting me by not reciprocating my totally irrational love for you."

There's a light tap on the bathroom door. She's found me. If only I could flush myself down the toilet and escape through the sewers of San Francisco. I'd rather see three-foot rats with razor-sharp teeth dripping with meningitis than face a woman I've hurt. But of course I let her in, because the only thing sharper than those rat teeth is guilt.

I return to my errant-king's throne. She sits on the floor in front of me and says the dreaded three brain-eating words: "Can we talk?"

"Sure, I'm happy you're speaking again. But before you say anything, just know that I'm this close"—pinching my thumb and index fingers almost together—"to losing it."

"I can either go home tomorrow or stay here for the rest of the time," she says. "But if I stay, I expect quality time with you and I need everyone here to be respectful of my feelings."

She looks at me hopefully, waiting to see how I'll respond to this request that she's clearly put a lot of time into properly formulating.

And so I give her—sweet, suffering Anne—a piece of my mind. "I think you've been really selfish. You say other people here aren't being respectful of your feelings, but have you been respectful of theirs? You say they can't touch me, but then you get to touch me? I think you came here with your own agenda and completely ignored what this living situation was all about."

She doesn't immediately respond, of course. Her lower lip juts out and she hangs her head and her face puffs and drops of water peel off her eyes. Eventually, the words dribble out: "So what do you want me to do?"

"Nothing. But just know, if you stay, then I can't be affectionate with anyone. I can't hold anyone's hand, I can't kiss anyone, and I can't sleep with anyone." Man, monogamy was better than this.

In Muslim countries where polygamy is allowed, some advocates say that it keeps husbands from having affairs. I used to think that was just sophistry, but I now know it to be true. Because any normal person with three or four wives is going to be too busy and emotionally exhausted even to consider adding another woman to the mix.

Anne stares at me sympathetically. Then she says, "This can be a growing experience, and we can become wise from these experiences."

"Well, I've definitely learned a lot from it."

"I want you to know something," she continues. For the next few minutes, she shares her timeline. Her father abandoned the family for a gay lover; her mother went crazy afterward; her uncle was an alcoholic; her first boyfriend raped her. Then she concludes, "You hurt me more than you can comprehend."

"I didn't know all that." My guilt is flowering again. I can't believe I've been put on that list of horrible traumatizers. Though now I understand why she hides beneath all that unflattering clothing: It's not unlike the sexual anorexic from rehab hiding behind her weight. "I don't think I'm healthy for you. But maybe this had to happen so you could be in reality about who I am and not in a romantic fantasy anymore."

And then what does she do: Does she leave? Does she get over it? No. She puts her hand over mine and drops her head gently into my lap.

We've just gone through the entire love-avoidant/love-addict relationship cycle that Ingrid and I experienced. And I only met Anne a month ago. It's accelerated dysfunction for the information age.

Anne wanted her one true love; I wanted my poly partner. We both struck out. In the dance of infatuation, we see others not as they are, but as projections of who we want them to be. And we impose on them all the imaginary criteria we think will fill the void in our hearts. But in the end, this strategy leads only to suffering. It's not a relationship when the other person is completely left out of it.

"I'm sorry about the situation," she says. "If you want me to stay, say it. Please be sure you're in my heart whatever happens. Everybody can make mistakes. And just so you know, I forgive you."

The heart of a woman is a beautiful thing. I'm ashamed by my previous words and behavior. "That means a lot," I tell her. "Let's just go to sleep and take some alone time to process everything that happened tonight, and we'll talk more in the morning."

Anne doesn't respond. Instead, she just lies in my lap content, like Hercules. And I fall asleep on the toilet. Like the piece of shit I am.

37

At some indeterminate hour of the night, I stumble out of the bathroom and make my way to the couch. A dream still lingers in the fog of my brain: I was driving a new car, but I lost control and smashed into a wall.

I pull the sheet over myself and set the alarm on my phone for noon. I have a call to make to Hawaii. To Isis Aquarian. One of Father Yod's wives.

I wake up shivering and wash my face with warm water, then call Isis and tell her I'm a fan. I'm not sure what that means, but she seems happy to hear it. So I let her know how I got her phone number (by contacting the editor of the book on Father Yod) and explain my current situation.

"It's not easy," she agrees. "After Father died and the family dispersed, no one was able to make it work with multiple partners."

I press her for an hour with every question I can come up with about life with Father Yod and what made it work then. She tells me that Father Yod was previously in traditional marriages. He started a vegetarian restaurant and a commune called the Source with his fourth wife, and the group eventually grew to two hundred people living together. Soon after, he realized that the rules of his relationship had to change.

"He'd been giving hints, but Robin"—his actual wife—"kept getting dramatic and freaking out," Isis explains. "She started hanging on him all the time and following him around because she knew it was going to happen. And then one day he just announced he was going to have extra women. It was his journey and he was the boss. But he was a very benevolent boss."

It's odd—she describes him almost the exact same way Kamala Devi described herself, as a "benevolent" authoritarian. I feel for his legal wife, the love addict whose heart he had to break in order to live his poly dream. But at least he was honest with her. I imagine that most men would do something similar if they became a virtual god to a community of free-spirited women.

What made the ensuing group relationship successful, Isis explains, is that unlike my situation, the women had already been living together in the community, so they were connected and bonded with one another in advance.

In addition, many had come from ashrams, intentional communities, and hippie lifestyles where they were used to more communal relationships. So the wives all got along—except, of course, for his legal wife, who wasn't happy with any of this.

"Was there any kind of hierarchy among the wives?" I ask. "Was one of them his primary?

"No. We each had our own specific role: Makushla was his mother angel and took on a mother role. I had his back as his bulldog and the archivist saving his legacy. Others had the role of having his child. We all had our role and within that position, we were the primary."

Now for the most awkward question: "And, um, how did the sex part work? Was it all together or one at a time or . . . what?"

Isis tells me the wives never had sex with each other—only one-on-one with him.

She goes on to explain that he chose each of his wives because he believed he had karma from a previous lifetime with them to resolve. "Some of the women were sixteen, but they had past lifetime threads with him," Isis elaborates. Evidently the Achilles' heel of cult leaders is that they think they're above the law. It's disturbing how, as soon as they reach the pinnacle of their power, one of the first things so many choose to do is sleep with—and often control the development of—underage girls. Even one of Muhammad's wives was a preteen. "Of course every woman in the family wanted to be with him, but he coupled many of them with other people they had karma with. So other men had multiple wives also."

"And you never fought about who got the front seat in the car?"

"That never happened because we were living as spiritual beings, not in our animal energy."

Apparently Father Yod did exactly what Orpheus Black recommended to me—and what I didn't do with my quad. He instilled his partners with a strong sense of family and of the future. In Father Yod's case, it was the belief that they were following an earthly god and ushering in a new era of humanity—in which they and their children would be prophets of the coming Aquarian Age. As a result, few people wanted to leave this exalted sanctum. It also helped that they donated all their money and property when they came to live with him, so they were pretty much stuck.

As I continue talking with Isis, I understand that what it takes to enjoy being the fulcrum is a high degree of narcissism and an unwavering certainty that your needs and beliefs are more important and enlightened than those of the rest of your community—and quite possibly the world.

Much to my dismay, as this picture emerges, I see that Father Yod may be more a model of what to avoid than to emulate: He demanded everyone's worldly goods, rigorously controlled his followers, and put their lives and their children's lives in jeopardy by not allowing them to use medicine because of his spiritual beliefs.

And this, sadly, may be the norm. In fact, most of the communes known historically as sexually liberal were actually very strict on the matter. At Oneida, a nineteenth-century utopian community that considered monogamy a sin, a committee approved hookups to make sure people weren't coupling off, and men were forbidden from having orgasms during intercourse without authorization. Similarly, the Kerista commune in San Francisco, where terms like *compersion* and *polyfidelity* were invented in the seventies, was another group run by a narcissist with strict rules, which included forbidding members from masturbating or having group sex.

"When he flew off the cliff, he was done and ready to move on," Isis says, referring to the hang-gliding accident that killed Father Yod. "And he left us because we wouldn't let go of him. However, to this day, I've kept my thread with him. I'm still his woman. I haven't been with anyone else."

I'm astounded by her dedication: He died four decades ago. I wonder if she also fits the love addict template. And if ultimately Father Yod—whose pseudonym is clearly a magnet for abandoned women—felt so consumed by the pressure of being the fulcrum for so many people that he eliminated himself.

"Do you have any final words of advice for anyone doing something similar now?" I ask.

"It made sense in the time frame of the sixties and seventies, but now I think it's a foreign thing. If you brought a woman into that situation today, I don't think it would work. Good luck, sweetie."

So that's it: Just good luck attempting to pull off the impossible?

I hang up, and look for more case studies online. In Hebrew, the word for co-wives is *tzara*, which tellingly also translates as *rival*. And in ancient Egypt, second wives were called *esirtu*, which means *rival* as well. Even Muhammad's wives were jealous. Stories of them smashing dishes, conspiring against a favorite wife, and gossiping about one another abound.

And then there's the Mormon prophet Brigham Young, who, like Father Yod, opened up his monogamous marriage soon after he felt a religious calling, except that he took on an astonishing fifty-three additional spouses. And they were almost the death of him. At one point, he told his wives to leave if they weren't happy, proclaiming, "I will go into heaven alone rather than have [you all] scratching and fighting around me."

As I read more about history's great fulcrums, which differ greatly from what I fear was an immature fantasy, I hear Belle talking to Anne in the living room.

"Do you want to sleep with Neil?" Belle asks.

"Yes," Anne tenderly replies.

"If you don't let us have sex with him, then you can't have sex with him. It's not fair for you to want to keep him for yourself."

At least Belle and Anne are taking Pepper's advice and working things out among themselves. Still, it's weird to hear them negotiating and manipulating to sleep with me as though I were some kind of prize. Perhaps Isis is still faithful to Father Yod not just because of the depth of her love for him, but also because she's still trying to win, to prove that she's the best wife.

I wonder why, after I completely fucked her over last night, Anne would still want to sleep with me. Or maybe that *is* the reason: Being fucked over is what she's used to. As long as she, like Isis today, is in love with someone who can't reciprocate, she may always be sad but her heart will always be safe—because no one can ever truly get to it.

Perhaps what I need to do is accept rivalry as an expected part of any new group relationship, then learn how to best manage it. So before venturing into the zombie lair, I decide to call one last person: Orpheus Black. He's figured out how to make a group marriage work in the modern world. He'll know how to handle the competitiveness.

"It's actually just Indigo and me right now," he responds when I ask for advice.

"What happened to the rest of your wives?"

"We're separated." He speaks these two words as if they're a confession—of regret, vulnerability, failure. I can relate.

"What happened to family and the future?"

"Someone stabbed it in the back."

After some prodding, he tells me that one of their former lovers spread rumors about him and manipulated his wives against him. The venom rotted the group and harmony turned to drama, so he decided to let his two non-legal wives go.

Immediately afterward, as a result of the stress and strain, he woke up one morning with amnesia. Not only could he not remember a thing that had happened, but he couldn't even recognize his actual wife, Indigo. This lasted two weeks.

Though he tells me he plans to rebuild his family again, I feel vindicated that even Orpheus, with all his experience and confidence, couldn't keep three women together and stay sane. Clearly, being a fulcrum is not easy even for very experienced people.

38

When everyone's awake and dressed, we take our usual places in the living room for a much-needed house meeting. I have a lot of apologizing to do.

But before I can speak, Anne beats me to it. "I'd like to say something," she begins. "I made a mistake."

"What mistake is that?" I ask.

"I want to stay. I promise to share things." She glances at Belle, who nods her approval. "I'm willing to share you. Yes, I want to stay."

One thing about polyamory is that it's never dull or predictable. Belle's negotiation was evidently a success.

"You manipulated her!" Veronika cuts in, glaring at Belle. "It's not fair to do that to Anne just so we can sleep with Neil."

If you'd asked any of them a month ago what they'd do in this exact situation, every one probably would've said she'd leave and never speak to me again. Yet here they are, breaking every law of logic, self-respect, and common sense. And perhaps it's a dynamic I set up by Svengali-ing these smitten women into playing a role in my sick fantasy.

I look at the strength in Veronika's eyes, the desire in Belle's, and the hope in Anne's. And I feel, for the first time since we arrived, completely clearheaded. Since last night, I've written, rested, and talked to Isis and Orpheus. Now is the time to make a powerful decision.

Father Yod made things work by not asking for or needing anyone's permission to set the rules for the family. Same with Hugh Hefner. Same with Oneida and Kerista and Orpheus Black. Everyone was subservient to the mission and the word of the benevolent dictator in charge. If someone didn't like the rules, they were presumably free to leave. So all I have to do is lay down the law—and that's how things will be going forward.

But I'm not Father Yod. I'm not Hugh Hefner. I'm not even Orpheus Black. And after what I've learned this week, I don't think I'd ever want to be them. I'm done with my Father Yod fantasies. There's only one right thing to do.

"Here's what I think," I tell Anne. "You very well could just suck it up and share me. But you'd be harming your spirit if you did. That wouldn't be true to who you are."

She looks into my eyes imploringly. "I think I can handle it."

"You can handle the hurt and the pain? Is that what you're saying?"

"Yes. Some things are more important." She speaks quietly, her body rigid but quivering, as if about to collapse into the black hole of itself.

"I don't want you to be a martyr. You tried that last night and look what happened. It's time to do what's best for Anne. And if you were to ask me what I think is best for Anne, it would probably be best that she goes home."

"But I can change," she protests, steeling her nerves, summoning her power. "I can work on controlling my emotions."

"If you had a daughter and she was in this same situation, would you tell her to try to control her emotions or to trust them?"

She thinks about it for a moment, then says softly, without the bravado of earlier, "To trust her emotions."

"Then why don't you take your mother's advice? You're a healer, and you spend a lot of time healing other people, but maybe it's time to start healing yourself."

I suddenly realize that those feelings of hatred I had for Anne the night before weren't actually about her at all. They were about my mother. And when Anne looks at me with those loving eyes, she's not Stalin trying to send me to an emotional gulag or a zombie trying to eat my brains. She just loves me. Whether rightly or wrongly, it doesn't matter. It's just love. That's it. Nothing to be afraid of.

The whole time I've been living with these three, I've seen love as a demand: "I need to talk to you," "Don't text when you're with me," "Tell her to order food for me," "Don't hold anyone else's hand," "It's not fair," "My turn to sit in the front seat."

I've seen love as a padded cell designed to take away my freedom. And that's because my "long-suffering" mother used love to exert control over me, which she enforced with guilt. In my relationship with Ingrid, I think as I sit illuminated by the beams of six expectant eyes, I interpreted her love as control and resisted it. First through cheating, and when that got shut down, through resentment, fantasizing, and emotional distancing. My whole life, I've been fighting against love for my freedom.

No wonder I've never been married, engaged, or even had a love that didn't wane after the initial infatuation period.

It's a depressing realization. I wonder why I'm just figuring it out now. Maybe I needed a situation this intense and overwhelming to force it to the surface.

I take a deep, Reid-like breath and look Anne in the eyes without resistance for the first time in days. And I apologize sincerely for my behavior. "I'd like to make amends for what happened yesterday," I tell her. "There's a process I recently went through called chair work. And it helps people get the bad things that happened to them out of their body and their psyche. I can sign you up for that, and help pay for it if you need me to. Because, whatever happened to you in the past, you should have professionals helping you treat it."

Gazing into her eyes without fear of my own annihilation, I notice a beautiful, loving, gentle soul looking back at me; a woman who's gone through hell and miraculously managed to keep her heart pure. And I feel bad for not seeing her as she is, but through my own distorted, reactionary lens. I should have behaved like this the whole time and seen the beauty in each of my partners instead of the flaws, empathized with their needs rather than feeling trapped by them.

And I most definitely should have done this with Ingrid instead of regressing every time she got too close.

"But don't you want me to stay so you can see if this type of relationship can work for you?" Anne asks. Now suddenly she gets what all this has been about. Apparently being understood leads to understanding.

"Honestly, my work is done. I'm sucked dry. I just don't have the constitution for a relationship like this. I don't think it would ever work for me with anybody."

I guess I've got my answer.

Now what do I do?

39

Excerpt from Anne's Journal

This week was my first time to the U.S. It was an adventure. Something new with much unknown. And for the first time, the unknown was not scary to me. My deep intuition was that it would bring me really important things.

I told Neil I wanted to be an experienced woman. But at the time, I had only a vague idea of how. I knew I wanted sex. And I was thinking about having new experiences, for instance being with another woman.

But when I arrived, I became afraid of being hurt and losing my self-esteem. And I didn't feel that breaking my boundaries would be a good idea. Will I be ready one day to break some of them? I don't know. I think I need time, and a reassuring and respectful context, to be able to disinhibit. Though I know if we had a normal relationship, it would have bored me and would not have been an effective way to evolve.

I could tell on the first day that there were many differences between us four. That created some misunderstanding. Seeing everybody touching, stroking, and whatever was weird to me. It felt like I'd landed on another planet. That was not the kind of relationship I imagined we would be having. Before I came, he told me there was something like that happening, but I didn't let my inner voice prepare me.

During our time together, we had to make choices. We hesitated and we didn't always know what was best for us. A great lesson this taught me was that if we place ourselves in our heart to make choices in new situations, we can't make any mistakes.

I think that one of the most important things I became aware of through this experience is what it means to be a woman.

Neil told me to listen to my heart and inner feelings. He had an insightful remark that was like: "If it was your daughter, what would you tell her to do? Behave with yourself as if you were your own mother."

I had a dream five years ago in which my boyfriend at the time gave me half of a moon. After that, I left him to go to a room where a mature man with a shaved head and a dark beard was waiting on a big red bed.

I met him and he gave me the second half of the moon. I now know what that dream means. The moon symbolizes the woman and the mother. And now I can say that the man on the bed was Neil, even if I didn't know him at that time.

So thanks to this experience and to Neil's advice, I finally understand and feel what being a woman is: to become my own mother.

I definitely feel the change. Since I now consider myself my own mother, I don't need to mother others anymore. I can now be in a relationship without trying to help someone. They can father themselves.

We laughed a lot in the last hours we spent together. I offered to do acupuncture on everyone, and I was glad to see that it comforted all of us and that we were finally at peace together.

When he dropped me off at the airport, Neil told me that he was worried we had wasted our time. And I answered that there was no wasted time but just time. And time is useful to experience and grow. This unusual relationship was a great thing to confront my issues, to know myself better, and to help me change. I can truly say it brought me a lot more than a normal one would have.

40

Formerly proud and erect, it has gone limp. Where once it was bursting with vitality, it now looks brown and lifeless.

The Survivor is not surviving very well in my care. I can't let Ingrid's indestructible plant die. I have to at least be able to take care of something successfully. As soon as I return home from San Francisco and see the neglected state it's in, I water it, move it into direct sunlight, and rush out to buy vitamin-enriched soil for it.

While I'm out, I check in with some of the guys from rehab. After reaching his eighteenth month of involuntary celibacy, Adam decided to contact Lorraine for additional counseling. Charles is separated and living in a motel. And Calvin tells me that things have been a disaster since he brought Mariana and his son to L.A. She's been depressed and misses Brazil, and he's been angry because he feels trapped and forced into the relationship by the child.

"Mariana wants to go back to Brazil, and I haven't been trying to discourage her," he confesses. "But I'm going to miss Flavio. Looking into the innocent eyes of your own child in the morning and seeing a big smile spread across his face is sublime! I hope you get to experience it one day."

"I hope so too," I tell him. "I don't think I've ever felt that kind of joy."

While Calvin's predicament was foreseeable, Troy's current situation no one saw coming. Not only did he start seeing his affair partner again, but she wants him to be monogamous with her.

"She wants you to break up with your wife?" I ask Troy to clarify.

"No, she knows I can't do that. She just doesn't want me having sex with my wife."

"That's insane. What did you tell her?"

"Well, I said no at first. Then she went on a date with some guy and it drove me crazy, so I gave in."

Fear of loss: It has motivated many weak people to make commitments they shouldn't have. "So you stopped sleeping with your wife?"

"If I was Adam, that would be easy to do." He chuckles cruelly. "But my wife and I have a decent sex life."

I struggle to get my head around what he's saying. "So let me see if I understand this. You're cheating on your wife with your affair partner. And now you're *also* cheating on your affair partner with your wife?"

"Welcome to my life."

That evening, I meet my friend Melanie for dinner. I've known her longer than anyone I've dated. She's been with me through it all, giving me the hard truth after every breakup—just as I've given her advice every time a man she likes gets flaky the moment a relationship appears on the horizon of their casual dating.

"Neil," she exclaims when I tell her about San Francisco. "You can't go on like this. Don't you want to get married and have children?"

"Yes, more than anything. I just don't want to end up like my parents. I want to find someone who adds to my life rather than limits it."

"I know someone like that," she says, brushing hair out of her face. She has a long black mane that cascades halfway down a frame so thin that an enthusiastic hug could snap it in two.

"Who?" I ask excitedly, hoping she knows someone perfect to set me up with.

And she answers with the one word I'm not ready to hear: "Ingrid."

I sigh and mutter something that sounds like "I know."

"She was so perfect for you, Neil." Melanie draws out the end of the sentence like a little girl whining for a puppy. "She's the only girlfriend of yours I met who loved you for you. I'm sure if you just showed her you could commit, she'd come back."

"That's the problem. We have two very different definitions of commitment."

I think about San Francisco, and wonder what my relationship with Ingrid would be like if I could hold onto the lessons I learned about love. If there's anyone in the world I'd want to have a child with, it's Ingrid. I flash back to watching the affection and tenderness she showed her shelter dog, Hercules—and think about how huge her heart is, how playful her spirit is, how great a mother she'd be. If only she'd been willing to budge just a little bit on the monogamy issue.

Or maybe Ingrid was right to stand her ground. Because right now, I feel like her prediction has come true: I am dying in the wild.

"You're sending the universe mixed messages," Melanie lectures. "You keep saying you want a family, but you're surrounding yourself with people you could never have one with. Can't you just let go of the whole nonmonogamy thing? For Ingrid."

Letting go would make my life so much easier. Maybe this whole thing was a bad idea. "Part of me really wants to. But if I tried to go back to Ingrid now and it actually worked out, I'd always wonder *what if*?"

What if I quit too soon, just before finding someone as open as Nicole or Sage? *What if* I found a nonmonogamous version of Ingrid? *What if* there's a stone I left unturned and it's the right stone? And most terrifying of all, *what if* I return out of fear and failure but not love and commitment?

What if, what if, what if . . . It's the ambivalent's mating call.

"You're going to lose her, Neil. A girl like that doesn't stay single for long."

Melanie excuses herself to go to the bathroom. When she returns a few minutes later, she looks distraught. "You're too late," she says, holding up her phone. "I just checked Ingrid's profile."

"What do you mean?" A cold sweat prickles through my skin.

"I hate to say it, but it looks like she has a boyfriend now."

She shows me a picture of a shirtless guy holding Hercules. He's a cross between James Dean and Thor, with hard ripples in places I never knew could grow muscles. In comparison to him, I look as appealing as the Hunchback of Notre-Dame. That's not being self-deprecating; it's just a fact.

Suddenly I feel profoundly alone. Not until this moment do I realize that I'd been assuming—so vainly, selfishly, and irrationally—that Ingrid was waiting for me or there would be some way to return to the relationship if things didn't work out. Whoever this superstud is, I hope that he's worthy of her heart, that he doesn't have doubts, that his skin doesn't crawl when she dotes on him, that he doesn't text random women or jerk off to PornHub at the slightest provocation, and that he loves Hercules instead of seeing him as a symbol of the hypocrisy of monogamy. I'm sure Ingrid looks back on our relationship as one long mistake.

I look at Melanie sitting across from me, trying to figure out what to say to make me feel better. And I fight back the sadness, the fear, the emptiness.

It wasn't the right relationship for me, I console myself. It was unhealthy. Love addict and love avoidant. Textbook dysfunction.

"Well, I guess that settles it, then," I tell Melanie with a smile as convincing as my mom's. "There's no going back."

It doesn't matter what it takes or what I have to do anymore. I'm going to find a relationship style that works for me, even if it kills me.

And, as it turns out, it almost does.

STAGE IV

▪ What Is My Species? ▪

*L*ISTEN, FRIEND," SAID ONE OF THEM
TO THE DUCKLING, ". . . NOT FAR FROM HERE
IS ANOTHER MOOR, IN WHICH THERE ARE
SOME PRETTY WILD GEESE, ALL UNMARRIED.
IT IS A CHANCE FOR YOU TO GET A WIFE;
YOU MAY BE LUCKY, UGLY AS YOU ARE."

—HANS CHRISTIAN ANDERSEN
The Ugly Duckling

A wise polyamorist once told him,
"Date your own species, Neil!"

But what is my species? he wondered.

He was alone in life.
He had just returned from San Francisco,
where he had discovered that being a
fulcrum was not his species.
But he had learned a lot.
And he had an idea.

He visited the most successful commune in the country.
And he stayed there a week, talking to everyone.
Some members had been there for over forty years.

"Our philosophy is that life is
perfect and I am perfect," said Ilana.

"When you live here, you don't ever
have to do anything you don't want
to do," said Colin.

They called their community
"an experiment in pleasurable group living."

And the living seemed pleasurable there.

So he wrote his own manifesto on group relationships.

And he moved into the tree house
that he had looked at with Rick a long time ago.

Nicole and James joined him there.

His friends Lawrence and Leah
from the polyamory meet-up moved in.

So did his friend Violet, her new
lover Angela, and three others.

Everyone was in some type of open relationship.

In the mornings, they did yoga and tai chi.

In the afternoons, they met with teachers to learn
intimacy, sensuality, and a powerful method of relating
to one another called nonviolent communication.

And in the evenings, they played.

Life was pleasurable.

But Pepper warned him:
"Group relationships of more than four
people rarely work. You have an
exploding complexity problem."

Pepper was right.

One afternoon, a housemate's jealous boyfriend had a psychotic break with reality and almost killed him with an ax.

Unfortunately, his assailant had missed the point of the nonviolent communication lessons.

When it was all over, he looked at what he had made.

And it was better than the San Francisco house.

But even with the assailant and his girlfriend gone, living in the commune was a full-time job.

It took a lot of work, communication, organization, and patience.

This was not his species.

He was alone again. But he had an idea.

"I should step into a relationship that already exists rather than trying to create my own," he said. "This way, I don't have to worry about making it work. It will already be working."

He suggested that Violet and her lover Angela stay with him for a little longer.

They did everything and went everywhere together.

And then they went to bed together.

They became a poly triad.

And it was nice because he wasn't the fulcrum: Violet was.

So there was no competition.

Pepper called it a "threesome vacation" and said it would never work in the long run.

Pepper was right.

Angela was just enjoying herself
between serious relationships.

And Violet, well, she had
a small drinking problem.

When it was all over, he looked
at what he had made.

And it was better than the commune.

But it was more fun than it was real.

This was not his species.

He was alone again.
But he had an idea.

He went to dinner with a successful bachelor friend.

"Think of the woman you've had the wildest sex with," his friend said.

He did.

"Now think about the woman you've had the best relationship with," his friend said.

He did.

"They're not the same person, am I right?" his friend said.

His friend was right.

"Your problem is that you still think of love and sex as things that have to go together," his friend said. "You need to separate them. Start a family with a good platonic friend who's your own age and keep sleeping with whoever you want."

His friend had an interesting point.

"It's like having a divorce but without the marriage," his friend concluded.

He asked his ladyfriends if they were interested.
He visited websites for women seeking sperm donors.
And he soon found someone special.

"I am a healthy, happy, successful professional
woman who recently woke up one day and yelled,
'I forgot to have children!'" she wrote to him.
"Now I find myself with the very real possibility
that I might not find my soulmate, yet refusing to
give up on the great gift of motherhood."

He met her for dinner.

"I'm an engineer, but I don't want my child to be all left brain," she said. "And you're a writer and right brain, so this is perfect."

"You have brown eyes," she continued. "So do I. I'd prefer blue eyes, but it's not a dealbreaker."

She went through nearly every aspect of his appearance and personality, remarking on which ones she wanted the baby to have and which ones she didn't.

This is a little weird, he thought.

But Pepper said that co-parenting arrangements can be very successful, and that this relationship could actually work.

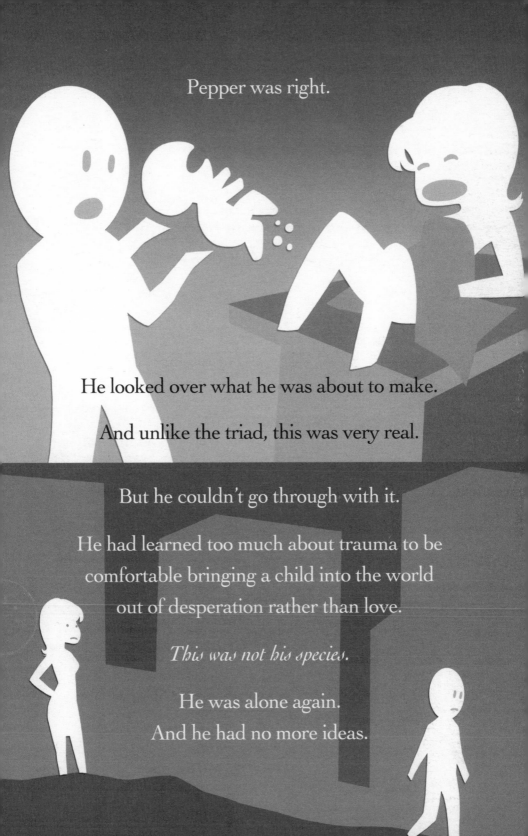

Pepper was right.

He looked over what he was about to make.

And unlike the triad, this was very real.

But he couldn't go through with it.

He had learned too much about trauma to be
comfortable bringing a child into the world
out of desperation rather than love.

This was not his species.

He was alone again.
And he had no more ideas.

He looked over the last few months of his life.

He had taken three women he barely knew and tried to start a harem with them.

He had taken nine random people, put them in a house, encouraged them to be together at all times, and expected them to get along perfectly.

He had taken a functional alcoholic and her love-addicted friend, and expected them to form a stable triad.

And he had taken a woman who was trying to customize a child as if she were ordering it from a build-a-burger restaurant, and expected her to be a great mother.

That's when he saw that he hadn't been in any real relationships since leaving Ingrid. He'd just been creating controlled experiments. And they never had a chance of working.

Why was he in such a hurry? Perhaps his biological alarm clock was ringing — so loudly, it was drowning out his common sense.

"You can't force a relationship to happen,"
he finally understood. "You just have to make a
space in your heart for one, then let go of
all expectations, agendas, and control."

And that's when he found his species....

MALIBU, CA

HOW ARE THINGS GOING?

NOT LIKE I PLANNED.

THIS WAS SUPPOSED TO BE A PERIOD OF FUN AND LIVING DECADENTLY, NOT A PERIOD OF PAIN. I THINK THE THING THAT YOU WANT TO GET THROUGH SEX YOU'RE NOT GETTING.

EVERYTHING WAS FUN WHEN I WAS JUST HAVING SEX. IT'S WHEN I STARTED TRYING TO HAVE RELATIONSHIPS THAT THINGS GOT BAD.

SO ARE YOU FINDING THAT THESE RELATIONSHIPS AREN'T ANY BETTER THAN MONOGAMOUS ONES, OR DO YOU JUST THINK YOU CHOSE THE WRONG ONES?

THE TRUTH IS THAT I HAVEN'T BEEN GOING ABOUT THIS RIGHT.

AND WHY IS THAT?

I'VE JUST BEEN COLLECTING PEOPLE WHO ARE OPEN TO THESE IDEAS, GETTING THEM TOGETHER, AND STRUGGLING TO MAKE IT WORK. AND IT TURNS INTO A BAD REALITY SHOW EVERY TIME.

IT ALWAYS DOES. IF YOU KEEP CHASING AFTER FANTASIES, YOU'RE GOING TO SPEND THE REST OF YOUR LIFE HAVING SHORT-TERM SEX WITH MULTIPLE DAMAGED PEOPLE AND PASSING ON THE IDEA OF ANY DEEP INTIMATE CONNECTION OR FAMILY.

YOU SEEM TO HAVE THE THESIS THAT ONLY A DAMAGED WOMAN WOULD WANT CASUAL SEX OR AN OPEN RELATIONSHIP. BUT THE WORLD IS CHANGING.

ALL I'M GOING OFF OF IS WHAT YOU'VE BEEN TELLING ME. NOTHING IS RIGHT OR WRONG. YOU'RE JUST NOT ANY HAPPIER.

BUT I'M GETTING CLOSER. I'VE SEEN SO MANY OPTIONS AND SO MANY PEOPLE MAKING THESE LIFESTYLES WORK FOR THEM. AND I'M FINALLY GETTING MY FOOTING IN THIS WORLD.

STAGE V
▪ Adventure ▪

ON OUR LIFE TOGETHER I WANT
YOU TO UNDERSTAND I SHALL NOT HOLD
YOU TO ANY MEDIEVAL CODE OF
FAITHFULNESS TO ME NOR SHALL I CONSIDER
MYSELF BOUND TO YOU SIMILARLY . . .
FOR I CANNOT GUARANTEE TO ENDURE
AT ALL TIMES THE CONFINEMENT OF EVEN
AN ATTRACTIVE CAGE.

—AMELIA EARHART
letter to her fiancé

41

This is how it goes.

We wake up together. Sometimes there's another woman under the covers with us; sometimes there isn't.

She cooks breakfast, I make smoothies, and we all feast in bed.

Once we're alone, she and I make love again. It is better, stronger, and more connected than it was with our play partner there. Multiples are for adventure, but one-on-one is for connection.

We shower—sometimes together, sometimes not.

I spend the day writing. She goes to trapeze school or acting class or works on her online business. There's always something she's excited about doing. From one week to another, it's not usually the same thing. Her life passion is simply passion.

When the sun sets, we head to dinner. She drives; I deejay. Some nights, we have dinner for two. Other nights, we meet friends. Those friends usually include a few women we've met together.

If we're in the mood for an adventure, we adjourn to a bar or club. Afterward, we bring as many women back to the tree house as we can. When clothes start coming off, whoever is not into it leaves. Oddly, they usually apologize for not participating as they depart, as if it's a moral failing of theirs, and they promise to be more fun next time. Sometimes they return; sometimes they don't. If we choose to have a quiet night after dinner instead, we return home, we watch a movie, we fuck, and we talk about the future. Not always in that order.

She's so quickly become a part of my life that sometimes it feels like a dream. Everything I enjoy—sex, music, surfing, reading, writing, learning, traveling—she now enjoys with me. And everything I don't enjoy—cooking, driving in L.A. traffic, transcribing my *Rolling Stone* interviews—she's started doing for me. Sometimes she seems too perfect, as if she's been spawned by some sort of nonmonogamous *Weird Science*-type experiment.

I'm fairly certain she had a life before we met. But I can't seem to remember what it was. I can barely remember what mine was. She hasn't been back to her home in a month. It may not even exist anymore. I recall asking Lorraine in rehab what was wrong with a single man enjoying his intensity, but I never imagined that two people could be in the same box enjoying that intensity together:

"You know," I tell her one night, "I've spent months trying to figure out what kind of relationship is natural to me. Whether it's monogamy or polyamory or a group relationship or whatever. But I think I realized what I like."

"This?" she replies joyfully. "An adventure relationship! I think that's what I was looking for when we first met. Not defining it as monogamy or polyamory or swinging, but just having fun together without having to be part of some stupid social scene."

I appear to have found my species, not to mention the heart connection I told Rick about.

And so one of my first dates in this world becomes my last: Sage from Bliss.

42

It began while I was in the triad. Sage found my email address online, contacted me to say she'd be in Los Angeles, and left me her phone number.

Of all the women I'd met since breaking up with Ingrid, she was the only one who shared most of my values, who I regretted blowing it with, and who, though admittedly it may have had something to do with the ecstasy, I could imagine a long future with.

I met Sage for dinner a few weeks later. "What happened at Bliss?" I immediately asked. "I thought you were miserable."

"I thought you were. I kept thinking I was ruining the vibe because I wasn't as high as you guys. You were all having fun, and I just kept getting more tired and irritable."

It was a lesson in projection. We hadn't truly seen each other that night—just reflections of the stories we were telling ourselves.

It's hard to recall what else we discussed as we ate, because the hours flew by breathlessly. Not only could we not stop talking, we couldn't stop looking, laughing, lusting. With her metallic red hair, her charismatic self-assurance, and her I-just-drank-five-energy-drinks-but-I-only-have-eyes-for-you personality, she sparked like a human Tesla coil.

That first date ended in a foursome with my old friend and commune-mate Leah and a heavily tattooed ex-girlfriend of Sage's named Winter. I watched as Sage attacked Winter—eating her out, fingering her, spanking her, then flipping her over and fingering her from behind—and I thought, "I've met my match."

Soon, Sage, Leah, and Winter started going down on me—passing it, fighting over it, sharing it, talking dirty. When Winter artfully wrapped her necklace around it, playing with the tension, I couldn't hold out anymore. As they licked me and each other clean, I thought, This is the greatest experience of my life. All that time and money wasted on sex addiction therapy, all that drama and misery in San Francisco, even the attempted murder at the love commune—every disaster, misstep, and tragedy—it was all worth it for these few minutes.

I often reflect on Rick's warning that on their deathbeds, people always think about love and family. But I believe I will also be thinking about this moment. We are sexual beings; it was my sexual zenith.

I'd like to say that there was some negative outcome or consequence, that this was the nadir of my addiction, that it was fundamentally flawed because there was no true intimacy and we didn't wait seventeen dates before touching. But it wasn't. There were no negative consequences.

Or so I thought: People are such good liars, they even fool themselves sometimes.

Just before sunrise, as Sage and I made love once again, Leah and Winter slipped out to leave us alone. A few hours later, Lawrence texted, "Sounds like a great time last night. I'm very happy you and Leah finally had a chance to connect."

I thought carefully of the right response that would show appreciation without being either awkward or crude, so I wrote: "It was really a great experience on a number of levels, including that it was part of a good friendship with both of you."

Evidently it was the right answer, because he responded: "That's exactly what I was thinking. Poignant. I really appreciate our friendship."

He is the definition of compersion.

Of all my sexual experiences since Ingrid, this was the only one that was wholly enjoyable—before, during, and after. Perhaps that's because, outside of an irrepressible hope that Sage would somehow still be interested in me, I had no relationship agenda. In fact, it was Sage who instigated the foursome that night.

In the weeks that follow, my closets and drawers fill with Sage's clothes and her room in Brooklyn empties. There was a missing piece in my life—for romance, for passion, for companionship, for understanding, for connection, for freedom within a partnership—and Sage somehow senses it and molds herself right into that shape. Even needs I didn't know I had or would enjoy, she begins filling.

Meanwhile, our adventures pile up. We do things I haven't even seen in porn clips, things that made me want to do books with rock bands just so I could live vicariously through them, things I didn't know were physically or geometrically possible.

I never would have imagined that my sex life would become better, wilder, and more varied in a relationship than it was at the peak of my singledom. Finally, after everyone said it was impossible, I'm having my cake and eating it too.

Even Pepper gives the relationship a positive prognosis: "It's more common and it's sustainable because everything you're doing with other people is short-term and transient."

Yet most incredibly of all, the adventures are only a supplement to what appears to be a growing bond between Sage and me. In fact, perhaps the least healthy part of the relationship isn't the sex, but the fact that we're never apart. For the first time since breaking up with Ingrid, it feels legitimately possible to live happily and nonmonogamously ever after.

43

However, as we hit the three-month mark—that inevitable point when relationships begin to get real—I notice a change in Sage's behavior. It's so subtle at first, it wouldn't hold up in a court of law as an actual change. But I see it in the way she looks at me. It seems not loving anymore, but like someone trying to play the part of loving.

At first, I wonder if it's just in my imagination, stemming from a sense of unworthiness or the love avoidant in me trying to sabotage the relationship.

But then one day, when we return from a trip to New York, she walks into the house and opens the refrigerator. Something has gone putrid and is rotting. As she smells it, fire truck and ambulance sirens ring shrilly from the street outside. She screams. It comes out of nowhere—a room-shaking, from-the-soul shriek. It's not directed at the sirens, the refrigerator, me, or anything specific, but at the universe. Her voice drowns out the noise, the smell, my thoughts.

"What's wrong?" I ask as she sits on the couch afterward, sobbing.

She wipes her nose. She looks up at me with those loving but not loving eyes. She says, "I've been reading my diary—and I miss me."

"What do you mean?"

"I don't know exactly. I guess sometimes I miss my wild days, when I was single and could just do whatever I wanted."

Only too late do I realize why things have felt off lately. She cooks, she drives, she transcribes my interviews, she brings in a constant parade of women. I have my freedom—a caked-out relationship completely on my terms and on my turf—and what does she really have? Just me.

She's been so busy taking care of my needs, she's completely neglected hers. In fact, I don't even know what her needs are. I thought we were being wild, but I guess that to her, I was just being predictable, male, and selfish, and taking her for granted.

So I tell Sage what I wish Ingrid had said to me: "Why don't you be free then? We should both be able to do whatever we want. Why should the fact that we're dating keep you from that?"

And that's how our relationship becomes a truly open one.

It will lead to more pain than I could possibly imagine.

STAGE VI
▪ Open ▪

Yoda: The fear of loss is a path
to the dark side.... Attachment leads
to jealousy. The shadow of greed, that is.

Anakin Skywalker: What must I do, Master Yoda?

Yoda: Train yourself to let go of everything
you fear to lose.

—STAR WARS EPISODE III: REVENGE OF THE SITH
directed by George Lucas

44

I have done it all—harems, communes, swinging, pujas, moresomes. And yet I haven't.

Since leaving the cage of monogamy, I've searched for sexual freedom—and, on a few occasions, perhaps even found it. Yet not once have I given my partner comparable freedom. Though I haven't kept anyone shackled to me by rules, promises, and fears, the situation never arose on its own. And, on some level, I've been grateful for that.

But reality has caught up with me and delivered the news that freedom is not just for parties of one. You can have your cake and you can eat it, but one day you're going to have to share it, too.

Sage and I are at a fancy tapas restaurant in Los Angeles with my former commune-mates Lawrence and Leah as well as three of Sage's friends from her weekly acting class. The hostess leads us to a large circular table—the kind Corey Feldman would put in a hotel room. I sit next to Leah and Lawrence; two guys from Sage's class flank my other side.

Sage arrives at the table last, humming happily to herself. She's wearing white shorts and a tight black baby tee with sleeves that stop just below her shoulders. She doesn't just walk to the table, she swaggers.

She looks for a seat beside me and seems disappointed when she doesn't find one. So instead she sits across from me, next to the third person from her class. He's over six feet tall, with wavy black hair and the whitest teeth I've ever seen. He introduces himself as Donald.

I've never met anyone named Donald before, most likely because any reasonable person would shorten it to Don unless he was a small-town theater snob determined to move to Hollywood to make it as an actor. This thought forms in my mind, with all its incipient hostility, before I can stop it. And this is probably because as soon as he's finished introducing himself to me, Donald's arm is on the back of Sage's chair and they're engaged in deep conversation.

I try to see my judgment for what it is—jealousy, insecurity, envy—and let it go. Sage has seen at least twenty different women with their tongues in my mouth since we started dating, so the least I can do is let her enjoy Donald's very sincere attention.

"So what made you decide to be in an open relationship?" I ask Lawrence and Leah, hoping to get some tips and stay distracted.

"I'd been in a monogamous marriage before and it didn't really work for me," Lawrence replies. "The whole time we were together, I was faithful. But I felt physical pain in my body from not having all that juice and excitement and connection in my life. When I came out of that, I decided I wouldn't ever do that again."

"I remember you were really upfront from day one that you were non-monogamous," Leah says. "There was no moment where I thought, Maybe I can persuade him to be monogamous with me. You made it clear: It's either this or we can't see each other. And I felt enough for you that I decided to give it a try."

From the corner of my eye, I see Donald's arm. It's no longer on the back of Sage's chair. It's now resting on her shoulder.

"Do you ever feel jealous with Lawrence?" I ask Leah.

"I wouldn't describe it as being jealous, but definitely some insecurity and paranoia." A waiter reaches over the table to set our food down, scoping out Sage in the process. Maybe he'll get her number later. Suddenly everyone's my rival. "But at one point something clicked inside me, and I started seeing Lawrence as a genuine person who has my best interests in mind and I realized that most of the insecurity came from my own childhood fear of being abandoned."

So maybe I'm feeling jealousy because I'm not secure in the relationship right now. I'm worried that Sage opened it up because I wasn't enough, because she was bored by the things that I've been enjoying, or, even worse, because she was so attracted to Donald.

It's been a week since that decision, and neither of us has been with anyone else. All we've done is discuss our values around being open. I told her that honesty is important to me and we need to always share our reality with each other. She told me that respect is important to her and she needs to always be put first. So we decided to build our open relationship on a foundation of honesty, freedom, and respect. It's exactly what I've always wanted. And what I like most about it is that, as Pepper advised, there are no rules, just intents.

As I watch her with Donald, though, I become painfully aware of the positive side of rules: They provide clear, fixed boundaries that keep us feeling safe.

"Did you like the jicama-wrapped guacamole?" I ask Sage across the table, trying to force a connection. But she doesn't hear me. It may be because her other two friends from acting class are engaged in a loud, silly improv game with each other. So I repeat the question, but to no avail. Now I feel ignored. Something I can't control is going on with my ego.

I try to focus on what Lawrence is saying: "If she's out and says she's met a guy and wants to explore it, I say, 'You're an adult. You don't need my permission.' The frame we have is that we're both adults and we trust each other's judgment, otherwise we wouldn't be together."

I suppose I just need to trust Sage's judgment. But what if she judges him as more compatible with her than I am? Do I trust that? I guess I'd have to.

"Okay," I ask Lawrence, "so if I'm feeling jealousy right now, what do I do?"

In my imagination, I never thought I'd be upset if Sage wanted to spend the night with another guy, as long as I knew about it. But in reality, it's a completely different experience. And this is just a man with his arm around her.

Suddenly, I have a little more empathy for the guy in the commune who tried to murder me.

"If you're feeling insecurity or jealousy, that's for you to manage," Lawrence answers. "It's not her job to manage your discomfort—unless she's doing something that's disrespectful or hurtful. One tool I've used is to understand that even if Leah deeply loves another person, it can only be additive to our relationship."

"In what way?"

"Think of it like this: You have a love muscle, and if you work it out more, it increases your capacity to love. And you can bring that energy and quality back to your relationship. The alternative to that would be my marriage, where I shut down my capacity to love and feel and have sex in order to stay monogamous."

Maybe I just have to eliminate my scarcity mentality about love, which is telling me right now that Sage has only so much to give and could run out. Lawrence's point of view makes much more sense. Perhaps on some level, the demand for exclusive love is an immature demand, the desire of the needy child who hungered to be the sole object of its parents' attention, affection, and care.

"So," I confirm with Lawrence, "if she's happy, it's not like she's going to go home and be sad because she got all the happiness out of her system?"

"Right. After being in the same situation fifty or a hundred times, pretty soon you won't be so scared or overwhelmed. You'll recognize the sensation as something that's going to pass. In my worst moments, I think of tying myself to the mast so I don't get sucked in by the sirens of jealousy and dashed against the rocks. There's nothing good that comes of jealousy. If someone's going to leave you, they're going to do it whether or not you're jealous. In fact, they're much more likely to do it if you are jealous."

It makes a lot of sense, so I try to lash myself to the mast and stay focused on Lawrence and Leah. When dessert comes, however, I can't contain myself any longer. I look over at Sage and squeak, "How do you like the flan?" And she completely ignores me again, like I'm invisible or more likely not speaking loudly enough. Donald's leaning in so close, their faces are almost touching.

"What do you do if Leah sleeps with a guy who you think is a douche-bag?" I ask Lawrence.

"If he's a douchebag, either there's something else she's getting from him or it's for her to figure out. I don't have to fuck him, so it's not my problem."

I imagine walking on the beach alone tomorrow morning while Sage is in bed with Donald and two women she's brought home for them to share. A queasy feeling spreads through my chest, knees, fingers, toes, eyeballs. I thought I'd learned and been through enough by this point to control myself better. But this is actually the first time I've had to walk the path of uncomfortable jealousy that Shama Helena told me about—and that the women in the San Francisco house went through with me.

When we finally get up to leave, I dash to Sage and ask her, "Did you have a good dinner?"

"Yeah, it was great." She smiles.

"I just want to make sure you were comfortable with Donald."

I'm hoping she'll tell me that she was uncomfortable and just being polite. But she doesn't. "Yeah, I enjoyed talking to him. We've never really had the chance to connect in class."

"Okay, good." Not good.

As we reach the door, she stops and stands with one knee bent forward, which has the enticing effect of creating a nearly perfect triangle between her legs. I walk out to see if she'll follow me, but she doesn't. She just waits near the exit for Donald, posing like a water-fountain nymph. And it hits me in the stomach like a baseball bat. It feels like she's choosing him over me.

I pause on the stairs between the restaurant and the valet stand to see if she'll stop on her way out to join me. And, as with every secret test a person gives someone they care about, she fails it. When Sage leaves with Donald, she walks right past me and they head to the valet together. And I could swear a smile flickers across his face.

I broke up with Ingrid precisely because I believed so much in romantic freedom, because I swore by the principle that one person should not own another's body, because I was so firmly convinced that possessiveness was a fungus rotting relationships. So why, I wonder as Sage mercifully enters the passenger seat of my car to return to the tree house, is it eating me up so much inside now that I've finally reached the promised land of my ideal free relationship?

45

Three days later, Sage tells me she's flying to Mexico for a long weekend with Donald and a friend of his with an equally unshortened name, Jonathan.

And there's nothing I can do to protest. I've already given her permission. In a moment of fear and paranoia, I wonder if the offer was on the table before we opened up the relationship.

But rather than dwell on doubts, I focus on the opportunity. This is my chance to truly let go of possession and jealousy, to allow someone I'm with to have fun even if it doesn't include me. Once again, it's exactly what I asked for and already it's not what I expected. Clearly, I was supposed to be the one going to Mexico with two actresses.

I once dated a woman who always said she wanted to marry someone rich. She ended up marrying a flat-broke musician. His name was Rich. The universe listens—and it gives you not just what you want, but what you deserve. It's the forager's karmic law.

"When's the trip?" I ask Sage. We are in the kitchen, where she's not just cooking breakfast, she's performing it, putting on a show whenever she reaches for a glass in a high kitchen cabinet or cracks open an egg. She's wearing black-framed glasses, and a blue hoodie that's been washed to maximum softness and unzipped to show the handles of her collarbone. I look at her with respect, lust, gratitude, fear. She's gotten inside me, to a deep place where my cultural, genetic, and developmental programming resides, and plugged herself in.

"Tomorrow." She quickly adds, "It's just for three days."

And now, I worry, she's about to unplug herself. I feel a pang in my heart. It's too soon. I don't have time to mentally prepare for this.

"Did they buy your ticket for you?" Jealousy is all over my voice like a coat of spray paint. I need to shut up.

"Yes, but I told them I won't sleep with them."

The words are meant to be reassuring. They have the opposite effect.

I remind myself that this is what I wanted. And her spontaneous, adventurous nature has always been one of my favorite things about her. It's part of the package of Sage.

The problem many people have is that the exact quality that originally attracted them to their partner becomes a threat once a serious relationship begins. After all, this quality was the open door through which the romance started, so now they want to close the door, lock it, and throw away the key before someone else tries to come in after them.

So rather than trying to crush Sage's spontaneity, I need to appreciate it. And besides, I've enjoyed a steady stream of new women, so why shouldn't she enjoy some fresh male attention? I need to be more Lawrence about this.

I ask her for the flight and hotel information, just in case something happens.

The airline, she informs me, is United. And the hotel is Temptation.

"Temptation? What kind of name for a hotel is that?"

"It's an adults-only hotel," she explains cavalierly. "They don't allow kids."

I try to be compersive about it. I also make a mental note to research the hotel online. Maybe it's just a place for vacationers who want peace and quiet without screaming children everywhere.

Unfortunately, the Temptation website is everything I hoped it wasn't. The banner on it proclaims: "Topless optional. Fun. Tempting. Sensual."

It sounds like a permanent swinger party.

I suppose even if she were at a Chuck E. Cheese's resort, I'd still be wracked with anxiety.

Immediately after I drop Sage off at the airport the following morning, something in me breaks. It is the safety harness tying her to me. I'm shocked and disappointed by my reaction. Yet I can't control it. I check the time on my phone anxiously, waiting for the exact moment she's supposed to land in Cancún. Then, seven minutes after that time, I text to make sure she's okay.

Minutes crawl by with no response. Maybe her plane was delayed. Or maybe she doesn't have an international service plan on her phone. Or maybe she's just not thinking about me.

To kill time, and keep the abyss of *maybe* from engulfing me, I stop by the post office and pick up my mail. In the stack, there's a letter from my mom marked PERSONAL. Our last conversation didn't go well: She said she was searching the house for Viagra and Cialis because she was convinced that my father was having an affair and there was "no way he could do it on his own." When I tried to end the conversation, she got upset and hung up on me. So I can only imagine what she must have sent in an attempt to get the last word in.

Then I return home and wait. Until, finally, two hours and twenty-three minutes after I texted Sage, she responds: "Thanks, I got here safely and am okay."

At least she's "okay." Okay is better than murdered and stuffed into a dumpster. It's also better than having the best time ever. But the message is so vague. I read it again. There's not one word of affection or emotion. Not even an emoticon. And nothing about the guys she's with. I feel so in-the-dark. So . . . disconnected.

At Lafayette Morehouse, the commune I visited to prepare for my group relationship in the tree house, I learned two useful terms. One was the concept of getting *strange ass*, which is when someone in a relationship has sex with a new person; often, this can add to the passion of the primary partnership. The other was *new relationship energy*, which refers to the obsession and fantasy that typically accompany a new affair—and often feel threatening to someone's primary partner.

So I tell myself that she's just going to get some strange ass, that any new relationship energy will eventually fade, and that this will make our connection more passionate in the long run.

It doesn't help.

So I turn to Lawrence again and take him out to dinner, hoping to stay preoccupied, get more support, and absorb some Lawrence-ness.

"I've been thinking about what's bothering me," I tell him. "It's not that I don't trust Sage. It's that I don't know what Donald's intentions are. Did he take her there as a friend or because he wants to sleep with her?" As I ask the question, the answer seems obvious. "I mean, what do you do if you think the guy isn't respecting you or he thinks he's stealing your girlfriend and somehow better than you?"

"If some dude thinks he got one over on me, it's his idiocy." He pauses, probably trying to empathize with someone as emotionally backward as me, then adds compassionately, "There's definitely a transition period where you have a lot of emotions to work through. So you may have some scary insecurities about whether the other guy is better for her than you or whether he's using you to connect with her. Just know that it's part of the adjustment process."

I suppose it makes sense: It takes time to get good at a new relationship skill. And this definitely is one. It goes counter to practically everything I've ever read, heard, thought about, and observed since childhood. Men aren't supposed to share women. They're supposed to fight and compete over them. Menelaus launched the Trojan War after his wife Helen ran off with Paris; Sir Lancelot's affair with King Arthur's wife led to war between the two; and in numerous tales, from *The Odyssey* to the Hindu epic *Ramayana,* men participate in contests to win marriage to a princess or queen. There can be only one victor, not two or three. It's a lot of programming to rewire.

But evidently not for Lawrence. "Leah's so great that I want other people to get the pleasure of experiencing what I get to with her," he explains. "And I'm so in love with her, I want her to do what makes her happy."

It's a beautiful and strangely romantic sentiment. As he speaks, I struggle to change my perspective, to find the pleasure in emotional pain that Corey Feldman discussed, to let my love not for myself but for Sage guide my feelings.

And that's when I realize, I don't actually want an open relationship. I just want a half-open relationship. It's completely unreasonable: I want to be with whomever I want while my partner is stuck with me. I'm clearly not as evolved as Lawrence, as emotionally stable as Pepper, as approval seeking as James, or as masochistic as Corey Feldman. Maybe I'm not looking for an alternative relationship, but just a selfish patriarchal one that's hard on her emotions but easy on mine.

I've learned nothing.

46

On her second night in Mexico, Sage calls briefly from a club to say she's drunk and she loves me. I absorb the world *love* greedily, like morphine for my pain.

"How's it going?" I ask nervously.

More than anything, I hope Sage will say she's having a horrible time and can't wait to come home. But of course she doesn't. "I'm amazed by how much fun I'm having," she yells into the phone. "And the guys are treating me like a princess. It's basically the opposite of our relationship. I'm the only girl, and I have two guys with me all the time taking care of me. They gave me a nickname." It's hard to hear her over the music. It sounds like her nickname is . . .

"Arch Low?" I ask.

"Marshmallow."

I try to imagine any type of sexual connotation that may have and draw a blank. It's better than Arch Low, which could conceivably be a position that involves two men.

We talk for a few more minutes, then she says she has to go. "This club is incredible," she shouts. "They brought me behind this screen and I danced in front of eight hundred people. Then this dwarf started pretending to hump me."

"That sounds awesome." I try to be positive. "I wish I were there." I don't say the rest of the sentence: ". . . so I could chuck that dwarf across the fucking club."

So this is what having an open relationship is like: lying on the couch in your underwear eating a peanut butter sandwich while your girlfriend is at a clothing-optional resort in Mexico getting pampered by male slaves and dry-humped by dwarfs. I've really been missing out.

I want to invite one of our play partners to spend the night, but that would be the definition of addictive behavior: using sex like a painkiller to avoid uncomfortable emotions. Besides, I'm so agitated, I don't think I'd be able to stay present with anyone.

I place my sandwich on the floor. I've lost my appetite. A pain shoots through my chest and I twist my body in agony. It's as if there's an itch in my heart that I can't scratch. I recall the conversation we had at Bliss, in which she said that she'd consider it "unmanly" if a guy she was dating allowed her to sleep with other men. In giving her freedom, have I lost her respect?

I was so sure this was the relationship my life was leading to. But freedom doesn't taste quite as sweet without security. Perhaps this is the flip side of love avoidance: I have a need to feel needed, even if I don't actually like it.

I look at the clock. It's only 8 P.M. I have Lorraine's cell phone number. I've never called her out of the blue for help. It seems vain to even consider it. She deals with addicts whose lives are at stake. I'm just an idiot who let his girlfriend go to Cancún with two studly actors.

"How have you been treating yourself?" Lorraine asks when she answers the phone. It's the perfect therapist greeting: one with a message. It is not about what's happening or what's new or how life's treating me. Those are things that can't necessarily be controlled. All you can control is your response to them, how you treat yourself.

"Not so well," I tell her, then explain the situation.

She listens without judgment. When I finish, she responds, simply, "I would recommend becoming a scientist of your own lows."

"What do you mean?"

"If you're in pain of the heart, enter into the pain and try to find its source rather than letting the pain drive you, or trying to escape from it or overcome it."

"Okay." The empathy in her voice and the logic of her words soothe me. I already feel better. "I think it was just a momentary panic. Thanks. I'll let you go."

"Remember that beneath the fear of enmeshment, the love avoidant is secretly terrified of abandonment."

That makes sense: Any mother who's enmeshing is also, on an emotional level, abandoning.

"Just remember," she adds soothingly, "that the only people who can be abandoned are children and dependent elders. If you're an adult, then no one can abandon you except you."

"Thank you. I won't bother you again."

"I'm happy to help. I'll be in L.A. next month. Let's plan on another dinner with your friend Rick."

"I'd like that a lot. Did I thank you already?"

"Yes, you did."

"Thank you."

"Good night."

I hang up, lie back on the couch, and try to dive into the feelings I'm experiencing. They're pretty easy to identify, because they're all shades of the same emotion: fear.

The first fear that comes up is that of not being enough—of thinking that Sage is having more fun without me, that these guys are taking better care of her, that she has more in common with them, that they look healthier in bathing suits, that they appreciate her more, that they're better in bed than me. If even half of this is true, then it makes my second fear almost a certainty: abandonment. Perhaps she's discovering that she's happier without me around or, even worse, she's barely thinking about me and the call was just the obligation of a love avoidant acting out of guilt. The third fear is that I'm not cut out for nonmonogamy, and I'm a hypocrite who wants to fuck other women but not allow my partner her own freedom.

Except I'm not a hypocrite. I actually agreed to this. It's just much harder than I thought it would be.

Behind all three fears is the deepest one of all: that Joan in rehab was right, that I have an intimacy disorder and this whole quest has been a symptom of it.

I imagine Sage returning to her hotel room drunk, lying on her stomach in the luxurious Temptation bed while her two manservants strip off their shirts and start massaging her. Slowly she becomes more aroused, raising her hips into a low arch as the men position themselves on either—

"Love and let go," I tell myself, the phrase appearing in my mind, the ghost of an old lesson from an old teacher. I take a few deep, calming breaths. "Love and let go."

Everything I've been complaining about as illogical in monogamous relationships is truly not logical. I was right about that. But what I didn't take into consideration is that it's emotional. My brain knows that whatever Sage is doing won't affect our relationship—and even if it does, then it means it's not the right relationship. But my heart won't listen. Suddenly, I understand why the women in San Francisco agreed to a group relationship in theory, but then seemed to want me to themselves as soon as they experienced it.

Before going to bed, I decide to open the letter my mom sent. Inside, there's just a single sheet of notebook paper. I recognize the handwritten numbers on it as my own. It's clearly a punishment I was given as a teenager,

though I have no memory of it. I just hold it in my hands and stare at it in astonishment, wondering what kind of person would want her son to think this about himself:

54	I am a dumb jerk	81	I am a dumb jerk
55	I am a dumb jerk	82	I am a dumb jerk
56	I am a dumb jerk	83	I am a dumb jerk
57	I am a dumb jerk	84	I am a dumb jerk
58	I am a dumb jerk	85	I am a dumb jerk
59	I am a dumb jerk	86	I am a dumb jerk
60	I am a dumb jerk	87	I am a dumb jerk
61	I am a dumb jerk	88	I am a dumb jerk
62	I am a dumb jerk	89	I am a dumb jerk
63	I am a dumb jerk	90	I am a dumb jerk
64	I am a dumb jerk	91	I am a dumb jerk
65	I am a dumb jerk	92	I am a dumb jerk
66	I am a dumb jerk	93	I am a dumb jerk
67	I am a dumbjerk	94	I am a dumb jerk
68	I am a dumb jerk	95	I am a dumb jerk
69	I am a dumb jerk	96	I am a dumb jerk
70	I am a dumb jerk	97	I am a dumb jerk
71	I am a dumb jerk	98	I am a dumb jerk
72	I am a dumb jerk	99	I a dumb jerk
73	I am a dumb jerk	100	I am a dumb jerk
74	I am a dumb jerk	101	I am a dumb jerk
75	I am a dumb jerk	102	I am a dumb jerk
76	I am a dumb jerk	103	I am a dumb jerk
77	I am a dumb jerk	104	I am a dumb jerk
78	I am a dumb jerk	105	I am a dumb jerk
79	I am a dumb jerk	106	I am a dumb jerk

It doesn't help much. But it explains a lot.

When I text Sage the next morning, she doesn't respond. Later, I go to lunch with a colleague who's helping me with the final edit of the Mexican drug war book, and I'm so tightly wound with stress that I'm barely able to pay attention to what he's saying. Instead, I just wait—listening, straining, praying for the reassuring ping of an incoming text from Sage.

As soon as the meal ends, I check my phone messages, just in case one somehow snuck past me. Nothing. And it feels like a javelin hurtling through my chest. She must really be having the time of her life. I commit the cardinal sin of texting her again.

Finally, close to midnight Cancún time, Sage texts that she's going to bed soon and will call me from the airport tomorrow.

It's a long night.

The following afternoon, she phones as promised during a layover. The guys, for some probably shady reason, are on another flight the next day. "I missed you," she says right away. The consoling words achieve their intended effect and the stress begins to drain out of me—that is, until she speaks the next words. "And don't worry, I didn't have sex with anyone or give anyone a blow job."

Her words are too specific. I instantly assume she gave everyone hand jobs.

"I had the best time," she continues. "They love being subservient to me. I think that's their fetish. They enjoy waiting on me and being told what to do and, like, sucking on my toes."

I'm instantly creeped out. But what matters, I tell myself, is not how I feel but how she feels. "Did you like it?"

"It's fun being pampered, and I am attracted to them."

Though the word *attracted* makes me wince, as she keeps talking, I actually do get a jolt of happiness for her. Her boyfriend before me was extremely domineering and controlling, so maybe getting fussed over by subservient men was healing for her. She's such a people pleaser that she deserves having people focused on pleasing her for a change.

Immediately following this thought, however, a cold front of negativity arrives: If she likes getting pampered by douchebag Donald and his friend at a cheesy Cancún resort, dancing while being admired by eight hundred people and one dwarf, and getting her toes sucked by submissive males— then maybe she isn't the right person for me.

Compersion is a struggle. It goes against every fiber of my being. I don't know if my resistance to it is cultural or evolutionary or both, but I work to overcome the emotional obstacles. I've done a lot of extreme and experimental things these past few months, and surely I'd be just as likely as her to go to a resort and enjoy getting pampered by two doting women. At least she's honest about it.

My ex-girlfriend Lisa once said that every woman wants the same thing in a relationship: to be adored. So Sage had a great weekend of adoration, and maybe this will help me remember never to take her for granted or stop showing my appreciation of her.

But then she says, "And I never realized how much we text each other."

"What do you mean?"

"They commented on it whenever I pulled out my phone."

And that's when the dam breaks, when the compersive adult becomes the wounded child. Before I can stop myself, I punch the wall and scream. I don't even understand why her words hurt so much until a few seconds afterward, when the emotion subsides and the shame kicks in. This whole weekend, when I was suffering because she wasn't texting, I assumed she was just busy having fun. But that wasn't why she didn't text: It's because some guys she was with didn't approve of it. And so the story I hear is that their feelings mattered more than mine, that not being judged by them was more important than reaching out to connect with me. And it pisses me off.

"Are you okay?" she asks.

"Yeah. You could always have snuck away to text me, you know."

"I know, but I was having such a nice time and in this fantasy bubble. And I was worried that talking to you would somehow ruin it or change things."

Another hammer blow. So she *purposely* disconnected. How can I still feel compersion when I'm now the enemy of her fun? I am the bubble burster.

What I want to say in response is, "If calling me is that much of a downer, then let's just stop seeing each other." But what I say instead is, "I'm glad you had fun. But we need to be better about communication. Other guys shouldn't be telling you what's right or wrong about our relationship, and I can't understand why you'd even listen to them."

There is silence on the phone, followed by a guttural staccato sound and rapid aspirating. Shit, she's sobbing. She had a great time in Cancún, and now I'm making her cry. I'm doing exactly what she was worried I'd do: pop the bubble. No wonder she didn't call me. And no wonder I'm having a shame attack.

Guilt is about not being good *to* someone. Shame is about not being good *for* her.

"Why can't you understand?" she finally pleads. "I needed to do this for me."

"I *can* understand," I respond, "*if* you communicate."

As the words come out of my mouth, I realize I'm repeating the criticism that made her cry. Communication was something I needed, not her. She needed freedom. I'm sure Leah doesn't text Lawrence every few minutes when she's over at some guy's house: "I just unzipped his pants, lol," "I'm licking his ass, it tastes like kombucha," "Now I'm fucking him, miss you!"

Sage is absolutely right: I would've burst the bubble. If we spoke, I would've felt a need to give my opinion on everything, to make fun of the guys, to somehow control the experience or make sure she was thinking of me in some way—like Tommy with his running commentary when I had sex with his fiancée. No, I don't use rules to control people anymore. Now I just pretend to give them freedom, then use guilt and passive-aggressiveness to control them instead.

For a guy who doesn't want to be controlled, I never noticed how controlling I actually am. I'm acting just like my long-suffering mom. It's a depressing insight. Rick would probably love to hear it.

Healthy nonmonogamous relationships clearly require a high EQ—emotional intelligence—not to mention some seriously secure attachment. And unfortunately, I'm still not there. But it doesn't mean I can't successfully make the transition from half-open to open—from selfishness to selflessness—with more conscious practice. This is just the burning period. No one said it would be easy.

If I truly want to be compersive with Sage and not a total hypocrite, I need to take Lawrence's advice to heart and understand she's a grown woman who can take care of herself. But, I think immediately afterward, do I actually trust her to take care of herself? Can I even be trusted to take care of myself?

"Is there anything else you want to share?" I ask when the boarding announcement for her flight finishes blaring in the background.

"Mm-hmm," she begins in a timid voice. "Did you miss me?"

"Yes," I tell her. "I did."

47

Before picking Sage up at the airport, I meet Adam near his office to swim laps together. I fill him in on the ups and downs of the relationship with Sage.

"At least it's an honest relationship," he tells me. "And that's a good thing. But my question for you is: Is it real?"

It's a good question. One I've been avoiding.

"I honestly can't tell you if it will work in the long run. But it's the most real relationship I've had since Ingrid. And it's everything I said I wanted in rehab. But it's driving me crazy. "

As we change in the locker room, I ask Adam if he's ever tempted to reach out to the woman he had an affair with.

"I'll tell you, Neil, I think about her every day. And I can't say that I wish it never happened, because it was the happiest part of my life. That's unfortunate. And on some level, my wife knows that."

Adam, and most people, seem to believe that if a relationship doesn't last until death, it's a failure. But the only relationship that's truly a failure is one that lasts longer than it should. The success of a relationship should be measured by its depth, not by its length.

We shower, then head to the pool. As we do, we pass a tall, toned woman in a one-piece bathing suit. "I'll tell you, if she threw herself at me, it would be hard to resist," he comments. "When you're not happy in your marriage, you're vulnerable. So I just stay busy with work and she stays busy with the kids."

He tells me about a book he recently read called *His Needs, Her Needs* by Willard F. Harley, a clinical psychologist who writes that a man needs five basic things from his wife: sexual fulfillment, recreational companionship, physical attractiveness, domestic support, and admiration.

"I don't think she's meeting a single one of those," Adam says.

"What does he say a woman's needs are?"

Adam explains that a woman's five basic needs are affection, conversation, honesty and openness, financial support, and family commitment. It seems antiquated to write that a woman needs her man's money but not his sex and he needs her domestic support but not her conversation; however, this seems to resonate with Adam. I get the feeling sometimes that he wasn't looking to be swept off his feet in his relationship, but to have the floor under his feet swept.

"I gave my wife the book and pointed out three pages that explain why I had my affair, just so she could understand the things we're missing from our marriage," he laments. "But she hasn't taken the time to read them."

As we ease ourselves into adjacent lanes, Adam tells me that he's had insomnia lately and an itchy red rash on his right hand. "The dermatologist said she can give me all the medicine there is for it, but it's stress related and won't go away until the stress clears up."

And that's when I realize: He's not a sex addict. "You know how they taught us that addiction is something that hurts your life and spirit, that gets progressively worse, and that you can't stop doing even though you know it's not good for you?"

"Yeah," he says.

"I just realized that you're a marriage addict."

"I think I am. I just can't let it go for some reason."

"Maybe you need to go to rehab for that."

"Along with a lot of other married people," he replies and swims off ahead of me.

On the way to pick up Sage, I call a few of the other guys from rehab, and only Charles is in good spirits after having evidently cured himself of sex addiction by ending his marriage.

"I stopped going to meetings," he says in what, for him, is an upbeat voice. "And I've been so happy, I'm like a little kid. I walk with my head up. I look at people. It's like someone turned the lights on and I don't have this confined, sad feeling that I can't go out and do anything ever again." He pauses and then confides, "And I finally finished *The Game*."

"You approve of it?"

"No, but I used it to meet a woman at the car wash the other day. We're going on a date tomorrow."

48

They say that absence makes the heart grow fonder, but according to science, even more powerful than the large space between you and the one you love is the small space between that person and someone else. In studies on sperm competition, males ejaculated more and harder after their partner had been with a rival. In her book *Mating in Captivity*, psychologist Esther Perel advises that the way to keep romance and sex hot in a relationship is through separation, unpredictability, and fear of loss.

So, theoretically, Sage's return should be the ultimate in hardwired passion and makeup sex.

Unfortunately, that's not how it initially goes down.

When Sage emerges from customs, she's talking to a man with a deep tan and a gaunt, weathered face. The passionate reunion I've been craving doesn't occur because he stands next to us, watching awkwardly.

"This is Mike," Sage says after tepidly hugging me. "We met on the plane. He's a director."

I try to take the high road. It's not easy because I desperately need the reassurance that even if Mexico wasn't strange ass, it was strange feet and it didn't hurt us. But now there's a random leather-faced guy lurking over us like a bodyguard. "Great," I tell him. "Sage acts. Did you guys exchange numbers?"

"Yes, we did," he says.

"Well, pleasure meeting you."

As we walk to the parking garage, Sage explains, "He offered to get me a job on one of his films."

"That would be great. Let's see if he comes through on that." Then, a final twist of the knife: "Guys will say anything to get what they want."

Her face darkens. "Maybe he saw something in me that was special." She lingers on the last word and stares at me, as if accusing me of seeing her only as an object of desire and not of talent.

And she's right. I wasn't speaking in a spirit of openness. I was speaking to close things, to create doubt, to expose him as a potential fraud, to poison her mind against a possible rival.

If I want this openness to work, I need to be more neutral about other men. I'd resent her talking shit about some woman I met. Like Lawrence said, she can discover the truth on her own. I don't have to sleep with him. These underhanded attempts at control stop today.

Relationships are like divining rods for locating one's faults and weaknesses.

As we drive home in awkward silence, I worry about how many of these guys are going to be in our lives now—phony actors and creepy directors and dirtbag producers who leech onto every fresh female who comes to Hollywood with a dream. A friend once met with a top Hollywood producer who told her he could "fast-track" her career. He explained that it just involved spending a little extra time with him at night, and then with some of his "influential" friends.

When we get back to the house, I kiss Sage and she kisses me back. I lead her to the bed and she follows me. I take off her clothes and she lets me. I go down on her and she spreads her legs for me. I enter her and she makes sounds for me.

The woman who left for Mexico is not the same as the one who came back from Mexico. She isn't making love to me; she's simply agreeing to sex.

However, just as I'm about to withdraw in disappointment, she gets on top of me, closes her eyes, and rides me enthusiastically. To anyone watching (such as Tommy), it would look like passionate lovemaking. But I know her too well. Her eyes are shut firmly and her mind is elsewhere. She's fantasizing about being on top of someone else. I'm sure of it. Maybe one of the guys from the trip or Leatherface from the plane.

So this is what it felt like all those times for Ingrid when I was connected sexually but disconnected mentally.

"Is everything okay?" I ask as we lie together afterward, so close together and so far away.

"I'm fine."

"You know what fine means?"

"No."

"Never mind."

She was supposed to have more love to give after these experiences. Her sexuality was supposed to be more alive, intense, and free. But instead there's less love, less sexuality, less Sage.

It feels like I lost her. And I don't even know what I lost her to.

49

That evening, we walk down the beach to eat at Paradise Cove. The waves gently polish the sand and the sky sparkles with stars, planes, planets. There's not another person in sight. Just Sage and I, and the long shadows caught in the beams of our flashlights as we trudge in silence.

I feel like I'm leading a prisoner to the gallows, only I don't know what crime's been committed or which of us is guilty.

One of the side effects of rehab is that I've become as unhealthily obsessed with people's childhoods as I am with their relationship species. So, as Lorraine taught us, I look into Sage's relationship with her opposite-sex parent for clues to our relationship. And the pattern is clear: When she conformed to her father's unreasonable expectations of her, she was daddy's little girl—until she asserted her independence and he lost his temper with her, often violently. After he threatened to kill her when she was a teenager, she even spoke to a hit man about getting rid of him once and for all. So it makes sense that she molds herself into the perfect girlfriend and takes care of my needs, but then begins to lose herself, grows resentful, and rebels.

If this is true, then opening the relationship wasn't about freedom, it was about escape. And that's exactly what she appears to have done. So I'm not actually leading a prisoner to the gallows. I'm leading an escaped convict back to prison.

Hopefully Leatherface isn't a hit man she hired to kill me.

Every now and then, the sound of her phone breaks the stillness and she types a response. Until, finally, I can't take it anymore. "Can I ask you something?"

"Sure."

I don't know how to frame the question without sounding jealous. It may be impossible. So, with full awareness that I sound like every woman I've tried to run away from, I continue: "Is there something going on with that guy from the plane?"

"What do you mean?"

"I don't know—like, did anything happen with him or did you guys do something?" I struggle to soften the harshness of what I'm thinking.

"No, nothing. We just talked."

"Is he someone you're interested in dating?" I hate myself for asking these questions. I'm not sure whether I'm trying to find the wall she's built between us so I can tear it down or so I can use it as an excuse to retreat. Quite possibly it's both. This is the dance of two love avoidants: Let me tear your wall down so I can build my own in its place.

"Well, I think he could be a good connection for me. And he did say he'd get me a job, so that would be great."

"That would be a good break," I mumble, careful to keep my pledge and let go of control. Meanwhile, my mind plays out every horrible scenario imaginable. They culminate in everything from her crying to me because he kicked her out of the car after she gave him a blow job, to me at home alone watching the Academy Awards as she arrives on his arm in an expensive designer dress.

Suddenly, Sage's phone pings. She checks it instantly.

"Is that him?" I ask. I've lost my grip on the functional adult. I am the wounded child, scared of losing love.

"No."

"Who was that, then?" I hear my voice asking this and I'm powerless to stop it. People often say to trust your feelings, but emotions can be even stupider than thoughts.

"My sister," she says.

I don't believe her. Both my emotions and thoughts agree on this.

And so I say something I've never spoken to anyone, the magic sentence capable of destroying any relationship, the four words Ingrid spoke to me shortly before we broke up: "Show me your phone."

"No," she says.

"Now I'm sure you're lying. Just show it to me."

She raises the phone to chest level and her fingers dance frantically all over it.

"Don't delete a single message or we're through!"

I've made an ultimatum. I've hit rock bottom.

Sage wheels around and starts walking back to the house. It's something I would do—run away rather than face responsibility for my behavior. It's the first thing I did when Ingrid caught me cheating: I told her I'd call her back later.

I run after Sage, promise not to get upset, coo everything I can to reassure her—until finally, like a child caught hiding a cookie behind her back, she thrusts the phone toward me.

"I'm worried you'll hate me and never want to talk to me again," she says.

I brace myself for the worst.

My heart is pounding so loudly, I feel like it's going to explode. There's no way for this situation to have a good outcome. If he didn't text, then I'm crazy. If he did, then I'm right. And whether I'm crazy or right, something is still wrong with the relationship for us to even be in this situation right now.

On her phone, I see dozens of texts from him, all from today. The first one that catches my attention is worse than anything I braced myself for: "I've never done anything like that on a plane before."

Agony, revulsion, and horror rise in me like vomit. There's another text from him about how they have a magnetic connection that he can't deny.

They talked for hours on the plane, she tells me. They had a powerful chemistry, she tells me. His face was so close to hers that they just started kissing, she tells me. It came out of nowhere, she tells me. Next thing she knew they were in the lavatory fooling around, she tells me. They didn't have sex or remove any clothing, she tells me. She stopped him out of respect for me, she tells me. And then, finally, she tells me that she wanted to wait to discuss it with me but didn't know how to say it.

As the words and tears tumble from her, rough waves of emotions and thoughts crash and collide in me. There is anger, because she lied to me. There is jealousy, because of the chemistry she had with him. There is disgust, because it seems so cheap. There is understanding, because it's pretty much what I did with Nicole and how James reacted to it. There is even relief, because I wasn't crazy to think there was more to the story than she was telling. And there is fear, for so many reasons.

"I told him about you and our relationship. That's why he wanted to meet you in the airport," she concludes.

But chief among these emotions, there is complete and utter bewilderment.

"How could you? I don't get it."

Her lower lip starts to quiver. I'm going to make her cry again. I don't care. And I care.

"We're in an open relationship," I continue.

Silence. She fights back the tears and glares at me.

"You can do anything you want."

Her arms fold across her chest in defiance.

"The only thing I asked for was honesty."

Her forehead creases into lines of hatred.

"You lied to me and cheated on me in a fucking open relationship with no rules."

The tears come now, burning with resentment.

I am her father. I am the ruiner of fun. I am the enemy of freedom. I am the bubble burster.

At least to her I am. But we have a free and open relationship. It was completely unnecessary for her to sneak around and lie to me. That's the whole point of all this. If she'd just told the truth, then it would have been my responsibility to deal with my reaction to it. But clearly, as my experiences with Nicole and with her French friend Camille should have warned me, an open relationship is no cure for drama and cheating. And Sage did say she'd cheated on her last boyfriend.

As I move through all this, Sage stands stiffly, her arms still crossed petulantly. I hug her to re-connect, but she remains stubbornly rigid. I wonder if she feels like I did with Ingrid: enmeshed, overwhelmed, trapped, like running into the water and drowning herself.

My first thought is that I need to let this relationship go. But it seems hypocritical to break up with her for cheating when even Ingrid gave me a second chance. And this is the most unrestricted and adventurous relationship I've had so far. Aside from the lying, she's doing it better than I am. I want the freedom to go to Cancún with two beautiful actresses who worship me. I want the freedom to fool around with a strange woman I randomly meet on the plane. In fact, when I flew home from rehab, that's exactly what I was fantasizing about.

Besides, it's not like I set up a situation in which Sage was safe to tell me the truth. As soon as we were alone, I was snarky, judgmental, and manipulative.

As I pull away, the violence explodes from her. She pounds my chest with her fists and stomps in the sand, like a child. "I want to be in your arms all the time," she yells. "I need that more than anything. I feel like I belong there"—she kicks an arc of sand into the air—"but I also want to have my cake and eat it."

I try to disentangle her words: She wants me but she doesn't want me. She needs the security of the relationship but she doesn't want the responsibility of it. She wants my commitment but she wants her freedom.

And slowly the truth dawns on me. I've gotten what I deserve: someone just like me.

50

That night, Sage and I talk for hours, until it seems like we've broken through our walls and can finally see who each other really is: the strengths and weaknesses, the gifts and wounds, the hopes and fears, the mother issues and father issues. Afterward, we have sex with a level of connection and depth that's equal parts intimacy and relief. I'm not sure if it's love—perhaps we are too wounded to even be capable of loving each other—but it's definitely passion. The sperm competition theorists were right after all.

As I watch her sleep, her cheeks flushed pink with warmth, her light dusting of freckles no longer covered by makeup, and her face bathed in the innocence that belongs to those in slumber, an overwhelming empathy flows through me. And I understand that I just need to embrace her as if she were myself, to expect her to behave no differently than I do in matters of the heart and flesh. Every restriction in my life has been an invitation to a rebellion. It's time to fully and finally commit to freedom and the risks inherent in it: to giving Sage hers and to enjoying mine.

Three days later, Sage goes on her first date: with Mike from the plane. I try not to think of him as Leatherface anymore. That was the old, non-compersive me. That night, I don't ask her where she's going or when she's coming home. And I don't text her while she's gone. Leashes are for dogs and leather families.

In the meantime, I invite one of our play partners over for the night. And that's when I discover the next challenge of having an open relationship: As Pepper predicted, I feel oddly guilty because I've been so conditioned to believe that sleeping with someone else while my girlfriend is away is wrong. Even if my girlfriend is away probably fucking someone else.

To my surprise, Sage returns home before midnight and joins us in the living room, telling me that her feelings for Mike are gone. When I ask why, she says, "I think it's because I've felt filled up by you since our talk."

According to Colin, one of the communards I studied with at Lafayette Morehouse, "The best way to have strange ass is to be sure the primary woman you're with is totally gratified and you have her agreement. She has to feel she has a surplus of you."

In the weeks that follow, Sage and I try to adhere to this dictum. We try to keep each other full. We try to let go of possessiveness. We try to communicate through the inevitable discomfort, fear, and jealousy. And we try not to date others who don't respect our relationship or who want to become our primary.

Try is the critical word here, because managing feelings is like taming lions. No matter how successful you think you are, they're still ultimately in control. During a foursome one night, Sage bites my cheek, then disappears into the bathroom and throws a water bottle against the wall. Another night, we visit a bondage club where some guy who looks like Glenn Danzig spanks and punishes Sage for half an hour. I feel so emasculated as I watch her enjoy being masterfully dominated that I pick a fight with her for no good reason on the way home. And roughest of all, one night Sage goes out with her ex-girlfriend Winter and doesn't return for two days.

There are times during the relationship when I don't like myself. There are times when I don't like her. And there are times when we're in perfect harmony, sharing our strange-ass stories, then making love one-on-one and finding it much more satisfying.

Through the ups and downs, adventures and misadventures, I tell myself that this is just the burning period, that I'm managing powerful emotions like guilt and fear much better as a result of all the failed nonmonogamous relationships that led up to this, that comfort is just around the corner.

And then one night, as we lie in bed together, Sage turns to me, her eyes glistening, and says, "I want to have your child."

Though her words are more the result of momentary passion than judicious premeditation, I elatedly wonder if I've actually found it: a relationship that fits all four criteria I laid out when I started this journey. It's not sexually exclusive, it's honest (now), it's emotional, and it's capable of developing into a family. Though I wonder what we're supposed to say when our kid walks in the room and sees a bunch of women spread-eagled on the bed: "Son, when a man and four women love each other very much . . ."?

A few minutes later, however, I remember the entirety of the final condition: The relationship has to be capable of evolving into a family *with healthy, well-adjusted children*. And not only is it still too early in the relationship to know if it's sustainable, but our lifestyle is too intense and unstable for kids to be around it. And without the partying, is this really a relationship?

When I call Rick to discuss the viability of getting more serious with Sage, he responds cryptically, "Deepak Chopra says that if you want to stop smoking, you have to change the way in which you smoke. In other words, if you smoke with coffee or after sex, stop smoking with coffee or after sex. Then, when you smoke at other times, really feel all the sensations in your body. And you'll see it for what it really is: putting poison in your lungs."

"So what's the analogy for my situation?"

"Maybe you need to try only having sex with Sage and no one else for a little while, and really feel what it's like to be with her. See what the truth of the relationship is—and if you're real friends with her or just sex-addict friends."

"That's a good idea. I'm going out of the country next week, so I'll do it as soon as I'm back." It's a bittersweet trip that I'm not completely looking forward to: hiking Machu Picchu, which I'd originally booked with Ingrid.

"Why wait until then?"

"Because Sage is bringing me twins as a birthday present before I leave."

"God help us all."

51

Their names are Josie and Jenn. They have tiny breasts, tiny noses, and tiny brains. We fooled around with them a few weeks earlier in the bathroom at a hotel suite party.

When they arrive, however, a problem becomes immediately apparent: One has a cold sore on her upper lip. And I don't want to risk getting herpes—even for twins.

Fortunately, her doppelgänger has clean lips.

"Let's do something you guys have never done before," the safer twin, Josie, says, brightening the mood as she drops onto the couch.

I rack my brain to think of something I haven't done before. Nothing comes immediately to mind. Not a single sexual stone left unturned—at least, not one that I really want to turn. It's been almost a full year of swing parties, harems, communes, and moresomes. On top of all that, Sage and I have been to S&M dungeons, gang bang parties, orgasmic meditation sessions, and bondage courses in our explorations. I even slept with the twins' mother one night after she emailed me out of the blue. My penis is literally rubbed red and raw from the nonstop activity.

Sage, too, seems to be at a loss.

Suddenly, inspiration strikes her. "I've never pissed on anyone before," she exclaims.

Josie doesn't jump at the opportunity, but she doesn't say no either. However, after a few seconds, Sage realizes, "Yes, I have."

As we rack our brains for something new to do together, Josie leaps off the couch. Where she was sitting, there's a small, spreading, bright-red stain. Her period has started.

"We can always do some coke," she offers apologetically as she makes her way to the bathroom.

Sage accepts the invitation. I decline.

"I don't have a septum anymore. Look!" Jenn, the twin with the cold sore, says after removing a small baggie from her purse. She pushes on the bridge of her nose and it squishes flat against her face. "Like Michael Jackson," she laughs. "Except mine's from doing too much coke."

"It just burned your septum away?" I ask, incredulous.

"Pretty much."

"Can I touch it?"

"Go ahead."

She thrusts her nose toward me proudly and I mash it like a big wobbly button.

One of the most dangerous side effects of cocaine is that it causes people to talk about themselves nonstop. And soon the twins are chattering away about the celebrities they've slept with and the rich men they've used, as Sage hangs on their every word. If the male game is getting sex, they school her, the female game is withholding it. When there's something they want—such as emotional control or financial commitment—they dangle sex just out of reach, creating a finish line that appears to draw closer with every meeting yet always remains one elusive step away.

As Sage nose-vacuums the last line of white dust off the coffee table, Jenn cackles, "That's not a line, it's a chapter." She turns to me. "Do you mind if our dealer comes over with more?"

I press her nose, hoping it works like an off button.

Worst birthday ever, I think as I head downstairs to sleep alone. On the nightstand, there's a tube of Neosporin, which Sage recommended using to treat my friction-sore dick. I rub it on, feeling annoyed and neglected. This is what it's like to date my *own* twin: She's so busy trying to fill the emptiness inside her that she has no time to fill the emptiness inside me.

To cheer myself up, I decide to gently masturbate myself to sleep. It's my birthday present to me.

I close my eyes, take a few breaths, relax into the pillow, find a comfortable grip away from the tender area, and prepare to sink into fantasy.

I try to imagine a woman I'm attracted to and haven't slept with yet, but no one comes to mind.

I try to think of a sexual fantasy I haven't experienced yet, but can't come up with a single one.

I try to think of something that will turn me on, but I draw a complete blank.

I have nothing to masturbate to. I didn't even think this was possible. For the first time in my life, my fantasy coffers are empty.

I think back to the challenge Rick originally posed almost two years ago: Am I any happier?

I've had a lot of excitement, even a lot of pleasure. But I don't think I've truly had any happiness.

Researchers at Princeton University did a study on the correlation between money and happiness. As people's incomes rose up to $75,000 annually, their happiness increased. But at incomes beyond that, people on average did not become happier.

Perhaps the same is true of sexual partners.

Coming on more tits is not going to make me any happier.

It seems I've mistaken being out of control for freedom.

When I asked Lorraine how I'd know if this journey was true to my authentic self, she warned: Wounds bring drama and trauma, not comfort.

It doesn't take long to determine what the past year has brought.

"There is nothing frenzied about debauchery, contrary to what is thought," Albert Camus once wrote. "It is but a long sleep."

It is time to wake up.

52

"The obvious clinical facts demonstrate that men—and women—who devote their lives to unrestricted sexual satisfaction do not attain happiness, and very often suffer from severe neurotic conflicts or symptoms. The complete satisfaction of all instinctual needs is not only not a basis for happiness, it does not even guarantee sanity."

—Erich Fromm, *The Art of Loving*

53

A foreign correspondent I met in Haiti while working at *The New York Times* once told me a story about a colleague of his, which has always stuck with me, although I was never able to independently corroborate it:

When he was on assignment in Central America, he was kidnapped by rebels. Government troops discovered their location and planned a rescue operation. Rather than give up the hostages, the rebels decided to kill them.

So one of the gunmen pushed the reporter to his knees and pressed a pistol against his head.

In that moment of finality, the reporter thought not of his wife at home, but of his high school sweetheart. A woman he hadn't spoken to and had barely even thought of in over ten years.

Suddenly, an explosion shook the shack. Moments later, government forces burst in and rescued him.

Afterward, the reporter reflected on that unexpected moment of truth. He had been given a second chance at life, and there was no doubt what he needed to do. As soon as he got home, he called his high school sweetheart. She told him that she was divorced. So the reporter left his wife and married her.

As I hike the Inca Trail to Machu Picchu without Ingrid, I can't stop thinking about that reporter's story. It may not be a fairy-tale happy ending, but it's a real-life happy ending. Life is a test and you pass if you can be true to yourself. To get the first question correct, all you have to know is who you are. A life is just one letter away from a lie.

I originally invited Adam to join me, but his wife said that if he was going to take a vacation, it should be with the whole family. Then I tried Calvin, who said yes, and made plans to go to Brazil afterward to see his son. Sage also wanted to come, but the trail permits were already sold out.

"I have a favor to ask," Calvin begged just before the trip. "Make sure I don't go mongering in Peru."

"I promise," I told him. Then I searched *mongering* online until I found his particular definition of the word: whoring, especially in a foreign country.

For the first couple of days, the walk is uncomfortable. Not just because of the length of the trek and the steepness of the ascents, but because I had sex with Sage before I left, and the skin on the shaft is blisteringly red from overuse and stings from the slightest touch. Whenever I change clothes, I have to cradle it gently, like a broken bone. There's Neosporin in my first-aid kit, so every few hours when I take a break to pee in the underbrush, I surreptitiously rub some on.

Calvin and I are accompanied by a mandatory guide, Ernesto, a squat Andean man with legs sculpted from a lifetime of hiking these mountains. As we tramp mostly uphill, through arrows of rain and blankets of heat, chewing coca leaves to ameliorate altitude sickness, our minds clear and we share our dreams, fears, and ambitions.

There is, however, a space between us where something is missing. It is just big enough to fit Ingrid. And with every peak that juts through the clouds, every ruin that emerges in the clearing, every smell that perfumes the morning dew, I wish she were there to share it.

I don't think about Sage being here and seducing random female hikers into camping threesomes. I can just imagine her asking the guide how to turn coca leaves into cocaine. To my surprise, since snapping out of my decadence-induced stupor on my birthday night, I'm not even worried about what she's doing at home and who she's doing it with.

"So how've you been doing with the mongering?" I ask Calvin as we reach a small plateau.

"It's been a while. I haven't seen an escort in probably six months."

"Maybe that's because you were living with one."

"I think that's what ruined it for me. For my birthday, Mariana dressed up like the day we met and thought it would turn me on, but it repulsed me. I didn't want anything to do with it." He stuffs a handful of coca leaves into his mouth and continues. "The odd thing is that since I stopped, I've been drinking a bit—and getting angry at people who don't follow the rules, like if they don't use their turn signals to change lanes."

We walk in silence for a while as the forest screams with life around us, both probably thinking about how his behavior supports the addiction theories he supposedly disproved.

"I have a weird dream last night," Ernesto says softly.

"What was it?"

"I should not say it maybe."

To make him more comfortable, I share one of mine. "I've been having this recurring dream lately where I'm playing football. And I'm visualizing the penalty kick that's going to score the winning goal. But when the time comes for the actual kick, I barely connect with the ball and it dribbles just a few feet in front of me. And every time, I'm jolted awake by my feet kicking the sheets."

"Bad dream," Ernesto replies. "Your mind, it knows the right thing to do; but your body, it doesn't listen. Maybe I tell you mine." He lowers his voice, even though there's no one around us. "So . . . I dream that a girl from the Amazon is in Cusco to look for me, and I am very worried that my wife finds out she is there."

"Were you worried because you'd slept with her?"

"An affair, yes."

"Is this girl someone you're seeing in real life?"

He hesitates, then responds tersely, "Yes."

We discuss his affair and all the others his friends have when they leave their homes to work as guides and porters. "There's a book I want," he says. "It is about strategies for these women. Very helpful."

"Is it *The Game*?" Calvin asks.

"No." We pause to lean against a large outcropping of boulders, drink water, and wipe sweat while he searches his memory for the book's name. Then suddenly, it comes back to him. "I think it's called *How to Cheat*."

Men everywhere, it seems, are the same.

As the hours pass, my lifelong antipathy to jogging and unnecessary walking catches up with me, and I tire and fall behind the guys, sweat prickling my sun-roasted neck. Calvin and Ernesto clear a ridge and when I reach it ten minutes later, I don't see them.

I trudge on, but soon my head starts to spin. I feel incorporeal, like at the beginning of my ecstasy trip, but with the addition of a headache. Maybe it's dehydration or altitude sickness or exhaustion, or all three. I pull the water bottle from my bag and drain the small puddle that remains. I slow to a zigzag trudge, worried that I'm going to veer off the ledge and tumble into the valley far below.

And I wonder: If I collapsed right now and I needed someone to get help before dehydration or heatstroke or pulmonary edema killed me, which of my current or former girlfriends could I rely on?

My ex-girlfriend Katie would probably get angry at me for abandoning her by collapsing. My ex Kathy would start hyperventilating, and I'd end up having to rescue her. And Sage . . . I imagine that she'd stay by my side. But for how long until she got restless, began worrying about what she was missing by being there, and took off to save herself?

Only Ingrid would stay with me, trying to find help until my dying breath. Ingrid.

In that moment, the dizziness briefly lifts. And with my lungs full of crisp smog-free air, with my vision clear and unobstructed by advertising, with my ears open and unclogged by chatter, with my mind clear and unclouded by distractions, a thought I've been trying to keep buried charges to the surface of my mind on a tidal wave of emotion: *I blew it*.

Sex is easy to find—whether through game, money, chance, social proof, or charm. So are affairs, orgies, adventures, and three-month relationships—if you know where to look and are willing to go there. But love is rare.

I was so blind. I really thought that when I broke up with Ingrid, it was about wanting freedom. I didn't see at all, despite everything I'd learned, that it was about not wanting to be loved so much. I did exactly what Lorraine warned me not to: I let the grounded adolescent run my life.

Whatever I have with Sage, it is not love. She molds herself into the perfect partner for me because she wants something back—affection, attention, and whatever little social status comes from being a writer's girlfriend. And I mold myself into the perfect boyfriend because I want the sexual adventures. Maybe the reason I didn't take Rick's Deepak Chopra advice is because if I did, then I'd see the relationship for what it is: not poison like smoking, but immature like breaking up with your wife and buying a sports car after finding your first gray hair.

Except if married men have mid-life crises, men who haven't ever truly been able to commit have no-life crises. And if they're able to see clearly for even just a moment, they start to realize that they're losing more than they're gaining each day they remain stalled on the scenic road of growing up.

When I finally huff up to the mountain pass, I see two figures sitting just on the other side of it: Calvin and Ernesto. I drop my backpack to the ground, collapse in the shade, and swallow Ernesto's water and Calvin's aspirin. Then I wait for my body to return to equilibrium.

Though it was more a brush with discomfort and anxiety than with death, there's one thing I didn't think about in that moment of truth: the wild foursome with Sage, Leah, and Winter. No, I thought about Ingrid.

I thought about returning the sports car, going home, and begging for forgiveness.

At the campsite on our final night, as Ernesto, Calvin, and I drink tea and snack on Andean guinea pig under the swaying glow of a lantern, I pull out a deck of Skittykitts and suggest a game, hoping it will distract me from my thoughts.

"I wish Ingrid were here," I sigh to Calvin. "She'd love playing Skittykitts with us right now."

Calvin mumbles something noncommittal. He's probably sick of me whining about her.

"And she's so funny. By now, we'd have dozens of private jokes. You saw how she lit up the table when she came to rehab! I hope I haven't blown it."

"You'll get back together with her," Calvin says matter-of-factly. "I know it."

"I hope so." I close my eyes and a deep sense of despair overwhelms me. What's the fun of hiking Machu Picchu, of walking a trail carved centuries ago, of waking to see the sun cresting over a mountaintop and the clouds below, of eating Andean cuisine and playing Skittykitts in a tent underneath the glow of a lantern, if I can't share it with someone I love?

That is the price of freedom.

As we begin our descent to the lost city of Machu Picchu the following morning, the reception indicator on my phone returns to life with a single bar.

And I text Ingrid: "Freeeeeeeedom!"

54

After I send the text, followed by another letting her know Machu Picchu has no magic without her, a surge of familiar fear comes over me. That night, I dream of having a threesome with two random tourists.

Why won't my libido leave me alone?

Before checking my phone for Ingrid's response, I try to steady my nerves. So many people much wiser than myself—Prince Charles, Bill Clinton, General Petraeus—have cheated on their wives. Can I really hope to succeed where the world's leaders have failed?

I don't know. But what I can do that they didn't is make the choice to be honest, to communicate my vulnerabilities with Ingrid, and to get support if I'm struggling. Fuck my doubting mind. I can do this.

I check my phone. Nothing. But I know in my heart that she'll keep her word from what seems like so long ago.

When we reach the fabled city, nestled among the mountaintops, there's still no response from Ingrid. Nor is there one when the sun sets. Maybe she didn't get it. Maybe I misspelled *freedom* and didn't use the right number of e's. Maybe she's happy with her new boyfriend. Maybe she's forgotten about me. Maybe I made a mistake.

Definitely I made a mistake.

The next day, there's still no response from Ingrid.

The following day, nothing.

57

The day after that, I realize she's never going to respond.

That night in the Spaceship Room, I told Ingrid I needed time to explore and learn and make a choice—and finally I've made it. But love is not like roulette. You can't bet on a spread.

As I'm packing to return home on my last night in Peru, I receive a message not from Ingrid, but from my ex-girlfriend Kathy, who says she urgently needs advice. Like Ingrid, Kathy was abandoned by her father, who was caught living in secret with another woman and other children.

When I call, Kathy explains tearfully that her ex-boyfriend Victor was recently diagnosed with liver cancer. He's a notorious player from Miami who broke up with her because he wanted to fuck other women. But while he was delirious on medication in the hospital, his family said he kept calling out her name. When Victor regained his senses, the doctor told him the cancer had advanced so much that, at age forty-four, he had only three months left to live.

Victor didn't react to the news by deciding to go on a fucking spree for his last days on earth. He didn't get a bunch of women together so he could experience the wildest foursome ever. Instead, he told his family, "That's what I get for being a player all my life. I need Kathy. I need to apologize to her."

"So he called me last night and asked me to go to the Caribbean with him," Kathy continues. "He said he wants to spend the days he has left with me."

"What'd you tell him?"

"I told him I needed time to decide. He threw my love away when he wanted to have fun and now that he's dying, he wants me back? I'm scared it's going to be too painful to get close to him again and then lose him again."

"You're right. It would be good for him to have you there, but it wouldn't be healthy for you."

And that's when I understand why Ingrid hasn't called back.

It's predictable, even stereotypical, that a love avoidant like me would hit a bottom and reach out to the love addict, only to start the cycle anew and waste another year of our lives. Or that a love avoidant, as soon as his next girlfriend says she wants to have a family together, would start pining for the one who got away.

As for my big Machu Picchu epiphany, while the longing for Ingrid may have been real, everything else about it was pitiful. Love isn't about wanting someone to save my life or see a vista with me or make me laugh or any of those selfish reasons I've always given for loving Ingrid. Those are just things she can do for me or ways she makes me feel. Love is . . .

Actually, I have no idea what love is.

Ingrid's right. She's doing what's healthy; I'm not.

All I've got is a healed dick and a defective heart.

58

When I return home, I receive a wedding invitation in the mail. I check the calligraphy on the back of the envelope. It says *De La O*. Ingrid's last name.

My muscles go weak and I drop the card to the ground.

I am a dumb jerk.

Door

4

ANHEDONIA

STAGE I

▪ Emptying Out ▪

William: You must be very lonely.
Do you know what it is you're searching for?

Keoma: Myself, I guess. I don't know. I need to
find out who I am, to give the simplest of my actions
a reason. I know my being in this world has some
significance, but I'm afraid when I find out what it is,
it'll be too late. In the meantime, I'm a vagabond.
I keep traveling. Even when the earth sleeps,
I keep traveling, chasing shadows.

—KEOMA
directed by Enzo G. Castellari

1

"You set out to do something and you did it. You accomplished everything you ever wanted. You had every single kind of sexual adventure and relationship you ever dreamed of. And you're still not happy or fulfilled."

The voice is wise. The voice is cruel. The voice is right. It belongs to Rick, who sits at the Italian restaurant Giorgio Baldi in his uniform of white T-shirt, black shorts, and frayed loafers.

"That's because he hasn't been in any relationships with real intimacy. He's one up and they've been way one down. They're toys. He won't get hurt playing with a toy. But these women, they will."

This voice is also wise. It is also cruel and right. It belongs to Lorraine, who's in town running a workshop. I notice for the first time how heavily creased the lines around her lips are, as if strained from dispensing so much wisdom.

I struggle to take it in. The hardest truth to swallow is the one that follows a full meal that one thought was truth but turned out to be the opposite.

"Can't you see?" Rick turns to address me directly. "All your relationships were doomed to fail! It didn't matter what kind you tried, whether it was with one person or a hundred." His eyes blaze with the fire of conviction he gets when channeling the gods of harsh truth. "Because it's not relationships that are broken. It's you!"

And that's when it sinks in: The battle is lost. I feel a wrecking ball swing through my head, smashing all the open relationships, the swinger orgies, the free-love communes, and the threesome adventures. If Rick had told me this any earlier, I wouldn't have been able to hear him. I would have argued, resisted, and tried to prove him wrong. But for the first time, I have no *what-if* arguments and scenarios left to debate him with.

All that remains is me, sitting with my family of choice, my heart in pieces over losing Ingrid and my mind flagellating itself for every bad decision since leaving rehab.

As for Sage, I returned from Machu Picchu, ready to break things off . . . and she was already gone. She sent a long email explaining apologetically that she felt she was losing her identity in our relationship and needed to find herself. So she decided to move back to Brooklyn with her ex-girlfriend Winter, who she's now apparently dating again.

Even though I was about to do almost the exact same thing to Sage, it came so unexpectedly and on the heels of losing Ingrid, that I was emotionally wrecked. I suppose when a bandage covering an open wound is peeled off, it's going to bleed a little.

"So what should I do?" I ask Rick and Lorraine. All evening, they've been destroying what remains of my ego, exposing my every thought as a fraud and my every emotion as infantile. Almost two years have passed since I went to rehab. I tried sex addiction recovery and it didn't work for me. I tried monogamy and it didn't work for me. I tried nonmonogamy and it didn't work for me. So what's left?

"You need to try the only thing you haven't experienced yet," Lorraine suggests.

"What's that?"

"Anhedonia."

I repeat the word clumsily. I've read many big books with big words, but I've never come across *anhedonia* before. Whatever it is, I don't like the sound of it.

"It's the dark place of not feeling," she elaborates. "People feel dead in the place of anhedonia. They can't experience joy."

I think back to Henry's ninth emotion. That's what it's called—not the death emotion, but anhedonia. "Why would I want to experience that?"

"Because in order to return to homeostasis and have any clarity on who you are and what you need, you have to detox from the intensity of these one-up, one-down relationships. You've been through a constant cycle of intensity, from your relationship with your mother all the way up to your relationship with Sage." She pauses to order a glass of wine, and for some reason I'm surprised, as if drinking is taboo for addiction therapists. "You'll find that being committed to your authentic life supersedes the intensity."

I sit in silence, processing this. In my heart, I know she's right. I spent all year thinking that if somehow I found the right relationship, my problems would magically disappear. But the one relationship I didn't try was the one with myself. For a love avoidant, I've done a good job of constantly having some sort of girlfriend for the last eight years. Maybe that's because there's no better place to hide from intimacy than in a relationship.

When I last sat with Rick and Lorraine, it felt like every door in the world was opening to me. Now they're all shut, locked, and sealed with concrete—including, most painfully of all, the only one I want to walk through, the one leading back to where I started.

"But what should I do about Ingrid's wedding?"

"Don't worry about Ingrid for now," Lorraine says as the wine arrives, her words searing my addled heart. "Just let yourself be emptied out and deal with whatever comes up in the process. I'll help you. Then we can fill you up with the things you need—and you can see how you really feel about Ingrid then."

People do lemon juice and cayenne pepper diets to clean out their insides, so why not a cleanse for the psyche? Then I can start consuming healthy thoughts and experiences. That is, as long as Lorraine isn't going to fill me with the sexual shame Joan was peddling. I know I can't heal myself alone—I barely even trust myself anymore—but I can't help feeling that rehab was as harmful as it was helpful.

"What kinds of things do you want to fill me up with?" I ask, to be certain.

"With freedom."

That's the last word I expected to hear her say. "What do you mean?"

Lorraine places her glass on the table, takes my hand in hers, and looks into my eyes. She then replies slowly, making sure each word lands meaningfully, "In life, we are born innocent and pure, beautiful and honest, and in a state of oneness with each moment. As we develop, however, our caregivers and others load us with baggage. Some of us keep accumulating more and more baggage until we become burdened by all the weight, trapped in beliefs and behaviors that keep us stuck. But the true purpose of life is to divest yourself of that baggage and become light and pure again. You've been searching for freedom this whole time. That is true freedom."

I thought I'd at least healed something during rehab and my year of sex addiction therapy, but clearly all I did was identify my issues and then go consciously live an unconscious life. It takes more than advice, books, meetings, therapy, and rehab to change. It takes more than even a powerful, unwavering, full-bodied desire to do so. It takes humility. And there is nothing more humbling than the past year, and the realization that I've

made a mess of everything and may never experience true happiness, love, and family if I keep trying to do things my way.

The underlying cause of most unfulfilled lives is that we are simply too close to ourselves to see clearly enough to get out of our own way.

"Why don't you come back to the hospital and continue working on yourself?" Lorraine offers.

My enthusiasm instantly fades as I imagine going back to rehab with Joan. I'd rather move back in with Belle, Anne, and Veronika.

Lorraine reads my mind. "But privately, just with me."

"Really, you'd do that?"

"It may be your last chance." She tilts her wineglass to her wise lips and lets the last drops fall into her throat. "I'll be working with your friend Adam in a few weeks. If you'd like to, you can join us. But be vigilant: You're at great risk right now of jumping into another relationship. And if you can't refrain from relationships and sexual contact throughout this entire process, then I'm going to recommend you check back into rehab."

A triumphant smile flashes across Rick's face. And the adapted adolescent in me, the grounded teenager who's been running my life so poorly this last year, makes a last desperate attempt to save himself: "So basically," he asks, "you want me to castrate myself?"

"Yes," Rick replies coolly. "We do."

2

In the weeks that follow, as I wind down my life and wait to get help from Lorraine, masturbation saves me.

You want to ask out someone you recently met? Masturbate first, then see if you still want to spend six hours wining, dining, and entertaining her, desperate for an outcome that's not only going to disappoint you if it doesn't occur, but may even disappoint you if it does.

You want to call an escort? Masturbate first, then see if you really want some junkie who looks nothing like her decade-old Photoshopped images to give you a lazy hand job.

You want to call a former fuck buddy? Masturbate first, then see if you still want to invite her over, have sex that isn't as good as you remembered, then spend the rest of the night figuring out how to politely get rid of her without hurting her feelings.

Masturbate when you want to break the rules of your relationship or your celibacy agreement—and you'll soon discover that once your desires are fulfilled in your imagination, the need to live them out in real life suddenly doesn't seem so urgent. Once the brain's reward center has gotten its hit of dopamine, it doesn't need another one—at least not for a little while.

They say that viewing porn correlates with depression. I'm not sure whether it's a cause or a symptom, but now I understand why it's so appealing: It's not just a world where sex is easy, but also where sex doesn't involve dealing with someone's emotions before, during, and after the experience.

She doesn't yell at you if you aren't faithful and you start watching another porn clip. She doesn't shame you for your taste in women, your fetishes, your performance, or your body, income, and faults—unless being shamed happens to turn you on, in which case she's glad to do it all night. And she doesn't mind if you come before it's done, then roll over and go to sleep and never talk to her again. It's just instant sexual gratification with no waiting, no rejection, no emotion, no commitment, no obligation whatsoever—plus infinite variety.

The strict sexaholics and sex addiction therapists definitely wouldn't agree with the jerk-off solution, and it's delaying my entry into the pleasure-less world of anhedonia, but it serves its purpose as a Band-Aid keeping me faithful to myself and my promise to Lorraine before seeing her again.

The only problem is that after the orgasm, I'm still stuck with myself—and my mistakes. I think about Ingrid's footsteps clomping outside the front door, her mocking shouts of freedom, the glee she took in blocking my path when I tried to enter a room, and the warmth of her body, heart, and spirit. All she tried to do was bring joy and laughter into my life. And in return, I gave her the best of what I had to offer: resentment.

One lonely evening, after my porn pity party, I bring a stack of unopened mail and random bills to the bed. That's when I come across Ingrid's wedding invitation again.

Perhaps it's time to come to terms with her marriage and move on to the last stage of grief, acceptance. I turn the envelope nervously in my hands for a few moments, wondering if she's marrying the James Dean-on-steroids guy. Then I slide an index finger along the flap, my heart thudding loudly, my body bracing for the shock.

I scan the card and see the words *Hans De La O*. She's marrying her brother?

No, idiot, her brother is getting married. And for some reason—maybe accidental, maybe spiteful—you've been invited.

My heart bursts open and hope rushes through me, chasing away the darkness. When Ingrid and I were dating, her shy brother told me that he'd never had a girlfriend. Something must have changed. And now I've been granted one last opportunity to see Ingrid again. This just may be the best day of my life.

There's only one problem: Though I've displayed a modicum of self-control by avoiding sex and relationships these last few weeks, I'm still exactly the same. If I truly want to change, not only do I need to cut the porn out—it's certainly not doing anything positive for my mind—but I need Lorraine's help. More than all the sex and alternative relationships in the world.

The next morning, Lorraine calls unexpectedly. "There's something I want you to do for me," she says.

"Anything," I respond. And I mean it.

Dr. Hasse Walum doesn't look like the kind of scientist who churns out eighty-page research papers that are barely decipherable to anyone without a Ph.D. in biology. He has long, stringy Kurt Cobain hair, a boyish face sculpted like Ryan Gosling's, and the relaxed poise of a young Marlon Brando.

Over dinner, I ply him with cocktails until, finally, I ask what I'm there to find out. When she called, Lorraine suggested that, since I liked talking to experts so much, I should see Walum. "He's a famous geneticist," she explained. "And I want you to ask him a question."

Not surprisingly, considering her perceptiveness, it was a question that's been playing on a loop in my head for the last two years. One which, even now as I'm praying for a miracle when I see Ingrid again at her brother's wedding, has been lurking in the shadows of my mind: Is being monogamous something that's genetically determined or do I have a choice in the matter?

When I asked for Walum's contact information, Lorraine replied, "Oh, I don't know him. I've just read about him."

As I researched Walum, I wondered what Lorraine was up to. Everything he stands for seems to contradict what she's been telling me. His experiments, along with similar research conducted by his colleagues at Emory University, have led to the discovery of the exact biological factor responsible for monogamy. Evidently, if you have long receptors in the brain's reward center for the hormone vasopressin, then you're more likely to be monogamous. If not, then you're a born player.

One science writer, summarizing these findings, concluded: "Devoted fathers and faithful partners are born, not made or shaped by a father's example."

If this is true, then there's no point in seeing Lorraine again or even going to Hans's wedding. I'm as nonmonogamous as I am male, and stuck with my own species whether I like it or not. I wonder if this is a ruse of Lorraine's to test my sincerity and see if I'm willing to change on the basis of faith alone in defiance of proof, evolution, genetics, and experience.

After a few drinks with Walum, I pop Lorraine's question: "Do you think monogamy is genetically determined?"

The answer seems obvious, considering what I know already about Walum. But his response surprises me. "Not entirely," he says. And I find I'm relieved to hear those two words. "There have been studies where scientists have taken young rodents away from their parents, and as a result, they get a much lower amount of the receptors."

"How about with people?"

"They've done similar research with humans, looking not exactly at receptors in the brain, because that's really difficult to do in people, but at plasma levels of oxytocin and vasopressin. And kids in orphanages have lower levels. So, generally, good parenting will promote better oxytocin and vasopressin systems in the long run, and these are linked with more closely bonding individuals when it comes to romantic relationships. We haven't published it yet, but that's exactly what we're looking at right now."

It makes sense: If you have a healthy bond with your parents, you'll have a healthy pair-bond with others as an adult—which, considering my upbringing, doesn't bode well. "So let me ask you: If you're an adult *and* you don't have a gene coding for long vasopressin receptors *and* you've been badly parented, is there any hope?"

"I think so," he says, and a second wave of relief rises above the first. "A messed-up childhood makes it hard, and it gets even more complicated as you get older, but it's not set in stone. We haven't found anything that's completely genetic. Not even these really hurtful diseases like autism and schizophrenia, or things like intelligence. There's still some sort of environmental factor involved. So you get to change things."

It seems I am in control of my romantic destiny after all. Now I see why Lorraine wanted me to speak to Walum: to crush my last reservoir of resistance and skepticism—the argument that monogamy and fidelity are evolutionarily unnatural or culturally anachronistic or just not lifestyles I was built for. She probably doesn't want to hear me intellectually debating those points all through therapy again.

Walum orders another drink, then runs a hand through the thick hair that genetics has blessed him with. "Can I ask why you're raising these specific questions?" he inquires.

I tell him about the last few years of cheating, rehab, failed monogamy, failed nonmonogamy, regret, and repentance.

"That's the sad thing for women," he says afterward, shaking his head. "You can't be perfect enough for a man not to want to cheat."

It's a surprisingly cynical comment, one that seems to come more from experience than from research, so I ask him: "What's your relationship situation?"

He heaves a sigh and confesses, "I think I experience relationships as more difficult than other people do."

He slumps back in the booth and I lean in, sensing that he may be going through a crisis similar to mine. "So if you could design the perfect relationship for yourself, considering the genetic, evolutionary, and behavioral factors we've been talking about, what would it be?" I ask.

"I can't really answer that at the moment."

"You must have a secret plan. Everyone has one. I used to have a few until I experienced them in real life."

Walum thinks for a while, then gives his answer: "Being a loner. That's a solution." He forces a smile.

"Considering that you're a biologist, that wouldn't be a good evolutionary strategy."

"Yeah," he admits, "so that's no good." Then he sighs and says, "I don't really know. Actually, that's my answer. Maybe that's one of the reasons I'm studying these things—to understand why I feel the way I do myself."

Suddenly, Walum's no longer a vaunted scientific researcher, but a guy just like me, trying to figure out why something as simple as loving someone is so complicated in real life.

"So is it hard for you to be faithful?" I press.

"Not exactly. I would never be unfaithful. But in relationships, I feel limited because I'm missing out on other things. It's a bit tragic. You can be with someone that you really, really like and still feel a bit sad that you can't have anything else."

"So you get depressed because you feel trapped?"

"More or less."

"Can I ask you a personal question? Did you have to take care of your mother growing up?"

"Not when I was really, really young, but later on, definitely."

"Emotionally or physically?"

"Primarily emotionally."

"Interesting."

And so I end this last week exactly where Lorraine wants me. I recognize that I can make every argument in my head against monogamy. And they may even be right: It probably isn't natural. But none of this is going to make me happy or bring me closer to Ingrid—or, if she won't have me, to any meaningful connection.

The person who is too smart to love is truly an idiot.

With my last pillar of intellectual resistance demolished, I fly to Lorraine to be healed, to become worthy of Ingrid, to become worthy of myself, to find out who I am beyond the perpetually turning wheels of desire, manipulation, and intellectualization that have run my entire life.

4

"It's time for you to get your life back," Lorraine announces, rising in front of us in a green-and-brown dress like Mother Earth herself. "Your childhood is a terrorist and it's holding you hostage."

Adam and I sit in plastic chairs arranged side by side in an administrative building off the site of the rehab hospital. Calvin, who I invited with Lorraine's permission, is also with us. Except this time, we're not here as sex addicts and there are no red tags hanging from our necks. Lorraine has decided to try a new type of workshop, one that's not designed specifically for people with addictions but for all men and women who, like us, spend their lives running in circles like dogs chained to a stake in the ground. And that stake is trauma.

"All of you share something in common," Lorraine continues. "Each of you had a mother who was unhappy and who you could not help. And that has been the starting point for your three very different journeys away from intimacy and connection."

As she speaks, all our confusions and complications suddenly seem so clear and simple. Our lives are like children's building-block games in which objects are stacked one by one on top of each other. You can build the tower to a certain height without a problem, but as it continues to grow, eventually the instability of the foundation will cause everything to come tumbling down.

But, I wonder, how do you fix the base when you've stacked so much on top of it already? As Walum put it, the older you get, the more complicated it becomes.

"The goal this week," Lorraine concludes, "is to get the three of you unstuck."

She starts with Adam, pulling out his genogram and trauma worksheet, which he brought for her to reexamine. "Are you happy in your marriage?" she asks him.

"No, I'm really not. What I had with this other woman showed me the happiness I was missing."

"Is your wife happy in the marriage?"

"I . . . I don't think so." Adam purses his lips and shakes his head. This is the conversation I've been having with him over and over. If anyone can get through to Adam, it's Lorraine.

"Have you ever, even before your affair, been happy and content with your wife?"

"Not really. I was way too young to get married. I think one of the reasons I got so involved with the football leagues was just to do something away from her."

"So don't you think"—and here Lorraine holds Adam's genogram in front of him—"that it's time for someone in your family to make a stand and take care of their own needs for once? Look at your parents: Your mom is unhappy and medicating with romance novels and pills while your dad walls off and keeps busy. This is a behavior that's been passed down for generations. And it only takes one courageous person to stop the cycle of silent suffering and sacrifice."

"But how?" He seems genuinely stumped.

"By being true to yourself. People always ask how supposedly good German people could have been complicit in the atrocities of the Nazi regime. And one part of the answer is: the family system. Children in that time were taught to be obedient to their fathers, that Father is always right, and that they must make sacrifices for the parents to whom they owe their entire existence." She pauses to make sure we get it. "And then what happens? The government demands loyalty, obedience, and sacrifice, until you have a nation of people violating their internal value system for the Fatherland."

We sit in silence and take in her words, their apparent truth, and the profound way in which trauma shapes history. "I'm passionate about what I'm doing," she continues, "because I believe that functional parenting is the secret to world peace. And the only way to make functional parents is to heal psychological wounds with the same urgency that we heal physical wounds. Do you get what I'm saying?"

She looks almost beatific as she speaks. "I get it," Adam responds enthusiastically.

"So then, tell me, are you are willing to stay in your marriage, even at the cost of sacrificing yourself and hurting your children?"

He closes his eyes and exhales slowly through his nose. Then he bites his lower lip and shakes his head. "I agree with what you're saying one hundred percent, but I can't leave. I just can't. Not while the kids are still in the house."

Lorraine's gaze bores into Adam's being. "Then I want you to repeat after me: 'I will stay in this relationship . . . even at the cost of sacrificing myself and all my needs . . . and hurting my children.'"

Backed into a corner, Adam blanches. Tears well up in my eyes as I watch him grapple with the truth. This is exactly what my parents have done—to themselves, to my brother, to me.

Finally, Adam crosses his arms over his chest, opens his mouth, and, to everyone in the room's surprise, repeats Lorraine's every word. Calvin and I stare at him slack-jawed. And this is the moment when I finally understand why I had such a hard time committing to Ingrid after rehab: Even when we see the truth, trauma still prevents us from reaching it, like a rockslide blocking the road to our future.

Lorraine turns to us and says, not with the anger we were expecting but with acceptance and empathy for Adam, "Do you see how strong this is? How trauma can destroy individuals and nations and generations?"

More than our relationships are at stake here, I think. The future is at stake.

As Lorraine swings the door open to dismiss us for lunch, we see a sight that makes our hearts freeze: Joan.

Joan looks intently at each of us, singeing us with the coals of her eyes, then says, unsmiling, "Welcome back, gentlemen."

Turning to Lorraine, she tells her, sweetly: "See me in my office tomorrow morning."

It is the quickest group castration in history. Even Lorraine seems rattled. A brief shudder runs through her head and shoulders, like a dog shaking off stress. Then she snaps at us, "Be back here in an hour."

When we return, she goes to work on Calvin. "Your problem is that you want unconditional approval and admiration from women," she says bluntly. "When you're with someone you pay for or a young helpless dependent, you get that. But in a healthy relationship of two people with equal internal power, sometimes your partner doesn't agree with you or support your behavior. And that's where the real relating begins."

"So I'm supposed to date someone who doesn't like me?" Calvin asks, genuinely confused.

"No, you're supposed to grow up emotionally so that when someone you love doesn't constantly worship you or do what you want, it doesn't cause your entire sense of self to crumble."

As Calvin takes this in, his eyes ring red and he reaches for the Kleenex. By the time Lorraine turns her attention to me, the sun has already set. I promise myself that I will listen to her with an open mind, that I'll be less stubborn than Adam about whatever truth she's about to confront me with.

"Just like Adam has to separate from his wife to take care of himself, there are some things you need to cut off as well," she tells me.

"Besides sex and relationships?"

"Absolutely, though of course that depends on what you've decided you want since we last spoke."

"I talked to Hasse Walum, like you told me. And I just want to overcome my past so I can have a loving relationship and live my authentic life." More specifically, I want to do these things with Ingrid, but this doesn't seem like the best time to bring it up.

"How many women who you've been sexual with are you still in contact with?"

"A lot, but I haven't been seeing them."

"Then let me ask you"—here it comes, the verbal aikido that will use my words to topple my beliefs—"is it possible to live your authentic life if you have inauthentic people around you?"

She's backed me into a corner, just as she did to Adam and Calvin. Or more accurately, we've already backed ourselves into these corners and she's just helping us see the walls.

"Probably not," I tell her, then correct myself. "No, definitely not."

"That's right. To empty out completely, you need to let go of all the negative messages you received about yourself as a child. And you need to separate from the lifestyle you created as a reaction to them. So if you want to take back your life, you're going to be best served by ending contact with every female you've ever sexualized."

"Oh god," I begin, my voice cracking. The pathological accommodator in me is terrified of rejecting so many people; the adolescent is reminded of being grounded; the player is afraid to die. No wonder I was able to keep my pledge to Lorraine relatively easily these last few weeks: They were just the first baby steps into anhedonia.

At least I now know the answer to my building-blocks question from earlier: The only way to fix a tower with a faulty base is to knock it down and rebuild it over a stronger foundation. "So what would be the most compassionate way to do that?" I ask.

"Why don't you think about all the different ways women get in touch with you and all the ways you seek them out, and seal those doors shut permanently?"

A lump forms in my throat. On the blackboard, Lorraine writes stage two of her detox plan. All I have to do are four things:

1. Change my phone number

2. Change my email address

3. Block all social networks on my computer

4. Don't give my new information to anyone with tits

And that's when I reach for the Kleenex.

6

There are the women I've slept with; the women I've fooled around with but haven't slept with; the women who don't want to sleep with me but hopefully one day will change their minds; the women who want to sleep with me but I don't want to sleep with them, though maybe on a lonely night I'd reconsider; the women who want to sleep with me and I want to sleep with them but there's a complicating factor like distance or a boyfriend; the women I want to sleep with but I slept with their friend and now it's a little awkward; and all the women I haven't met yet but would want to sleep with if I met them.

All told, it's a lot of women. Nearly a lifetime of work: thousands of dollars squandered at bars and restaurants, thousands of hours spent calling and messaging and emailing, thousands of times saying things like "Does Friday work for you?" and "My ex and I ended things on good terms" and "I have to show you this video on my computer" and "I didn't think this was going to happen either."

Whenever I haven't been working, whenever I haven't been studying, whenever I haven't been watching movies or reading books or playing video games, this has been what my waking life—and some of my sleeping life—has been about.

And so I sit, frozen in the hotel room in front of my computer, a hoarder reluctant to part with the detritus of his past. Going sexually sober for a limited amount of time was a reasonable challenge, but making a permanent break with every single one of my options is terrifying when I'm not in a relationship. Yet if I want one last shot at happiness with Ingrid when I see her again—assuming she hasn't completely moved on—then I must prepare for the trip before leaving, not after.

"Let me help you," Adam offers. I stand up and he takes my seat, downloads a program that restricts access to specific websites, then shields the keyboard from my eyes as he types in a password.

"I'm blocking all pornography, social networking, and dating sites from your computer," he informs me. "I used this program with my kids. If there's anything you want to post on these sites for your friends, you can send it to me and I'll post it for you—if it's appropriate."

In just minutes, my pipeline to variety has been sealed shut.

"Now for the email," Adam says cheerfully, clearly at home taking care of someone else's needs.

"Can we do it in stages?" I sit down on the bed. I'm getting dizzy, light-headed, nauseous.

"You gotta rip off the Band-Aid."

"So are you gonna let me file divorce papers for you and your wife, then?"

He's not amused.

Adam sets up a new email address for me. I make a list of less than twenty people—family, close friends, colleagues—to give it to. Then he changes the password on the old email account to lock me out, and we write an auto-responder letting everyone else from my past know I can no longer be reached there.

"Man, this is weird," I tell Adam. "Feel my hands. I'm shaking."

I'm like an alcoholic going through the d.t.'s.

"Fortunately for you, there's nothing I can do with your phone right now. But not only do you need to get a new number, you also need to get a flip phone that doesn't have Internet access."

"I'll do that when I'm home," I respond, grateful for the small reprieve.

"Think of yourself as Tarzan," he suggests, repeating advice that Lorraine once gave him. "You can't hold onto the vine behind you and the vine in front of you forever. At some point, you have to let go of the past to move forward."

Suddenly, my world has become much smaller. And after the initial fear and panic of letting go subside, I realize it's also become much easier to manage.

W̲hen we return to the workshop the next day, Lorraine looks more dispirited than I've ever seen her.

"Most of the therapists here are as bad as the patients," she vents before
the session begins. Something must have happened with Joan this morning,
and it likely has to do with us. "They think their degrees and certifications
give them permission to be one up and constantly in the adapted adolescent. Last week, Joan shamed one of the men's groups and told them that
waitress was a sexist word. I talked to her about it, and I think reporting me
was her way of retaliating." There's a weariness in her voice that I haven't
noticed before. "There are so many rules and politics here that I can't do
what I need to help people."

We thank her for her dedication and courage. What we don't say is
that, like Adam, it seems she's stuck in a relationship that doesn't meet her
needs.

And she's therapist-enmeshing us.

For the next three days, Lorraine perseveres, and soon her powers return—
until the moment comes that I've been both dreading and hoping for. She
puts each of us into a light trance to go through a more intense version of
chair work that she calls an "emotional root canal." I yell at my mother, my
father, and the bully who fondled me. And like last time, the thick black
curtain in front of my mind parts to reveal the truth.

And I see that I've been making sex the most important criterion in my
relationships at the expense of my own happiness. There wasn't one point in
this last year where I searched for a deeper kind of emotional connection or
a greater kind of love. It was all about exploring a single aspect of relationships: sexuality. And even in that one aspect, I failed.

At the puja and in the sex-positive community, I found countless women
who were sexually liberated and open, and required only one thing—that
they be empowered and in control of the context, because that's how they
felt safe enough to truly let go. And I was uncomfortable with that. Did I
ever really see who Kamala Devi was or did I just see my mother? Could San
Francisco have worked if I wasn't so hell-bent on making it go exactly my
way and resenting anyone who threatened that? Why was the relationship

with Sage so great until she wanted her freedom and I lost my absolute control? And why, in so many of these experiences, could I not let go when I felt vulnerable around women—not to mention other men?

The answer: I was never actually pursuing sexual freedom. I was pursuing control, power, and self-worth. I was either acting like my mom or making someone into my mom. But rarely was I actually myself. Because, as I witnessed on ecstasy, the feeling that I'm not acceptable as I am is so fucking overwhelming that I'm terrified to let go and just be myself with anyone.

I've been the benevolent dictator of not just everyone else, but also my own fucking self.

As this last insight hits home, I dissolve into a puddle of tears. Lorraine waits as I wipe my nose on the back of my hand, then she speaks slowly and gently: "All the things you've been trying to get from these relationships— freedom, understanding, fairness, acceptance—are exactly the things that you never got from your mom. So every time you load all that unfinished business onto your partner, you're setting yourself up for another disappointment. Because as an adult, the only person who can give you those things is you. Do you understand that?"

"Yes," I tell her. "I do."

And I really do.

She invites Adam to the chair next, and proceeds to blow his mind. When he opens his eyes afterward, they're brilliantly beaming. And in a happy-go-lucky voice that differs from his usual beaten-down and measured tone, he exclaims, "I want some ice cream!"

His inner child, whose needs he's been repressing his whole life, has finally spoken up. It's probably been decades since he's allowed himself to enjoy even a morsel of sugar.

This process is the closest thing I've seen to a miracle.

An hour later, we're eating ice cream.

"I've missed me," Adam says between shovelfuls of an Oreo-topped sundae that Lorraine went out and bought for him. Calvin sits mutely nearby, shell-shocked from his own epiphany, which is that if you become the hero in an enmeshed family as an adult, accepting that role will occupy the space your heart has available for a relationship. So Lorraine insisted that he draw strong boundaries with his parents, even though he feels that they need him right now.

Meanwhile, I work up the nerve to tell Lorraine about the wedding invitation from Ingrid's brother. When she doesn't seem to disapprove of my attending, I ask her the question that's been worrying me since Machu Picchu: "How will I know I'm truly ready this time and not one of those love avoiders who wants to be in a relationship when he isn't in one, then wants to be free when he's in a relationship?"

Lorraine responds cryptically, "Do you know the story of the Prodigal Son?"

Adam nods his head vigorously, melted ice cream dribbling down his face. He knows his Bible well. Lorraine tells us her version of the story anyway:

"A father has two sons. The older one is a good son. He does everything he should, pleases the father, and stays on the farm to take care of it. The younger one leaves the family, spends all his father's money on prostitutes, doesn't stay in touch, almost starves to death, and then, finally, returns and begs to be allowed to take care of the farm with his brother again.

"When the father throws a huge celebration to welcome his youngest son back home, the older brother asks, 'What about me?' And do you know what the father replies?"

"He says that a Christian should always be merciful and allow someone to repent?" Adam tries.

"Perhaps. But I like to believe he also said something else: 'You worked on the farm because you felt like you should; your brother came back to work on the farm out of choice. And that is the more meaningful of the two.'"

She pauses and lets it sink in for all of us. "Love is something about a person, some connection with them, that makes you willing to change."

As Adam scrapes the sides of his bowl clean, I realize why monogamy never worked for me before. It's always been something that I felt my partner expected or made me do. If I treat it as a choice this time as opposed to a demand, then maybe I can be the Prodigal Boyfriend.

Lorraine sees the hope illuminating my face and quickly warns, "You, my friend, are on a deadline to love right now. If you want any hope of being in a relationship with Ingrid again, you're going to have to attack your trauma with all the commitment you have and every tool there is before that wedding. Only after you've learned how to be alone without loneliness will you be ready for a relationship."

"What other tools are there?" I ask.

She lists them for me: a litany of therapies designed to work on different senses. They're unfamiliar—word combinations I've never heard before. But I write them down like a prescription.

"My biggest worry," I tell her, "is that after I did the chair work with you last time, I felt just like this. I had so much clarity and hope. But when I returned to my normal environment, I totally reverted to my old thoughts and behaviors."

She holds her fingers to her lips and considers the dilemma for a moment. "As you peel away the layers of the false self, you're going to start feeling the pain inside that it's protecting you from. So you're going to get very raw and uncomfortable before you get better. I think you may have gotten stuck in those feelings last time and that's why you left Ingrid. But if you can process all that old pain in an adult, healthy way this time, you won't need your old walls and defenses anymore."

It's a lot to take in and I struggle to understand it all. Then I decide I don't need to understand it. I just need to do it.

There's only one problem: "What if afterward, I go to the wedding and I'm truly ready in my heart and soul to commit, and Ingrid's with someone else or doesn't want to be with me again?"

Lorraine's eyes smile into mine, makeup cracked over the lids like dry earth, as she answers without hesitation: "If she doesn't want you back and she's the catalyst for this change, then she's the best thing that ever happened to you."

8

Curtis Rouanzoin waves a thin metal rod back and forth in front of my eyes as I recall memories of my mother. He then places headphones over my ears and plays tones that jump from the right earpiece to the left one as I keep remembering and feeling pain, remembering and feeling pain—until I'm just remembering.

Lindsay Joy Greene ducks as I send my fist flying into the air with all my strength, releasing anger that feels like it's been trapped in my wrist for decades. I do it over and over again with each hand, until I just don't need to anymore.

Olga Stevko spends eight hours hypnotizing me. I walk around her office, entering the minds of my parents in search of the things they didn't get from their parents. Then I imagine flowing these qualities to each person in my family back seven generations and then forward to me in the moment I was conceived, until I feel like I actually grew up with them.

Greg Cason gives me homework. Lots of it. Thought records, goal sheets, written exposures, gratitude diaries, behavioral experiments—each one chipping away at my fears and pathological accommodation until I can see them as the delusions they are.

Barbara McNally tells me to close my eyes; picture myself and my mother in a room with a white light coming from me and an *X* over her; and then imagine yelling, "Give me the fucking keys!" as I punch her in the face repeatedly.

I am at war. It is a strange fucking war. But I am winning.

"On a scale of one to ten, how strong is the emotion attached to the memories we've been working on?" Curtis Rouanzoin asks one day. The procedure I've been going through with him is called EMDR, or eye movement desensitization and reprocessing, which looks at the way trauma is stored in the brain and attempts to properly process it.

"If it used to be a ten, now it's an eight," I tell him.

Lindsay Joy Greene is trained in a therapy called SE, or somatic experiencing, and she's been locating trauma trapped not in my brain, but in my body, and releasing the stored energy. One day she asks, "On a scale of one to ten, how much anger do you feel when you recall the memories we've been discussing?"

"If it used to be an eight, now it's a seven," I tell her.

Olga Stevko practices her own variant of NLP, or neuro-linguistic programming. Where the experientials with Lorraine were about debugging my operating system, her process is about rewriting the original code. For example, she tells me that inside my mother's words, "Never grow up to make anyone as miserable as your father makes me," was a hidden command: *Never grow up*. As she helps me grow up, it brings my trauma down to a six.

Greg Cason specializes in cognitive behavioral therapy, which takes it to a five. And I don't know what to call Barbara McNally's method and her bottomless quiver of techniques, but they work, they're original, and they bring the emotion associated with those memories to a four. And I do so much more: I beat pillows with baseball bats. I tap on energy meridians. I make shadow maps of my dark side. I try psychodrama. Not all of it works, but none of it hurts.

One morning, I notice that half the boxer shorts in my dresser are gifts my mother has given me for various birthdays and holidays. Most are novelty themed with semisexual jokes on them, like male and female gender signs with the words "change often" next to them. Though I feel a pang of guilt as I scoop them up and toss them in the trash, I recall Barbara McNally telling me that this kind of guilt is a good thing. It means that I'm finally doing the work of separation.

While I'm at it, I throw away all the keys to old cars and apartments that I've saved in some unconscious attempt to prove to my mother that I won't ever lose them.

As Lorraine predicted, I feel fragile and vulnerable during this shock-and-awe campaign, as if my skin has been removed and all my nerves exposed. The slightest stress—be it a small criticism from a colleague, an obstacle standing in the way of a project I need to complete, someone asking me to repeat myself, a restaurant being out of my favorite dish—fills me with disproportionate anxiety and rage. Even if a person says something nice to me, I misinterpret it as rude and disrespectful. And every night, I toss and turn, obsessing over the events of the last few years, unable to fall asleep.

"This isn't making me happy," I complain to Rick one dark morning.

"The purpose is not to feel good or have fun," Rick reminds me. "It's to force feelings to surface so they can be examined, and to find the deeper causes for your behavior. In that respect, it's working amazingly well. How you feel during the process is the least important part. So you can feel good to the extent that you're doing the work to learn about yourself and you're willing to look at the feelings that come up. That's the part to hold on to."

So I push through the pain and fight harder. It eats into my bank account, but in the long run I'm saving thousands of times this amount of money on bad dates, dramatic relationships, short-lived marriages, poor decisions, and the false friends I'm trauma-bonded to.

I am motivated by the mistakes of the past, the hope of a better future, the desperate dream of Ingrid, and the feeling deep down that finally, after all this searching, I'm doing the right thing. Not just for Ingrid or for my relationships, but for me. Instead of trying to find other people to complete me, I am finally completing myself.

Today, I'm doing something even more excruciating than therapy. I'm sitting at an STI clinic, preparing to get tested for literally everything.

As I wait to see the nurse, I think of all the women I was with while dating Sage: the one whose period started shortly after I went down on her, the one who dropped her ass on me before I had a chance to put a condom on, the one who the rubber slipped off inside, and then all the women who went down on me while I basically had an open sore on my dick. And what if that sore wasn't from friction?

Then there's Sage: She said she was clean, but who knows when she was last tested?

I don't think I could show my face to Ingrid again if I caught something during this time. What if this whole quest for freedom has instead sentenced me to death? What if instead of having my cake and eating it, I end up having no cake and nothing to eat?

I call for my test results several stress-filled days later. As the nurse looks for them, my heart curls into a tight ball. My forehead knits. Even my dick is tense, as if a guillotine blade is about to drop onto it.

Finally, she returns to the phone. "You're negative for HIV, chlamydia, gonorrhea, and . . ." I silently rejoice, but then she hesitates, as if about to say something awkward. The rejoicing ends.

"This is odd," she continues. Fuck, I knew something was wrong. What if it's incurable? "You tested negative for herpes."

"Negative?"

"Just about everyone has herpes," she says, as if it's the equivalent of pimples.

And in that moment, I'm grateful to my parents for their immune system. "Thank you," I tell her. "I think I love you."

"I love you too, honey," she says and hangs up, my blood-drawing angel.

One advantage to monogamy: no more terrifying STI tests.

Relieved and reprieved, I continue the war on my past.

There are, of course, experiences that I can't access: preconscious, early childhood, and forgotten imprints. And surely a great deal of the damage is done in those crucial first few years. But when I ask about it at a weekend workshop just outside Los Angeles run by a trauma-healing center called The Refuge, I'm reassured that what I remember is a window into what I've forgotten—that the patterns likely stayed the same, that a narcissistic parent was always a narcissistic parent.

On my way home from The Refuge workshop, I stop by my friend Melanie's birthday party at a West Hollywood bar. Since starting this voyage into anhedonia, it's one of the only social events I've attended. I'm wearing jeans and a hoodie, feeling very anti-social, and planning to just give Melanie her present and then duck out.

But as soon as I walk in the door, I spot trouble: Elizabeth, the tech entrepreneur Melanie introduced me to years ago—the one who said she'd have sex with me only if I agreed to marry her.

"I've been trying to reach you," she says in greeting. She's wearing a low-cut green dress and black strappy stilettos.

"I changed my number," I tell her, polite but curt.

She continues, unfazed: "I've had a little to drink, so I can tell you this. You're part of the reason I broke things off with my boyfriend. I made a list of the qualities I look for in men. Then I made a list of the potential men in my life. Then I compiled all the data on a graph, and you rated highest in every category except one."

I get the sneaking suspicion that she prepared this ambush in advance. "Let me guess," I respond dispassionately. "Stability."

"That's exactly it." She holds eye contact. "The first thing I thought when I broke up with him was, Now I can fuck Neil Strauss."

I've never been hit on this aggressively. Either she's relaxed her marriage criteria or she's a subscriber to the twins' dangle-the-sexual-carrot theory of seduction. The old me would be intrigued enough to find out which; the new me is intrigued for a fleeting moment, but fortunately he makes better decisions. "Unfortunately, you're too late, because I'm off the market."

I start to walk away, but she asks after me: "You're not still in love with that blond girl, are you?" She sneers the word *girl* as if she's saying *peasant*.

I stop and tell her, "I am, actually." The words are much easier to articulate than I would have imagined.

"I don't think she's at your level." Elizabeth is undeterred. "I saw a photo of you two online. Her nail polish was chipped."

Now that I'm not seeing Elizabeth—or any woman—as a means to a sexual end, I'm astonished that I was ever interested in her. If I were dying of altitude sickness in Machu Picchu, she's the type who'd leave if she saw a rich guy landing in a helicopter nearby. "That's the great thing about Ingrid," I inform her. "She doesn't define herself by her looks. One day, she sent me photos she'd put into some apps, and they showed what she'd look like fat and old."

This is when Elizabeth says the one thing that, until recently, would have affected my last ounce of resolve like kryptonite. "Since our talk, I've decided that I want a more open relationship. I don't want to keep a man from exploring his sexuality or having experiences with other women. I think it's natural for a man to want variety."

"Well, I hope you find someone." I'm grateful to find myself unmoved by her words. Either I'm healing or I'm just really irritable from all this wound-scraping. "Good seeing you again."

Instead of saying goodbye, she kneels at my feet, a still life of submission. She then slowly ties the loose laces on one of my shoes, gazing up at me the whole time, edging into the space between my legs and then freezing there for a moment to give my mind's eye the exact picture it needs to imagine what could still happen tonight.

This is the moment the red demons and I always talked about, wondering if we could resist the lure of easy sex with a beautiful woman.

Elizabeth slowly rises to her feet, letting her freshly polished nails linger on my arm as a testament to her superiority over Ingrid. Sensing victory, she purrs, "My mother always used to say, 'If you thought it, then you already cheated.'"

"Well, I'll just have to live with that." I bid her a final goodbye and walk off to greet Melanie. Fortunately, it turns out I can resist.

As I head home a little later, feeling like the target instead of the player, I'm unexpectedly elated. This is the first time I've turned down sex from a potential partner I'm physically attracted to and, more so, a nonmonogamous relationship. And I have no regrets. If Ingrid knelt on the ground to tie my shoelaces, it would be because she wanted to tie my shoelaces, not because she wanted to seduce me into thinking she'd be the perfect wife.

I think back to the photos that Ingrid texted me, the ones with her face altered to look unflattering. The message that accompanied them read: "Let's grow old and fat together."

I wondered in Peru what love was. That is love. It's when two (or more) hearts build a safe emotional, mental, and spiritual home that will stand strong no matter how much anyone changes on the inside or the outside. It demands only one thing and expects only one thing: that each person be his or her own true self. Everything else we attach to love is just a personal strategy, be it effective or ineffective, for trying to manage our anxiety about coming so close to something so powerful and uncontrollable.

I return to the tree house, which is free of chaos and clutter, and to bed, which is free of cigarette smoke, condom wrappers, and wet spots from spilled drinks and other fluids. And I realize that I made a mistake by equating variety with freedom.

I'm off all social and dating apps and websites. That's freedom.

Less than twenty people have my email address. That's freedom.

My phone barely makes a sound. That's freedom.

I have my life back. That's freedom.

I didn't catch anything communicable. That's a fucking relief.

I am truly alone, bereft of options for the first time since puberty. And, oddly, I don't mind at all. It turns out that leaving all my options open has kept me too busy juggling them to really live. Studies on choice even affirm that having too many options leads to less happiness and satisfaction.

I think back to my childhood—to the irrational rules and the bedside conversations and the constant criticism—and I feel nothing. On a scale of one to ten, it's now a one.

10

The following week, something snaps.

It begins when I'm talking to my mother on the phone. We haven't spoken for a while because I've been avoiding anything that could interfere with the work I'm doing. But when she mentions that this year will be her forty-ninth wedding anniversary, I walk right into her trap and ask, "Do you want anything special for your fiftieth anniversary?"

"No," she replies with scorn. "Why would I want anything honoring that?" She pauses, then decides, "Well, there is something you can do for my fiftieth anniversary: Shoot your father." She laughs, as if it's funny, then adds as an afterthought, "Actually, if you wanted to shoot him for my forty-ninth anniversary, that would be fine too."

Her comment doesn't bother me or make me feel like I'm being asphyxiated, nor does it cause me to feel sorry for her or for Dad. It just rolls off me, like a child's attempt to recruit a stranger in a personal vendetta.

That's when I see our relationship as if it were a movie—with distance, detachment, and clarity. It's a black comedy about a mother who feels victimized by her husband, yet too broken to do anything about it, so nearly everything in her life, including her own son, becomes a weapon to use or an ally to recruit in her private, solitary war against this oblivious man.

As I end the conversation with her, not only do I let go of any remaining expectations that she'll be nurturing or mothering, but I let go, without guilt, of any obligations I owe her as my mother. And it is this moment of release—of changing her role in my life from mother to adapted adolescent—that ultimately frees me.

With that original trauma bond broken, in the days that follow, I'm possessed by a feeling I've never experienced before. In fact, it's hard to actually call it a feeling. It is the absence of feeling.

Sometimes I'll sit on the couch and just listen to the sounds outside, look around the room and through the window, and think about nothing. Or I'll move through the house in slow motion, disconnected from my usual sense of urgency, going about everyday behaviors like brushing my teeth as if they're the only things I have to do in my lifetime. It's like zoning out, except there's nowhere to zone out to. It's as if there's nothing in my head. I don't even know if I feel good or bad. I'm beyond good and bad. I just am.

When I try to sleep at night, my breathing seems light, like it's not filling my lungs with the oxygen they need. My heartbeat seems faint, like it might stop at any time. My mind seems slow, as if my neurons are degenerating and I'm drifting into a painless death.

I've finally emptied out. I've Forrest Gumped myself. I am truly in anhedonia—if not in a void beyond it.

There's just one problem: Lorraine never told me what I was supposed to fill up with afterward. So I email her to find out.

She doesn't respond.

A few days later, I try her again.

And still there's nothing.

I'm reminded of Ingrid's deadly silence, yet it doesn't feel like abandonment.

I'm too empty to feel even pain. I am, as Lorraine predicted, deeply alone, but without a trace of loneliness.

As the week passes without a response from Lorraine, I start to wonder quite apathetically if she's turned me into a zombie, doomed to spend the rest of my life brain-dead.

I call her and leave a message, asking in a slow, confused voice what the next step is and how to fill up. But still she doesn't respond.

And she never will.

STAGE II
• Filling Up •

TIME COMES WHEN YOU'RE
ALL ALONE, WHEN YOU'VE COME TO THE END
OF EVERYTHING THAT CAN HAPPEN TO YOU.
IT'S THE END OF THE WORLD. EVEN GRIEF,
YOUR OWN GRIEF, DOESN'T ANSWER YOU
ANYMORE, AND YOU HAVE TO RETRACE YOUR
STEPS, TO GO BACK AMONG PEOPLE.

—LOUIS-FERDINAND CÉLINE
Journey to the End of the Night

11

I look into his face. The first thing I notice is the smile, all gums and crooked teeth. Then there are the black glasses, too large and harsh for his face. And most tragically, there's the hair, cut amateurishly short with crooked bangs and random wavy lumps. Yet despite all this, there's something about him that's delightful to look at. It's not just his innocence and naïveté, but his eagerness to please, to learn, to become.

And that's when it happens: Something finally moves in me. It appears to be a feeling. It's hard to tell whether it's love or sadness. Quite possibly it's both. But it's pure. A love and a sadness—for him, for myself.

I'm looking at an elementary-school class photo of myself, age eight, which I dug out of an envelope buried in my file cabinet. I can't remember the last time I looked at my childhood photos.

I am filling up, and I'm doing it on my own.

Both Adam and Calvin called earlier in the day, panicked because they were experiencing their own crises and hadn't heard back from Lorraine either. Fortunately, Calvin gave me the clue I needed. He read the last email Lorraine had sent him, which concluded with the advice: "You have your own internal therapist that is far wiser than any external therapist you could consult. You just need to find that voice and listen to it."

It seemed like her way of saying goodbye, though we had no idea why. Maybe we were taking up too much of her time; maybe this was tough love; or maybe Joan had gotten her suspended for working with patients who'd left rehab AMA. Whatever her reasons may have been, those final words were worth taking seriously.

So I sat in my zone-out couch and reflected on what had brought me up to this point. The first steps were doing a timeline and genogram, which allowed me to identify my wounds. The second steps were the intense therapeutic processes, which emptied and cleaned out the wounds. So the third step must be to fill in the holes left by them.

But fill them with what?

Something Lorraine said the first time we did chair work drifted into my mind. She asked me to protect and look after my inner child.

So I rose from the sofa and rummaged around the file cabinet until I found my old photos. When I truly saw for the first time the wounded child I'd been working so hard to heal, that's when the feelings began to come back.

I used to think that the term *inner child* was a ridiculous metaphor invented to remind responsibility-burdened adults to lighten up occasionally and just have fun. But it turns out that the inner child is very real. It is our past. And the only way to escape the past is to embrace it.

So before going to bed that night, I put the photo in a frame and place it next to my bed. And I vow that from this day forward, that child will be protected. He will be loved. He will be accepted. He will be trusted. And all this will be given unconditionally. He will not be taught to hate and fear. He will not be criticized for failing to live up to unrealistic expectations. He will not be used as a Kleenex or aspirin for someone else's feelings of loneliness, fear, depression, or anxiety.

The next morning, I start filling him—and me—with the things I needed but never had as a child. When I have a negative thought about myself, I gently replace it with a positive truth. When I make a mistake, I forgive myself. When I'm too thin-skinned or thick-skinned, I gently guide myself back into moderate reality. And when I regress, I silently soothe myself as if teaching a child not to be afraid of the dark.

Just as I told Anne to be a good mother to herself, I'm reparenting myself. It's somewhat pathetic that at this age, I need to properly learn how to be an adult. But if the problems I have in relationships are the result of developmental immaturities, then by nurturing these stunted parts of myself into a growth spurt, perhaps I'll finally attain the happiness and stability that have eluded me through them all.

So with this small crack of light shining into my numbness, I start creating a new life.

Each day, I try to take care of the six core needs Lorraine told me about: *physical,* by surfing and eating healthily; *emotional,* by allowing myself to experience and express feelings without being either hypercontrolling or out of control with them; *social,* by spending time with Adam, Calvin, Rick, and other growth-minded friends; *intellectual,* by reading literature, listening to lectures, starting a film discussion group, and, most importantly, simply listening more; and, most alien of all for me, *spiritual*, through transcendental meditation, which a friend of Rick's teaches me.

But the biggest challenge is the sixth core need: *sexual*, especially since I'm chaste and porn-free right now. So while continuing with the rest of my self-care regimen, I decide to skip this one. I've fulfilled enough sexual needs to last several lifetimes. And maybe it's for the best that Lorraine never responded, because now it's truly my life that I'm rebuilding. I've cleansed the childhood wounds and I'm filling the holes inside. All my life, I've been trying to fill the wrong holes.

12

Six days before Hans's wedding—and just a couple of weeks into my new self-care regimen—I wake up and the last remnants of torpor, deadness, and apathy have lifted like storm clouds. In their place, I see a blue sky I forgot was ever there.

I've finally been un-Gumped. All those nights I lay in bed during anhedonia feeling like my heartbeat and breathing were fading to nothing, I wasn't dying or even close to it. My switching speed was simply slowing down, and the lack of constant stress, anxiety, and intensity felt alien to me.

Suddenly I realize that the dichotomy between the false self and the authentic self that all these recovery people talk about is meaningless. It's a value judgment that's impossible to determine. A better way to think about it is the destructive self and the creative self: the *you* that damages your life and the lives of others, and the *you* that brings forth the best in yourself, is connected to others, and is in harmony with the world around you.

All morning I'm struck by epiphanies. It's as if by emptying out and then simply taking care of myself, truth is pouring in spontaneously and effortlessly, without my having to consult experts to find it.

"You seem happier and more at peace than I've ever seen you," Rick says when I meet him for lunch at Coogie's a few days later. "And there's something else different about you too, but I can't put my finger on it." He looks me over slowly, nodding, as if giving a spiritual CAT scan. "Maybe you healed something in you."

He's not the first person to say that. Nearly everyone I've seen lately has noticed a change—not in my appearance, but in my being. Things I never before thought I could change—such as my tendency to snap into anger when hemmed in by irrational rules—have completely evaporated. Where before I was anxious, frenetic, and nervous, now I'm more present, still, accepting. I'm hardly a Buddhist monk, but I'm more at peace with the world and with myself.

"I know. I feel different. I thought this was just to change my beliefs about sex, but it's shifted everything."

"How you do anything is how you do everything," Rick responds, with a calmness that for once I mirror. "Do you see now that the way you choose to live your life affects everything about it? A cheat here and there is not just a cheat here and there. It's a break in the continuum of who you are and the person you are in the world."

"I get that. I think I have a good understanding now of why I cheated."

"And why is that?" The words sound vaguely challenging, like a test to make sure I really have changed.

"It's actually a list of things."

I pull out my phone and show him a memo I wrote one night in bed during anhedonia:

WHY I CHEATED

1. I didn't communicate or keep boundaries with Ingrid, so I acted out due to fear of engulfment.

2. I didn't share my sexual preferences with Ingrid or give her space to share hers, so I acted out due to unfulfilled sexual desires.

3. I blamed her for "not allowing me" to fuck other people, so I acted out due to a denial of personal responsibility for my behavior.

4. I had feelings of worthlessness and low self-esteem deep down, so I acted out for acceptance and validation.

5. I had no spirituality and a faulty intellectual paradigm, so I acted out because I believed we're no different from any other animal and that's what animals do, and the consequences don't really matter to the universe.

For once, Rick is speechless. A smile slowly spreads across his face. And after what feels like eternity, he tells me, "I think you're going to understand what I mean now when I tell you the secret to being faithful."

"What's that?"

"Don't trade long-term happiness for short-term pleasure."

I add that phrase to my notes. It's a good mantra to remember.

"Think of intimacy as a fire," he continues. "The more logs you add to it, the bigger it gets. And the bigger it gets, the less you want to throw water on it."

"My problem before was that the bigger the fire got, the *more* I wanted to throw water on it. I was so scared it would consume me."

Rick studies my face. Words are easy to say, but am I capable yet of living by them? Another test percolates in his mind. He is a producer not just of music, but of lives. "If things don't work out with Ingrid, in order to give your next relationship a chance, I would recommend building intimacy and making a deep emotional commitment *before* beginning a sexual relationship. I think that should be your new challenge: to wait three months before having sex with your next girlfriend."

He waits for my reaction. When I accused Rick and Lorraine of trying to castrate me after they first suggested anhedonia months ago, it only confirmed to them my unhealthy obsession with sex. This time, though, I don't overreact. If I want to have a heart-based relationship, his challenge makes sense. It takes time to let go of our projections and unmet developmental needs so we can see our partners as they really are and for them to see who we are.

"You know, three months sounds like a long time," I tell Rick. "But if I'd done that in the first place, I probably wouldn't have wasted so many years of my life in the wrong relationships."

Yet as I speak those words, I feel a small flutter of discomfort with the idea, and a rising fear from deep inside that surprises me: Will someone want to commit to me without the sex and the oxytocin of orgasm? This would mean that she'd actually have to like me for who I am.

And a powerful voice from somewhere else inside me rises and cradles the fear like a child, telling it, simply, "Yes, she will."

13

After watching John Frankenheimer's *All Fall Down* with my movie group that night, I'm struck by a troubling chain of thoughts: I emerged from anhedonia with not so much a decision but a *knowing* that I was ready for an adult relationship with Ingrid. But what if I've changed so much that my wounds and her wounds are no longer complementary, and we're not attracted to each other anymore? Or what if she's angry at me and just over it? Or what if she's madly in love with that James Dean guy? And even if she is single and doesn't hate my guts, how is she going to believe I've changed? I've told her that before, only to break her heart later.

So I decide to bring proof to the wedding. I spend the next few days gathering the materials I need. In a box marked "#1," I insert a framed photograph of the Survivor. "Thank you for the plant," I write on the back. "It has taught me that I can take care of things. The following packages are not gifts, but expressions of my commitment to you. I've worked hard on who I am and on becoming a better person. And I've learned that with love, anything can bloom. But with ambivalence and fear, a living thing will die. So no one who truly loves and is loved can ever be in a cage."

In box two, I place my old phone, along with a note explaining the new number, who I've given it to, and that I'm now giving it to the person I care most about in the world as well. Inside box three is the receipt for the program blocking all my social networking and the bounceback message from my old email address. Box four takes half a day to prepare: I set up a spaceship room similar to the one she'd made in our old guesthouse, and take a photo of it for her. Box five contains my most prized possession, my only key to the private beach where I surf—my version of the filing cabinet key of trust she gave me. And inside box six is a locket with photos of me as a child on one side and her as a child on the other, with a message: "Little Neil was scared. Adult Neil is not. The only fear he has is of losing you. Let's be great parents to our inner children together."

I wrap each box, and place them all in a larger box. I'm leaping out of the plane without a parachute, committing to her on the basis of faith alone, loving her without requiring her love—and either it's the most romantic thing I've ever done or the most stalker-like. Possibly both.

Some schools of attachment theory assess the way people behave in relationships on a continuum, rather than by clear-cut categories like in rehab. They place people on a graph divided into four quadrants, running from low anxiety to high anxiety on the x-axis and high avoidance to low avoidance on the y-axis. Each quadrant determines a different attachment style: High avoidance and high anxiety would be *fearful-avoidant attachment,* similar to love avoidance; high anxiety and low avoidance would be *preoc-cupied attachment,* similar to love addiction; high avoidance and low anxiety would be *dismissing attachment,* a more extreme form of love avoidance in which relationships are rejected almost altogether because no partner is perceived as worthy. So for fun, I take a test to determine which style I have, answering each question as honestly as I can. And I'm relieved when I fall into the fourth category: low avoidance and low anxiety.

"Combining your anxiety and avoidance scores, you fall into the *secure* region of the space," my analysis reads. And though it's just an online test, it's also the first positive psychiatric evaluation I've had in a long time.

I then read through my notes from the last few years. I look back on every conversation, meeting, book, appointment, intensive, and internal epiphany I've experienced. And I start writing a compendium of all the lessons I've learned.

It is my center, an incomplete guide to love for the incomplete man, a map to success not just in my relationships but to safely handling all the outer and inner forces that can threaten them. It is my reminder to take care of myself, communicate my needs, stay away from the dark side, and keep from getting sucked back into my childhood reality. And it contains much more: ways to cope with the urge to cheat, to avoid turning my partner into my parent, to prevent over-reactions, to resolve conflicts, to make sure I'm growing closer to my partner over time instead of into a stranger.

My progress on it, however, is interrupted by a soft knocking on the front door.

"Who is it?" I ask cautiously, hopefully.

"It's me," a woman's voice says shyly.

"Ingrid?"

"No," the voice responds. "It's Sage."

14

Excerpts from An Incomplete Guide to Love
for the Incomplete Man

1. No matter what the situation may be, the right course of action is always compassion and love.

"I flew in to talk to you. Can you just open the door?"
I want to hide. I want to run. I can't let this get in the way of my plans. But there are plans and then there is life. And life trumps plans every time.
"What are you doing here?" I ask as empathically as I can.

2. As long as at least one partner is in the adult functional at any given time, most—if not all—arguments can be avoided.

"This is crazy, I know. I've been trying to reach you to apologize. I made a mistake. I love you." Pause. Silence. "I got scared, so I ran away, but I'm not scared anymore. I want to be with you. I hope you care about me enough to at least give me five minutes of your time."

I hesitate for a moment, widening the space between the emotion I'm feeling and acting on it. The emotion I'm feeling is fear. I'm worried she'll do something that will affect my newly won clarity or my chances of getting back together with Ingrid. So I summon all my adult brain cells to a meeting in my neocortex and remind them that no one can hurt me without my permission.

3. Recognize when you are backsliding into a childish or adolescent behavior. Then pinpoint what old story is being triggered and tell yourself the truth of the situation. Let go of the lie.

From a distant flank of my brain, however, the small, ragged remains of a once-formidable army of guilt tries to invade. She flew all this way, so I must not disappoint her or hurt her. I squash the voice instantly as the pathological accommodation it is—the old belief that because my mom loves me, I must never do anything to make her suffer. And just about everything makes her suffer.

Love is a cage only when you feel indebted to it, constrained by it, responsible to its owner.

4. Accept what is.

With one army vanquished, the next attacks: the terror of self-doubt. What if this is how I sound when I see Ingrid? What if Ingrid thinks exactly what I'm thinking right now? What if she's right?

What if . . . Today I will expunge those two words from my vocabulary and replace them with *I will accept it if.*

I will accept it if this is how I sound when I see Ingrid. I will accept it if Ingrid thinks exactly what I'm thinking right now. I will accept it if she's right.

5. Instead of saying "I'm never going to cheat again," say, "Today, I'm not going to do that thing that makes me feel weak and shameful about myself again."

And then the final phalanx marches toward me, the most dangerous of all: desire. It tells me how great the sex with Sage was and how fun the threesomes were. And I attack it with the best weapon there is: experience. I remind it that besides the lonely night with the twins, the adventure before that involved a neighbor who brought her giant husky over, and Sage and she made love while the dog tried to make love to me.

Perhaps the corollary to Rick's secret is that the fantasy of other people is almost always better than the reality.

I open the door and guard the threshold. Sage stands before me in full club makeup and a black dress, with her hair freshly dyed and her legs perfectly tanned. She's clearly spent a lot of time working on herself. And, more worryingly, there's a suitcase at her feet.

She reaches out to hug and kiss me, and I back away. I will not feel sorry for her. I will not be turned on by her.

6. You can't have a relationship with someone hoping they'll change. You have to be willing to commit to them as they are, with no expectations. And if they happen to choose to change at some point along the way, then that's just a bonus.

Words start tumbling out of her mouth, concluding with her desire to move in and start a family with me. It sends a chill up my spine, because this is exactly what I want with Ingrid if things work out between us.

"You want to move in, stay with me forever, and start a family together?"

"Yes," she says, her eyes widening with equal parts sincerity and supplication.

I picture what the future would actually be like with Sage: I imagine us married and raising children—until one day when she feels trapped again, she runs away to Fiji without warning, leaving me to explain to the kids that Mommy left to search for herself and I don't know when she's coming back. The winds of ambivalence will continue blowing her back to me and away again, back and away, back and away.

They say that love is blind, but it's trauma that's blind. Love sees what is.

7. Communicate and maintain healthy boundaries. This means finding the proper balance of filtering and protecting your self, thoughts, feelings, time, and behaviors without either closing off behind walls, or becoming overwhelmed or overwhelming.

She looks forlorn and expectant, and every now and then tears fall from her eyes as she tells me that she spent her savings to fly out here. Until recently, this was my nightmare: having to meet other people's expectations—especially when doing what's right for me hurts someone else's feelings. But it was her choice to come here, so there's nothing to feel guilty about. This is my chance to implement the boundaries I've learned, to enforce them when they're trespassed so I don't feel enmeshed, to break old habits and reinforce new ones.

"This isn't cool," I tell her. "You can't just come by without letting me know."

"But your phone number wasn't working. How can you be so cold? You said you loved me. It doesn't just go away like that."

She has a good point. I flash back to Lorraine's words: You won't get hurt playing with toys, but they will. "I have a lot of love for you," I tell her. "But the relationship just"—I don't know how to best put it—"is over. It ended exactly when it should have."

8. Ask yourself throughout the day, "What do I need to do in this moment to take care of myself?" If you can be aware of what legitimate needs and

wants you're not attending to, and then take actions to meet them on your own—or ask your partner for help if you can't—that is the road to happiness.

"Is there someone else?" she asks.

"There is. But she won't talk to me."

"Is this a joke? You're crazy."

"I used to be crazy," I tell her. "I think I'm finally getting sane."

"Can I at least sleep here?" She takes a step closer and I inhale her unique blend of pomade, sex, and moisturizer.

9. No one can make you feel anything and you don't make anyone feel a certain way. So don't take on responsibility for your partner's feelings and don't blame your partner for yours. The most caring thing to do when they're upset is simply to ask if they want you to listen, to give advice, to give them space, or to give them loving touch.

"What?" It's amazing: Even when you set a boundary, people still want to trample across it.

She says, "I have nowhere to stay. Can I at least stay in the spare bedroom and we can talk when you're ready?"

I remind myself . . .

She says, "I took a cab from the airport."

. . . that Sage is not my mother and . . .

She says, "I promise I'll leave after we talk."

. . . I am not responsible for her happiness.

So I draw the boundary more firmly. "It's not okay to stay here. I'm sorry, but I made a commitment to myself and I need to honor it."

10. Love, honor, and affirm yourself. Whatever your decisions, actions, feelings, and thoughts throughout the day may be and whatever outcome they may lead to, if you are healthy, then they are ultimately healthy.

The words register on her face and she starts to protest. The old me would want to hug her, to say we can talk later, to let her crash here, to promise that we can still be friends, to make any number of mistakes. But now all that goes through my mind is a question: Is it in my highest good?

And none of these is in my highest good. So I remain resolute like stone and she melts into water.

The tears mix with her mascara, running black down her face. They are not my problem. They are her problem. And she will get over it. Or she won't. But the most compassionate thing I can do is let her make her own decision based on the truth. And the truth is that I love Ingrid.

I just hope that Ingrid loves me.

11. And, above all, always remember to breathe and be in the moment.

But I will accept it if she doesn't.

15

I stand outside the unheated garage where Ingrid's stepdad made her live with nothing but an old torn-out car seat as furniture while her brother and stepbrothers lay on warm beds in warm rooms. I make sure my jacket sits firmly on my shoulders, my purple shirt cuffs jut ever so slightly out of the sleeves, my matching tie is just a touch off-center, and the bottoms of my pants hang neatly over my shoes. I am Sage. I've come begging.

I walk through the kitchen, where Ingrid's stepfather made her cook and scrub for hours every day, punishing her if she dared to sit down. She was allowed to eat only after the rest of the family finished their meal. At the end of the kitchen, there's a door to the backyard, where Ingrid's stepfather would force her to chop the heads off chickens and would laugh as she vomited at the horror of the act. She is my Cinderella.

And hopefully in her fairy tale, I am the frog she has kissed and transformed into a prince.

I look around for her, the box I wrapped last night in my arms. There are two long tables decorated with flowers, surrounded by women in red dresses and men in dark suits. Four of those men are her stepbrothers. I hope Ingrid's been telling them nice things about me. But somehow I doubt it.

I circle the yard looking for Ingrid, hopeful not to see James Dean and careful not to make eye contact with any of her stepbrothers. But she's nowhere to be found. I don't belong here. I should leave.

"Hey, brother," I hear a voice saying.

I turn around and see Hans near the bar, waiting for the ceremony to begin. I congratulate him and thank him for inviting me. I want to ask why he sent me the invitation, but I'm afraid he's going to say it was an accident.

His hand presses against the small of his back and he stretches as if in pain. When I ask if he's okay, he looks around furtively, making sure no one else can overhear. Then he tells me he went to a strip club with his friends for a surprise bachelor party the night before. He got so drunk that he started dancing on the pole and carrying two strippers across the stage. But he fell, dropped the dancers, and threw out his back.

"Don't tell my bride," he cautions.

"She doesn't know?"

He smiles at me conspiratorially. "I told her I hurt it at work."

And so another marriage is born with a lie. It is the great lie—that husbands and wives have no sexual interest in anyone except each other. I know deep down that I haven't conquered my desire for other women—I don't think that's possible without getting Hasse Walum to lower my testosterone levels—but I've removed what was psychological: the fear of loving, the terror of being loved, the compulsion to cheat, the cowardice of lying, the weak sense of self, the pathological accommodation, and all the defense mechanisms that kept this system in place and me too blind to see it.

I want to ask Hans where Ingrid is, if she knows I'm coming, and if she's excited or angry or nervous or just doesn't care. But this is his day, his passage into a new life, so I leave him to prepare for it.

That's when I see their mother, who gave up a television career in Mexico to become a housewife in the United States. She sacrificed everything to get away from the cheating first husband who tried to murder her. But his replacement rarely lets her leave the house, have any friends, do anything but chores, or even be a mother to Ingrid and Hans. She is trapped not in the past, but in a fear her future will replicate her past. So in the end, perhaps her ex-husband did kill her. She lives in a coffin in Sylmar. Its headstone reads: Security.

Yet even she cheats, though she doesn't see it as such. Sometimes she tells her husband that she's going to see a neighbor, but instead sneaks out to see Ingrid and Hans, the children she had with her first husband. Jealousy is an unforgiving adversary, still controlling the border long after it has won the war.

I am back in the reality of relationships, where partners "bend the rules" and tell "little white lies" to get their needs met. The ideal I've been striving for is not the way people have relationships in the real world. Perhaps, as I promised my friends in rehab, I actually have gone out and designed a new type of relationship. Yet not one in which I get to fuck all the women I want, as I'd hoped, but one in which I live in truth and without fear or guilt.

I think about how I snuck out on Ingrid so long ago, telling her I was going to Marilyn Manson's house the night before our trip to Chicago, the night before her birthday. And I feel disgust with myself for ever having done that. I used to think I was a good person, but how could a good person do something so reprehensible?

The answer: compartmentalization. The act of putting shameful activities in a small sealed box in our brain, where they remain safely hidden, even from our own intelligence and conscience.

I hope her mom's not upset I'm here. "Congratulations," I tell her slowly. She doesn't speak English—her current husband never let her take lessons— though she understands basic words. "You must be very proud of Hans."

She smiles with a delicacy that reminds me of Ingrid and then says softly, "She needs you."

They are the only English words I've ever heard her speak. I stand before her stupidly for a moment, fighting down the surge of emotion. "We need each other," I sputter.

She nods wisely and kindly at me, as only a mother can, a mother who sees something that her children are too inexperienced to recognize.

And that's when I spot her, emerging from the back porch of the house, all white and all blond—a color combination shared by no one else at the wedding. She is pale like a ghost but radiant like a goddess. She's not just more beautiful than I remember, she's more exquisite, commanding, otherworldly.

It's too far away to see the expression on her face as she steps into the darkness between the back stairs and the party. Hercules follows obediently, wearing a red bow tie. I break into a wide smile and hope to see it reflected back in her face. As she comes closer, I don't detect anger or fear or disappointment or disgust or any of the emotions I was afraid she'd have. She too is smiling.

I've been so stupid.

This is the one, I tell myself. This is the woman I'm going to marry.

I just hope I've truly changed.

16

Excerpt from Ingrid's Mind

And there he walks through the crowd of a Mexican fiesta. I recognize his shirt and tie. They're the same ones he's worn at almost every book signing since I've known him. Purple shirt and purple tie hugging his body.

I quickly run into the house and bypass my aunt, who's waiting for the bathroom. As soon as the door opens, I stumble in, pushing everyone out of the way so I can look at myself one last time before he sees me.

I check my hair, reclip my extensions, fix my push-up bra, and debate whether to use my pink lipstick or keep the red. Red screams, "Take me, you fool, and kiss me passionately." And pink says, "These lips are delicate and soft, handle with care."

So I choose the red. I leave the bathroom and walk through the kitchen. But when I see my reflection in the stainless-steel refrigerator door, I quickly grab a napkin and rub off the red lipstick. Then I put on the pink, and now it's a mess and my lips say, "Take fool kiss delicate handle."

The last year was hard for me. When Neil and I broke up, I felt like everything I had was taken from me. I was angry and disappointed because I gave and gave and gave, and then I was left with nothing. I felt disconnected from the world. There was an emptiness in my chest. I kept trying to figure out what was wrong with me that would cause him to do that.

I dated a lot to forget the feeling. I rebounded with a bartender/underwear model. But one day after we had sex, he pretended like he was a gorilla, flaring his nostrils and pounding his chest while naked for an uncomfortably long period of time. I grabbed my clothes, left politely, and never saw him again.

After that, I met a sweet guy who wrote speeches for presidents. I just wanted to have fun and not feel the pain, but he wanted more from me than I was ready to give. So I broke up with him, then started dating a magician I met at the Magic Castle. When I split up with him, I realized that maybe the relationship I needed to be in was with myself.

When Neil texted me from Machu Picchu, I wanted to run back into his arms. But I was scared I'd be cheated on again. And I wasn't ready. I'd just broken up with everyone and felt too vulnerable.

Being alone was the best thing I ever did for myself. I've always gone from one relationship to another, hoping the other person would help me figure out who I was or complete me and make me feel whole. But it never worked out that way. When the other person didn't make me feel whole, I was left with an even bigger emptiness inside. It took the pain of the last year to realize that I needed to stop being a half trying to find my other half, but to be a whole on my own. I had to learn how to love myself. I had to learn to value myself. And I had to learn that I mattered.

I'm not sure if I'm whole yet, but I'm more complete. And so when Hans asked for help thinking of wedding guests, I suggested Neil. I told Neil that if he ever texted me "freeeeeeedom," I would be there. I didn't say when. I had to be ready, too. And so I made and sent him the invitation myself. I wanted to see him one more time, just to be sure I wasn't making a mistake and walking away from the love of my life.

Before leaving the kitchen, I stand behind the window and try to catch one last glimpse of Neil before our eyes meet. My hands are sweating and I feel a burst of anxiety. There's still time for me to call a taxi and leave. Or run through the front door and climb up my favorite tree, where I used to hide from my stepdad as a kid.

I'm worried that this is a mistake. As my grandmother used to say: You can't change a person unless they're in diapers.

Though another one of her favorite sayings is: With patience, even the grass becomes milk.

Being with Neil felt like having the most beautiful bird from the Amazon, full of colors and life but kept in a cage that was too small for his wings to spread. I'd sit next to the cage every morning and sing with him, but he was always looking out the window. I told him when we separated that it was time to open the cage and set the bird free. But every morning afterward, I looked through the window and hoped to catch a glimpse of him flying by.

So now here I am, looking through the kitchen window and into the yard, and I see Neil flying outside. I see his tender eyes and his sweet smile. He touches his face just below his left eye with his index and middle finger, rubbing back and forth. And as I smile at the memory of that nervous tic of his, I open the screen door and step outside to fly with him.

I just hope he's changed.

Door

5

FREEDOM

I will die kissing your crazy cold mouth,
caressing the lost fruit buds of your body,
looking for the light of your closed eyes.

And so when the earth receives our embrace
we will go blended in a single death, forever
living the eternity of a kiss.

—Pablo Neruda
Cien sonetos de amor

The Survivor sits on my window ledge, brilliantly green and thriving.

Beneath it, Ingrid and I sit on a couch that's been cleaned obsessively, removing all DNA traces of communes, triads, and open relationships. Hercules is sprawled on the floor next to a beautiful white Maltese dog that Ingrid also rescued.

On the table, there's a box wrapped in silver paper. I undress it, slit the packing tape with a pen, and open the cardboard flaps.

There are five small wrapped presents inside, each marked with a different number. A scroll of burnt parchment lies on top of them.

"Go ahead, read it," Ingrid urges.

> *Ladies and Gentlemen,*
>
> *You are cordially invited to the funeral of our greatest and biggest room fixture, Jacob "The Elephant" Goff, age 3, of Malibu, California.*
>
> *A celebration of life service will be held today at 9 P.M. in the community where he lived uninvited. Mr. Goff the Elephant will be buried with some of his most precious items.*
>
> *Sincerely,*
> *Messrs. Freedom & Trust Mortuary*

At first, I don't understand. Why are we burying an elephant?

She places her hand warmly over mine. "You worked hard to win back my trust, so I've been working hard to forgive."

It's the elephant in the room—my past cheating, sneakiness, and lying. And just as I gave Ingrid a present at her brother's wedding to prove that I've changed, the five individually wrapped boxes in front of me three months later are her way of saying that so too has she.

Though Disney cartoons and romance movies end the moment the lovers reunite, leaving the audience to assume they lived happily ever after, in real life this is the moment the story truly begins.

It's when Sleeping Beauty asks Prince Phillip, "How many princesses did you kiss while I was asleep?"

It's when the Little Mermaid yells at Prince Eric, "An enchantment spell? That's the worst excuse I've ever heard. You were about to marry that other girl!"

It's when the princess who kissed the frog asks the resultant prince, "Be honest: While you were a frog, did you have sex with any female frogs?"

Without the intensity to keep them busy, the common enemy to unite them, or the obstacles to intensify their longing, these legendary lovers now face the biggest challenge of all: dealing with each other—and the differences, be they great or slight, in their values, upbringings, opinions, personalities, expectations, preferences, and imperfections. Especially when the aftermath of every such adventure is trauma.

And so, as one might expect, Ingrid did not freely give me her trust after we reunited. On our first day back together, she threatened to leave if I didn't change my social networking status to reflect that I'm in a relationship—even though I no longer have access to the account. On the second day, she threatened to leave after seeing photos of Sage on my computer. On the third day, she threatened to leave if I didn't let her look through my phone. And on the fourth, she said that the memories of the past were too painful for her to want to date me again.

That's when I realized that as a love avoidant, I'd placed Ingrid on a pedestal, thinking that because she was so attached and I wasn't, she must somehow be better at love than I. But in reality she was just sitting on the other end of the same dysfunctional seesaw. After all, she has at least one fatal flaw we both agree on: She chose me as I was back then.

"I never saw it before, but I definitely have a pattern, too," she realized when we discussed this. "My boyfriend before you was totally enmeshed by his mother. She'd call all the time, asking him to do things for her, and he'd drop everything to take care of her. I stayed with him for five years, even though he never let me use the word *boyfriend* or say we were dating or even see him more than twice a week."

And so I found a former colleague of Lorraine's named Vince, zipped up my wetsuit, and watched as he put Ingrid in the chair and began the process of healing the father-abandonment wounds that led to her love addiction.

As she sat yelling at her father, tears streaming down her face, I realized that we had the exact same parents: enmeshing moms and abandoning dads. Except where my mother wants my father dead, her father actually tried to kill her mother.

It's odd how relationships work like that: Love is not an accident. It is a delicate union of two complex, complementary puzzle pieces that have inadvertently been created by different manufacturers.

I was told, "When it's love at first sight, run in the other direction." And I tried that. But I ran right back into her. And now as we sit side by side, starting down a new path together, I unwrap the gift marked #1. Inside, there's a small wooden coffin lined with white satin. Ingrid's handwritten instructions say to leave it open.

The second gift is a small, gray plastic elephant. The note with it reads: "This is the Elephant in the room. He will no longer be in the room with us, because he will be resting in his coffin. The fear, doubt, and anger he created will no longer hurt us or be intrusive to the love we have for each other. I love you."

My face swells as I place the elephant in the coffin on its side. It fits snugly, its feet and trunk close to the edges.

The next package contains two small metal birdcages, each with tiny metal birds in them. "The Cages symbolize being restrained, unable to speak your mind, misunderstood, and alienated," Ingrid's note explains. "These two beautiful Birds placed inside cages with nowhere to go, left alone and lonely, symbolize us as children, as teenagers, and as adults. We are burying this because we are no longer alone or lonely. We have the freedom to fly anywhere we want."

Awed by her wisdom, thoughtfulness, and creativity, I place the two caged birds in the coffin: one at the elephant's head and the other at its rear.

In such a short amount of time and with much less struggle, Ingrid is already on this journey with me. And together we are learning that, to paraphrase the relationship writer Harville Hendrix, the unconscious purpose of a long-term relationship is to finish childhood. Or, as psychiatrist Eric Berne puts it even more succinctly, "Love is nature's psychotherapy."

The next gift contains a dozen miniature metal hands. "The Hands symbolize judging, lack of boundaries, and control. This is how we felt as children and sometimes as adults. Today we are burying this and letting go of the people who pointed fingers at us, the people who tried to control us, our own lack of boundaries, and our attempts to control each other."

I sprinkle the hands over the elephant, the cages, the coffin floor.

The fifth package contains two metal keys with words on them: Secrets and Memories. "These are the Bad Keys," her parchment explains. "The Secrets Key means we no longer have to keep secrets for anyone who ever hurt us. When this key is buried, we will let go of the secrets that are hurting us inside and no longer take on responsibility for other people's problems. The Memories Key is for our bad memories. We are letting go of our attachment to them. We will no longer keep these memories locked up inside and allow them to rule us."

As I slide the keys around the elephant, I finally understand what the true intimacy that Joan spoke about in rehab actually is: It's when partners stop living in the past—in their trauma history—and start having a relationship with each other in the present moment. Love, it turns out, is not something to be learned. It's something we already have, and we must unlearn in order to access it.

Her instructions then read: "Take a moment or two before closing the coffin. You will not be able to open it once it is closed, so take pictures and do whatever you want for the next few minutes or hours. But close it before the day is over."

I stare at the coffin and the beautiful, carefully thought-out items inside. I look at the little elephant, the trapped birds, the many hands, and, finally, the keys, until a single word in the coffin fills my vision: *secrets*.

And I think that if I truly want the past buried, now is the time to set free any last secrets. The moment is so perfect, but like everything perfect, it is fragile.

I tell her nervously, awkwardly, slowly: "I want you to know that there was other bad stuff in the past besides Juliet"—the woman I cheated with. "I didn't know then that I couldn't still love you and sneak around behind your back. I didn't understand. But I understand now."

As she takes this in, her face freezes and her spine stiffens, like a cat reacting to a sudden noise. I look at the Secrets Key and think of what else I'm holding back. "I know you dated some people while we were apart, and

I just want to let you know that besides some of the stuff we've already discussed, I had a lot of other experiences."

"What kind of experiences?" she asks warily.

The beautiful solemnity of the ritual is shattering. But this is what it means to tell the truth: It is to give someone else her freedom, to allow her to have a reaction even if it leads to negative consequences for you, to give her the voice that lying takes away.

In the past, I've had a remarkable gift for turning even the most minor manifestation of fear or disapproval from my partner into a personal catastrophe. But instead, I use the four adjustments to turn shame into reassurance.

Shame is about being bad for someone; reassurance is about being good to yourself.

And not only does it make more sense to respond with compassion instead of criticism, it's also much easier on everyone involved. It may be the key to a longer, happier life.

I tell Ingrid about the poly people, and learning the four adjustments and the concept of relationships based on intents. I tell her about the swingers, and learning that my sexual fantasies can add to a relationship if I include my partner in them rather than trying to protect her from them. I tell her about the harem house, and learning that love is not a terrifying monster making unreasonable demands on my life, but a beautiful friend making occasional requests that I have the option to accept or deny. And I tell her about the open relationship, and learning not just to let go of jealousy and control, but to explore my painful emotions rather than avoiding them like an addict.

As Ingrid listens, she oscillates through a spectrum of feelings: anger, fear, sadness, until, finally, she lands on love. "I never thought I'd say this," she sighs, sliding closer to me and stroking my head. "But maybe all those things you did weren't a relapse after all but were part of the healing."

"I'd like to think so."

As Lorraine once put it, recovery is not about perpetually living in joy and harmony, but about shortening the time it takes to return there when you inevitably fuck it up. And for this reason, I'm grateful for the opportunity that every conflict Ingrid and I have provides to practice this.

"It's just incredible how different you are now," Ingrid says after I share this with her. "You're much more calm and mature and patient and understanding. Sometimes I'm waiting for you to get upset or annoyed, and it doesn't come. It's magical. You're like a butterfly. You spun your little cocoon and you transformed. Even your eyes are different. I can see your heart through them."

Most love stories are about two people who belong together, but are blocked by an obstacle keeping them apart: their cultures, their social standing, their families, a rival lover, a manipulating villain, an unexpected tragedy. But in real life, love stories are more complex. People want love, but after they get it, they become scared or bored or uncertain or resentful. And when they get pain instead of love, they don't leave. They cling to it more strongly than they would to pleasure. And so in life, the real obstacle keeping two lovers apart is not external. The battle to be fought is within.

And so, I think as I take in Ingrid's words, in the end, love is not about finding the right person. It's about becoming the right person.

I put my hand on the lid of the coffin. "This is it," I tell her. "We're saying goodbye to the past. Is there anything else you want to know?"

"Let's close it," she says.

First, I take a photo:

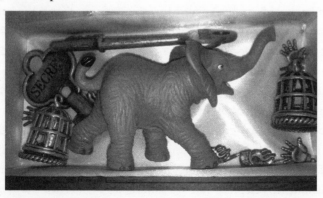

And then I shut the lid.

The elephant in the room is gone.

"There's one last package," Ingrid says.

She hands me a palm-sized box that she's kept separate from the rest of the gifts. Inside are a note and four keys of various shapes and sizes, each with a different word on it. "These are the Good Keys, the ones you keep," the note reads. "The Love Key is to remind you that you are worthy of love and you always have access to my love. The Heart Key is the key to the biggest heart on earth: yours. The Life Key is the key to opening our lives for each other. And the Journey Key is for the path to our happiness."

While reading these beautiful words, I notice the complete absence of my old feelings: suffocation from her love, doubt that I have a good heart, fear of opening our lives to each other, and anxiety about her expectations of me. Instead, every word rings like truth. Neither haunted by the past nor worried about the future, I'm finally grateful for the present.

It turns out that relationships don't require sacrifices. They just require growing up—and the ability to stop clinging to immature needs that are so tenacious, they keep the mature needs from getting met.

I find some paracord in the kitchen, thread a length of it through the key ring, and hang it around my neck so I can keep the keys close to my heart.

"I trust you with these keys," she says.

"I will be worthy of them this time."

There's one last instruction on the scroll: to bury the coffin. Unable to find my shovel in the garage, I grab two large spoons from a kitchen drawer instead.

In the backyard, on top of a hill so small it's more of a bump, there's a soft patch of dirt surrounded by fragments of discarded slate. We kneel around it and start scooping. The dirt is soft and yields easily. We dig until the grave is ten inches deep, safe from being discovered by the tree house's next tenants. In olden days, this was supposedly a Chumash burial ground.

We throw a spoonful of dirt over the coffin and she says a few words. "Dearly beloved, we are gathered here today to bury Jacob 'The Elephant' Goff. He was a very loyal companion. He never left our sides. We wanted to get rid of him, but he turned out to be the best thing that ever happened to us. Without this elephant, we wouldn't have each other. May God have mercy on his soul."

We fake-cry as we gather the dirt spooned around us and fill the hole, until the elephant is gone and buried without a trace of its existence left above ground.

Then we share a moment of silence, basking in the solace of letting go. Ingrid speaks first: "Uh-oh, I accidentally buried my car keys."

I laugh, squeeze her tightly to me, and kiss her between the sparkling, mischievous eyes I so sorely missed.

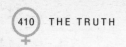

"I love making you laugh," she grins. "You have this amazing smile and your cheeks fill up. I have this picture in my head of us as old people, and me doing something to make you laugh."

"I picture that too." And if I had the choice between laughing or having different foursomes for the rest of my life, I'd take the laughing every time.

"I kind of want to call Juliet and tell her, 'Thanks for everything,'" Ingrid says as we walk back to the house.

As I take her hand in mine, I realize that before trauma healing, I always wanted more—more women, more success, more money, more space, more experience, more possessions. Not once did I stop and say, as I do now, "I have enough."

Epilogue

WHEN THE WILD CARD IS PLAYED, IS IT STILL WILD?

We drive in silence. My father and I. It is my last day as a single man.

I wait for him to give me advice, to say something about my impending wedding, to offer anything he's learned from fifty years of marriage. But he says nothing. I suppose I shouldn't have expected anything different: He never told me about the birds and the bees until I was twenty-two, and his advice was, "Take your time. Go slow. And don't rush it."

To break the silence, I ask what his father was like.

"He was very quiet and didn't say much. He usually worked all the time."

"What's your favorite memory of him?"

"I guess it was when we were fishing together one day, just in silence."

I think about how lonely that must have been, and I suppose, in correlation, how lonely I was. "What about your mom? What's your favorite memory of her?"

He struggles to remember something about his mother, who was a busy Chicago socialite. "I guess I don't have any strong memories of her, either positive or negative."

In my enmeshing conversations of old, we would discuss the theory that because Dad's mother was self-absorbed and his sister was the family favorite, his self-esteem was so low and his fear of women so great that he felt as if the only people he could have power over were the helpless—the handicapped. Clearly, on some level, my foray into the world of seduction—to get what I believed was a psychological advantage over women—was my own attempt to do the same.

"I did have a live-in babysitter, though," he adds, "and I guess we were closer."

I'm surprised to hear how similar our childhoods were—with a distant father, narcissistic mother, favored sibling, and babysitter raising us. And I think about how similar our adult lives almost were.

My relatives often tell the story of a family portrait I drew in kindergarten.

Sketched in crayon on construction paper, there are stick figures representing myself, my little brother, our babysitter, and each of my parents. Then there's a large red line that begins in the center of my father's legs, drops straight to the ground, and finally stretches out in a wide circle around the family. It is my father's penis. Even back then, I somehow knew that our entire family was subordinate to its influence, living in the shadow of its enormity.

And so there is one question that's burning my insides. I work up the guts to ask my father and get some closure on the subject after more than two decades.

"So how did you become obsessed with people with physical disabilities?"

That's what I want to ask, but I don't. Whatever his answer may be, it's a discussion his wife should be having with him, not me. The part of it that concerns me—growing up around a marriage rotted by it—is over with.

I reflect on something Ingrid told me the day I knelt in the sand on a deserted beach in Kauai and asked her to marry me. "You didn't come from a loving family. I didn't come from a loving family. But now we have a chance to make a loving family together."

My father and I lapse back into silence. We haven't quite bonded. I don't know if that's even possible. I can't recall him ever being comfortable with emotional intimacy or physical affection. Trying to bash my head through his wall will only result in brain damage. But at least I've knocked on his door for the first time to see if he wants to let anyone in.

Lately, I've started thinking of the things my parents didn't do perfectly as *variables* that make me an individual rather than as *trauma* that makes me a patient. It's not healthy to walk through life identifying oneself as a victim and others as perpetrators.

"Your mother wants to talk to you," my dad says when we return to the beach house Ingrid and I are renting for the wedding.

She sits in an armchair, with her feet up and a cane at her side. "Is there going to be a photographer at the wedding?" she asks.

"Of course."

Her face tilts to disapproval. "Did you tell him not to take any photos of me?"

"I did." This is the only request of hers I honor. Since she found out about my dad's fetish, she hasn't allowed anyone to take a single photo of her.

"I used to think I was so beautiful," she sighs. "But now I just feel like a freak."

In rehab, I told my group how I used to try to convince her otherwise, to tell her that if she were blond and Dad had a fetish for blondes, she'd be completely fine with it. But this time, I let the comment pass unnoticed, as she herself wants to be. And I accept the fact that she is too old to change. One day soon, she won't be here anymore.

In the notes about love that I compiled during anhedonia, one of the most important was not to date someone hoping she'll change. So perhaps I can apply the lesson to my relationship with her also and accept her as the person she is, not the one I'd like her to be, and be grateful that she loved me as much as she knew how.

"Thanks so much," I tell Rick when he visits on the morning of the wedding. "You made this possible."

"I don't want any of the blame!"

"Any blame would be on me."

"On this we agree."

We walk outside to the patio and sit on deck chairs facing seaward. "At one point, I was ready to give up and stop discussing all this with you," he says, looking over the ocean to the horizon. "It's tragic. The wounds that humans get are so strong that they're like robots operating on childhood programming. And even if they learn the truth about themselves in therapy and rehab, they still cling to their false beliefs and make choices that don't serve them—over and over again." He shakes his head at the cosmic absurdity of it all. "It takes hard, conscious, diligent work to genuinely change."

I have a feeling it's the closest thing to a wedding congratulations I'm going to get from Rick, so I accept it as such. The reception, Ingrid and I agreed, should be small, so that we actually have time and energy to pay attention to each other. I've invited only the people who made it possible: my immediate family, Rick, the red demons, close friends like Melanie, and a few dating coaches and relationship healers. The former gave me the tools to meet Ingrid, the latter to commit to her.

However, Lorraine, to whom I owe more thanks than anyone, never RSVP'd to the invitation. I made some calls to find out what happened to her. From what I could gather, she was disciplined for having what's known as a *dual relationship* with clients (both social and therapeutic). So now she's in a more administrative role at the hospital, and—not unlike Adam—she's too scared to leave and spread her wings on her own. Yet I hope that one day I'll be able to speak with her again and thank her for saving my life—just as she has saved the lives of countless others.

Beyond showering, shaving, and putting on a tuxedo, there's not much for me to do to prepare for the wedding. So in the afternoon, Adam, Calvin, and Troy come by the house and we change into swimsuits.

"How are you doing with the whole monogamy thing?" Troy asks as we walk down the hillside to the beach together.

"You know, I think I blew it up into too big a deal. I hate to say this, but Joan was right: I was just throwing intellectual barriers in my way to avoid being vulnerable and committed." In a big, connected world, it's easy to find enough people with the same trauma profile to agree with you, then simply discount, ignore, or attack all evidence to the contrary.

"But what about the male dilemma—the whole 'sex gets old and so does she' thing?" Troy asks. And I'm embarrassed for ever having thought of anything so shallow and misguided.

"I think that's only true if two people see each other as objects or employees. If they're emotionally healthy adults, then there's no dilemma that they can't work out together. They're not going to even notice each other aging but just getting happier." I pause to reflect on it. What I saw as getting old before wasn't truly a fear of physical decline but a fear of becoming unhappy like my parents. And I'm definitely not worried about that anymore. "Growing older and happier with Ingrid is one of the things I'm most looking forward to in life right now."

A strange thing happened: As I dealt with my enmeshment issues, I became less concerned about wanting sex outside the relationship. And as Ingrid dealt with her abandonment issues, she became less concerned about losing me if I happen to feel attraction to another woman. In fact, once she saw that I was completely happy and fully satisfied to be exclusively with her, anything became possible.

As a result, we developed the relationship I'd been looking for the whole time, only I didn't know what it was: a relationship without fear. Without fear of intimacy, without fear of suffocation, without fear of loss, without fear of speaking our truth, without fear of being hurt, without fear of boredom, without fear of change, without fear of the future, without fear of conflict, and even without fear of other people.

The opposite of fear is not joy. It is acceptance. And that is what we've replaced the fear with. So our commitment today is to neither monogamy nor nonmonogamy. Those are other people's values and dichotomies. Our commitment is solely to nurturing, supporting, and honoring three important entities in our lives: me, her, and the relationship. Whatever it takes and however we may change.

Call it a non-dualistic relationship.

"How are you handling all the temptation?" Calvin asks. His eyes direct my gaze to a woman with long black hair, pink headphones, and a zebra-striped bikini jogging past.

"I still get tempted, but I just decide to wait a little while before opening any doors or doing anything stupid. Soon the temptation goes away, and I realize the trust I have with Ingrid—and where that can go—is much more powerful than a few moments of pleasure, followed by a lifetime of shame."

I've come to realize that there's no so-called *natural* way to be in a relationship. The whole idea that we can study the past or other cultures to determine what's right for us today is ridiculous. Because nearly every society of simians tells a different story of mating and sexuality—and every point of view can be supported with evidence from some other tribe or species. There isn't just one true and proper way to love, to relate, to bond, to touch. Any style of relationship is the right one, as long as it's a decision made by the whole person and not the hole in the person.

The path of ambivalence leads nowhere.

"So what would you do if the most beautiful woman in the world hit on you right now?" Troy asks.

"And what about porn?" Calvin adds.

"Or what if Ingrid loses interest in sex altogether?" Adam tries.

It's interesting: All these issues that were so important and perplexing in rehab don't actually matter anymore. The answer to all of them is, They're the wrong questions. "Here's what I'm doing," I explain. "I'm honest about everything and so is she. There are no secrets. So we'd just discuss those things, like we should have in the first place. In fact, the exact things I used to be the most scared to talk about actually brought us closer together once we got past the initial awkwardness. It was the *not knowing* that was driving her the most crazy. Eventually she felt safe enough to share her deepest fantasies, and it turned out that some of them weren't all that different from mine anyway."

The beach ends at a cliff that marks the northern tip of Point Dume.

Just around the cliff is a wide, empty beach, and I ask the guys if they want to swim around to the other side.

"I don't want you to die on your wedding day," Adam replies, and seems to mean it.

We take off our shirts and wade into the water in a safer spot. The waves crash ten yards out from the shore and we playfully tumble with them to the sand a few times.

"How are things with your wife?" I ask Adam as we sit on the shore afterward, drying off in the sun.

"She finally started having sex with me again," he says.

"No way. So was it worth the wait?"

"I'll tell you, Neil, it really wasn't. On a scale of one to ten, it's a three at best." Troy laughs cruelly. So many men like Adam complain that their wives won't have sex with them, yet so few of them would be satisfied if their wives did. Because the problem isn't actually the sex; it's the relationship between the people having it.

"You should watch instructional videos together," Calvin suggests. "Or get her really drunk."

"That's okay. I really can't change my wife. She is who she is, and I have to start thinking about what's next."

"Wow, really?" I exclaim.

"You know," he says, burying his feet in the sand, "recently I had to wear a Holter monitor because my heart started randomly fluttering—sometimes for five minutes straight. So either I leave this marriage or I have a good risk of a heart attack."

"So which are you going to choose?"

"I've rehearsed the conversation I'm going to have with the kids, but I want to wait until our youngest is out of the house in two years and then do it."

"Two years?" Calvin interjects. "You could be dead by then! What's wrong with you?"

"What about you, Calvin?" Troy rises to Adam's defense. "As soon as you develop feelings for someone, you can't even have sex with them. What are you doing about that?"

"More than you're doing about your affair."

I listen as Calvin says that he wants to find his soulmate and Adam says that he truly is ready to move on and Troy says that the modern human isn't designed for lifelong monogamy. Their voices mingle with the sea, blurring, blending, and ringing like music.

As we walk back up to the house so I can change into my tuxedo, I get the feeling that this is the last meeting of the red demons. It takes commitment to change. For only in commitment is there freedom. And it is time, finally, to commit.

Check-in: the only emotion on the list of eight that I never checked in with at rehab . . . love.

Special Note to Ingrid

I hope you ignored the message at the beginning
of the book and read everything. I wrote that
years ago, when I started working on this, when
I knew so little about love, sex, relationships,
and intimacy. But I want you to know the real me.
After all, you're stuck with me for a long time.
No matter what Helen Fisher says.

GRATITUDE

There are times when I'm in the bathroom with Ingrid getting ready for the day, and I'm so happy I get what we've come to call an ROL—a *rush of love*. In those moments, I think about how Rick tried to convince me I was missing out on a bigger happiness and how cynical I was about it. I had no way of understanding what he meant until I experienced it for myself. And now, not a day goes by that I'm not grateful.

So I would like to thank from the bottom of my heart (now that I know I have one) everyone who made it possible. And for those who want to use this experience as a starting point for your own explorations, here are a few first steps you can take as you find your unique path. Note that I don't agree with all of the recommendations of these experts, so feel free to cherry-pick whichever are most useful to you.

Many of the concepts can be found in the works of Pia Mellody, James Hollis, Virginia Satir, John Bradshaw, Kenneth Adams, Marshall Rosenberg, Marion Solomon, Harville Hendrix, Salvador Minuchin, Peter Levine, Bessel van der Kolk, Robert Firestone, and others. I also recommend taking Patrick Carnes's Post-Traumatic Stress Index test online to understand the ways your past haunts your behavior today. (Use the original PTSI test, not the revised PTSI-R.) And you may want to email Barbara McNally (the one in Venice, CA) and urge her to publish her own book, because her teachings and wisdom were a big influence as well.

If you want to go deeper, choose your practitioners carefully. So much of what passes for therapy is an expensive, endless series of weekly appointments progressing not toward healing but toward income security or ego gratification for the therapist. If you're lucky, you'll find someone like Lorraine to be a kind of primary-care therapist who will develop a treatment plan designed to heal a particular core issue—one that includes other practitioners and methods. And remember that once the change begins, psychological maintenance, self-correction tools, and consistent self-care are necessary to keep from backsliding.

Note that there is probably no therapist who would read this book and agree with everything in it. I have selected and conveyed various ideas in an immense canon of work with only one goal in mind: to share the ways in which they spoke to and influenced me. My adaptations, adjustments, and interpretations of these concepts do not necessarily have any relation to the way they were originally written or intended. They are simply what I needed to believe to get right with myself.

Though there are countless competing theories, classification systems, and schools of thought dedicated to understanding and treating the human mind—many claiming that they are newer, better, or more scientific than others—all that ultimately matters is what works for you. So be open-minded and try everything for yourself firsthand rather than accepting received opinions, including mine.

I'm currently keeping an open and expanding list of recommended websites, workshops, and practitioners at www.neilstrauss.com/thetruth. I also have a detailed reading list there, as well as information on trauma-healing workshops that offer scholarships for those who don't have book advances to spend. And although I've tried to obfuscate the details for most rehab centers, meetings, and therapists in order to protect the privacy of the patients, addicts, and certain practitioners I met, if you reach out to neil@neilstrauss.com, someone will be happy to point you in the right direction. (I've slowly removed the phone and Internet restrictions created during anhedonia, but I still try to stay offline.)

If you're interested in finding your own relationship species and want to avoid making the mistakes I did in these pages, heal yourself *before* exploring different styles. You're likely to fare a lot better. If you're healthy, whatever type of relationship you choose will also be healthy. Be aware, however, that the underground scenes change quickly—for example, the Bliss parties aren't what they used to be—so do some independent research before plunging in. In an early draft of this book, when I thought it was going in another direction, I put together an appendix of all the different relationship styles I could find, and you can grab that at www.neilstrauss.com/goodtimes.

There are many people who helped read, critique, fact-check, or otherwise opine during the years it took to write this book. The following are just a few of them: Rico Rivera, Tim Ferriss, Ryan Soave, Michelle Piper, Christopher Ryan, Chris Collins, Jaiya, Rodrigo Umpierrez, Molly Lindley, Suzanne Noguere, Andrea Dinsmore, Nola Singer, Jackie Singer, Brian Fishbach, Sy Rhys Kaye, Jared Leto, Paul Hughes, Judith Regan, Michael Wharton, Steven Kotler, Jim Galyan, Chelsey Goodan, John Mills, Alexander Hoyt-Heydon, Jack Sadanowicz, Chris Hurn, Brad Rentfrow,

Billy O'Donnell, Aaron Werth, Victor Cheng, Kira Coplin, Elizabeth Hill, Lucy Brown, Christina Swing, Thann Clark, Anthony Miller, Jay Stinnett & the Mago staff, The Society, Mary Ellen Junkins, and the late and great Eleanor Starlin.

Special kudos to Ben Smolen and to the razor-sharp Phoebe Parros for research. And to design collaborators new, the clairvoyant Laurie Griffin, and old, the wizardly Bernard Chang. Finally, of course, a massive thank-you to my extended family at HarperCollins, particularly my longtime and ~~mostly~~ extremely patient editor Calvert Morgan and my new publisher, Lynn Grady.

Everyone else I'd like to acknowledge is already in the book. I'd especially like to thank them for putting up with me as I drove them nuts during this process of growing up.

And, finally, I'd like to welcome Tenn Strauss to the world. As I write this, he is three weeks away from being born. Last night, I wrote him a letter, letting him know that no matter what may happen over the course of his life, he was conceived and brought into this world with pure love and absolute joy.

I hope he grows up to make someone as happy as his mom makes me.

ABOUT THE AUTHOR

NEIL STRAUSS was born. He is currently living. One day he will die. His website www.neilstrauss.com will outlive him. He knows this because he reserved the domain as part of a ninety-nine-year package. It was a once-in-a-lifetime kind of deal.

Speaking of which, as a reward for finishing this book to the very last page, you can grab the deleted chapters there and read all the gory details of the near-murder at the love commune: www.neilstrauss.com/goodtimes.

ALSO BY NEIL STRAUSS

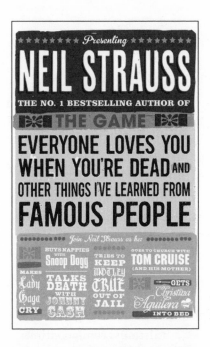

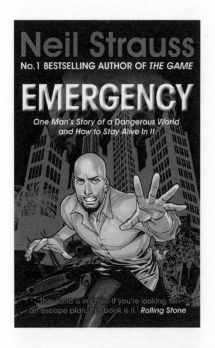

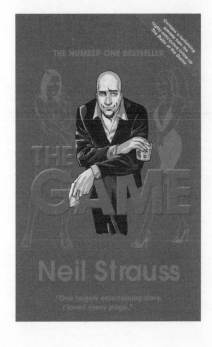

*T*he best thing we can do for our relationships with others ... is to render our relationship to ourselves more conscious. This is not a narcissistic activity. In fact, it will prove to be the most loving thing we can do for the Other. The greatest gift to others is our own best selves. Thus, paradoxically, if we are to serve relationship well, we are obliged to affirm our individual journey.

—JAMES HOLLIS
The Eden Project